CHANDLER PUBLICATIONS IN
ANTHROPOLOGY AND SOCIOLOGY
Leonard Broom, Editor

CONSULTING EDITOR FOR
BASIC STATISTICS FOR SOCIAL RESEARCH
Richard J. Hill

Basic Statistics for Social Research

Basic Statistics for Social Research

DEAN J. CHAMPION
DEPARTMENT OF SOCIOLOGY
University of Tennessee

CHANDLER PUBLISHING COMPANY
An Intext Publisher • Scranton, Pennsylvania 18515

STANDARD BOOK NUMBER 8102-0004-x
LIBRARY OF CONGRESS CATALOG CARD NO. 69-13164

PRINTED IN THE UNITED STATES OF AMERICA
Book design by Joseph M. Roter

Contents

Tables in the Text

Figures

Preface

This volume originated as a result of a desire to provide social scientists with an easy-to-understand collection of statistical methods which could aid researchers in their investigations. The criterion "easy-to-understand" required numerous decisions concerning what to include and what to exclude, plus other decisions pertaining to the level of the textbook in terms of its statistical sophistication. In making decisions such as these it is impossible to please everyone equally. The author will be the first to admit this book is not and was never intended to be a comprehensive compilation of statistical methods.

The likelihood that a majority of social scientists and students of social science are not expert mathematicians reinforces the need for an understandable textbook dealing with statistical methods. The social scientist of today often finds it difficult to read recent articles in the professional journals because of increased emphasis on elementary and advanced statistical usage. This text is geared to help to increase a reader's understanding of what statistical methods are and what they are supposed to be used for.

Most social scientists will find that several of the statistical methods included here will be helpful in their particular data analyses. If the student can add, subtract, multiply, divide, and take square roots, he will find no section in this book difficult to understand. All symbols and notations are fully described and defined. Formulas and directions for using them are conveniently provided at many points. In this respect the text functions as a cookbook, but, hopefully, with a purpose above and beyond simply revealing "how to bake the cherry pie." The student should emerge with an increased understanding of why one statistical method was chosen over another. Assisting him in making these kinds of choices is a central function of this volume.

While the request may seem unusual, the author suggests that the reader peruse Chapter 11. This chapter, while found at the end of the text, serves to briefly review what the author is up to as far as the rest of the book is concerned. It is an important chapter which any beginning student cannot afford to ignore.

This text is different from most others in that it brings the most basic statistical principles and descriptive methods under the same roof with parametric and nonparametric statistical procedures. The extended treatment of nonparametric statistical methods is generally not found, unless the student turns to a specialized book on the subject. The general case is that most books emphasize either parametric or nonparametric statistical methods, but not both. An objective of this book was to achieve a balance between these different methods.

The author believes that social scientists need a statistics book where examples are used which are pertinent to their specialty areas. While most of the examples used here are hypothetical, the reader should have little difficulty deciding whether he can use this or that statistical technique for a particular research problem.

Appreciation is extended to all of the author's colleagues at the University of Tennessee, who were frequently stopped in the hall and asked questions about the manuscript and the content and direction of it. Included among these are Professors Robert A. McLean and Richard M. Duvall, who read various portions of the manuscript. Miss Laurie Rees was most helpful in assembling a large part of the bibliography. The author owes a special thanks to Dr. Richard J. Hill at Purdue University, whose editorial assistance made it possible for this book to take shape and reach its final form. Finally, the author wishes to thank the many publishers and authors who provided permission to use their material in this book. I am indebted to the Literary Executor of the late Sir Ronald A. Fisher, F.R.S., Cambridge, to Dr. Frank Yates, F.R.S., Rothamsted, and to Messrs. Oliver and Boyd Ltd., Edinburgh, for permission to reprint tables from their book *Statistical Tables for Biological, Agricultural, and Medical Research;* these materials appear in adapted and abridged form in Appendix A of this book as tables A.4, A.5, and A.7.

Dean J. Champion

University of Tennessee

Basic Statistics for Social Research

1 Introduction

There was a time when explanations of events rested solely upon one's opinions and impressions, and little attempt was made to verify these explanations empirically. Now, though many of us frequently use our impressions to guide us toward what we believe to be good explanations of the phenomena around us, there is a growing tendency for us to rely upon the general method of *science* to supply answers to our myriad of unsolved questions. And despite some disagreement about the specifics of the method of science, there is agreement on several basic points.

First, science specifies *systematic observation of events* as necessary to the understanding of those events. In science, untangling the threads of life's complexities requires that we analyze observations.

Second, science requires that we be objective as we posit explanations for the phenomena around us. Objectivity specifies a detachment from feeling or emotion, together with a vigorous confrontation of reality, of what is observed. In addition, objectivity implies an absence of particular values.

There are at least two different demands for objectivity. The first has to do with being objective in our *observations* of phenomena. (Studies of racial prejudice are replete with instances of people endorsing stereotypes of specific minority groups, of seeing what they want to see and believing what they want to believe. Observations of this type are not objective.) The second demand has to do with *interpretation.* After we have observed phenomena, we interpret what we have seen. To be consistent with the method of science, we should be "value-free" in the interpretation of what we observe. In other words, we are required to accept what we observe even though it may be contrary to what we originally believed to be true.

Consider the story, possibly apocryphal, of a university president challenged by a campus parking problem. He hired a team of investigators to study the relation between whether or not students drive cars and what kind of grades they received in their classes. But he further directed the research team to find evidence according to which low grades would appear to be related to driving cars. He wanted to provide substantive "evidence" to the parents of prospective students that their cars should be left home. Thus the research team was to violate the scientific rule of objective observation by overlooking unwanted findings.

The university president stood ready to make an unobjective interpretation of the study results since he was already committed to reporting, in a brochure to parents, that the *facts* showed students who drive cars get lower grades.

It is difficult for any person to be completely objective. Nevertheless, the scientist, *as far as he is fully aware,* tries to be as objective as possible when observing and interpreting phenomena. Obviously, the scientists' choice of problems for study and their approach toward solving the problems are, to some degree, subjectively determined. However, the general method of science does help us to be consistent and systematic as we collect and analyze data.

The techniques and methods developed by mathematicians and statisticians can help us to be systematic and objective in the solving of our problems. A book such as this reflects the social investigator's borrowing from the mathematical statistician. But there is some disagreement, even among statisticians, as to just what statistics is and what its functions are. Later in this chapter, some attempt will be made to explain why such disagreements exist. For our purposes, however, *statistics is the general body of methods used to assemble, describe, and infer something from numerical data.* Data may be defined as any set of observations that have been collected. Of course, *good* data will have been collected systematically and objectively.

There is also some disagreement as to how much background students need in order to be able to apply statistical tools appropriately to research problems. Some feel that the student should know how each statistical formula was originally derived; in this approach, much of the student's energy is expended in learning mathematical proofs for various equations. Other investigators are willing to forgo this experience in favor of making immediate application of statistical methods. Sound arguments favor each position. The position taken in this book, however, is more closely identified with *application* rather than with understanding of how each statistical method is theoretically and mathematically derived. The concern here is practicality.

ABOUT THIS BOOK

This book will provide the reader with an array of statistical techniques and tests used by social scientists—not a comprehensive compilation, but hopefully a representative one. It will provide:

(a) the primary assumptions underlying each statistical technique presented, with accompanying limitations and suggestions for application;
(b) some useful references for finding less common statistical techniques and tests for unusual problems in data analysis;

(c) a helpful set of tables to aid in statistical interpretation; and
(d) some selected questions at the conclusion of each chapter with solutions to the mathematical and statistical problems immediately following Chapter 11.

This book will not:

(a) discuss the theoretical derivation of statistical formulas; nor
(b) include statistical procedures requiring knowledge beyond simple addition, subtraction, multiplication, division, and square-root skills. (Table A.1 of Appendix A includes the squares and square roots of all numbers from 1 to 1,000.)

The target of this volume is the beginning student of human behavior interested in acquiring elementary facility in dealing with technical social reports and in analyzing data collected from social research. To satisfy this interest, many common procedures will be presented which are needed primarily during that stage of an investigator's work known as *data analysis*. Knowing which techniques and tests are available allows one to plan the best strategy for the analysis of his data. The tests covered here include but a small portion of the many statistical methods currently available. However, having some familiarity with these techniques and tests will be helpful toward understanding statistical procedures outlined elsewhere, some of which are considerably more complex.

Social-science examples will be emphasized in this volume, because students often have difficulty in trying to relate to their own situation an example taken from another field such as agriculture, business, or botany.

It may help to view statistical techniques as *strategies* for solving problems in the social-research process. And just as many strategies can be used in becoming successful financially, so likewise many statistical techniques and tests (strategies) can help in solving research problems. Each financial strategy has accompanying advantages and disadvantages if used in any particular situation. The same is true with statistical tests. Naturally, we want to pick the *best* strategy for the problem we want to solve—not always an easy task. Some people have called this process an "art."

Our choice of strategy—statistical technique or test—is based upon at least two things: first, what the particular statistical test is geared to do, and second, what the relative advantages and disadvantages of the technique are. There are many statistical tests. Some are designed to do the same thing as others. Among similar tests there are differences, however, which we can evaluate by paying attention to the particular advantages and disadvantages of each. As each statistical test is presented in this book, the accompanying advantages and disadvantages will be given.

One goal of this volume is simplicity. Step-by-step procedures will be presented for the application of each statistical technique. If a particular test requires knowledge of some procedure previously discussed, reference will be made to such prerequisites.

SOME OBJECTS OF INQUIRY IN SOCIAL RESEARCH

As one of the social sciences, sociology studies human behavior as it is affected by group *variables*. Small groups and their problem-solving behavior, census tracts, group processes at work in the formation of delinquent gangs, family interactions, and the like are included within the scope of sociological study.

When actually carrying out a research project, the social scientist studies these phenomena by paying attention to variables. A variable is simply anything that can assume more than one value. Sex is a variable because it can vary between male and female. Income is a variable because it may have many different magnitudes. Groups vary in size, populations vary in life expectancy, and criminals vary according to the types of crime they commit.

Additional objects of inquiry in social research include the social characteristics of interaction situations and the variables that seem to make a difference in these situations. Answers to problems such as these are derived in a number of ways. The techniques of social research are helpful here. Interviews with people can provide some answers, while observation of the interaction setting can provide others. The anthropologist lives with a remote tribe to learn about its culture. Small groups working on problems or other activities are observed by social scientists through one-way mirrors in order to identify group process. Public-opinion polls are conducted by social-research organizations to determine community sentiment for or against a particular political issue. We can examine the biographies of people from the past to help answer questions pertaining to present social phenomena. There is a wide variety of ways in which data may be collected and analyzed.

To add clarity and confidence to one's findings and observations, statistical procedures can be used under certain conditions. These procedures provide the researcher with a set of standards and rules by which to describe and evaluate what has been found. Of course, these statistical procedures can assist the investigator to be more objective in his inquiry and more systematic also. When applied correctly, they are unyielding in the decisions they give, unaffected by the emotions and sentiments of the researcher.

The use of statistical techniques requires that the data be presented in a meaningful numerical language. The variables may be counted, weighed, measured, or otherwise numerically displayed; but they must be susceptible to some kind of valid numerical treatment.

Two major kinds of variables with which we shall deal in subsequent discussion are *discrete* and *continuous* variables. Discrete variables are those which have a set of finite or fixed values. Sex can assume only two values—male and female. Religious affiliation varies according to denomination or sect. Sex and religion are called discrete variables because they contain only a limited number of specific values. When variables are continuous, we say that the values they can assume are infinite. Age and income are continuous variables. We can fraction age into years, months, weeks, days, hours, minutes, seconds, and smaller time units. Income can be fractioned similarly. Often, for convenience, many continuous variables are treated as though they were discrete. The chief convenience is that it is easier to understand relations between variables which have been "grouped" (a technical expression whose meaning will become clear). Social class is one such variable. It has been said that there are as many social classes as there are families. But for convenience, social class is often treated as though it were discrete: social scientists group people into various strata according to certain characteristics which they have in common; thus, upper-middle class, lower class, working class, white- and blue-collar class, and the like.

A person's education is also treated in this fashion. For convenience, we may group people according to how many years of formal schooling they have obtained, how many units of college credit they have accumulated, the number of degrees they hold, and the "prestige" of the institutions from which the degrees were obtained. But education is a continuous phenomenon. We are hard-pressed to say just exactly where a person's education ends. For some of the statistical techniques to be discussed, differentiation between discrete and continuous variables will have little importance, but for other techniques, such distinctions are necessary in order that the appropriate statistical procedure can be selected.

WHAT ARE STATISTICAL TECHNIQUES?

Statistical techniques embrace the entire body of methods used to assemble, describe, and infer something from numerical data. These techniques perform two general functions: description and inference. Statistical procedures allow the investigator to *describe* what he has found. They allow him to categorize and identify systematically what he has collected. The batting "average" describes a ballplayer in this sense. These techniques also allow the investigator to say something about many elements by examining a few taken from them. The investigator "infers" something about a large population by examining only a portion of that population. *Statistical inference* is the name given to this function. Statistical techniques, then, allow us to describe things systematically and also to infer something about a larger collection of them.

A statistical technique should not be confused with a *statistic,* which is a characteristic of any *sample of elements.* A sample refers to any collection of elements taken from a larger *population* of them. Some confusion exists, in part, because many investigators loosely refer to statistical techniques, methods, or tests as "statistics." We shall use the phrase "statistical technique" (method or test) to refer to the procedures learned in this text, in order to avoid such confusion.

When the investigator studies the entire population of elements, the characteristics of that population are called *parameters*. The figure below will make this distinction more clear.

Figure 1.1. The Distinction between a Population and a Sample.

Population (100%)	**Sample (25%)**
All members of the upper class in the United States	Some members of the upper class in the United States
Some Characteristics of Elements	
The percentage of males in the upper class in the United States	The percentage of males in the sample of the upper class ir. the United States

Sample and population characteristics, statistics and parameters, are represented by different kinds of symbols throughout this text. Statistics are represented by Roman (English alphabet) letters ($\overline{X}$, s, t, and the like), while parameters are represented by Greek letters (μ, σ, τ, and the like—mu, sigma, and tau). The distinction between statistics and parameters will become more apparent when statistical inference is discussed in Chapter 6.

THE MODUS OPERANDI OF THE SOCIAL SCIENTIST

Involved in social research is the accurate description of groups and group members and the measurement of the qualities and characteristics shared by them. This is not always as easy as it may sound. We can easily count the number of people in a group and we can generally tell how many share certain visible characteristics (for instance, skin color, sex, color of shoes and clothing, or height), but how are we to measure less visible characteristics such as attitudes, prejudice, and intelligence? We cannot "see" an attitude. We cannot "see" prejudice. We cannot "see" intelligence. In other words, we cannot readily apply numbers to many social characteristics that may be important in disposing an individual to behave in a given way.

How do we measure and categorize characteristics that we cannot see directly? One method is to record the verbal, written, and/or physical responses of people to specific ideas or things. For example, we may want to find out the extent to which automation in the work setting will affect the level of job satisfaction of employees. (We are assuming that employees either like or dislike their jobs to varying degrees.) One way to learn whether employees like or dislike their jobs is to *ask* them. If we find that all of the employees like their jobs before automation, but all employees dislike their jobs after automation, we are led to suspect that some connection exists between liking the job and the presence or absence of automation in the work setting.

The sociologist also asks questions such as "What difference does it make for some people to think more favorably of their jobs than others?" In so asking, he is treating job satisfaction somewhat differently. In the first instance, the primary aim was to identify something which "caused" job satisfaction to change. In the second instance, the primary aim is to identify something which changes as a result of varying degrees of job satisfaction. This difference illustrates the fact that any variable studied may be treated as either *dependent* or *independent.*

A dependent variable is one which has its value affected by change in some other factor or factors. Whether one is satisfied with his job may depend upon the kind of supervision received from the boss. A student's marks in school may be dependent upon how much the student is motivated, how much he studies, and his basic intellectual capacity. Winning a race may depend upon the amount of training the runner does and the competition he receives from other runners. Obtaining a fellowship from a university may depend upon the student's previous academic record and the availability of fellowships, not to mention the competition from other students. These variables are all dependent upon other factors.

An independent variable, however, is one whose changes cause other variables to change in value. Automation may be treated as an independent variable if it is used to account for changes in job satisfaction of employees. Social class is an independent variable if it is used to explain why people behave toward others in certain ways. The independent variables associated above with getting high grades were the degree of motivation, the amount of study, and basic intellectual capacity. The independent variables for winning a race were the amount of training and the presence or absence of faster runners in the race.

Outcomes are usually interpreted as being dependent upon independent variables. Whether a variable will be used in your research as dependent or independent is for you to recognize according to whether it "acts upon another variable" or whether it is "acted upon by another variable."

Statistical techniques, then, are useful for helping us to describe the characteristics of individuals and groups, for inferring something about them, and for evaluating differences between them. Some techniques will be helpful in allowing us to learn how strongly one measured characteristic is associated with another. And still other techniques will help us to construct and evaluate our measuring instruments.

Throughout this and following chapters, it will become apparent that statistical techniques comprise a general system of tools designed to aid us in the analysis of our data. There are many different kinds of statistical techniques, each performing a particular service but in some instances overlapping the services of others. It will be important for us to recognize which statistical methods are appropriate for particular problems in data analysis. We generally determine whether one statistical technique is better than another for use in a given instance by paying attention to what kind of data we have, what we would like to find out, and what the assumptions are that we must meet.

MEETING THE ASSUMPTIONS

The problems confronting the social scientist today are quite different from the problems facing the early formulators of statistical techniques. Yet many of the same techniques are applied to current problems. The social scientist has learned to adapt these statistical methods for solving his current problems. Whenever a statistical technique is used for a purpose for which it was not originally intended, some question arises concerning the meaningfulness of the statistical results. Therefore, caution should be exercised in order to insure that the statistical technique is used for problems *similar* to those dealt with originally.

Underlying each statistical technique is a set of rules which we shall label as "assumptions." Before we can meaningfully use any statistical method, we must strive to satisfy *all* of the assumptions underlying it. *If we do not satisfy the assumptions, our findings and eventual conclusions may become meaningless and erroneous.* Sometimes, investigators feel that satisfying a few of the assumptions underlying a particular statistical technique justifies their using that technique. This practice is the equivalent of sloppy research, and the results are comparable to allowing a basketball game to proceed under football rules; a final score would result, to be sure, but the *meaning* of that score would be questionable.

One important requirement underlying all statistical techniques is that the investigator has data which meet the assumptions of a particular *level of measurement.* Some techniques require addition, subtraction, division, and multiplication; some require square-root procedures. Some data which the investigator has, however, may not be amenable to some of these mathematical operations. There are generally four *levels* of measurement. These are called the *nominal, ordinal, interval,* and *ratio* levels, respectively. Associated with each level are certain permissible statistical methods. Because social data are often scattered throughout these four levels, we must be careful to choose the statistical test equivalent to the particular measurement level we are able to achieve. In order to understand what is meant by *level of measurement*, a series of examples will be helpful.

The Nominal Level of Measurement

The nominal level of measurement is generally referred to as the "lowest" level of measurement. Any data a researcher may have are *at least* nominal. Having nominal data means that we can *categorize* elements in some way. We may categorize people according to race, ethnic origin, religion, political party, sex, or any number of other designations. About the best we can do with this level is to compute percentages and say that a certain percentage of the population is Catholic, German-born, Negro, Democrat, or of some other category. The measurement limitations of this level are such that we cannot imply that one category is better or worse, higher or lower, than another.

Some confusion exists at this level which centers around the meaning of numbers which we assign to represent the categories we create. For convenience, we often label categories with some number, as Catholic = 1, Protestant = 2, Jewish = 3, and so on. Sometimes investigators mistakenly try to manipulate these label numbers of categories mathematically. For example, let us assume that we have labeled the above three categories as shown. We may be interested in seeing if there is any relation between one's social-class standing and the particular religious system he adopts. We obtain a large sample of people from a given community and we interview them. We record the information from these interviews and begin to analyze it.

Because our sample is large, we want to simplify our analysis procedure in some way. One way of doing this would be to transfer the information to cards or tape for use in a computer system. We must, therefore, convert our information to *numbers*. In the case of religious preference, such numbers are arbitrarily assigned to each religious category and they in no way imply that a "1" is *less than* a "2." Nor can these numbers be added, subtracted, multiplied, or divided: a "1" (Catholic) plus a "2" (Protestant) does not equal a "3" (Jew). The numbers themselves serve no other purpose than to differentiate one category from another. A "1" is *different from* a "2." Our conclusions are limited to such statements as there are more Catholics or more Protestants or more of some category in our collection of elements (sample) than any of the other religious categories. All statistical techniques require at least the nominal level of measurement before one can use them to analyze his data.

The numbers used to categorize elements on the nominal level also represent mutually exclusive categorization. A "1" is not a "2," a "2" is not a "3," and so on. The position of one category is in no way related to the position of another category on the nominal level.

The notion of exclusiveness may be illustrated by the following example. The category "sex" may be divided into two parts: male and female. We assign numbers to each of these classifications as a means of conveniently differentiating between them. Being a "1" or male means that a person cannot belong to the other subcategory simultaneously. Hence, we say that a "1" is exclusive of a "2." Numbers are arbitrarily assigned with no regard for order among the subcategories.

The Ordinal Level of Measurement

The ordinal level of measurement contains all properties of the nominal level. In addition, ordinal measurement includes the property of being able to say that one number is greater or less than another. In other words, the ordinal level of measurement permits the *ranking* of numbers from high to low. Now we are able to say that a "1" is higher (or lower) than a "2," that a "2" is higher (or lower) than a "3," and so on. We are not permitted to say *how much higher or lower* one number is from another, however.

For example, suppose we rank basketball teams in the Southeastern Conference as Table 1.1 shows. In this case, numbers are used to indicate one team's position above or below some other team. The numbers indicate which team has the most victories in any given season, but they do not convey how much better one team is than another. We cannot say, for example, that Tennessee is five times as good as Louisiana State, or that Vanderbilt is twice as good as Mississippi State. We can only say that one team is above or below the others according to how each team is ranked.

Table 1.1. Hypothetical Ranking of Basketball Teams in the Southeastern Conference.

Team	*Rank*
Tennessee	1
Vanderbilt	2
Florida	3
Mississippi State	4
Louisiana State	5

To take another example, suppose we measure a worker's apathy toward his job. For the particular questionnaire we use to measure apathy, we indicate that worker apathy scores range from 10 to 50. Three workers have apathy scores of 20, 25, and 48 respectively. In Figure 1.2, these scores are shown on a hypothetical *continuum*. A continuum is a

Figure 1.2. A Hypothetical Continuum of Apathy Scores.

straight line representing some characteristic from the highest to the lowest degree.

Is a person with an apathy score of 30 twice as apathetic as a person with a score of 15? We are not in a position to say. What may be said, however, is that one person, by virtue of his position on the continuum or his apathy score, is more or less apathetic toward his job than some other worker with a different score on the continuum. We cannot say *how much more* apathetic one person is compared to another. In Figure 1.2, notice the distance between the person with the score of 25 and the person with the score of 48. Also notice the position of the persons with the scores of 25 and 20 respectively. The distances between the three scores have been drawn irregularly purposely to illustrate that we are unable to say just how far one score is from another.

Attitudinal measures of various kinds are frequently of the ordinal type. Examples of other concepts which are usually measured at the same level include social class, occupational ranking or "prestige," and the influence of group leaders.

The Interval Level of Measurement

The interval level of measurement contains all properties of both the nominal and the ordinal levels. In addition, we may specify the *exact distances between numbers.* For example, we can view years of education as fitting interval measurement. Students having two years of college have exactly two years less than a student with four years. A person who is 5 feet tall is exactly 6 inches shorter than a person who is 5 feet 6 inches tall. In fact, there is an equal distance between people of the following heights: 5 feet, 5 feet 6 inches, 6 feet, 6 feet 6 inches, 7 feet. Also a person who is 20 is 10 years older than a person who is 10. The same distance exists between a person of 20 and a person who is 30 years of age.

If we could assume that our attitudinal scales were of the interval level, we could say, for example, how much more prejudiced one person is than the next, how much more anxiety one person has compared with the anxiety that another has. Some researchers in the social sciences are working on methods to transform ordinal concepts into interval ones. They label the measures they construct by such names as "equal-appearing interval scales" or "successive interval scales." One reason they are seeking these methods is that they would like to use certain statistical techniques which require that the concepts be at least of interval level. Generally, *the higher the level of measurement one can assume, the greater number of statistical techniques he will be able to choose from as he analyzes his data.* Simply put, this statement means that he will be able to do more with what he has. And carrying this reasoning to its logical conclusion, he will be able to learn more about his data.

The Ratio Level of Measurement

The "highest" level of measurement is called the ratio level. The ratio level contains *all* properties of nominal, ordinal, and interval levels. In addition, this level contains an absolute zero. This fact is quite important because it permits the investigator to make ratio statements. He can say that a score of 2 is *twice as large* as a score of 1, a score of 50 is twice as large as a score of 25, that in a set of scores 100 is to 200 as 150 is to 300. These are ratio statements. Among things which are amenable to ratio statements are income ($1.00 is twice as much as 50¢), sheer numbers of people, time intervals, and weight.

The interval level of measurement is very similar to the ratio level, but it has no absolute zero. For example, intelligence is measured in terms of I.Q. A person with an I.Q. of 140 is not twice as smart as a person with an I.Q. of 70. On the Fahrenheit scale of temperature measurement, 20° is not twice as warm as 10°. Intelligence quotients and Fahrenheit temperature measures are interval-level measures rather than ratio ones.

Some people argue that the difference between the interval and ratio levels of measurement is relatively meaningless, for when interval levels of measurement are found, the data are such that ratio statements can be made as well. Throughout this volume we will make reference to interval scales of measurement as representative of both levels, because no statistical technique presented in subsequent chapters requires measurement *beyond* the interval level.

Levels and Techniques

Summarizing briefly: The investigator determines the level of measurement used in making his observations. Once he determines this, he surveys the available statistical techniques to find those which are the most

Figure 1.3. Levels of Measurement and Appropriate Statistical Techniques to Use.

If the investigator has:	Then the kind of statistical techniques he can use are:
Nominal information	Nominal-level techniques
Ordinal information	Ordinal- and nominal-level techniques
Interval information	Interval-, ordinal-, and nominal-level techniques
Ratio information	Ratio-, interval-, ordinal-, and nominal-level techniques

appropriate for the given measurement level. The information in Figure 1.3 will illustrate this procedure. In this text, appropriate levels of measurement will generally be indicated as each statistical technique is presented. Meeting the appropriate level of measurement is an important assumption underlying all statistical tests.

Randomness

Another important assumption which many statistical tests require is that the elements selected for analysis be randomly chosen. Randomness generally means that we select our elements for analysis in such a way that *each has an equal and an independent chance of being drawn.* An equal and an independent chance means that each element has the same chance of being included in a given sample *and* that the draw of one element will not affect the chances of other elements being included in subsequent draws.

Randomness is particularly important when we wish to *infer* something about a general population of elements by examining a few taken from them. It is essential that the sample obtained for this purpose be "typical" of the general population from which it was drawn. Randomness helps to insure that the sample is typical in the sense that all elements have an equal chance of being included. Usually, tests which require randomness are called *inferential statistical tests.* Other tests and techniques not principally concerned with inference are called *descriptive statistical tests and techniques.* These describe the characteristics of a collection of elements. Randomness is an assumption underlying several statistical tests in this book.

There are several ways to obtain a random set of elements. First, each element in a specified population must be identified in some way, usually by being assigned a number. Some people have suggested that numbers standing for all elements of a given population be placed on perfectly round marbles and the marbles placed in a perfectly round urn. A blindfolded person then draws a given number of marbles from the urn, and the result is supposedly a random sample of elements from that population. During World War I the Selective Service System operated in a comparable fashion. Draftees were selected in some areas by drawing their names or numbers from a bowl.

Perhaps you have attended a drawing, where someone is selected from the audience to draw numbers from a bowl of some sort, in order to choose *randomly* the winner of a door prize. Such a method is comparable to the ones previously described. When a sample is obtained by this method, it is called *sampling without replacement* because the number, once drawn, is not returned to the bowl. When the numbers *are* returned to the bowl and subsequent drawings occur, the procedure is called *sampling with replacement.* The replacement has the consequence that an individual can be drawn again. But when the size of the population is quite large, say 1,000 or more, the chances of repeated drawing are relatively slight.

An alternative method of selecting a random set of elements is to use a *table of random numbers*. Table A.2 of the Appendix is a table of random numbers. In this table, (a) the digits included are not represented in any particular order or sequence, and (b) no number is represented any more often than any other number. Some people have suggested elaborate ways of entering the table to obtain a random number of elements. The easiest way is simply to pick a page and a starting place in any column of numbers. Because the numbers in the table occur in random frequency and sequence, the sample obtained from the table, regardless of where a person starts, will, by definition, be a random set of elements. There is the danger, however, of getting in the habit of turning to the same page every time a random sample is drawn. Researchers using a random-numbers table frequently find that the pages of the book they are using "automatically" open to the page they always use. If they do so, and if the same table is used often, the purpose for which the table was originally intended is defeated. The same elements will be drawn each time a supposedly random sample is selected.

Let us see how a random-numbers table is used. First, the investigator specifies his population and identifies it numerically. If there are 100 elements in the population, number labels from 1 to 100 are assigned, one to each element. To select an element for his sample, the investigator enters the table of random numbers from any point (any line and any column) and, since three digits define the total number of elements in the population (100), he considers the first three digits. Suppose the first three digits are 073. These mean that the investigator should draw the 73rd person from the population and include him in the sample. The next number *down* the column may be 711. Since there is no such element numbered 711 in the population, this number is skipped and the next one is examined. This next number is 011. The 11th person is selected and included as a part of the random sample. This procedure is followed until the desired number of elements for the sample is obtained. If the number of elements in the parent population is 5,000, then *four* digits are used. If the population is 10,000, then *five* digits are used in the table. The number of digits used in the table corresponds to the number of digits in the total population from which the random sample was obtained. The researcher may move up or down the columns of numbers as he selects his sample. He is obligated only to be consistent in the drawing of the sample. A sample thus obtained meets the requirements of a *random sample*.

Sample Size

In order to apply some statistical techniques appropriately in the data-analysis process, the investigator must obtain at least a certain number of elements from the population. Some statistical procedures require large numbers of elements while others are designed for small numbers of them. The number of elements required by a particular statistical technique will be indicated as each technique is presented.

What constitutes a large sample? How many elements make up a small sample? Such questions are quite normally asked during the primary stages of the research process. Many investigators label samples of size 100 or more as large samples, while samples with fewer than 100 elements are called small samples. Some statistical techniques treat small samples as 25 elements or fewer. The distinction between a large sample and a small one is often quite arbitrary. Some researchers think a sample of 200 elements is small while others regard it as quite large. In this book the sample size required by any particular statistical technique is generally indicated as the technique is discussed.

Sample size is often determined by the *sampling fraction,* or

$$n/N$$

where n = the number of elements to be included in the sample; and
N = the total number of elements in the population.

For statistical inference, a frequently recommended sampling fraction is 1/10 of the population. Although 1/10 is the recommended sample/population ratio, for extremely large populations such as the population of the United States, a considerably smaller sampling fraction may be quite appropriate. Further discussion of sample sizes will be found in Chapter 6.

Meeting assumptions, then, is a necessary step preceding the proper application of statistical procedures. The list of assumptions given here is not an exhaustive one. Others will be mentioned and explained at later points in the text where appropriate.

When some assumptions are *not* met for particular statistical tests, as when the investigator draws a nonrandom sample from a population of elements, he is obligated to select a statistical test requiring less stringent assumptions or *not to use statistical procedures at all.* Sometimes, the investigator will *assume* that certain assumptions are met, rather than go to the trouble of showing empirically that they have been satisfied. But for the reasons mentioned above, such practice should be avoided where possible. Good data analysis takes time, and there are *few* places where shortcuts are warranted.

SUMMARY

This chapter has sought to show briefly how statistical techniques may act as *aids* to the investigator in social research. The method of science which is employed by researchers means, in part, that we should try to be as systematic and objective in the collection, analysis, and interpretation of our information as we possibly can. Though statistical techniques help us to be more objective and systematic, they are not substitutes for careful and systematic data collection.

Before we can meaningfully use statistical techniques, *we must first identify the type of data we have as well as the goals of our research.* Having these two things clearly in mind makes it easier for us to determine whether or not we can satisfy certain assumptions underlying statistical techniques. If the assumptions which underlie statistical tests are not met, subsequent application of these tests in the data-analysis process is questionable, if not entirely wrong. It must be remembered that many of the statistical techniques we use in social research were originally developed for other purposes. This fact is even more reason for learning to be conservative in our use and application of statistical techniques in the research we undertake.

QUESTIONS FOR REVIEW AND DISCUSSION

1. What are some important assumptions underlying statistical tests? Why is it important to "meet the assumptions"?
2. What is the difference between nominal and ordinal scales of measurement? Between ordinal and interval scales? Give some examples from your own experience in addition to those provided in this chapter.
3. Can a social researcher legitimately use interval-level statistical techniques with ordinal-level information? Why or why not?
4. What is a "statistic"? What is a "parameter"?
5. What is a random sample? What are some ways in which random samples may be obtained?
6. What is the difference between "sampling with replacement" and "sampling without replacement"?
7. Label each of the following data as either discrete or continuous: (a) age; (b) the number of telephones in Los Angeles; (c) intelligence; (d) height; (e) religion; (f) political parties; (g) social class (explain); (h) family size.
8. What is a "sampling fraction"?
9. Is it always necessary to use statistical procedures in social research? Why or why not?
10. How does the scientific method help us to be objective in the analysis of our data?

2 Graphic Presentation

After he has collected information pertaining to a number of elements, one of the first steps an investigator will want to take is *to describe what he has.* For this purpose he has several procedures at his disposal. In this chapter, a number of procedures will be presented which permit the researcher to "visualize" his data.

It has been said that a picture is worth a thousand words. For this reason and others, the investigator turns to the use of tables, graphs, charts, diagrams, and figures to give his readers a richer grasp of his findings. These techniques are *aids* in helping him to conceptualize what he has found. One of these graphic aids is called a *frequency distribution.*

FREQUENCY DISTRIBUTIONS

A frequency distribution is the simple tally of scores or values of characteristics which have been taken from any collection of elements. The frequency distribution permits the researcher to see at a glance how certain scores taken from these elements are distributed.

Frequency distributions may be constructed for data at the nominal, ordinal, interval, and ratio levels. Suppose we wished to see how many people in a particular community are in certain religious categories. To begin with, we might interview members of a civic club in the community. We can construct a simple frequency distribution showing how many members of the civic club belong to each of three general religious categories (Catholic, Protestant, Jewish). Table 2.1 shows a frequency

Table 2.1. Religious Affiliation of Civic-Club Members (A Frequency Distribution).

Religion	*Frequency (f)*
Catholic	~~////~~ //
Protestant	~~////~~ ~~////~~ //
Jewish	~~////~~ ////
Total	$f = 28$

distribution which might be so constructed. In this table, we have simply tallied the number of people belonging to each of the three religious categories. The tallies which we make in the right-hand column of the table might be called "frequencies" or "observations."

We can do the same thing for ordinal information. For instance, suppose we wished to obtain a general idea of the distribution of social class in some city, organization, or small group. Again, to take a simple example, it might be the same civic club. Suppose we establish six categories of social class, and on the basis of several criteria such as income, occupation, education, and ethnic background, we make a tally of our observations as is shown in Table 2.2. By examining the frequency distribution

Table 2.2. Social Class of Civic-Club Members (A Frequency Distribution).

Social Class	*Frequency (f)*
Upper-upper Class	///
Lower-upper Class	/
Upper-middle Class	𝍸 /
Lower-middle Class	𝍸 𝍸 /
Upper-lower Class	////
Lower-lower Class	///
Total	$f = 28$

of social class as portrayed in Table 2.2, we are able to see at a glance the social-class composition of the civic club. Again, we have done nothing more than delineate several categories into which the elements we examine may be sorted or classified and tally our observations.

To illustrate a treatment of interval- or ratio-level information, suppose we were to study smoking patterns among various classes of workers. For purposes of illustration, we single out a group of blue-collar workers and ask them how many cigarettes they smoke per day. Let us assume that we have identified ten blue-collar workers who smoke. By asking them this question, we might obtain the information presented in Table 2.3. The information has not been systematically assembled. It is difficult for us to "make sense" out of this information in its present form even though we are dealing with only ten cases. We need a frequency distribution in order for us to understand more fully what we have found. Such a frequency distribution for this information appears in Table 2.4, in which we have simply rearranged the information in Table 2.3. We now observe that the number of cigarettes smoked per day among this sample of 10 blue-collar workers varies from 27 to 33. We have constructed a column on the left representing each *interval* between and including 27 and 33. A column of tallies on the right stands for the number of blue-collar workers in our sample who smoke a specified number of cigarettes. This column contains the *frequency* of workers who smoke particular numbers of cigarettes per day.

Table 2.3. The Number of Cigarettes Smoked per Day by 10 Blue-Collar Workers (Unorganized Data).

Blue-Collar Worker Number	*Number of Cigarettes Smoked per Day*
1	32
2	27
3	31
4	29
5	30
6	31
7	33
8	31
9	28
10	28

In Table 2.4 we have a better picture of the smoking behavior of these workers than Table 2.3 presents, and we can more easily compare this behavior with that of other samples of workers drawn from other occupational categories, perhaps white-collar office workers, doctors, or teachers. We have introduced *greater meaning and order* into the information we have.

Table 2.4. The Number of Cigarettes Smoked per Day by 10 Blue-Collar Workers (A Frequency Distribution).

Number of Cigarettes Smoked per Day	*Number of Blue-Collar Workers Smoking Specific Number of Cigarettes (f)*
33	/
32	/
31	///
30	/
29	/
28	//
27	/
Total	$f = 10$

The frequency distribution which we have just constructed in Table 2.4 is called a *frequency distribution for ungrouped data of the interval level.* When there are few scores and when the distance between the highest and the lowest scores is small (no more than 20 intervals), constructing such a frequency distribution is quick and easy. But what do we do when we have a larger number of different scores?

Frequency distributions can be constructed for larger numbers of scores as well. But to construct the same kind of frequency distribution as that in Table 2.4 would be cumbersome for even the most patient of social researchers.

A Frequency Distribution for Grouped Interval-Level Data

Suppose we had information which represents job-satisfaction scores of 50 Pennsylvania coal miners, as shown in Table 2.5. While we *could*

Table 2.5 Job-Satisfaction Scores for 50 Pennsylvania Coal Miners (Unorganized Data).

59	65	42	81	41	37	77	72	75	65	67	68	50
52	54	53	51	62	71	74	83	72	68	67	64	55
48	46	44	49	48	50	72	77	68	44	81	78	72
56	54	75	38	43	48	49	72	75	41	63		

set up a frequency distribution identical with that for ungrouped data in Table 2.4, we would find ourselves with values varying from 37 to 83. This technically *correct* frequency distribution would not be a very *practical* one. We would find that it was not much of an improvement over our original unorganized data; although more clear, we would still have difficulty evaluating our information.

To deal with this information more effectively we should construct a frequency distribution for grouped interval data. We decide to "condense" the number of possible values between 37 and 83. Condensing or "grouping" these values means to expand the size of the intervals between the high and low scores.

In the frequency distribution shown in Table 2.4, the interval size was 1; the frequencies were for 27, 28, 29, 30, 31, 32, and 33 cigarettes smoked. If we were to maintain and use an interval size of 1 in the present distribution of scores as originally proposed, we would have 47 intervals. But if the interval size were 2, we would then have 24 intervals of size 2 which would include all values between the scores of 37 and 83 (the lowest would contain only one value, 37). *As we increase the interval size, we decrease the number of categories into which our data can be grouped.* A rule of thumb to follow is that the number of intervals in a frequency distribution should be somewhere between ten and twenty. A number less than ten would be too few, while more than twenty intervals would again be somewhat cumbersome to handle. As a partial result of convention, many social researchers lean toward approximately fifteen intervals as a fairly manageable figure and as a happy medium between the two extremes.

To construct a frequency distribution for interval data which require grouping, the procedure outlined below may be followed. We shall illustrate this procedure by using the job-satisfaction scores in Table 2.5.

1. First we must determine the highest and the lowest scores in the distribution of values. The difference between these values plus 1, is called the *range,* and it will be discussed in greater detail in Chapter 4.
2. Next, we divide the range by some value between 10 and 20, generally 15. This will give us a value close to a whole number which can become the desired interval size. (Common interval sizes are 1, 2, 3, 4, 5, 10, 20, 30, 40, 50, 100, and so on.)
3. After determining the interval size, we begin a column on the left-hand side of a blank page with an interval which includes the *lowest* value in the distribution of scores and which begins with *a multiple of the interval size.* Working from the bottom upward, we continue constructing intervals until the one containing the largest score is reached.
4. The final step is to tally each score in the distribution according to the interval where the score would be found. Such tallying is done in a separate column to the right of the other column.

Following these steps with the information in Table 2.5, we find that the highest score in the distribution is 83 and the lowest score is 37, the range being $83 - 37 + 1 = 47$. Dividing 47 by 15 (a desirable number of intervals), we obtain an approximate answer of 3. Let us accept this value as the proposed interval size for our frequency distribution.

Next, we search for a number which is a multiple of the interval size, 3, that is, 3, 6, 9, 12, 15, or the like, and which will begin an interval that will contain the lowest score in the distribution, or 37. Beginning with 33 (another multiple of 3) will not help us much, because the interval 33–35 does not contain 37, the lowest score. Beginning with 39, another multiple of 3, to start an interval will give us 39–41. This interval will not contain 37 either. But if we begin the first interval with 36, the interval 36–38 *will* contain the lowest score, 37.

The reason we select a number to begin an interval which is a multiple of the interval size is that this procedure can act as a check on our work. If we make a mistake in the construction of our frequency distribution, the error can be detected more quickly. A common error is making one or two of the intervals larger or smaller than the others, such as the case with the following interval sequence: 36–38, 39–41, 42–44, 45–49, 50–52. The interval 45–49 is actually of size 5 and contains the values 45, 46, 47, 48, and 49. In this example, the regular interval size is 3; 50–52 is a *correct* interval size, but 50 is obviously not a multiple of 3, and an error is detected. Without a good system of constructing intervals for frequency distributions, such discrepancies would have a good chance of slipping by undetected, and the interpretation we make of the frequency distribution would be distorted to a degree.

Since each interval will contain three numbers, we set up the following frequency distribution as is shown in Table 2.6. Each interval in Table 2.6 contains three values. The interval 36–38 contains the values 36, 37, and 38, for example. This table is called a frequency distribution with an interval size of 3. Sometimes these intervals are referred to as "class intervals of size 3."

Table 2.6. Job-Satisfaction Scores for 50 Pennsylvania Coal Miners (A Frequency Distribution).

Job-Satisfaction Scores	*Tallies*	*f*
81–83	///	3
78–80	/	1
75–77	~~////~~	5
72–74	~~////~~ /	6
69–71	/	1
66–68	~~////~~	5
63–65	////	4
60–62	/	1
57–59	/	1
54–56	////	4
51–53	///	3
48–50	~~////~~ //	7
45–47	/	1
42–44	////	4
39–41	//	2
36–38	//	2
	$\Sigma f =$	50

The final step will be to tally each of the 50 job-satisfaction scores in horizontal proximity to the interval where each score belongs, and then to sum each of these sets of tallies in a frequency column as shown above. In subsequent tables, the symbol "*f*" will stand for the word *frequency*. Also, the symbol Σ (a capital sigma) will stand for "the sum of."

Interval Characteristics

At this point it is important to indicate some features of intervals which help us to better categorize information and which will serve as essential background for some of the statistical procedures to be presented in later chapters. We are generally accustomed to thinking in terms of *whole numbers* as they appear in Table 2.5. However, there are occasions when it will become necessary to deal with values *not* in whole-number form, as is frequently the case with continuous variables. Whenever we have fractions of numbers or decimal values such as 33.3, 2.86, or $4\frac{3}{4}$, we must be able to deal with these values in some systematic fashion.

Having a knowledge of the *upper and lower limits of intervals* will help us to categorize values other than whole numbers. Technically, the upper limit of the number "1" is 1.5, while the lower limit is .5. *Every number has an upper and a lower limit.* The upper and lower limits of three whole numbers are given below:

Number	*Upper Limit*	*Lower Limit*
55	55.5	54.5
7	7.5	6.5
2,158	2,158.5	2,157.5

Numbers containing decimal fractions also have upper and lower limits:

Number	*Upper Limit*	*Lower Limit*
.386	.3865	.3855
4.2	4.25	4.15
.0001	.00015	.00005

When we are dealing with larger intervals, say, of size 3, the following procedure is followed for identifying upper and lower limits of the intervals:

Interval	*Upper Limit*	*Lower Limit*
6–8	8.5	5.5
27–29	29.5	26.5
330–332	332.5	329.5

You may now be asking yourself *why* the investigator need concern himself with the upper and lower limits of intervals of various sizes? Suppose we were dealing with a series of numbers containing decimal fractions, and we were interested in constructing a frequency distribution for them. Where would we place the value 46.7 for instance? We would most likely place this observation in the interval containing that value. In Table 2.6, the interval containing 46.7 would be 45–47. But what about the number 47.5? Does it belong in the interval 45–47 or in the interval 48–50? The fact that the upper limit of the interval 45–47 is 47.5 and the lower limit of the interval 48–50 is also 47.5 presents a problem. In what interval should we place the value 47.5? A simple *rounding* procedure will determine where this value should be placed properly. Fractional values which are exactly halfway between one value and another, such as 38.5, 41.5, or 47.5, are rounded in favor of the closest *even* number. For example, 38.5 would be rounded to 38, 41.5 would be rounded to 42, and 47.5 would be rounded to 48. This is a generally accepted practice. Consequently, 47.5 would be placed in the interval 48–50.

Besides having upper and lower limits, all intervals have *midpoints.*

We are particularly concerned in this case with the midpoints of interval sizes of class 2 or larger. Midpoints divide the interval size into two equal parts. An easy way to determine the midpoint of any given interval is to sum the upper and lower limit of a particular interval and divide by 2. The midpoint for the interval 36–38 would be:

$$\frac{35.5\ (= \text{lower limit}) + 38.5\ (= \text{upper limit})}{2} = \frac{74}{2} = 37.$$

$$\text{Midpoint} = 37.$$

Often, midpoints may be determined by inspection. To improve accuracy and to guard against possible mistakes, however, it is recommended that the investigator take the time to carry out this simple computation. Midpoints will be essential in the computation of certain statistics from grouped data. Their value will become more apparent in Chapter 3.

Assumptions for Frequency Distributions

There are virtually no assumptions involved for the construction of frequency distributions for nominal-level data. We simply categorize the data and tally it. For ordinal data, a ranking of categories is implied. For either nominal- or ordinal-level data, we are not apt to apply the interval-determining procedure previously discussed. When we have interval-level data or "higher," we encounter no restrictions for the construction of frequency distributions.

Cumulative Frequency Distributions

Frequency distributions may be "cumulative." Cumulative frequency distributions represent nothing more than a systematic summing of all previous tallies at each interval level in a frequency distribution. Table 2.7 shows a cumulative frequency distribution for the data in Table 2.6.

The construction of a cumulative frequency distribution is quite easy. For instance, the interval 36–38 contains 2 frequencies. These frequencies have also been recorded in a third column labeled *Cf* in the table, which presents the *cumulative sum of frequencies*. The next higher interval, 39–41, contains 2 frequencies also. These frequencies are added to the frequencies of the first interval, and this value, 4, is placed in juxtaposition to the frequencies of the interval 39–41 in the third column. Each ascending interval contains a number of frequencies. These are systematically added to all previous frequencies and placed in the corresponding position in the third column. The last interval should contain the frequencies which, when added to the rest, will equal the total number of frequencies in the distribution.

Table 2.7. Job-Satisfaction Scores for 50 Pennsylvania Coal Miners (A Cumulative Frequency Distribution of the Data in Table 2.6).

Job-Satisfaction Scores	*f*	*Cf*
81–83	3	50
78–80	1	47
75–77	5	46
72–74	6	41
69–71	1	35
66–68	5	34
63–65	4	29
60–62	1	25
57–59	1	24
54–56	4	23
51–53	3	19
48–50	7	16
45–47	1	9
42–44	4	8
39–41	2	4
36–38	2	2
	$\Sigma f = 50$	

PERCENTAGES, PROPORTIONS, CENTILES, DECILES, AND QUARTILES

Frequently, investigators are interested in determining various cut-off points in their distributions of scores above or below which a certain *proportion* of the frequencies will be found. *Proportions are obtained by dividing part of the sum of frequencies by the sum of the frequencies.* In order to find out what proportion 40 is of 80, we must divide 40 by 80, obtaining 40/80 or .50. By moving the decimal place two spaces to the right and adding the word or sign for percent (%), proportions may be converted to *percentages*. In other words, a percentage equals a proportion multiplied by 100. By converting a cumulative frequency distribution to percentages or proportions, the investigator who has ordinal data can tell at a glance where a given proportion of frequencies lies. Such a question as "Which score in a distribution has 70 percent of the frequencies below it?" is easy to answer.

Any given point in a distribution of scores defines a particular *centile*. A centile identifies that point in a distribution below which a certain percentage or proportion of frequencies is included. For example, the 45th centile is that score in the distribution having 45 percent of the frequencies below it. The 83rd centile has 83 percent of the frequencies below it, and correspondingly, it has 17 percent of the scores *above* it. Centiles are written as C_{45} and C_{83} to represent the 45th and 83rd centiles respectively.

Sometimes *deciles* may be used. Deciles identify 10-percent points in a distribution of scores. D_1 is defined as the first decile and it has 10 percent of the scores in the distribution below it. D_5 is the fifth decile, and it has 50 percent of the scores above and below it.

The investigator may want to use *quartiles*. Quartiles define 25-percent points in any distribution of scores. Q_1 is defined as the first quartile, and is the value in the distribution having 25 percent of the scores below it. Q_3, the third quartile, has 75 percent of the scores below it and correspondingly has 25 percent of the scores above it.

The following relationship obtains between centiles, deciles, and quartiles:

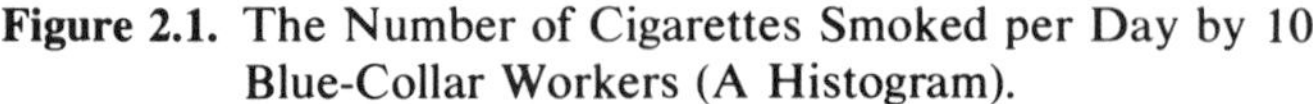

$$C_{50} = D_5 = Q_2.$$

Each of these has 50 percentage points in a distribution below it. Quartiles, deciles, and centiles will be used at various places throughout the text to aid in the computation of certain statistics. The computation of these values will be left to the following chapter and will be discussed in conjunction with *medians*.

THE HISTOGRAM

The histogram is a graph which presents visually the information found in frequency distributions. Figure 2.1 is a histogram representing the data in Table 2.4, the frequency of blue-collar workers who smoke particular numbers of cigarettes per day. The horizontal axis contains the

Figure 2.1. The Number of Cigarettes Smoked per Day by 10 Blue-Collar Workers (A Histogram).

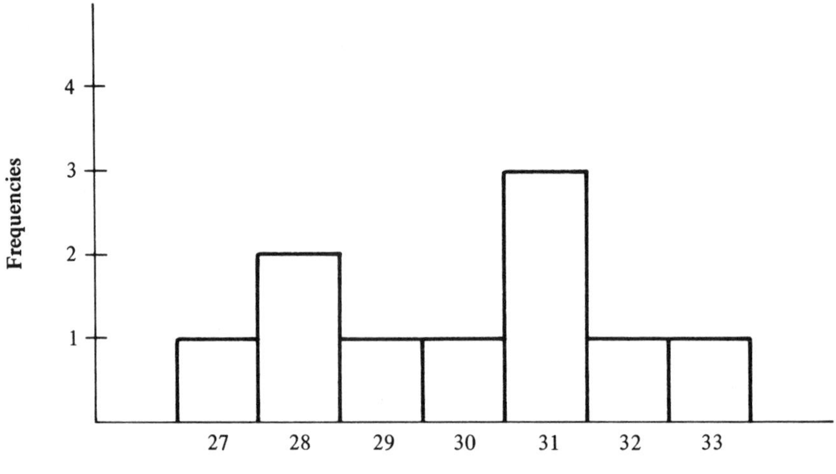

possible number of cigarettes smoked, within the range existing among the blue-collar workers. For grouped data, somewhere between 10 and 20 intervals can be placed conveniently along this axis by widening or narrowing the space allowed for each interval.

The vertical axis represents the frequencies of workers who smoke specific numbers of cigarettes. Over the value 28 are shown 2 frequencies, which means that 2 of these blue-collar workers say that they smoke 28 cigarettes per day.

More frequency classifications are included here than are actually needed for this example. This treatment illustrates the *flexibility* which the investigator has in dealing with larger numbers of categories and frequencies. Sometimes, when the number of frequencies is extremely large, percentages are used along the vertical axis.

Constructing a Histogram

The following procedure may be followed for the construction of histograms. Graph paper is recommended for this purpose.

1. Draw vertical and horizontal axes as shown in Figure 2.1.
2. On the vertical axis mark off equal segments which will represent frequencies. Label the segments with the appropriate numbers. The most frequencies found for any one value will be the number of divisions needed along the vertical axis. Label the axis (in Figure 2.1, "Frequencies").
3. Mark off the horizontal axis similarly. Divisions along this axis represent the range of values found in any distribution of scores. These segments may be labeled with intervals of any class size. Label the axis (in Figure 2.1, "Number of Cigarettes Smoked").
4. The height of each bar perpendicular to the horizontal axis is determined by the number of frequencies found at each value. In Figure 2.1, the value 27 has one frequency, and the height of the bar corresponds to where "1" is found along the vertical axis.

From time to time, the investigator will encounter situations where the intervals along the horizontal axis will be *unequal*. Such a situation might occur if, for example, a few scores were markedly different from the rest. Consider the following values:

1 2 3 4 5 6 7 8 9 10 11 80 95 117

These values might represent income, age, or any other classification. Constructing a histogram for these scores would be relatively easy up until the scores 80, 95, and 117 were encountered. What do we do with these? Should we keep numbering spaces along the horizontal axis until these values are included?

To deal with this problem, we may label a final interval as "10 or over" or "over 10." This interval should be made *larger* than the rest of the intervals along the horizontal axis. *How* large will depend upon the number of frequencies included in the interval. Sometimes, with grouped data, the investigator arbitrarily estimates the *proportionate size* of the unequal interval and includes the percentage of frequencies found within that interval.

THE FREQUENCY POLYGON

The frequency polygon is a graph in the form of a series of connected straight lines linking the midpoints of intervals along the horizontal axis; its height at these midpoints is determined by the number of frequencies according to the scale along the vertical axis.

Frequency polygons are very similar to histograms. If we were to take a pencil and place a dot at the top and in the middle of each vertical bar in a histogram, and then connect the dots with straight lines, we would have a frequency polygon. Figure 2.2 is a frequency polygon drawn directly from the data presented in Figure 2.1.

All steps for constructing histograms are followed until we draw the shape of the polygon. Midpoints of each interval are used instead of the upper and lower limits of the intervals. Straight lines are drawn which connect the dots. Lines which "close" the polygon are drawn at each end of the distribution of values along the horizontal axis. These lines are attached to the midpoints of the intervals immediately preceding and following the distribution of values. In the above example, lines are drawn to the midpoints of the spaces that would represent values 26 and 34,

Figure 2.2. The Number of Cigarettes Smoked per Day by 10 Blue-Collar Workers (A Frequency Polygon).

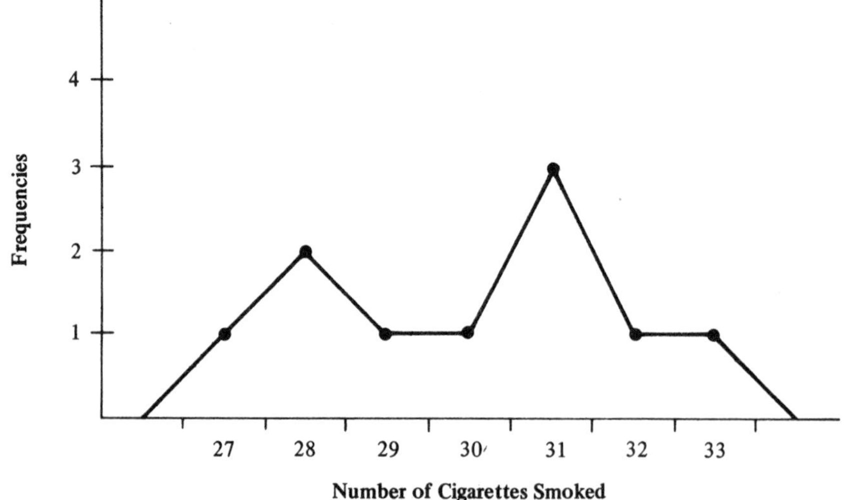

even though there are no frequencies recorded for them. These lines simply close the polygon.

Frequency polygons are designed to portray the shape of a distribution of scores. Knowing the shape of the distribution of scores will be helpful in selecting certain statistical techniques, as will be seen subsequently.

Assumptions for Frequency Polygons and Histograms

Perhaps the best way to identify the assumptions underlying frequency polygons and histograms is to begin with a review of the assumptions necessary for frequency distributions. A frequency distribution requires nothing more than that the data be of such a nature as to permit categorizing them. Frequency polygons and histograms have the same requirement. In addition, these graphs assume that the data for which they are drawn are of interval level. Equal units are identified along the horizontal axis of each. This assumption is frequently relaxed, however.

BAR GRAPHS

Bar graphs are horizontal bars representing the degree to which certain characteristics may exist among any collection of elements. Figure 2.3 is a bar graph showing the percentage of sons who follow their father's occupation according to social class.

Bar graphs are very easy to construct. We do not need to be concerned about the width of the bars as we do with histograms. As long as we are

Figure 2.3. The Extent to Which Sons Follow the Father's Occupation (A Bar Graph).

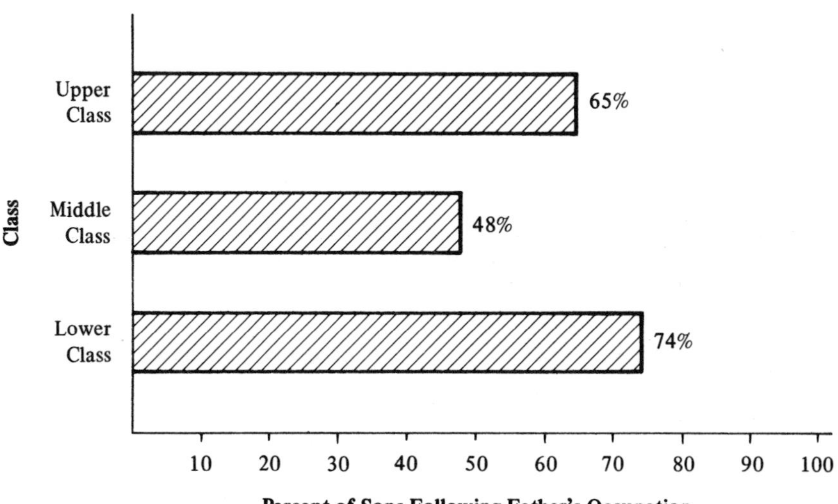

Figure 2.4. Percentage of Crimes Cleared by Arrest and of Those Not Cleared (A Bar Graph).

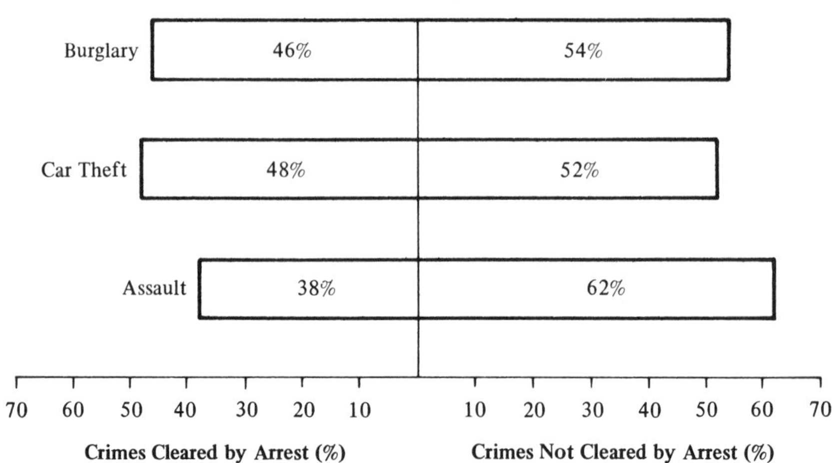

consistent in making our divisions along the horizontal and vertical axes, we are at liberty to design the graph as we choose.

The horizontal axis portrays "frequencies," in this case, the percent or "relative frequency" of sons following their father's occupation. The vertical axis portrays a particular category, in this case social class.

The horizontal bars in bar graphs may be extended to the left, to the right, or in both directions simultaneously as in the bar graph of Figure 2.4. This figure illustrates the percent (relative frequency) of certain crimes (category) cleared by arrest and the percent of those same crimes not cleared.

The bar graph is subject to little restriction. Nominal-level data may be used in these types of graphs. For this reason, they have been used extensively in helping researchers describe their findings. These types of graphs are probably among those most easy to construct.

PIE CHARTS

Pie charts are circular graphs which are divided into sectors representing fractions of the total circle. Figure 2.5 shows two ways in which pie charts can be used.

In the first instance, the F.B.I. uses pie charts as "crime clocks" to show the frequency of occurrence of certain crimes in the United States. *One hour* is represented by this chart. The second chart represents the distribution of religious faiths throughout the United States.

Pie charts also have assumptions identical to those for bar graphs. Any data which can be nominally categorized are amenable to the use

Figure 2.5. Two Pie Charts: (A) Crime Clock; the entire circumference represents 1 hour. (B) Religions in the United States; the entire circumference represents 100 percent.

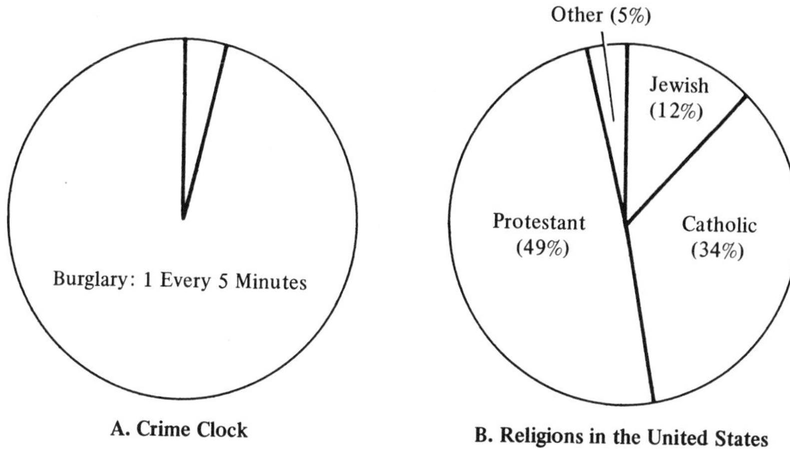

A. Crime Clock **B. Religions in the United States**

of pie charts. Their chief advantage is that they offer the reader a rapid visual appraisal of his data. Also, they serve to make a discussion of findings illustrative and meaningful. Their disadvantage is that they cannot easily accommodate many divisions of the data and they often become too complicated if more than five or six divisions of the circle are necessary.

SUMMARY

In this chapter, we have examined some of the primary graphic techniques used by social researchers to categorize and visualize some of the information which they collect. These graphic techniques are not statistical methods. They are simply aids which serve to help the investigator illustrate what he has found and which help him to determine the kind of statistical analysis he will want to make, if any.

In the following chapter, we shall examine some primary statistical techniques for describing distributions of scores numerically. Numerical presentation is made especially clear when graphs and charts are skillfully and simultaneously used in the research report.

QUESTIONS FOR REVIEW AND PROBLEMS TO SOLVE

1. What are graphs? Differentiate between a histogram and a frequency polygon.
2. Construct a frequency polygon and a frequency distribution for the following data:

70	29	45	72	38	56	47	42	33	59	56	45	71	68	32
55	51	69	69	59	58	41	38	34	33	51	51	56	45	56
65	67	34	45	42	34	26	49	55	70	58	47	49	54	63
65	67	67	47	46	34	29	43	74	38	28	26	58	69	64
62	47	38	49	70	45	62	55							

(a) Is the frequency distribution for these data better in the ungrouped or in the grouped form? Why?

(b) What is the size of the interval which you selected? What are some requirements for selecting interval size and the starting point of intervals in the construction of frequency distributions?

3. Draw a pie chart for the following information:

Negroes	12 percent
Caucasians	83 percent
Puerto Ricans	4 percent
Mexicans	1 percent

4. Draw a bar graph for the information in Problem 3.

5. What are the midpoints for the following intervals: (a) 24–27; (b) .85–.89; (c) 66–67; (d) 550–599; (e) 10–14; (f) .001–.003?

6. What are the lower limits of the following numbers (assume that these values have been rounded.): (a) 568; (b) 46.78; (c) .5; (d) .82; (e) 8,999.5; (f) .002; (g) 2.8?

7. Why should the investigator be concerned with upper and lower limits of intervals?

8. Write the proportion represented by the following centiles, deciles, and quartiles: (a) C_{34}; (b) D_7; (c) D_{10}; (d) Q_4; (e) Q_2; (f) C_{97}; (g) D_8.

9. Change the following proportions to percentages: (a) .331; (b) .01; (c) .0002; (d) .476; (e) .5; (f) .1000; (g) 100.0.

10. Change the following percentages to proportions: (a) 33.67%; (b) .998%; (c) .099%; (d) 3.841%; (e) 10.000%; (f) .0001%.

3 Some Measures of Central Tendency

It can be said of any frequency distribution that the scores tend to focus around some central value in that distribution. This characteristic of a frequency distribution is called *central tendency.*

When we seek to describe a distribution of scores in terms of some central value around which the scores tend to focus, we want to use some measure of central tendency. Three popular statistical techniques which define the central tendency of any distribution of scores are the *mode,* the *median,* and the *mean* or "average." *

THE MODE

The *mode* is a measure of central tendency which tells us which value in the distribution of scores is observed most frequently. For data in *upgrouped* form, we refer to the mode as the value or score which occurs most frequently. In the following series of numbers, 17 is the mode because it occurs more frequently than any of the other numbers.

12 14 15 16 17 17 17 18 18 19

When discussing the mode for *grouped* data, we refer to the mode as the midpoint of the interval containing the greatest frequency. In Table 3.1, we have portrayed the job-satisfaction scores of 50 coal miners. For these grouped data, the interval containing the greatest frequency is 48–50. This interval contains the scores 48, 49, and 50. Since the midpoint of this interval is 49, then 49 is said to be the mode for this distribution.

Sometimes in ungrouped data, more than one number will occur most frequently. If two or more occur "most frequently," as when each occurs 5 times, each of these numbers is given as the mode for the data. Where only two numbers thus occur most frequently, the distribution is said to be *bimodal.* The following set of scores contains two modes:

14 15 15 15 15 16 16 16 16
17 17 17 18 19

* In some statistics books, "average" comprises all the measures of central tendency. Here, note that "average" is equated with "mean."

Table 3.1. Job-Satisfaction Scores for 50 Coal Miners.

Interval	*f*
81–83	3
78–80	1
75–77	5
72–74	6
69–71	1
66–68	5
63–65	4
60–62	1
57–59	1
54–56	4
51–53	3
48–50	7
45–47	1
42–44	4
39–41	2
36–38	2
	$\Sigma f = 50$

For this distribution of scores, the scores 15 and 16 are given as the modes; 15 and 16 occur the most frequently.

If the same thing occurs for grouped data, the midpoints of the intervals containing the largest number of cases are *both* given as the modes for the data. The data in Table 3.2 are said to be bimodal. The modes for

Table 3.2. A Bimodal Frequency Distribution.

Interval	*f*
57–59	4
54–56	8
51–53	8
48–50	7
45–47	4
	$\Sigma f = 31$

this table are the midpoints of the intervals which contain the largest frequencies. In this case, the modes are 55 and 52, midpoints for the respective intervals of 54–56 and 51–53 which contain 8 cases each.

Assumptions for the Mode

Of the three measures of central tendency to be discussed in this chapter, the mode is the most unrestricted; that is, it has the fewest assumptions. Its use is appropriate for data of the nominal level or higher. The category which is represented most frequently or the value found most often in a distribution is defined as the mode of that distribution. In a distribution of religious faiths among a sample of people, for example, the modal religious faith would be "Catholic" if there were more Catholics in the sample than members of any other religious faith.

Advantages and Disadvantages of the Mode

The mode as a measure of central tendency is probably the easiest to compute. Compared to other central-tendency measures, it has the fewest restrictive assumptions. It gives the investigator an idea of the most "popular" value in a distribution of scores by identifying the value occurring most frequently.

Despite these advantages, we do not depend upon the mode as often as on the other measures of central tendency. While it is the most popular value in a distribution, it does not tell us certain things which we associate with the central tendency of a distribution of scores. The central value of a distribution of scores is not necessarily the most popular value or the mode. For example, Table 3.3 shows a frequency distribution where the mode is clearly not in the center of the distribution, but rather, toward the end of it. More descriptive measures accrue through the use of the median and the mean.

Table 3.3. A Frequency Distribution Showing a Mode away from the Center of the Distribution.

Interval	*f*
57–59	10
54–56	6
51–53	7
48–50	3
45–47	2
42–44	1
39–41	4
	$\Sigma f = 33$

THE MEDIAN

The *median* is defined as the measure of central tendency which divides any distribution of scores into two equal parts or proportions. (The median is numerically equivalent to C_{50}, D_5, and Q_2, respectively centiles, deciles, and quartiles.) In the following series of numbers, the median is 15 because it is that point which divides the series of numbers into two equal parts. There are just as many cases above 15 as there are below this number.

10 11 12 13 14 *15* 16 17 18 19 20

A preliminary step in determining the median for any distribution of scores is to arrange them *in order* from high to low. Situations will arise where an *even* number of scores is found. If an even number of cases occurs, the median is defined as the point which is equally distant from the two most central values. In the following series of numbers, 14.5 is the median. It is the value lying halfway between the two most central values.

13 14 15 16

An interesting problem occurs when there are *several* central values identical to one another. The following series illustrates this kind of distribution:

10 11 12 13 13 13 13 14 15 16

There is an even number of scores, 4 with the value of 13. In order to determine the median, we count over from the lower end of the distribution of scores until we reach the group of 13's. Theoretically, we need 5 scores from the left (or right) to identify the median. Since we already have the first three scores, namely 10, 11, and 12, we are only interested in 2 of the scores of 13. This may sound somewhat strange, but what we are doing is treating the string of 13's as occupying an interval of 1. The lower limit of the interval is the lower limit of 13, or 12.5. To this value is added half the interval ($\frac{2}{4}$ or .5) because we need only 2 of the 4 13's to identify the median value. This arithmetic becomes

$$12.5 + \tfrac{2}{4} = 13 \qquad \text{or} \qquad 12.5 + .5 = 13$$

The median is 13.

Working from the other end of the distribution of scores, we would *subtract* .5 from the upper limit of 13, or

$$13.5 - \tfrac{2}{4} = 13 \qquad \text{or} \qquad 13.5 - .5 = 13$$

Again, the median is 13. This operation will become more clear when we discuss determining the median from *grouped* data.

For data in grouped form, the median is defined as that value within any given interval which divides the distribution of scores into two equal

Table 3.4. A Frequency Distribution.

Interval	*f*	*Cumulative f*
45–49	5	30
40–44	6	25
35–39	8	19
30–34	7	11
25–29	4	4
	$\Sigma f = 30$	

parts. The first two columns of Table 3.4 show a frequency distribution for which we will compute the median. In this case, 5 intervals are shown of size 5. Summing the frequencies, we find that the total number of scores in the distribution is 30. The median for these data, then, would be the value that divides the distribution of scores into two equal parts, that is, 30/2 or 15; this value will fall within one of the intervals.

Computation of the Median for Grouped Data

1. First, we construct a cumulative frequency distribution from the original distribution of scores in Table 3.4, as is shown in the third column. From this cumulative frequency distribution we are able to tell which interval contains the score that divides the distribution into two equal parts. Examining the table, we find that the first 2 intervals, 25–29 and 30–34, contain 11 frequencies. If we add the frequencies from the next interval, 35–39, we will have more frequencies than we really need to reach the middle of the distribution: 11 plus 8 will give us 19. Since we need only 4 more scores to reach the necessary 15, we are going to have to divide the interval 35–39 in some way to obtain them. We are now going to make an important assumption. We are going to assume that the 8 frequencies found in the interval 35–39 share the interval *equally*. Each frequency has an equal share of the interval. If the interval size is 5, then each frequency "takes up" $\frac{5}{8}$ of that interval, and all of these frequency shares, when added together, should give us the interval size.

2. The next step is to add together the values of any 4 needed frequencies, thus: $\frac{5}{8}+\frac{5}{8}+\frac{5}{8}+\frac{5}{8}=\frac{20}{8}=2.5$. This is the part of the interval we need to make up 15 scores and to determine the median of the distribution.

We are now ready to identify the median of the distribution. Since the true limits of the interval 35–39 are 34.5 and 39.5 respectively, we add to the *lower* limit of the interval the portion of the interval we need (as we have determined from the number of frequencies required to divide the distribution into two equal parts). In this case, we add 2.5 to 34.5 and obtain 37, which is defined as the median for these data.

We could just as easily have computed the median for these data by working from the top of the distribution *downward.* Adding the frequencies for the intervals 45–49 and 40–44, we get 11. The next interval, 35–39, contains too many frequencies. Again, we need only 4 of these frequencies to make up the necessary 15 in order to divide the distribution into two equal parts. This time we *subtract* that portion of the interval needed from the upper limit of the interval 35–39, or $39.5 - 2.5 = 37$. Again 37 is found as the median for these data.

It is a good idea to remember that to work *downward* in a frequency distribution means to work from the larger interval values to the smaller ones, as 45–49, 40–44, 35–39, 30–34, and so on, and to work *upward* means to work from the smaller interval values to the larger ones, as 30–34, 35–39, 40–44, 45–49, and so on.

The median for grouped data of the interval level of measurement may be found readily by applying the following formula:

$$\text{median} = LL' + \frac{f_n}{f_{int}}(i)$$

where LL' = the lower limit of the interval containing the frequencies dividing the distribution into two equal parts;
f_n = the frequencies needed;
f_{int} = the frequencies found in the interval; and
i = the interval size.

In the previous example, the median would be determined as follows:

$$\begin{aligned}\text{median} &= 34.5 + \tfrac{4}{8}(5) \\ &= 34.5 + 2.5 \\ &= 37.\end{aligned}$$

Assumptions for the Median

Because the median divides a sequence of values into two equal parts, a ranking of values is implied. For this reason, data of a level at least equivalent to the ordinal level of measurement are appropriate for using the median. When the formula above is applied, the researcher must have interval-level data. It was observed in previous computations of the median that *intervals* need to be entered to determine precisely what the median should be. Therefore, the data should be of such a nature as to permit any kind of division, when necessary.

Advantages and Disadvantages of the Median

Of the three measures of central tendency discussed in this chapter, the median is the most stable, meaning, in part, that it is least affected by extreme scores occurring in a distribution. The following two sets of scores contain identical medians, but notice the scores at the extremes:

1	14	15	16	17	18	19	20	21	22	23	24	50	(A)
13	14	15	16	17	18	19	20	21	22	23	24	25	(B)

In set (A), the extreme values, 1 and 50, are quite different from the other scores. In set (B), the extreme values, 13 and 25, are very similar to the other scores. The fact that both sets have the median 19 demonstrates that the very extreme scores can occur at either end of a distribution but have little or no effect upon the value of the median. This quality of stability makes the median a very reliable measure of central tendency.

By comparison, the mode fluctuates more than the median. It defines only the most popular value in a distribution of scores and, therefore, it does not necessarily appear in the center of the distribution.

THE MEAN

The *mean* is defined as that measure of central tendency which is the average value of all values in a distribution of scores. The symbol for the mean is $\bar{X}$, and the mean for ungrouped data is found by using the following formula:*

$$\bar{X} = \frac{X_1 + X_2 + X_3 \cdots X_i \cdots X_N}{N}$$

where X_i = any score in a distribution of scores; and
N = the total number of scores in a distribution.

For data in ungrouped form such as the following scores, we can obtain the mean by summing the scores and dividing this sum by the total number of scores.

5 9 6 3 8 4 8 6 7 2

It is apparent that we do not have to place these scores into any particular order as we needed to do for the computation of the mode and the median. For these data we carry out the following operations:

$$\bar{X} = \frac{5 + 9 + 6 + 3 + 8 + 4 + 8 + 6 + 7 + 2}{10}$$

$$= 58/10$$

$$= 5.8.$$

5.8 is defined as the mean for these data.

Another way of writing the formula for the computation of the mean is:

$$\bar{X} = \frac{\Sigma X_i}{N}$$

where ΣX_i = the sum of the scores; and
N = the total number of scores.

For grouped data, the procedure for determining the mean is somewhat different.

Computation of the Mean for Grouped Data

In order to compute the mean for grouped data, we must first construct a frequency distribution such as that shown in Table 3.5.

* From here on, various symbols will be used to describe the operations involved in the computation of statistics. These symbols are part of a notation system. There are several kinds of notation systems, and this accounts for the fact that as a student examines a number of statistics texts, he finds various symbols referring to the same statistic. The basic principles involved in the computation of statistics remain the same, however. As new and unfamiliar symbols are presented, each will be defined.

Table 3.5 shows a frequency distribution with intervals of 5. In a column to be labeled x', *arbitrarily* select an interval which is believed to contain the mean for the distribution of scores. It is important to note here that *any interval can be chosen,* as long as the interval size is equal

Table 3.5. A Frequency Distribution.

Interval	f	x'	fx'
55–59	3	3	9
50–54	4	2	8
45–49	5	1	5
40–44	7	0	0
35–39	5	−1	−5
30–34	4	−2	−8
25–29	3	−3	−9
20–24	2	−4	−8
	$\Sigma f = 33$		$\Sigma fx' = -8$

for all intervals. Whichever interval we select as the *arbitrary reference point* will not affect the mean value for the distribution. The procedure is "self-correcting," so do not worry about making a "wrong" choice. In this case, the interval 40–44 has been selected arbitrarily.

Next, place a zero in the column x', opposite the interval selected. From this point, number *increasing* intervals, here 45–49, 50–54, 55–59, successively 1, 2, 3, and so on, until the "top" of the distribution is reached. Also, successively number *decreasing* intervals, here 35–39, 30–34, 25–29, successively −1, −2, −3 and so on, until the "bottom" of the distribution is reached. Again, remember that the original point selected, commonly called the arbitrary reference point or "guessed mean," was *arbitrarily* determined.

Next, multiply the frequencies by each corresponding value in column x'. The products are placed in a third column, fx'. For the interval 20–24, for example, there are 2 frequencies. This frequency 2 is multiplied by the corresponding value in column x', or −4, and the product −8 is placed in a third column, fx'. These products are then summed, giving a total of −8 in our example.

The following formula then may be used to determine the mean for grouped data:

$$\overline{X} = M' + \frac{\Sigma fx'}{N}(i)$$

where M' = the midpoint of the interval selected as the arbitrary reference point or guessed mean;

$\Sigma fx'$ = the sum of the products of the frequencies and corresponding plus or minus values in column x';

N = the total number of frequencies in the distribution; and

i = the interval size.

When the information in the table is substituted for these symbols, our formula for determining the mean for these grouped data is:

$$\begin{aligned}\bar{X} &= 42 + \frac{-8}{33}(5)\\ &= 42 + \frac{-40}{33}\\ &= 42 + (-1.2)\\ &= 42 - 1.2\\ &= 40.8.\end{aligned}$$

The mean for these grouped data is 40.8.

Another method for determining the mean from grouped data begins with the construction of a frequency distribution as before. But this time, we multiply the midpoints of each interval by the frequencies found in the interval. Summing these products and dividing by the total number of frequencies will give us the same result as the first method. The following example in Table 3.6 will make this procedure more clear.

Table 3.6. Frequency Distribution Showing Short Method for Computation of the Mean.

Interval	*Interval Midpoint*	*f*	*Mf*
55–59	57	3	171
50–54	52	4	208
45–49	47	5	235
40–44	42	7	294
35–39	37	5	185
30–34	32	4	128
25–29	27	3	81
20–24	22	2	44
		$\Sigma f = 33$	$\Sigma Mf = 1{,}346$

In Table 3.6, the midpoint for each interval has been determined. Each of these midpoints is multiplied by the number of frequencies found in the interval, and the products are placed in a third column, *Mf*. These products are summed and divided by the total number of frequencies in the distribution. (Having a desk calculator at your disposal is very helpful when using this method of calculating the mean.) The following formula is applied:

$$\bar{X} = \frac{\Sigma Mf}{\Sigma f}$$

where ΣMf = the sum of the products of the midpoints and frequencies found in each interval; and

Σf = the sum of frequencies.

Substituting values in the table for symbols in the formula gives

$$\overline{X} = 1{,}346/33$$
$$= 40.8.$$

The mean for these data is again 40.8. Both methods give approximately the same mean values. Slight discrepancies may occur due to rounding, but these will not be significant.

The first method presented here is perhaps the easiest to use, particularly when the interval size and interval frequencies are quite large. Consider the cumbersome task of multiplying income values, as midpoints of intervals, by their respective frequencies. Keeping the values to be multiplied as small as possible will help to guard against possible errors accruing frequently when larger values are manipulated.

The Mean of Means

It will sometimes be useful for a researcher to "average" several means. If the number of elements in each sample is *equal* to one another, the investigator may simply sum the means of each sample and divide by the total number of samples. This procedure is identical to that for computing the mean for ungrouped data. However, if there are *unequal* numbers of elements in each sample to be averaged, the investigator must handle this problem differently. Suppose we have the following data:

	$\overline{X}_i$	N_i	$(\overline{X}_i)(N_i)$
Sample 1	25	10	250
Sample 2	35	20	700
Sample 3	60	5	300
		$\Sigma N_i = 35$	$\Sigma X_i N_i = 1{,}250$

In order to obtain the average for the means from these three samples, we must *weight* each sample mean by its respective N_i. To do this, we simply multiply each $\overline{X}_i$ by its N_i as is shown above. Summing these products as well as summing the three N_i's, i.e., 250 + 700 + 300 = 1,250 and 10 + 20 + 5 = 35, we substitute these sums for symbols in the following formula:

$$\overline{X}_T = \frac{\Sigma \overline{X}_i N_i}{N_T}$$

where $\overline{X}_T$ = the mean of means;
N_T = the total number of elements of all samples; and
$\Sigma \overline{X}_i N_i$ = the sum of the products of each sample mean and its number of elements.

Therefore,

$$\overline{X}_T = 1{,}250/35$$
$$= 35.71.$$

The mean of the three means is 35.71.

Assumptions for the Mean

The primary assumption for using the mean is that the data to be averaged are at least of the interval level. Means computed for nominal- or ordinal-level data are meaningless. Often, people compute the means for *ranks.* A student ranks third in one class, fourth in another, and second in yet another. The sum of the ranks is 3 + 4 + 2 or 9, and the "average" rank is 3. Interval-level data assume that there is an equal distance between each interval or rank. To the extent that such is the case, the computation is valid. But where the ranking scale is of something less than an interval level of measurement, the computed average or mean of ranks is meaningless.

Advantages and Disadvantages of the Mean

One advantage of the mean is that it is a frequently used and hence a popular measure of central tendency. Most social researchers are familiar with it. But primarily because of its popularity, we should be even more aware of its overuse and misuse, particularly when we have data not meeting the interval-level assumption.

One major disadvantage of the mean is that it can only be used for data of the interval or ratio level of measurement. This limitation rules out the possibility of using the mean for data of the nominal or ordinal level. This disadvantage is a restrictive one. There are many instances in social research where means simply cannot and should not be used. For example, what level of measurement should be assumed in measuring *attitudes* has not been fully established. Yet, because of the popularity of the mean, many researchers insist on applying it to such phenomena. The use of some less stringent measure of central tendency is recommended when in doubt.

Another disadvantage of the mean is that it is affected by extreme scores. We can illustrate this disadvantage by citing *ages* of individuals. Suppose we have ten people with the following ages:

25 26 27 28 30 31 32 33 76 32

The mean for these data is the sum of ages divided by the number of people, 340/10 or 34. However, 9 of the people in this example are 33 years of age or *less*. It is apparent that one person, age 76, is primarily responsible for distorting the "average age" for the group. In this case, the deviant observation of 76 raised the over-all mean considerably. The mode and the median for these data are 32 and 30.5 respectively, values certainly more descriptive in the sense of being more *central.* This illustration suggests that when distributions are found containing a few deviant scores (observations departing markedly from the rest of the scores), the median is ordinarily to be preferred instead of the mean. Sometimes, the investigator may report *both* the mean and the median or *all three measures* of central tendency for the distribution of scores. This practice provides an even better picture of the distribution, and there is no reason why it should not be done.

SUMMARY

In this chapter we have examined three common measures of central tendency. These statistics reflect values around which all other scores in the distribution tend to focus. The most popular value or measure of central tendency is the mean, although it is not always the best measure to use, particularly in situations where extreme scores are contained in the distribution and/or when the assumptions of interval-level data are not met.

The mode, the most popular score, is by far the easiest statistic to find for both grouped and ungrouped data. It also has the fewest limitations for application. But frequently, the mode tells us the least about the central tendency of a distribution of scores. It may not reflect the central value of the distribution.

The median is better for data of the ordinal level, and it is relatively unaffected by occurrences of extreme scores.

The mean has the most stringent assumptions of the three measures of central tendency. Changes in any *one* score in a distribution of values will change the mean for that distribution. If the researcher finds that he can use the mean for any given set of scores, there is absolutely nothing preventing him from reporting all of the central-tendency measures in his research report. In fact, it may be better to do so where possible. Certainly the reader will not complain because of *too much* information!

QUESTIONS FOR REVIEW AND PROBLEMS TO SOLVE

1. Compute three measures of central tendency for the data below:

Interval	f
110–119	7
100–109	3
90–99	11
80–89	14
70–79	9
60–69	22
50–59	18
40–49	13
30–39	7
20–29	2
10–19	1
	$\Sigma f = 107$

2. What are some assumptions associated with the mode? The median? The mean? Which measures of central tendency would be best to use for social-class scores? For income? For religious preference?

3. What are the mean, mode, and median for the following ungrouped data:

88 93 89 91 89 88 89 91 91 90 91

4. What are some advantages of the median over the mean? What are some advantages of the mean over the median?

5. Compute the mean of the following set of means: $\overline{X}_1 = 126, N_1 = 8$; $\overline{X}_2 = 115, N_2 = 9$; $\overline{X}_3 = 105, N_3 = 4$; $\overline{X}_4 = 140, N_4 = 20$; $\overline{X}_5 = 121, N_5 = 6$.

6. What is the "guessed mean" and why is it important and useful in the computation of the mean?

7. Compute three measures of central tendency for the data below:

Interval	*f*
10	2
9	3
8	7
7	3
6	5
5	9
4	5
3	6
2	2
	$\Sigma f = 42$

8. Why isn't the mode always the best measure of central tendency?

9. What are the midpoints for each of the intervals in Problem 1 above? In Problem 7 above?

10. Compute the median for the following data:

16 71 76 82 119 750 825 1,026 1,029

4 Measures of Variability

In the preceding chapter, three measures of central tendency were discussed. These statistics identify certain central values in a distribution of scores. If we were to stop our work here, however, our description of any given distribution of scores would be incomplete. True, we have described the values around which all other scores in the distribution tend to focus, but we have not described *the way in which these scores are distributed around the central values.*

The following sets of numbers focus around an identical mean, $\bar{X} = 50$. But the way in which each set of scores is distributed around the mean is different.

$$46 \quad 47 \quad 48 \quad 49 \quad 50 \quad 51 \quad 52 \quad 53 \quad 54 \qquad \text{(A)}$$

$$10 \quad 20 \quad 30 \quad 40 \quad 50 \quad 60 \quad 70 \quad 80 \quad 90 \qquad \text{(B)}$$

Roughly describing these two distributions of scores, you might say that the scores in distribution (A) closely focus around the mean, 50, while the scores in distribution (B) are more widely scattered around the mean.

The ways in which scores scatter themselves around the central value in a distribution are more precisely defined by *measures of variability* or of *dispersion.* Measures of variability describe the *spread* of a distribution of scores. In this chapter we shall examine a number of measures of variability which will allow us to specify the extent to which any distribution of scores focuses around some central value.

Among the statistics to be discussed are the *index of qualitative variation,* the *range,* the *interquartile range,* the *quartile deviation,* the *average deviation,* the *variance,* and the *standard deviation.*

MUELLER'S AND SCHUESSLER'S INDEX OF QUALITATIVE VARIATION

The *index of qualitative variation (IQV)* is a measure of variation among attributes. More specifically, it measures the degree of homogeneity or heterogeneity of the attributes or qualities possessed by a given number of elements.

IQV is defined as 100 times the ratio of the total observed differences among elements to the maximum possible differences, or

$$IQV = \frac{\text{total observed differences}}{\text{maximum possible differences}}(100).$$

IQV can vary from 0 to 100 percent. The higher the percentage, the greater the variation among elements according to some attribute.

Suppose we have a group of 300 students that makes up the population of a small college in a Midwestern community. In order to learn about the qualitative heterogeneity of this small population, we need to compute an *IQV*. Let us assume that the attribute of interest is academic major. We want to know how heterogeneous the student body is according to academic major. We have the following observations:

Academic Major	*(A) (Observed Differences) Number of Students*	*(B) (Maximum Differences) Number of Students*
Physical Science	5	100
Social Science	45	100
Education	250	100
	$N = 300$	$N = 300$

Column (A) above shows the observed distribution of students according to academic major. Column (B) shows the maximum heterogeneity which would exist if students were spread equally throughout each academic-major classification. Our observed differences, however, show that a degree of homogeneity exists—considerably more students are Education majors than are majors in the other two subject areas. To identify the degree of heterogeneity numerically, we can compute an *IQV*.

In order to find the *total observed differences,* we must multiply the number of students observed in each category (academic major) by the number of students in each of the other categories. For these data, the total observed differences would be

$$(5)(45) + (5)(250) + (45)(250) = 225 + 1{,}250 + 11{,}250 = 12{,}725.$$

To obtain the *maximum possible differences,* we perform the same operation, but with the data in the maximum-differences column. For these data, the maximum possible differences would be

$$(100)(100) + (100)(100) + (100)(100) = 10{,}000 + 10{,}000 + 10{,}000 = 30{,}000.$$

Substituting these values for the terms in the *IQV* formula, we have

$$IQV = \frac{12{,}725}{30{,}000}(100)$$

$$= .424(100)$$

$$= 42.4 \text{ percent.}$$

In this case, we can say that there is about 42 percent of maximum heterogeneity among the students with respect to academic major.

To take another example, suppose we obtain information from another student body. We are interested this time in learning how heterogeneous one student body is compared to the other, according to academic major. The second student body has 600 students, and they are distributed according to academic major in the following way:

Academic Major	*(Observed Differences) Number of Students*	*(Maximum Differences) Number of Students*
Physical Science	200	200
Social Science	100	200
Education	300	200
	$N = 600$	$N = 600$

This time we notice that there is a more balanced distribution of students throughout each academic-major classification. In other words, there appears to be *more* heterogeneity in this population of students than in the first population which we discussed. Computing an IQV for these data will enable us to determine numerically which population is in measurable fact more heterogeneous.

First, we obtain the *observed differences:*

$$(200)(100) + (200)(300) + (100)(300) = 20{,}000 + 60{,}000 + 30{,}000 = 110{,}000.$$

The *maximum possible differences* are also determined:

$$(200)(200) + (200)(200) + (200)(200) = 40{,}000 + 40{,}000 + 40{,}000 = 120{,}000.$$

Then,

$$\begin{aligned} IQV &= \tfrac{110{,}000}{120{,}000}(100) \\ &= .916(100) \\ &= 91.6 \text{ percent.} \end{aligned}$$

In this case, we can say that there is about 92 percent of maximum heterogeneity among the students in the second student body with respect to academic major. The heterogeneity percentages for the two student bodies are quite different, 42 percent compared with 92 percent. The second student body is considerably more heterogeneous than the first as far as academic major is concerned.

Assumptions and Advantages of the *IQV*

IQV is specifically designed to measure variation among attributes or qualities, and therefore, it is quite useful for data of the nominal level of measurement. The investigator can compare the degree of heterogeneity of any attribute between any group or groups of elements. Such comparisons can provide supporting evidence for his research and can suggest explanations for the occurrence of certain events. When the investigator is able to assume a higher level of measurement for the data he has, however, he should use higher-level measures of variation to obtain the most information from his data.

THE RANGE

The *range* is a statistic which tells us the distance between the highest and the lowest (largest and smallest) scores in a distribution. More specifically, the range is defined as *the difference between the lower limit of the smallest score and the upper limit of the largest score in a distribution.* It should be remembered that the range was used earlier to help us construct frequency distributions for interval measures.

A formula for determining the range for any distribution of scores is

$$\text{range} = H_u - L_l$$

where H_u = the upper limit of the highest score in a distribution; and
L_l = the lower limit of the lowest score in a distribution.

If the highest score in a distribution were 50 and the lowest score were 25, the range for this distribution of scores would be:

$$\text{range} = 50.5 - 24.5 = 26.$$

The values 50.5 and 24.5 are the upper and the lower limits of the values 50 and 25 respectively.

Frequently, the range is simply defined as the highest observed score in the distribution minus the lowest observed score plus 1. This sometimes avoids the confusion resulting from having to think of upper and lower limits of intervals. It will give the same result as the first computation. For example, $50 - 25 + 1 = 26$.

For grouped data, the range is defined as the difference between the upper limit of the highest interval and the lower limit of the lowest interval in a distribution of scores. If the highest interval were 75–79 and the lowest interval were 20–24, the range would be $79.5 - 19.5 = 60$.

Assumptions for the Range

In order to be able to use the range in our research work, we must have interval-level information. This assumption is frequently violated when investigators use the range to construct frequency distributions for ordinal data. Technically, the range assumes that there are equal distances between all scores in a distribution. For ordinal-level data, we do not really know how great the distance is between any two values. We only know that one score is *higher* (or lower) than another, but not *how much higher* (or lower).

Advantages and Disadvantages of the Range

The range is a useful measure of variation in that it can be computed quickly and easily. It is also useful for allowing the investigator to determine the limits of a distribution of scores for the purpose of constructing a frequency distribution. It helps the researcher determine the number of intervals to employ in his frequency distribution as well as the most appropriate interval size.

The range is an unstable measure of variation, however. It is computed on the basis of the highest and the lowest scores in a distribution, and one deviant value can increase the range considerably. For example, consider the two distributions of scores below:

10 11 12 13 14 15 16 17 90 (A)

10 11 12 13 14 15 16 17 18 (B)

In example (A), the range is $90.5 - 9.5 = 81$. In example (B), the range is $18.5 - 9.5 = 9$. The difference in ranges, 81 and 9, is due to the one extreme score of 90. This property is an undesirable one. It makes the *comparison* of ranges from several distributions relatively unreliable. Better statistics for comparative purposes are presented below.

THE INTERQUARTILE RANGE

The *interquartile range* is defined as the distance between the first and third quartiles in any distribution of scores. These quartiles are points which identify the upper and lower 25 percent of the scores in a distribution.

To compute the interquartile range, we must first determine how many scores it takes to make up one quarter of the scores in the distribution. Using the information in Table 4.1, $N/4 = 68/4 = 17$. Therefore, 17 scores make up one quarter or 25 percent of the distribution.

To find the third quartile (Q_3) and the first quartile (Q_1), we must de-

Table 4.1. A Frequency Distribution Showing Quartiles.

Interval	*f*	*Quartile Points*
75–79	5	
70–74	7	
65–69	8	$66.4 = Q_3$
60–64	12	
55–59	11	
50–54	9	$50.1 = Q_1$
45–49	7	
40–44	6	
35–39	3	
	$\Sigma f = 68$	

termine both the values of the 17th score from the "top" of the distribution (or the 51st score from the "bottom" of it) and the 17th score from the "bottom" of the distribution. In determining the median for grouped data, we were actually trying to find Q_2 or the *second quartile*. The same kind of computational steps are involved in order to find Q_3 and Q_1.

For these data, we find the 17th score from the top of the distribution lying somewhere in the interval 65–69. Because there are 12 scores in the above 2 intervals, 75–79 and 70–74, we will need only 5 of the 8 scores in the next interval, 65–69, to make up 17 scores and determine the Q_3. Because we are working *down* the distribution, we shall take the *upper limit* of the interval we are entering for the 5 needed scores and subtract from it 5/8 of the interval.

The interval size in this case is 5, and 5/8 of 5 is equal to 3.1. This value is subtracted from the upper limit of the interval 65–69, that is, from 69.5, and the result is $69.5 - 3.1 = 66.4$. Thus 66.4 is defined as Q_3 for this distribution.

Finding Q_1 for this distribution is simply a counterpart of these procedures, but this time we shall be working *up* the distribution. Now we are looking for the 17th score from the bottom of the distribution. Counting from the bottom of the distribution, we find that there are 16 scores in the first 3 intervals. The next interval, 50–54, contains 9 frequencies. Since we need only 1 of these frequencies to make up the 17th score, we take 1/9 of the interval, that is, 1/9 of 5, which is approximately .6. Adding this value to the lower limit of the interval we are entering, or 49.5, we have $49.5 + .6 = 50.1$. Thus 50.1 is defined as the Q_1 for this distribution.

Now we simply determine the difference between the Q_3 and the Q_1 and this difference is the interquartile range as defined.

$$\begin{aligned} \text{interquartile range} &= Q_3 - Q_1 \\ &= 66.4 - 50.1 \\ &= 16.3. \end{aligned}$$

Thus 16.3 is the interquartile range for this distribution of scores.

Assumption for the Interquartile Range

The only assumption necessary for the computation of the interquartile range is that the investigator has interval-level data.

Advantages and Disadvantages of the Interquartile Range

The main advantage of the interquartile range is that it is a more stable measure of variability than the range if one wishes to use it for comparative purposes. Unlike the range, it does not depend upon the extreme scores in a distribution for its value. It does, however, take somewhat longer to compute than the range.

THE SEMI-INTERQUARTILE RANGE, OR QUARTILE DEVIATION

The *semi-interquartile range,* or "quartile deviation" as it is sometimes called, is half the interquartile range. Expressed symbolically, it is defined as

$$\text{semi-interquartile range} = \frac{Q_3 - Q_1}{2}.$$

All assumptions, advantages, and disadvantages of the interquartile range apply here as well. Naturally, then, the question is often asked, "Why divide by 2?" This question has an easy answer: *convention.* Frequently we find ourselves doing things because of custom or convention. The same is true for statistical usage. Through continued usage, some statistical procedures have become popular and widely accepted. What we do in this text is not always because of certain hard-and-fast cardinal rules. We often follow patterns and we often present things in particular ways because most people are familiar with them in these forms. At this and other places throughout these chapters, we will see the *power* of convention repeatedly. Convention plays an important role in how we structure and interpret the statistical world as well as other worlds—including our worlds of personal experience.

THE AVERAGE DEVIATION

Whenever we have a distribution of scores, assuming interval-level data, we can compute a $\overline{X}$ for that distribution. Knowing the $\overline{X}$ for any distribution of scores will enable us to specify *how much each score departs* from that $\overline{X}$. Any score different from the $\overline{X}$ departs by a certain distance from it. This distance, which can be expressed numerically, is labeled x. Therefore,

$$x = X_i - \overline{X}$$

where X_i = any observed score;
$\overline{X}$ = the mean of the distribution; and
x = a "deviation score."

Observed scores (X_i's) which are *lower* than the $\overline{X}$ value always have a negative (−) deviation score (x), while observed scores which are *higher* than the $\overline{X}$ value always have a positive (+) deviation score (x).

Supposedly, if we sum all distances each score departs from the mean, paying attention to the sign of each value (either + or −), we would end up with *zero.* Any number other than zero would mean either (a) that we started with an incorrect $\overline{X}$ value, (b) that we made a mistake in our computation of x, or (c) that there is some rounding error, in which case the departure from zero would be very small.

The following three scores have a $\overline{X}$ of 10.

Scores	x
9	−1
10	0
11	+1
	$\Sigma x = 0$

The scores 9 and 11 depart from the $\overline{X}$, that is, from 10, by 1 point. The score 9 is below the mean and is 1 value away from it, and therefore, it has an x value of −1. The score 10 is exactly at the mean, and since it does not depart from the mean it has an x value of 0. The score 11 is above the mean and is 1 value from it, and therefore it has an x value of +1. Summing the x's gives us zero. *All deviations from the mean, when summed, will equal zero.* Expressed symbolically,

$$\Sigma x = 0$$

where x = any score deviation from the $\overline{X}$ of a distribution.

Sometimes, the investigator will want to know how far, *on the average*, the scores in a distribution depart from the $\overline{X}$ of that distribution. We know that if we add all score deviations from the mean, we will arrive at zero. In order to compute the *average deviation* of all scores from the mean of the distribution, therefore, we ignore the sign (+ or −) of each deviation score. When we ignore the sign associated with a set of values, we refer to these values as *absolute*. Expressed symbolically, an absolute deviation from the mean is $|x|$. The symbol $|\ |$ means that we ignore the sign of the values it surrounds. By ignoring the sign of all deviation scores, we can add all deviations from the $\overline{X}$ and divide this sum by the total number of scores in the distribution. Expressed symbolically, the average deviation is:

$$AD = \frac{\Sigma|x|}{N}$$

where $\Sigma|x|$ = the absolute sum of all deviations from the $\overline{X}$; and
N = the number of scores in the distribution.

The statistic AD tells us the average distance each score in the distribution departs from the mean. For our previous example, the average deviation for the scores 9, 10, and 11 is $\frac{2}{3}$. On the average, each observed value, here, 9, 10, and 11, departs $\frac{2}{3}$ or .67 from the $\overline{X}$, 10. This computation is

$$AD = \frac{(1 + 0 + 1)}{3}$$

$$= \frac{2}{3}$$

$$= .67.$$

For a larger number of elements, such as the information in Table 4.2, the same procedure is followed. The $\bar{X}$ for the data in Table 4.2 is 7. In a

Table 4.2. Absolute Deviations from the Mean.

X = *any score* ($N = 7$)	$\lvert x \rvert$ = *absolute deviations from the* $\bar{X}$, 7
12	5
10	3
9	2
7	0
4	3
4	3
3	4
$\Sigma X = 49$	$\Sigma \lvert x \rvert = 20$

column labeled $|x|$, we determine how far each score departs from the $\bar{X}$, 7, as is shown. Summing the absolute values in this column, we obtain 20, which we then divide by the total number of scores, 7, to get the *average deviation*. Using these values in Table 4.2, in the AD formula, we compute:

$$AD = \frac{\Sigma|x|}{N}$$
$$= \tfrac{20}{7}$$
$$= 2.86.$$

The average deviation for these data is 2.86. On the average, then, scores in this particular distribution depart from the mean by 2.86.

For grouped data, the average deviation is found similarly. But in this case, interval midpoints are used as deviation scores from the $\bar{X}$. A mean is computed; then each interval midpoint is analyzed to determine how far it deviates from the mean. These deviation values are multiplied by the frequencies found in the respective intervals, and these products are summed and then divided by the total number of frequencies. The answer is the average deviation. For example, suppose we had the information provided in Table 4.3. Computing the AD for these data, we have:

$$AD = \tfrac{222}{50} = 4.44.$$

The average deviation for these data is 4.44.

The primary assumption for the average deviation is that the investigator has interval-level data. Where it is necessary to specify exact distances from the mean and where means must be computed, the interval-level assumption must be met.

Deviation is meaningful only when the researcher has at least interval-

Table 4.3. Determining the Average Deviation for Grouped Data.

Interval	f	$\lvert x\rvert$ ($\overline{X} = 13$)	$f\lvert x\rvert$
21–23	5	9	45
18–20	7	6	42
15–17	8	3	24
12–14	10	0	0
9–11	8	3	24
6–8	7	6	42
3–5	5	9	45
	$\Sigma f = 50$		$\Sigma f\lvert x\rvert = 222$

level data to analyze. The average-deviation statistic indicates the extent to which variation exists within any distribution of scores. It is relatively easy to compute and interpret. One of the difficulties of the average deviation is that it tends to vary greatly from distribution to distribution. There is little *standardization,* if any, associated with the average deviation and the other measures of variability which we have discussed. This fact alone greatly restricts the use of these measures in research work. Because better measures of variability are presently available, the average deviation is seldom used any more.

THE VARIANCE AND THE STANDARD DEVIATION

Perhaps the most "standardized" measure of variability is the *standard deviation, s.* In order to more fully understand the standard deviation and how it is computed, we shall briefly examine another measure of variability which is closely related to it. This measure is called the *variance,* and it is defined as *the mean of the sum of all squared deviations from the mean of any distribution of scores.* To briefly illustrate, suppose we have the following 5 scores which have a $\overline{X}$ of 8:

Score	x	x^2
12	4	16
10	2	4
8	0	0
7	−1	1
3	−5	25
40 = score sum	$\Sigma x = 0$	$\Sigma x^2 = 46$

Remember that when the average deviation was computed, the x's were summed (ignoring the sign) and divided by the total number of elements. The x's reflect the distance by which each score departs from the mean. The variance is based upon a different approach to "deviation." In this case, all x's, as deviations from the $\overline{X}$ of the distribution, are *squared.* These squares are summed, and this result, Σx^2, is divided by the number of elements, in this case 5. The result is called the variance, and the formula is as follows:

$$\text{variance} = s^2 = \frac{\Sigma x^2}{N}$$

where Σx^2 = the sum of the squared deviations from the $\overline{X}$; and
N = the total number of elements in the distribution.

For the data above, the values are substituted for symbols in the variance formula:

$$s^2 = \tfrac{46}{5}$$
$$= 9.2.$$

Thus 9.2 is the variance, s^2, for these data.

The computation of the variance will be a necessary step for the computation of the standard deviation. The variance itself, however, has not been widely adopted as a popular descriptive measure of variation. Compared to the standard deviation, the variance does not lend itself to as direct an interpretation. The relation between the variance and the standard deviation is simply that *the standard deviation is the square root of the variance.* Expressed in symbols:

$$\text{standard deviation} = s = \sqrt{s^2} = \sqrt{\frac{\Sigma x^2}{N}}.$$

The standard deviation s is more desirable as a measure of variation than the variance s^2, primarily because it has certain properties which enable the investigator to make more meaningful comparisons between scores, both within the same distribution and between different distributions. Also, there are tables available which, in order to be interpreted properly, depend upon a knowledge of the standard deviation of the distribution. These properties will become more evident when we examine *standard scores* and the *normal distribution* in the following chapter. For the time being, let us turn to another problem, namely, computing variances and standard deviations from *grouped data.* It should be apparent that whichever statistic we compute, the variance or the standard deviation, the relation between them is a simple one, and we will always know one with a knowledge of the other.

Computation of the Standard Deviation for Grouped Interval-Level Data

Whenever we have interval-level data in grouped form, such as the information in Table 4.4, we can use the following procedure to find the standard deviation.

Beginning with a frequency distribution as shown in Table 4.4, we first determine the "step" or interval deviation of each interval of frequencies from an *arbitrary reference point. We may select the midpoint of any*

Table 4.4. Standard Deviation for Grouped Interval-Level Data.

Interval	f	x'	fx'	fx'^2
20–21	2	5	10	50
18–19	3	4	12	48
16–17	5	3	15	45
14–15	9	2	18	36
12–13	20	1	20	20
10–11	34	0	0	0
8–9	13	−1	−13	13
6–7	6	−2	−12	24
4–5	5	−3	−15	45
2–3	3	−4	−12	48
	$\Sigma f = 100$		$\Sigma fx' = 23$	$\Sigma fx'^2 = 329$

interval in the distribution as our arbitrary reference point. It makes no difference for the final result. In this case, we have selected as our arbitrary reference point the interval 10–11.

Beginning with this point, 10–11, we number all *increasing* intervals, here 12–13, 14–15, 16–17, and so on, 1, 2, 3, 4, successively until the top of the distribution is reached. All intervals *below* the arbitrary reference point are successively numbered −1, −2, −3, and so on, until the bottom of the distribution is reached. The arbitrary reference point receives the value 0. These numbers are placed in a column labeled x', as is shown in Table 4.4.

Next, we multiply each set of frequencies by each corresponding x' value, paying attention to the sign (+ or −) of the numbers. These products are placed in a third column labeled fx'.

Then, we multiply the values in the fx' column by each corresponding value in the x' column. These products are placed in a fourth column labeled fx'^2. Summing the values in columns f, fx', and fx'^2, we are now able to substitute values for symbols in the following standard-deviation formula for grouped data:

$$s = \sqrt{\frac{\Sigma x^2}{N}}$$

where $\Sigma x^2 = (i)^2[\Sigma fx'^2 - \frac{(\Sigma fx')^2}{N}]$; and

$i =$ the interval size.

To find Σx^2, we have

$$\begin{aligned}\Sigma x^2 &= (2)^2[329 - \frac{(23)^2}{100}] \\ &= (4)(329 - 5.29) \\ &= (4)(323.71) \\ &= 1{,}294.84.\end{aligned}$$

Then

$$s = \sqrt{\frac{1{,}294.84}{100}}$$
$$= \sqrt{12.9484}$$
$$= 3.6.$$

The standard deviation for the data in Table 4.4 is 3.6. It is apparent that we computed the variance in the process, and that its value is 12.9 as shown with the radical.*

What Does the Standard Deviation Mean?

The standard deviation represents, in terms of score values, a certain distance from the mean which theoretically includes a constant proportion of scores in the distribution. We can say that when we begin at the mean and move a distance specified by a standard-deviation value in either direction, we will include within this distance a certain proportion of the scores of the distribution.

The full meaning of the standard deviation will become clear when we discuss the normal distribution in the following chapter. For the time being, we will say that the standard deviation is a very popular and useful measure of variability.

Assumptions for the Standard Deviation

The primary assumption underlying the standard deviation is that the investigator has interval-level data at his disposal. If the scores to be manipulated and analyzed are below the interval level of measurement (that is, of the ordinal or nominal level), the standard deviation cannot be meaningfully applied. Other assumptions will be treated in Chapter 5.

Advantages and Disadvantages of the Standard Deviation

The interval-level assumption underlying the computation of the standard deviation restricts its use in the social sciences considerably. But when dealing with data that meet this assumption, the standard deviation is quite popular; tables exist (see Table A.3 Appendix A) which enable the investigator to interpret standard-deviation values with relative ease. Standard-deviation values are *always* used in relation to some $\bar{X}$.

Computation of standard deviations constitutes a preliminary step for certain other statistical procedures to be discussed in subsequent chapters. Other measures of variation are considerably easier to compute, but much more use has been made of the standard deviation.

---

* For simpler numbers, 1–1,000, see the Table of Squares and Square Roots in Appendix A, Table A.1.

SUMMARY

This chapter has explored certain measures of variation which describe the "spread" of a distribution of scores. Most of these statistics (with the exception of the index of qualitative variation) require that the investigator have interval-level data if they are to be meaningfully applied.

Of all the measures of variation discussed, the standard deviation is by far the most widely used in sociological research. A primary advantage of the standard deviation is that tables are available which make interpretation more meaningful. For nominal-level information, few measures of variation are available. The index of qualitative variation has been presented as a measure of attribute heterogeneity rather than as a measure of score dispersion.

In the next chapter, the normal curve will be discussed, particularly in conjunction with the standard deviation, and the relation between these ideas should become apparent.

QUESTIONS FOR REVIEW AND PROBLEMS TO SOLVE

1. For the following data, compute the interquartile range and the standard deviation. What is/are the mode/s?

Interval	f
85–89	4
80–84	7
75–79	9
70–74	13
65–69	20
60–64	7
55–59	20
50–54	17
45–49	12
40–44	6
35–39	2

2. What is "variability" or "dispersion"? What are some measures of variability?

3. Which is the best measure of variation to use for each of the following levels of data: (a) nominal; (b) interval?

4. What are some advantages and disadvantages of the range? Of the interquartile range?

5. Compute an index of qualitative variation for the following data:

Class	f
English	35
French	65
Russian	25
Greek	75

6. What are some advantages of the standard deviation over the other measures of dispersion? What are some primary assumptions underlying its computation?

7. Differentiate between measures of central tendency and measures of variability in terms of the information they provide about a distribution of scores.

8. Compute an average deviation for the data in Problem 1. What is the interpretation you can make here? How does it compare with the standard deviation for the same data?

9. Compute the standard deviation for the following raw scores: 8, 13, 14, 19, 21, 33, 67, 69, 88, 91, 95.

10. Give some examples of how *convention* determines the way things are done in statistical methods. What are some "dictates" of convention as far as measures of variability are concerned?

5 Standard Scores and the Unit Normal Distribution

In previous chapters we have discussed frequency distributions, two characteristics of them, and measures of these characteristics. These characteristics are central tendency and dispersion or variability. In this chapter we shall discuss a particular kind of frequency distribution known as the *unit normal distribution.* Understanding the various aspects of the unit normal distribution is a fundamental prerequisite to the understanding of subsequent discussions of statistical inference and to the testing of hypotheses.

Consider a simple frequency distribution. It will be remembered that frequency distributions can be graphically portrayed. Such graphs assume many different shapes. For example, some graphs show distributions of scores where many frequencies focus around very high scores and taper off toward the lower ones. Such is the case with the frequency distribution shown in Table 5.1. The frequency distribution in Table 5.1 is shown

Table 5.1. A Frequency Distribution.

Interval	*f*
65–69	45
60–64	27
55–59	12
50–54	8
45–49	6
40–44	3
35–39	2
30–34	2
25–29	2
20–24	1
	$\Sigma f = 108$

as a histogram in Figure 5.1. The continuous line joining the midpoints of the tops of the intervals in the histogram is called a *curve.* "Smoothing" a frequency polygon for these data will produce a similar curve.

A frequency distribution like that in Table 5.1 is said to be *skewed.* Skewness means that the distribution is not symmetrical—that the tails or ends of the frequency distribution do not taper off *equally.* in both

Figure 5.1. A Curve Superimposed over a Histogram.

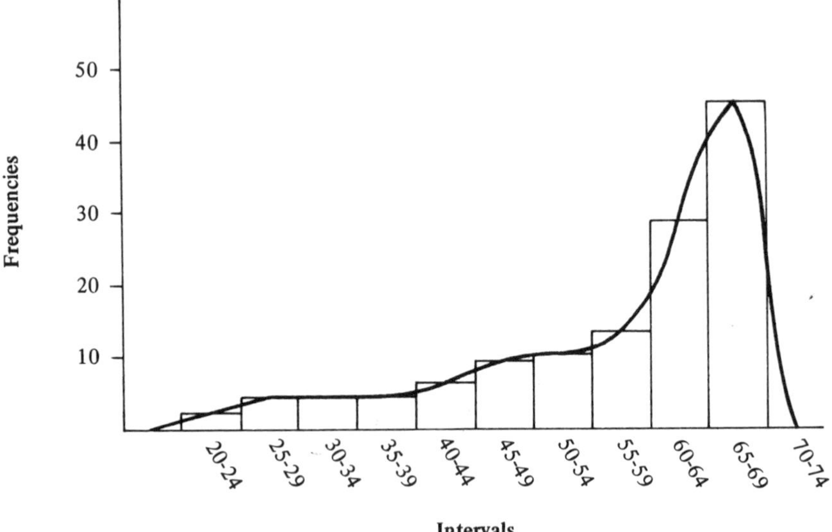

directions. The curve in Figure 5.1 is said to be skewed to the left, because the frequencies taper off toward the left. A curve which is skewed to the left is also said to be *negatively skewed.*

If we were simply to reverse the frequencies from the way they originally appeared in Table 5.1, we would have a frequency distribution represented by the curve drawn in Figure 5.2. This distribution is also said to be skewed. This time, however, the frequencies taper off toward the right end of the distribution. Such a curve is said to be skewed to the right or *positively skewed.*

When a curve is free of skewness such as the one shown in Figure 5.3, it is said to be *symmetrical,* and the frequency distribution for which it was drawn is also said to be symmetrical. The curve in Figure 5.3 is also said to be *normal.* Not all symmetrical curves are normal, but all normal distributions are symmetrical. The use of the word "normal" does not mean to imply that other curves are *abnormal.* The word "normal" as here used refers to the type of curve and distribution having certain mathematical properties.

Mathematicians have developed a formula for the unit normal curve which is given as follows:

$$Y = \left(\frac{1}{\sigma\sqrt{2\pi}}\right)e^{-\frac{1}{2}\left(\frac{X-\mu}{\sigma}\right)^2}$$

where $\pi = 3.1416$;
$e = 2.7183$;

Figure 5.2. A Curve Superimposed over a Histogram.

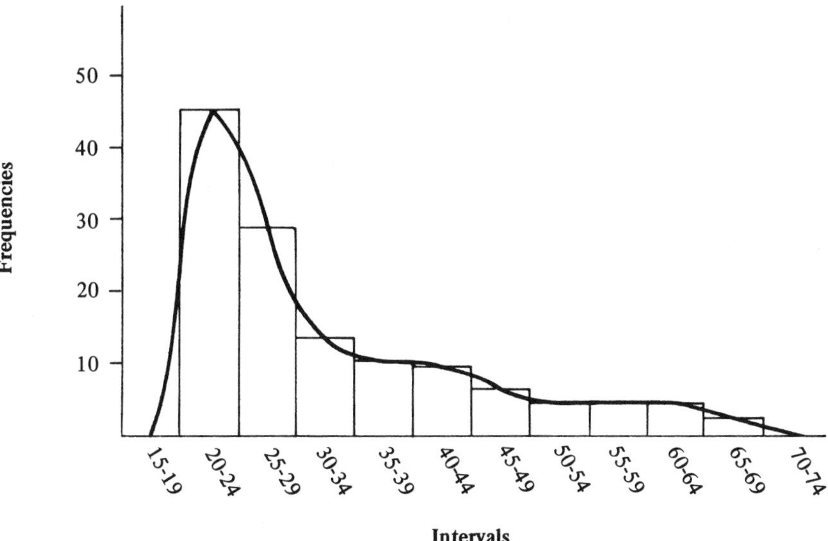

σ = a parameter equal to the standard deviation of the distribution;
μ = a parameter equal to the mean of the distribution;
X = abscissa—the measurement or score marked on the horizontal axis; and
Y = ordinate—the height of the curve at a point corresponding to an assigned value of X.

The curve based upon this formula has a number of desirable properties which are of particular interest to the social scientist, properties which are useful in that they define a series of constant attributes. The total area

Figure 5.3. A Normal Curve.

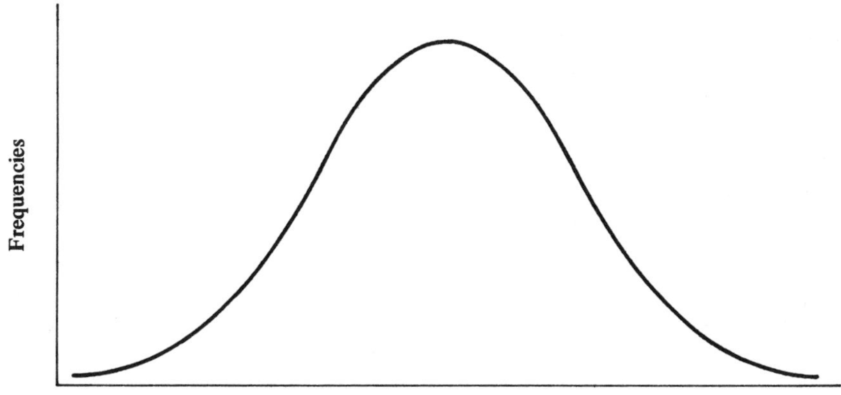

included under the normal curve can represent the total number of elements in any population. This area can be considered as being equal to unity. Because of this property, it is possible to determine the proportion of frequencies contained between any two scores along the horizontal axis by determining the proportionate area under the curve between the two scores.

It is apparent, then, that the normal curve can serve a general *comparative* function. This property will soon be illustrated. It will be seen that when we have a particular kind of normal curve, then certain statements which can be made concerning the normal distribution can also apply to our data. Before examining this particular type of normal curve, we must first of all give some attention to the standardization of scores taken from different, approximately normal, distributions.

STANDARD SCORES AND THE NORMAL DISTRIBUTION

Whenever we encounter scores taken on some characteristic from two different populations of elements, we are unable to compare them directly, much as we are unable to compare incomes of individuals from different countries. Because of differences in the means and in the standard deviations of these populations of elements, a *larger* absolute score does not necessarily mean a *higher* score relative to the means of the two distributions. Scores from different populations are directly comparable only when the means and standard deviations of both populations are identical to one another. Such is seldom the case in actual research.

In order to accurately compare the scores taken from different populations, we need to convert them to some common standard. Such a standard is found with the *unit normal distribution.* The unit normal distribution is a particular kind of normal distribution. It has a mean, μ, equal to zero and a standard deviation, σ, equal to 1. Some raw-score distributions can be converted into distributions which approximate the unit normal distribution and which have the same two parameters, namely, $\mu = 0$ and $\sigma = 1$. Comparing scores from different populations after such conversion poses no significant problem, because each population is reduced to virtually the same standard of measurement. "Standardizing" a distribution by converting it to a distribution with $\mu = 0$, $\sigma = 1$ is legitimate only if the original raw-score distribution is approximately normal and resembles that shown in Figure 5.3.

When raw scores are converted to a common standard, they are called *standard scores* or *Z scores.* Standard scores are expressed in terms of *standard-deviation units. Every raw score can be given an equivalent standard score.* The relative positions of such raw scores taken from different normal distributions can then be identified within the unit normal distribution and can be compared with one another.

To change a raw score into a Z score or standard score, the following formula can be used:

$$Z = \frac{X_i - \overline{X}}{s}$$

where X_i = any raw score;
X = the mean of the distribution from which the raw score was obtained; and
s = the standard deviation of the distribution from which the raw score was obtained.

As long as we know the mean and the standard deviation of the distribution from which any raw score is obtained, we can compute a Z score.

A Z score can be interpreted in terms of the number of standard-deviation units that measure its distance from the mean of the distribution. A Z score of 1.00 is one standard deviation above the mean, a Z of 2.50 is $2\frac{1}{2}$ standard deviation units above the mean, and so on. A Z score may be either positive or negative, according to the side of the mean on which the particular score is found. A positive Z score is a score above the mean. A negative Z score is a score below the mean.

The distance between any Z score and the mean of the distribution includes a corresponding proportion of the distribution. For example, the two Z scores $+1.55$ and -1.55 include equal proportionate segments of the normal distribution, but these Z scores are located on different sides of the mean. Figure 5.4 shows a normal distribution and the positions of positive and negative Z scores in relation to the mean. Table A.3 of Appendix A gives Z scores ranging from 0.00 to 5.00 and the corresponding proportionate areas of the unit normal curve included by each of them. Z scores are usually reported by carrying out mathematical work to three decimal places and then rounding to two places. The whole-

Figure 5.4. A Normal Distribution Showing Positive and Negative Z Scores.

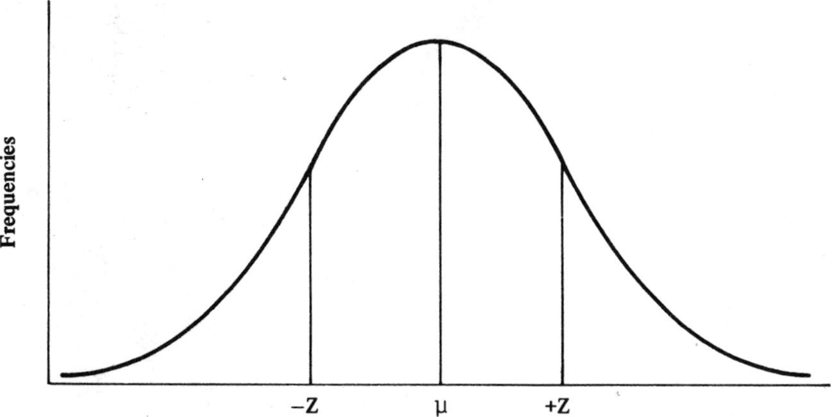

number digit and first fractional digit of the Z score are line labels in the left-hand (Z) column in Table A.3, while the second fractional digit is a column heading across the top of the table. The number at the point where the line and column intersect in the body of the table is the proportionate area of the normal curve included between the mean and the Z score. The following examples should make the use of this table more clear:

Z Score	*Area Included between Mean and Z Score*
0.12	.0478
1.78	.4625
−2.90	.4981
1.15	.3749
−1.15	.3749

The sign (+ or −) simply tells us whether or not a score is above or below the mean of the distribution. The proportionate area included by Z scores of the same size, *regardless of the sign,* is the same.

Uses of Standard Scores

Suppose two university students are taking introductory sociology courses from two different professors. At the end of the term they compare final-examination grades. John receives a grade of 85 while Bill receives a grade of 92. Without a standard for comparison, it would *appear* that Bill did better on his final examination than John. But *larger* scores are not necessarily to be equated with *better* scores.

If we were to convert each of these scores to standard scores, we would be in a better position to compare them. We need to know the final-examination means and the standard deviations for each of the sociology classes. This information is provided below:

	John's Class	*Bill's Class*
Class mean	75	88
Raw score	85	92
Standard deviation	6.5	4.0

With this information, we can transform each student's raw score into its equivalent Z score:

For John:

$$Z = \frac{X - \bar{X}}{s} = \frac{85 - 75}{6.5} = \frac{10}{6.5}$$

$$= 1.54.$$

For Bill:

$$Z = \frac{X - \bar{X}}{s} = \frac{92 - 88}{4.0} = \frac{4}{4.0}$$
$$= 1.00.$$

By examining the students' respective positions in each class according to their Z scores, it is apparent that John did better *relative to the other members of his class*, than Bill did *relative to the members of his class.* It is extremely difficult to say that either did better than the other, however. The tests may have been quite different in the degree of difficulty. Also, the classes may have differed markedly in ability. So many variables could have affected the performance of each student on the test that it is difficult if not impossible to determine who actually did better *compared with the other.* Compared with the members of their classes, however, is a different story. John, the student with the largest positive Z score, did better than Bill, relatively speaking.

We may wish to compare both students according to the normal distribution by superimposing one's Z score over the other's. We have done so in Figure 5.5. The reader is again cautioned about drawing conclusions

Figure 5.5. John's and Bill's Scores Compared on the Normal Distribution.

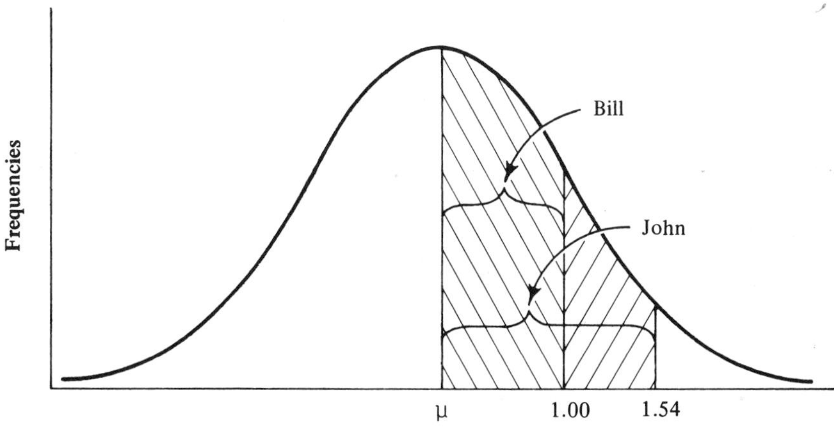

as to which student actually did better than the other *in relation to each other* rather than in relation to their respective classes.

Because the area under the normal distribution can be considered as unity or as 100 percent of the cases, we can also determine the percentage of students in each class whose scores lie below or above each standard score shown in Figure 5.5. We may do this by finding what proportion of the distribution is included between the mean and the Z score of each student.

John's Z score is 1.54. This includes .4382 of the distribution above the mean. Since the mean is located at the center of the distribution, we must *add* the proportion of the area under the curve and below the mean to the included proportion of the curve area above the mean, in order to determine John's over-all position in the distribution of test grades. Since half of the distribution is on the lower side of the mean, we must add .5000 to .4382. We can now say that approximately .9382 or about 94 percent of the students' scores lie below John's score, while about 6 percent of the class scores lie above it.

Doing the same for Bill's score in the same Figure 5.5, we find that the area included between the mean and his Z score of 1.00 is equivalent to .3413. Since his score is also above the mean, we must therefore add .5000 to it. Bill's score is at a point where .8413 or about 84 percent of the class scores lie below it, while about 16 percent of the class scores lie above it.

By changing a set of raw scores into standard scores, we are able to perform a number of meaningful operations. One of these operations, comparing scores taken from different frequency distributions, has been presented. Other operations are also possible.

Suppose we are trying to find the proportion of scores included between two Z scores. Using the Z scores of 2.36 and -1.71 as our example, we need to determine the proportion of the area under the curve that is included between the mean and each Z score. The distance between the mean and a Z of 2.36 includes .4909 of this distribution area, while the distance between the mean and -1.71 includes .4564 of the distribution area. Since one Z score is *above* the mean and the other *below* it, it follows that we must *sum* these two proportions to determine the total area of the distribution included between them. The proportion of the distribution included between the Z scores of 2.36 and -1.71 is $.4909 + .4564 = .9473$. We can say that about 95 percent of the scores or cases are included between these two Z scores. This analysis is illustrated in Figure 5.6 below.

Let us take a different example. Suppose we wish to determine the proportion of scores included between the Z scores of -2.25 and $-.93$. In this case, both Z scores lie below the mean. Again, we must find the proportion of the distribution included between each Z score and the mean. The respective proportions of the curve included by these Z's of -2.25 and $-.93$ are .4878 and .3238. We are interested in the proportion of the area included between these scores and therefore, we must *subtract* the smaller proportion from the larger. Subtracting .3238 from .4878 gives us .1640; thus about 16 percent of the scores lie between the two Z's of -2.25 and $-.93$. The illustration in Figure 5.7 shows the area included by them.

Suppose we need to determine a person's *raw score* from his Z score.

Figure 5.6. The Area of the Distribution between Two *Z* Scores.

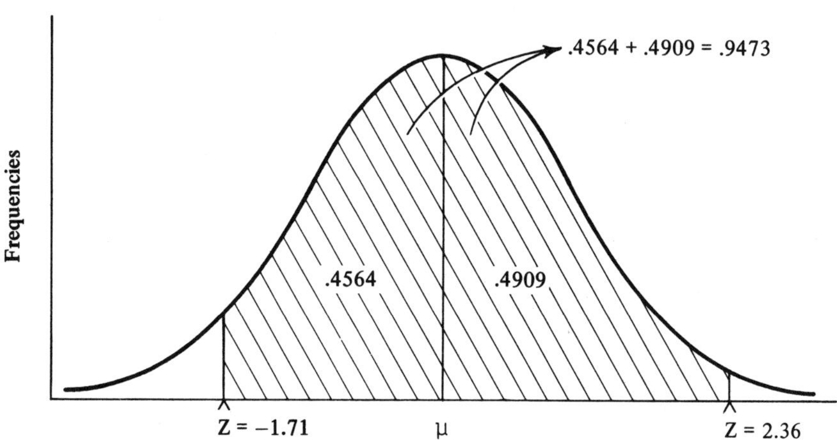

Is this possible? Yes, if we know the mean and the standard deviation of the raw-score distribution. To determine a person's raw score from his *Z* score, we simply multiply his *Z* score by the raw-score standard deviation, then add this product to the raw-score mean if it is positive or subtract this product from the raw-score mean if it is negative. The formula for this procedure is

$$\text{raw score} = \overline{X} + (Z)(s)$$

where $\overline{X}$ = the raw-score mean;
Z = the standard score; and
s = the raw-score standard deviation.

Figure 5.7. The Area of the Distribution between Two *Z* Scores on the Same Side of the Mean.

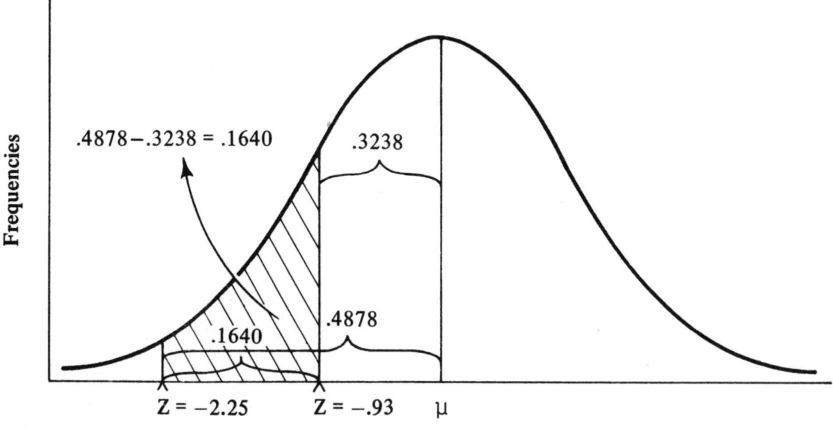

For example, suppose a person has a Z score of 1.75. Further suppose that the raw-score mean and standard deviation of the distribution from which his Z score was obtained were 50 and 3.68 respectively. Multiplying the standard deviation by his Z score, we obtain

$$(3.68)(1.75) = 6.44.$$

We add this value to the $\bar{X}$, 50, obtaining the following result:

$$50 + 6.44 = 56.44.$$

The person's original raw score should be 56.44 or a close approximation of it. If the raw scores are whole numbers, then his score would be 56.

Bear in mind that we are performing algebraic addition in applying the formula above. The Z score will sometimes be negative, hence the product $(Z)(s)$ is likewise negative. If the Z score in the example we have just computed had been -1.75, then the product $(Z)(s)$ would have been -6.44; the complete arithmetic calculation would have been

$$50 - 6.44 = 43.56$$

and the raw score would have been 43.56, approximately 44.

Advantages and Disadvantages of Standard Scores

The primary advantage of standard scores is that they may be used to compare raw scores taken from different distributions. The data, however, must be at least of the intervål level of measurement.

The major disadvantage of standard scores is that a *normal distribu-*

Figure 5.8. Comparing Areas of the Curve of a Skewed Distribution.

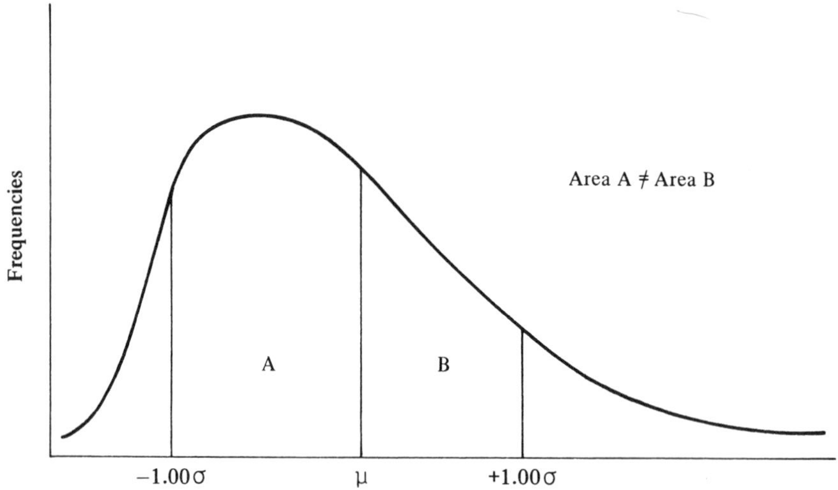

tion must be assumed. When this assumption is not met, a standard score cannot be interpreted in terms of a standardized proportion of the distribution from which it was computed. When the distribution is skewed, the area within 1 standard deviation to the left of the mean is not equal to the area within the same distance to the right of the mean. For example, the distribution in Figure 5.8 is skewed. Area *A* is not equal to Area *B*, even though each area is included by 1 standard deviation from the mean. This illustrates that when skewed distributions are encountered, a greater proportion of scores is found away from the skewed end of the distribution when comparing areas between identical *Z* scores on either side of the mean.

Some general statements may be made about skewed distributions, however, no matter how skewed they are. First of all, the area included within 2 standard deviations on either side of the mean of a skewed distribution will always amount to at least 75 percent of the total area under the curve. Second, at least 90 percent of the total area under the curve will always be included within 3 standard deviations on either side of the mean. In Figure 5.9, a skewed distribution is shown. It can be demonstrated statistically that the above statements will hold, regardless of how skewed the distribution may be.

These statements lend themselves to general application—the researcher will be able to make some general interpretations of his findings regardless of the degree of skewness in any distribution of scores he encounters. Such general interpretations will be quite helpful in obtaining an impression of the nature of the distribution.

Figure 5.9. A Skewed Distribution Showing General Areas Included by *Z*'s of 2.00 and 3.00 on Either Side of the Mean.

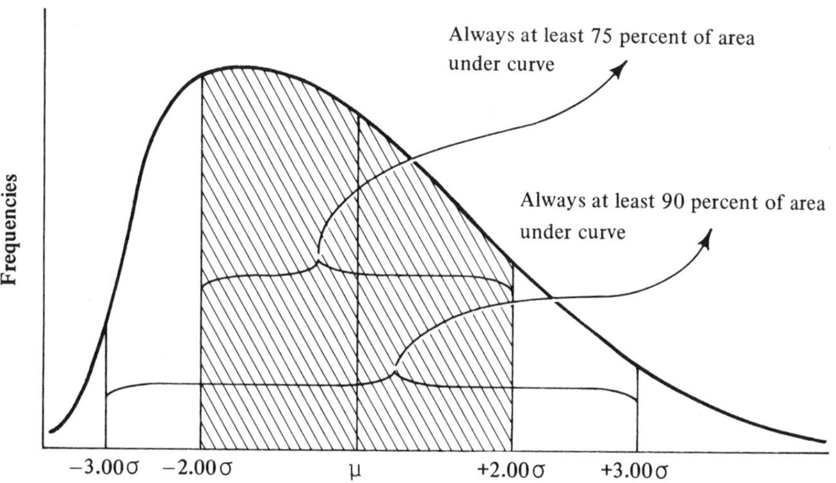

THE UNIT NORMAL DISTRIBUTION

It was previously mentioned that the unit normal distribution has a number of desirable properties which are useful to researchers. These properties are *constant,* which means that they never change from one unit normal distribution to the next. Six of the more important of these properties will now be discussed.

1. *The mean of the unit normal distribution is always equal to zero and the standard deviation is always equal to 1.* Figure 5.10 shows a unit normal distribution with a $\mu = 0$ and $\sigma = 1$. This distribution is often referred to as the "unit normal distribution" or the "standard normal distribution." Standardization is necessary if we are going to successfully compare scores taken from different raw-score distributions.

Let us examine the monetary systems of a number of countries, for example. Suppose we find a person in China with 1,000,000 yuan. (During World War II it took almost that many yuan to purchase a loaf of bread.) Further suppose that we find a person in Russia with 1,000,000 rubles. And let's say that we find a third person, this time from Egypt, who has 1,000,000 piastres. Do we conclude that all three are equally wealthy? When these persons enter a bank in the United States for the purpose of exchanging their money for United States currency, does the bank teller give each person an identical sum of 1,000,000 United States dollars in exchange for their money? Of course not!

During periods of excessive inflation in a country, the money may become relatively worthless. A person in Russia with 1,000,000 rubles may be considered very rich and may have high status. A person in China with 1,000,000 yuan, on the other hand, may be considered commonplace, average, even poor, compared with the rest of his countrymen. The

Figure 5.10. A Unit Normal Distribution.

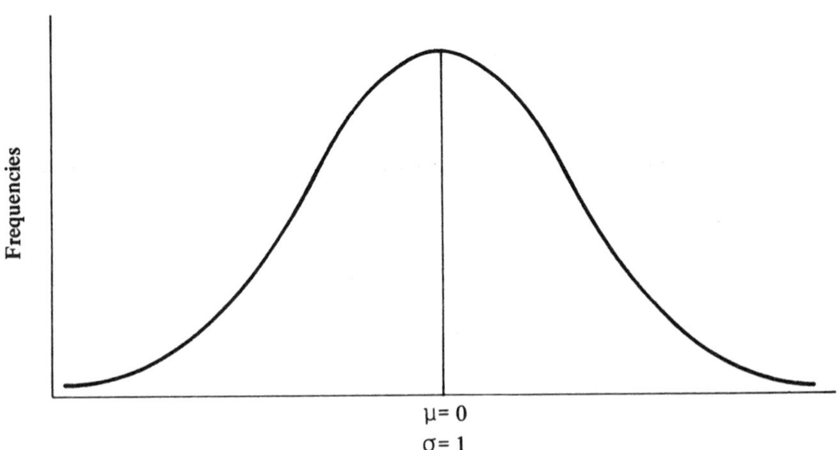

point is that each of these "assets" has been taken from distributions based on a different unit of measurement, the yuan, the ruble, and the piastre. In order to determine how each of these persons is positioned in his society in comparison to the other two, we must reduce their incomes to some common standard. This will allow us to compare them according to some common scale of measurement.

By changing the scores of individuals or values of observations taken from different frequency distributions into the same standard, scores from different distributions may be readily compared with one another *according to such a common standard.* A unit normal distribution with a $\mu = 0$ and $\sigma = 1$ provides a common standard by which to compare scores taken from different frequency distributions.

2. *The mean, median, and mode of the unit normal distribution all occur at the same point, namely, at the highest point of the curve in the center of the distribution.* In Figure 5.11 and Figure 5.12 are two curves, one normal, the other skewed. Notice that in the unit normal curve, the mean, mode, and median, three central-tendency measures, are located at the same point in the distribution, whereas in the skewed curve, the mean, mode, and median occur at different points.

3. *The total area underneath the curve and contained within the unit normal distribution can be defined as unity.* Parts of unity are represented as proportions of the total area underneath the curve and within the distribution. In a distribution like that of Figure 5.11, all scores or values are found underneath the curve. Cutting off the horizontal axis at known points also cuts off known proportions of the total area of the distribution. Such cutoff points along the horizontal axis are called "standard scores" or Z scores, and each Z score is an established distance from the mean of

Figure 5.11. A Normal Distribution Showing Three Central-Tendency Measures.

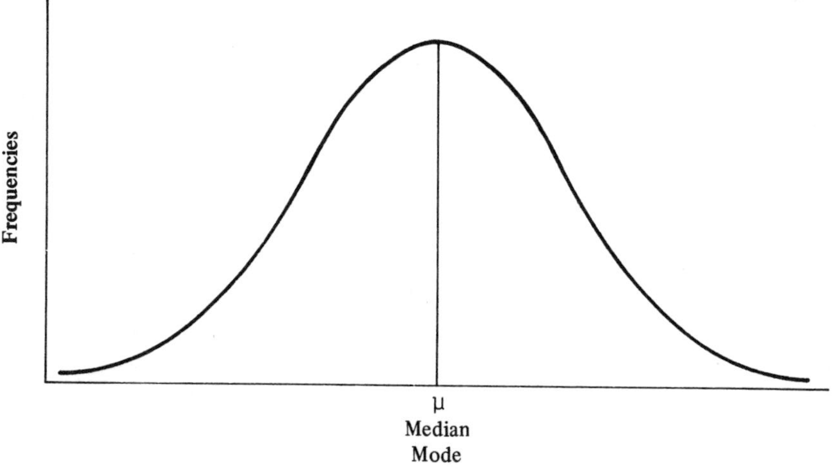

Figure 5.12. A Skewed Distribution Showing Three Central-Tendency Measures.

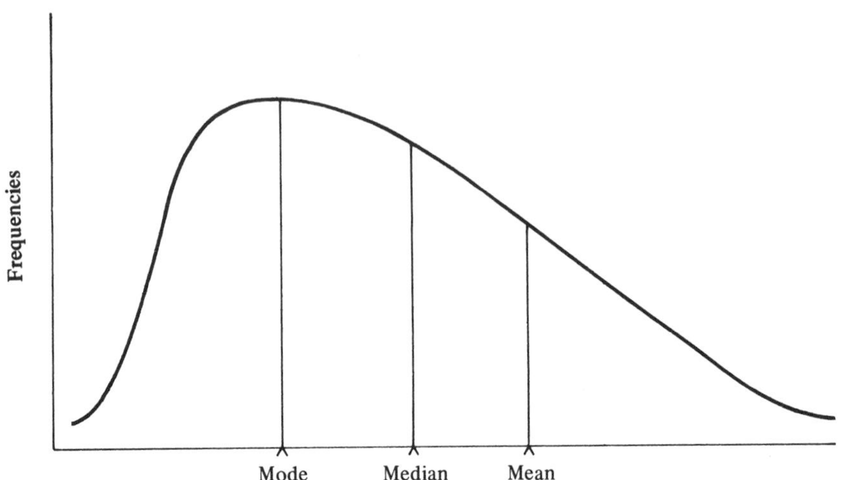

the unit normal distribution and includes a constant segment or proportion of it. No matter into how many segments the normal distribution is divided, the sum of the segments will always equal unity.

4. *The unit normal distribution is symmetrical and "bell-shaped."*

5. *The unit normal distribution is asymptotic.* This statement means that the ends of the distribution extend toward infinity, that the ends of the distribution always approach the horizontal axis but never quite touch it. For this reason, the ends of the unit normal curve in each of the figures above are shown as *not* touching the horizontal axis of the distribution. All observed distributions in social research will have defined upper and lower limits, however. This should make no difference if N is large, even though the range of the normal distribution is theoretically infinite.

6. *The area under the curve between a point at a given distance from the mean of the unit normal distribution is equivalent to the area under the curve between a point the same distance on the other side of the mean.* For example, a distance of 2 standard deviations to the left of the mean is equal to a distance of 2 standard deviations to the right of the mean, and the area included within these distances on either side of the mean is identical. This equality is a property of the *symmetry* of the curve. Figure 5.13 illustrates this more clearly.

On the basis of these characteristics of the unit normal distribution, certain conclusions may be drawn. First of all, the unit normal distribution is a *theoretical distribution.* It does not exist in reality, but the distributions of many real phenomena may approximate it.

Second, we are restricted as to what kind of data the unit normal distribution can be used for. The use of the mean and the standard deviation requires that we have data of at least the interval level of measurement.

Figure 5.13. A Normal Distribution Showing Equal Areas Included by Identical Standard Deviations on Either Side of the Mean.

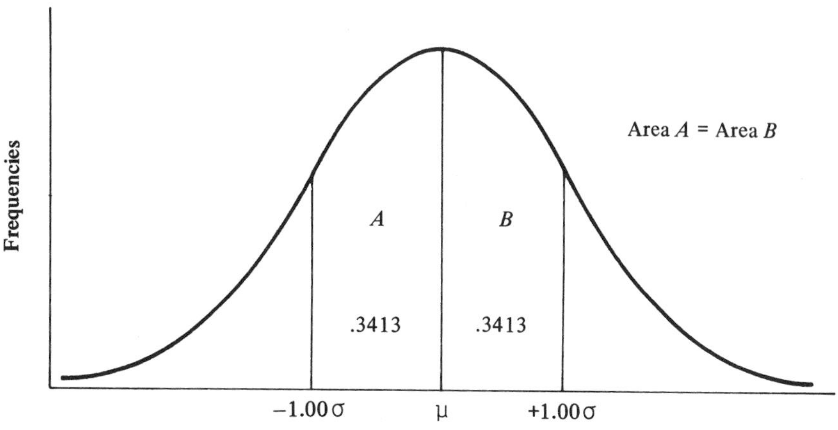

KURTOSIS

Technically, there is only *one* unit normal distribution and curve. But frequently observed distributions often differ from normal or from each other according to their peakedness or *kurtosis*. Some curves are flat, some tall, others more nearly normal in form. The curves are illustrated in Figures 5.14, 5.15, and 5.16. Tall curves such as the one in Figure 5.14 are called *leptokurtic*. Flat curves such as the one in Figure 5.15 are called *platykurtic*. More nearly normal-shaped curves such as the one in Figure 5.16 are called *mesokurtic*. The mesokurtic curve in Figure 5.16 most closely resembles the *standard form of the normal curve*.

Figure 5.14. A Leptokurtic or "Peaked" Curve.

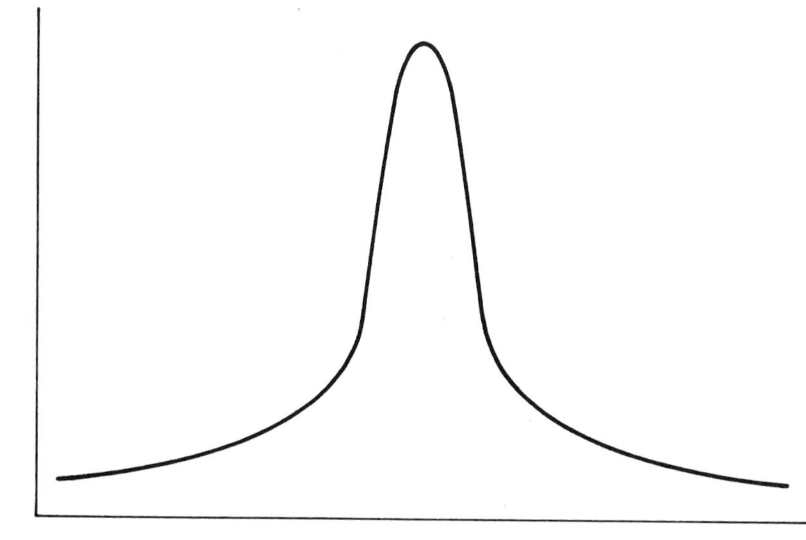

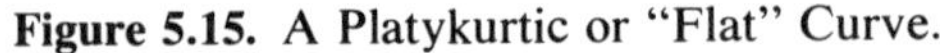

Figure 5.15. A Platykurtic or "Flat" Curve.

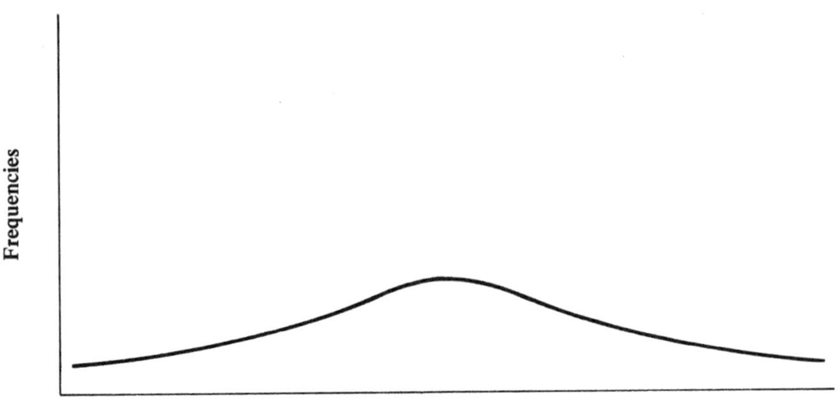

Figure 5.16. A Mesokurtic Curve More Nearly Normal in Form than a Peaked or Flat Curve.

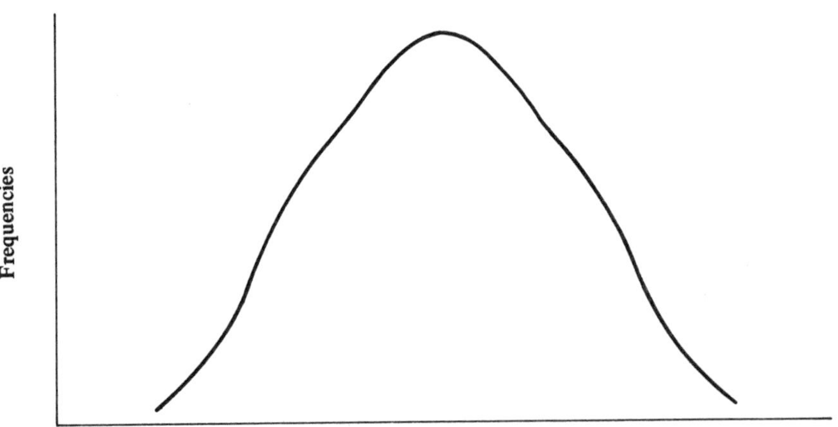

Leptokurtic and platykurtic curves are different from the normal curve. More scores are included under a leptokurtic curve within 1 standard deviation on either side of the mean of the distribution than in the comparable area of the normal curve. On the other hand, fewer scores are found under the platykurtic curve within 1 standard deviation on either side of the mean as compared with the normal curve. While neither of these curves is skewed or asymmetrical, they suffer limitations similar to those of skewed distributions. The researcher cannot use Z scores for comparative purposes.

THE PROBABILITY FUNCTION OF THE UNIT NORMAL DISTRIBUTION

The unit normal distribution is a probability distribution. The proportionate statements pertaining to segments of the normal distribution are the equivalent of probability statements. When we say that approximately 68 percent of the distribution is included between 1 standard deviation on either side of the mean, we can also say that the odds are 68 out of 100 that an observed raw score will be found between these two Z scores. When we extend the limits of Z to $+2.00$ or -2.00, we can say that the odds are about 95 out of 100 that a score will be found between these two Z scores. Three Z's away from the mean on either side of it will include most of the scores in the distribution, and therefore, it makes sense to say that at least 99 times out of 100 we will obtain a score which will fall between a Z score of -3.00 and one of $+3.00$.

It is very important at this point to remember this function of the unit normal distribution. In many statistical procedures to follow, the final test will be a Z test to determine the probability of obtaining a particular Z score. *Remember that we may directly translate a Z score into a probability which is estimated by reference to an area of the unit normal distribution.*

SUMMARY

In this chapter we have examined the normal curve and the unit normal distribution. The unit normal distribution is a probability distribution. This expression means that probability statements can be made about raw scores and raw-score populations which approximate normality.

Standard scores are the units of measurement along the horizontal axis of the unit normal distribution. These scores permit the investigator to more effectively compare scores taken from different raw-score distributions. Standard scores constitute a transformation of raw scores from different distributions into common units which can be more effectively compared.

These scores are very useful because tables have been devised which indicate the proportion of the unit normal distribution included between any given standard score and the mean. To the extent that we may assume that the raw-score distributions are normal and that the level of measurement achieved is at least interval, raw scores may be transformed into standard scores or Z's and compared with one another.

QUESTIONS FOR REVIEW AND PROBLEMS TO SOLVE

1. What proportion of scores lies between the following Z scores: (a) -2.38 and $.71$; (b) 1.14 and 1.75; (c) $-.45$ and $.45$; (d) 1.89 and 2.26; (e) 2.33 and -1.45?

2. What are four constant attributes of the unit normal distribution, and why are these attributes of value to social scientists?

3. With a $\bar{X} = 110$ and an $s = 12$, determine Z scores for the following raw scores: (a) 95; (b) 122; (c) 133; (d) 87; (e) 115.5; (f) 128.1.

4. What is skewness? Kurtosis? Draw a leptokurtic curve. How does a leptokurtic curve differ from a normal one?

5. With a $\overline{X} = 48$ and an $s = 3.5$, determine raw scores for the following Z scores: (a) -1.36; (b) 2.21; (c) .63; (d) -0.11; (e) 1.64; (f) 1.96; (g) 3.00.

6. Can a platykurtic curve be symmetrical? Why or why not?

7. Two students have taken final examinations in sociology and each has a score of 87. They are in different classes. What can you say about these two scores in relation to one another?

8. Why are different areas found within 1 standard deviation on either side of the mean of a skewed distribution? What can be said in view of the skewness of a distribution with respect to the area included by a specified number of standard deviations?

9. What raw scores are equivalent to the following proportions of the normal-curve area, with $\overline{X} = 50$ and $s = 5$: (a) $-.4456$; (b) .3413; (c) .3312; (d) .0626; (e) .4775?

10. Referring to Question 7 above, suppose you knew that the mean and standard deviation in one class were 75 and 7 respectively, but that in the second class, the mean and the standard deviation were 77 and 6. Which boy did the better relative to the other members of his class?

6 Hypotheses, Hypothesis Testing, and Statistical Inference

Two primary functions of statistical procedures are to describe elements and to help us make decisions about them. In the first few chapters of this text our concern has been with the descriptive function of statistical procedures. In this chapter, the purpose is to show how statistical decision making is done.

Many researchers see the decision-making functions of statistical techniques as the most important, for theories are accepted or rejected, modified or reformulated, in the making of decisions. It is essential to understand what is presented here in order to understand discussions of the statistical procedures in subsequent chapters.

HYPOTHESES

There are different kinds of *hypotheses.* The most familiar hypotheses which we see in social research are probably those called *research hypotheses.* Research hypotheses are derived from the theory of the social investigator and generally state a specified relation between two or more variables. An example of a research hypothesis might be "There is an inverse association between variables X and Y." More specifically, "When job satisfaction decreases, labor turnover increases." The symbol H_1 is used to identify research hypotheses.

Another kind of hypothesis is called the *statistical hypothesis.* The statistical hypothesis is usually constructed to enable the social researcher to evaluate his research hypothesis. Often the statistical hypothesis is stated in *null* form. Such an hypothesis might be "There is *no* association between variables X and Y." Hypotheses such as this are referred to as *null hypotheses.* In contemporary sociology, null hypotheses are usually, though not always, statements of no difference. The symbol H_0 is used to represent hypotheses of this type.

Below are some examples of the symbolic statement of statistical hypotheses with their corresponding research hypotheses.

Null Hypotheses:

$$H_0: \quad \mu_1 = \mu_2 \qquad \text{(A)}$$

$$H_0: \quad r_{1,2} = .00 \qquad \text{(B)}$$

Research Hypotheses:

$$H_1: \qquad \mu_1 \neq \mu_2 \qquad \text{(A}'\text{)}$$

$$H_1: \qquad |r_{1,2}| > .00 \qquad \text{(B}'\text{)}$$

Null hypothesis (A) is that there is no difference between two population means. Research hypothesis (A′) is that there is a difference between the two means. Each null hypothesis H_0 has at least one alternative hypothesis H_1, which is usually, though not always, the opposite of what the null hypothesis states. Null hypothesis (B) is that there is no association between variables 1 and 2. The research hypothesis (B′) is that there is an association between variables 1 and 2.

In statistical work, hypotheses usually specify the occurrence of an event and are capable of being rejected. Only those hypotheses which are amenable to empirical test are of interest to the social statistician. The specified *event* is usually a numerical value representing an observed or theorized difference between elements such as age differences, differences between means, medians, or modes, differences between ranks of elements according to some variable, or the like; it may be a coefficient of association.

Null hypotheses are often confusing to the beginning student. He often asks "Why state the hypothesis contrary to what you believe is true?" While we might again use *convention* as a partial explanation, we can provide a better answer by saying that *the null hypothesis constitutes a model which is used to test the research hypothesis.* By "testing" hypotheses we mean that we are able to determine to some degree their truthfulness or falsity.

All of the statistical techniques to be discussed throughout the remainder of this text are geared to testing hypotheses. We test hypotheses by specifying conditions under which the hypothesis will be rejected or not rejected. If a hypothesis is not to be rejected, then the outcome of the test of the hypothesis must have conformed to certain conditions which were specified *in advance of our making that test.* Being able to specify certain conditions in advance of the statistical test of any hypothesis makes it possible for the investigator to *predict* outcomes of events. Predicting an outcome *does not guarantee* that the event will turn out as predicted. But what *is* accomplished is that the investigator will be able to objectively assess the outcome in terms of certain *decision rules.* If the outcome does not conform to what was predicted and is not consistent with the decision model, the researcher decides to reject the hypothesis in favor of some alternative hypothesis. Decision rules, then, are requirements which must be satisfied in order for statistical hypotheses to be rejected or not rejected.

DECISION RULES

All models for testing statistical hypotheses provide a set of decision rules which specify the conditions under which the hypothesis will be rejected or not rejected. Before we can adequately specify which decision rules must be invoked before any given hypothesis is tested, *we must have a knowledge of all possible outcomes of the statistical test.* The possibility of one or another outcome is where "chance" enters into this process as an integral feature.

Some outcomes are *expected* more often than others. When a mother gives birth to quintuplets, the event is quite unusual, but giving birth to twins is less extraordinary. For a married couple to have three boys and three girls *seems* more likely than for the couple to have six boys or six girls.

To take another example, suppose you enter a raffle for a turkey. You purchase 10 tickets while 90 other people purchase single tickets. The 100 ticket stubs are placed in a large container. Of these stubs, 10 are yours. In other words, you have purchased 10 chances of winning while each of the other people has purchased only 1 chance. In a subsequent drawing, the draw of one of your tickets would be a more likely event than the draw of a ticket purchased by some other specified single individual. We would say that the chances of drawing your ticket from the container would be 10 in 100, because of the 100 tickets in the container, 10 are yours. The chance of drawing any specified other person's ticket from the container would be 1 in 100, because each other person has only 1 ticket in the container. If you had purchased all of the tickets placed in the container, then there is no doubt (the chance would be 100 in 100) that one of your tickets would be drawn. The more tickets you place in the bowl, the more you increase your chances of being drawn. The same is true with our observations of social events. When we conduct studies in social research, we are concerned as to whether our observations are likely or "expected" or are unlikely or "unexpected." *Decision rules help us to decide how to judge the observations.*

Decision rules involve specifying *the sampling distribution of a statistic, the level of significance,* and *the critical region or "region of rejection" in the sampling distribution.*

The Sampling Distribution

Every statistic has a *sampling distribution.* This should not be confused with a distribution of a sample (which is the distribution of observations or values for any given characteristic in a sample, such as the final examination scores of students in an introductory sociology class, the ages of males in a large audience, or social-distance scores for a select aggregate of people from several social classes). *A sampling distribution is the distribution of all possible values any statistic may assume, based upon random sampling of a specified size from a specified universe.* It may also be defined as a frequency distribution of a statistic.

For example, suppose we were to randomly draw samples of size 2 from a population of 5 individuals. The number of possible samples of size 2 which could be drawn from this population *with replacement* is

$$N^n$$

where N = the total number of elements in the population; and
n = the sample size.

In this case, there are N^n possible samples of size 2 which can be drawn from a population of 5, or $(5)^2 = 25$ possible samples.

Let A, B, C, D, and E represent each of the five elements in the population. Then we can make up the list of possible samples of size 2 which could be obtained from them. Further suppose that for each element in

Element	X	*Possible Samples of Size 2*				
A	6.00	AA	BA	CA	DA	EA
B	5.00	AB	BB	CB	DB	EB
C	4.00	AC	BC	CC	DC	EC
D	3.00	AD	BD	CD	DD	ED
E	2.00	AE	BE	CE	DE	EE

the population, a $\bar{X}$ is determined which stands for the number of times per week an employee receives direct orders from a supervisor on the job. We can then compute and list the $\bar{X}$'s for all possible samples of size 2. The sampling distribution of the $\bar{X}$'s of these samples of size 2 for this population is illustrated in Table 6.1.

Possible Sample $\bar{X}$'s for Samples of 2

6.00	5.50	5.00	4.50	4.00
5.50	5.00	4.50	4.00	3.50
5.00	4.50	4.00	3.50	3.00
4.50	4.00	3.50	3.00	2.50
4.00	3.50	3.00	2.50	2.00

A sampling distribution is a *theoretical distribution.* It specifies probabilities of obtaining certain observations for samples of any given size. In Table 6.1, probabilities have been determined for each of the observations. The observations in this case are the sample $\bar{X}$'s. They range in value from 2.00 to 6.00. It is apparent from the data in Table 6.1 that some $\bar{X}$'s occur more often than others. For example, a $\bar{X}$ of 2.00 constitutes 1/25 of the total number of observations. For a given sample such an observation is less likely to occur than, say, a $\bar{X}$ of 4.00.

Corresponding probabilities have been calculated for each of the above

Table 6.1. Sampling Distribution of $\overline{X}$'s of Samples of Size 2 from a Population of 5.

$\overline{X}$'s	f	*Proportion*	*Probability*
6.00	x	1/25	.040
5.50	x x	2/25	.080
5.00	x x x	3/25	.120
4.50	x x x x	4/25	.160
4.00	x x x x x	5/25	.200
3.50	x x x x	4/25	.160
3.00	x x x	3/25	.120
2.50	x x	2/25	.080
2.00	x	1/25	.040
	$\Sigma f = 25$	1.00	1.000

observations. The probability of obtaining a sample with a $\overline{X}$ of 2.00 is .040, or 4 times out of 100. The probability of obtaining a sample with a $\overline{X}$ of 4.00, on the other hand, is .200, or 20 times out of 100. That we will obtain a sample with a $\overline{X}$ of 2.00 or 6.00 is an event less likely than that we will obtain a sample with a $\overline{X}$ between 2.50 and 5.50. The chances of obtaining a sample with a more central value of $\overline{X}$ are greater than those of obtaining a sample with a $\overline{X}$ on the periphery of the distribution of $\overline{X}$'s.

Obtaining the sampling distribution for the data above was a rather laborious procedure. Imagine what the sampling distribution of the mean would be like for a population of 100 and a sample size of 30? The possible number of samples of size 30 to be obtained from a population of 100 with replacement would be $N^n = (100)^{30}$. Fortunately, we do not need to construct a sampling distribution every time we need one. Statisticians have worked out sampling distributions of various statistics which are frequently used in social research. The sampling distributions of several statistics are included in some of the tables in Appendix A of this text.

For large, normally distributed samples, the sampling distributions of many statistics will be symmetrical. Not all sampling distributions are symmetrical, however. For example, the sampling distribution of the correlation coefficient (see Chapter 10) is not symmetrical under all conditions.

The sampling distribution of any statistic specifies probabilities associated with the occurrence of any statistical value. A major decision rule involves the identification of a sampling distribution which will help in the support or rejection of statistical hypotheses.

The Level of Significance

When hypotheses are formulated, the researcher decides, *in advance of* the statistical test of the hypotheses, the *level of significance* at which the hypothesis will be rejected.

The level of significance refers to the probability that we are wrong in rejecting null hypotheses. For example, if we hypothesize that there is no difference between two sample means at *the .05 level of significance*, and if we determine further that there *is* a difference between the means at the .05 level, we are saying that 5 times out of 100 we are *wrong* in rejecting the null hypothesis that no difference exists between the two means. Rejecting a true hypothesis is known as *Type I error*. The researcher specifies the level of significance at which he will reject the null hypothesis in advance of the actual statistical test of that hypothesis. If he sets the level of significance too low, say at .10, .20, or .50, there is a good chance that he will find himself rejecting the null hypothesis even though it is true. On the other hand, if the level of significance is set too high, say at .001, .0001, or the like, then there is a good chance that the researcher will fail to reject the null hypothesis even though it is false and should be rejected. Failure to reject a false hypothesis is called *Type II error*. With this dilemma in mind, the researcher tries to set a level of significance which will allow him the greatest opportunity to reject false hypotheses and to avoid rejecting true ones.

Setting such a level is often a difficult process. For one type of problem the level of significance may appropriately be .001, while for another type of problem the level of significance should be set at .10. Fortunately, *convention* again comes to the researcher's aid. Commonly used levels of significance are .05 and .01. There is nothing sacred about these particular levels of significance. They are simply those levels of significance most frequently encountered in social research. Many investigators feel that 5 chances out of 100 of being wrong are good odds to proceed by. Some investigators prefer the higher and more rigorous levels of significance such as .01 and .001. The chances of failing to reject null hypotheses when they ought to be rejected *increase* as the researcher raises the level of significance from .05 to .01 to .001. The researcher is at liberty, however, to choose whichever level of significance he wishes as a part of the decision rules governing the rejection or nonrejection of hypotheses in his study. He is cautioned of the danger involved in making too rigorous decision rules, however, just as he is cautioned to beware of making the decision rules too weak.

The Critical Region, or "Region of Rejection"

The level of significance at which an hypothesis is rejected defines a particular area of the sampling distribution of the statistic. This area is called the *critical region* or the *region of rejection*. Let us examine the normal distribution to see how this might apply to all sampling distributions, regardless of their shape. Figure 6.1 shows a normal distribution. The ends of the distribution are called "tails." Critical regions are found in the tails of the distribution. Observations which fall in the tail ends of the normal distribution, or critical regions, are less likely than observa-

Figure 6.1. The Normal Distribution Showing Critical Regions.

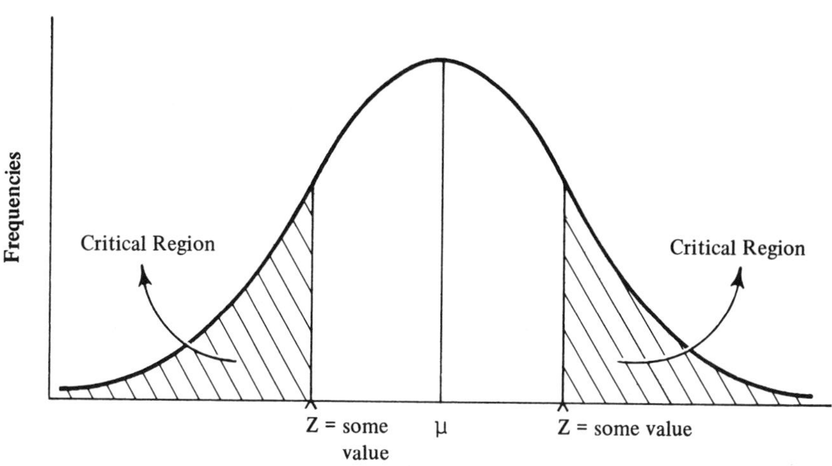

tions which fall somewhere near the center of the distribution. When both ends of the normal distribution are used in hypothesis testing, the researcher refers to such tests as "two-tailed." "One-tailed" tests refer to situations when only one end of the normal distribution is used.

Suppose we were to use the .05 level of significance in the test of some hypothesis. We would use 5 percent of the total area under the normal curve as the critical region, or rejection region. The .10 level of significance would mean that we would be using 10 percent of the normal-curve area as the critical region, the .01 level of significance would mean that we would be using 1 percent of the normal-curve area as the critical region, and so on. A one-tailed test would involve one end of the normal distribution. This is illustrated in Figure 6.2. It is observed that a Z of 1.64 cuts off a distance from the mean of .4500, leaving .0500 in the tail

Figure 6.2. Critical Region for a One-Tailed Test.

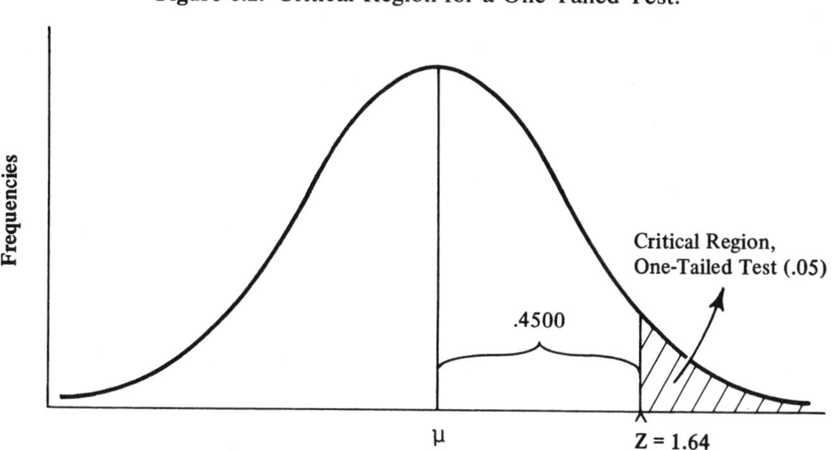

end of the curve. This 1.64 is said to be a *critical value* of Z for a one-tailed test at the .05 level of significance. Where two tails of the curve are used in hypothesis testing, we must split the level of significance into two equal parts, and the resulting proportions will be found in each end of the curve. Splitting .05 into two equal parts will leave .0250 in each tail of the curve, as is illustrated in Figure 6.3. A Z of 1.96 cuts off an area from the mean equal to .4750, leaving .0250 in the tail. $Z = 1.96$ is said to be the critical value of Z for a two-tailed test at the .05 level of significance. When a two-tailed test is used, the sum of the proportions of the curve in the tails of it is equal to the level of significance used in testing the hypothesis. From this discussion it is evident that Z values will somehow be used in hypothesis testing, and in relation to the unit normal distribution. The hypotheses provided as examples at the beginning of this chapter may be tested by means of a "Z test." Such a test is used in conjunction with the unit normal distribution and in a manner not altogether dissimilar from our previous use of Z scores.*

Usually, though not always, the critical region for a two-tailed test is divided into two equal parts. If the level of significance is .10 for a two-tailed test, a critical region of 5 percent will be found in each tail of the curve. Often the researcher will have some idea as to the direction of the hypothesis, and accordingly will be able to use one-tailed tests of significance. Sometimes the researcher may wish to put unequal portions of the critical region in different ends of the distribution, particularly if he believes that the direction of a hypothesized difference will tend toward one end of the curve rather than toward the other end of it. A discussion of the theory underlying such unusual splits of the critical region is beyond the scope of this text, however.

It should be apparent that when the direction of a hypothesis is known or suspected, that is, when the researcher knows or suspects that a score should be above or below a particular mean, then a smaller Z is needed in order to define the critical value. This condition suggests that the more information you have pertaining to the hypothesis, the "easier" it will be to reject null hypotheses. When little information is available, as when the researcher has no idea as to the direction of a particular hypothesis, Z values necessary for rejecting null hypotheses are larger, wherefore the observations need to be further away from the population parameter than if direction could be predicted.

Briefly summarizing: The decision rules which are established in advance of the test of any particular hypothesis involve the identification of a certain kind of sampling distribution, the specifying of a level of

---

*Z scores and various types of Z tests, to be discussed subsequently, perform different, yet similar, functions. Chapter 7 will present the Z test in detail, showing how it is used in hypothesis testing. The similarities between various Z interpretations will become more apparent.

Figure 6.3. Critical Region for a Two-Tailed Test at the .05 Level of Significance.

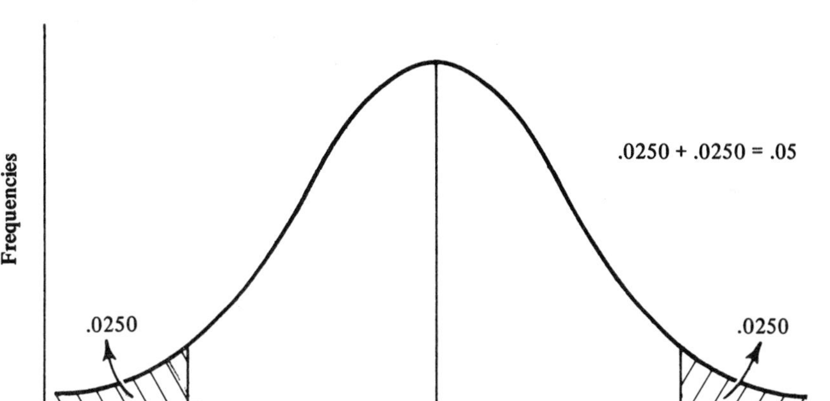

significance, and the establishment of a critical region within the appropriate sampling distribution. Primarily on the basis of these three criteria, statistical hypotheses are rejected or not rejected. All of the techniques to be presented in subsequent chapters require that these decision rules be specified in advance of the test of statistical hypotheses.

A WORD ABOUT SAMPLING DISTRIBUTIONS

Every statistic which has been identified has a sampling distribution. The sampling distribution of the mean has been discussed and you have already seen an application of the normal distribution. Other sampling distributions exist, such as the binomial distribution, the t distribution, the F distribution, and the χ^2 distribution. These distributions have one thing in common: *they can be interpreted as probability distributions.* Critical regions may be established within any sampling distribution and levels of significance may be set for the purpose of rejecting or not rejecting hypotheses. The selection of a sampling distribution depends primarily upon the statistical method chosen and the objectives of the research design.

STATISTICAL INFERENCE

Perhaps the most crucial aspect of statistical work is *the making of decisions about observations.* We have already found that there is an element of risk in the making of decisions. For example, we may set a level of significance too high or too low, and we may fail to reject false hypotheses and/or reject true ones. But if we are able to determine the extent to which this risk exists prior to and during the test of the statistical hypothesis, we will have a clearer picture of the interpretation we should make of our findings. We will have a clearer picture of what may be said about our observations. We certainly do not want to say things about our findings which simply aren't true, nor do we wish to mislead anyone reading our research report to believe that we have significant findings when, in fact, the findings are not significant. Each time we test a hypothesis, then, we should be able to calculate the degree of probable error of our results. This measure will be very informative to our readers. For now they will be able to see just how conservatively they should interpret our findings.

Many decisions which we make are based upon a *sample* of observations. Reviewing this discussion briefly: A sample is a set of observations taken from a larger population of them. The larger population is often called the "parent" population or *universe*. This term simply refers to a class of objects sharing certain characteristics, and about which we seek information. The universe may consist of all Boy Scouts, all students at UCLA during the 1960–1970 decade, all lower-level employees at Plant X, all residents of Jonesville, all members of the Optimist Club International, all policemen in Montana, and so on. Because of the limitations of time, money, and manpower, we are frequently obligated to take information and observations from a sample rather than from the entire universe of elements.

Try to imagine the cost, time, and manpower involved in interviewing all persons over 21 years of age in the United States at any given point in time. Such a task would almost be impossible as well as extremely impractical. So researchers settle for a sample of elements taken from the larger population or universe. The logic is that if a sample of elements is drawn from the universe in a random and representative way, then statements which may be made about the sample also may be made about the larger population of them. The Nielsen television ratings are geared to reflect what the entire nation thinks about certain television programs; the information is elicited by examining the television-viewing habits of 1,000 New England families. The case for sampling in this instance is based upon the "representativeness" of the sample. This particular New England sample closely resembles the nation at large.

Statistical inference derives from the fact that we wish to *infer* something about a population by examining a sample of elements taken from it. Before we can accurately infer anything about a population by examining a sample of elements taken from it, we must make sure that at least three procedures are followed as closely as possible. These are outlined below.

1. *We must make sure that each element in the parent population is identified or known.* Often this condition is very difficult to meet, but a truly random sample of elements from a population cannot be legitimately obtained unless all elements in that population have been enumer-

ated or identified. If the population is quite large, it may be impossible to identify all elements in it. City directories are often used to identify all residents in a community. But people die, move away, move in, change marital status, and do any number of other things to adversely affect the accuracy of such sources of information. When we are unable to reach and select for our sample certain members of a particular universe, the resulting sample of elements is said to be *biased*. This term means that the sample is to some degree unrepresentative of the population from which it was drawn. It is apparent that the accuracy of any inferences about a larger population rests, in part, upon how the sample was obtained and how representative it is of the larger population.

2. *We must obtain a sample which is random.* Randomness helps us to reduce bias by providing, as much as possible, the opportunity for each element to have an equal chance of being included in the sample. Any good research-methods text will discuss several varieties of sampling procedures to obtain such samples. With samples obtained in this fashion, we are often in a position to estimate, according to probability, how closely the sample statistic resembles the population parameter. This problem will be discussed in the next chapter.

3. *We must draw a sample of sufficient size to warrant generalizing to the larger population.* Increasing the size of the sample will cause the sampling distribution of the $\overline{X}$ to become more normal, regardless of how skewed the original distribution happens to be. This tendency accords with a mathematical argument known as the law of large numbers, which demonstrates that increasing the sample size causes the sampling distribution of the mean to tend toward the normal. Several statistical techniques presented in subsequent chapters specify that if $N > 30$, the normal distribution is approximated and the Z test may be used to test hypotheses. This advice is based on the law of large numbers. On the other hand, some statistical techniques are appropriate for small N's, say less than 30. Required sample sizes will be specified in all cases to follow, and the reader is cautioned that deviation from these requirements undermines the purpose and value of the statistical techniques used. Violations of the rules underlying statistical techniques should be accompanied by statements to that effect, in order to prevent the readers of an investigator's material from being misled by the way he has used any given technique.

Statistical inference, then, is the process of saying something about a large population of elements as a consequence of examining a sample of them.

THE STANDARD ERROR OF A STATISTIC AND CONFIDENCE INTERVALS

Earlier in this chapter it was indicated that *all* statistics have sampling distributions. Measurements made on samples taken from a larger population are called *statistics*, and a sampling distribution is associated with each of the statistics computed.

Like a frequency distribution or a distribution of sample characteristics, sampling distributions have standard deviations; these standard deviations of sampling distributions are more commonly referred to as *standard errors*. In many of the tests of significance to be presented in subsequent chapters, it will be necessary to compute standard errors of certain statistics in order to tell whether or not a particular observed value is a significant one.

Standard errors of *sampling* distributions can be used to perform a function similar to that performed by standard deviations of sample distributions. In the formula for computing a Z score, for example,

$$Z = \frac{X - \overline{X}}{s}$$

the standard deviation is used to interpret *how far above or below the mean a given raw score lies*. Dividing the mean and raw-score difference by the standard deviation gives a Z score which, in turn, may be transformed into a proportion of the normal distribution which can be transformed into a probability statement.

The standard error of a statistic (or more accurately, of the sampling distribution of a statistic) gives us some idea, according to probability, as to how closely a sample statistic should approximate the population parameter within stated probability limits. In estimating these limits we use the standard error of that statistic. The following illustration uses the standard error of the mean as an example.

Suppose we draw a random sample of people from a given population. The sample size is 50 and the mean age of the sample is 30, with a standard deviation of 4. The standard error of the mean is computed as follows:

$$s_{\overline{X}} = \frac{s}{\sqrt{N-1}}$$

where s = the sample standard deviation; and
N = the sample size.

Substituting values in the formula with our information above, we have

$$s_{\overline{X}} = \frac{4}{\sqrt{50-1}} = \frac{4}{\sqrt{49}} = \frac{4}{7}$$
$$= .57.$$

The standard error of the mean in this example is .57. It should be noted at this point that if the sample size were to be *increased*, the size of the standard error of the mean would *decrease*. This relation is part of the reason why researchers like to use large samples. Larger samples reduce the size of the standard error, or the error involved when estimating a parameter by using a sample statistic.

Up to now we have simply shown that standard errors may be computed from sample statistics. We have not yet demonstrated their research utility.

Continuing with the above illustration, suppose that we are further interested in knowing the proximity of the parameter to the statistic which we have computed. Although the population parameter is unknown, we can make a good guess from knowledge of the sample statistic. We know that according to chance or probability, the statistic which we have computed from the sample will probably be within a certain distance from the parameter. We use the standard error of the mean to set up a reasonable distance, given a certain probability.

With an $N > 30$, the sampling distribution of the mean approximates the normal distribution. We may therefore use Z values with the sampling distribution of the mean. It will be remembered that Z values cut off certain proportions of the normal distribution, and that these proportions are comparable to probability statements. For a review of this discussion, see Chapter 5.

Knowing the mean and the standard deviation of a distribution of scores, we are able to specify how far above or below the mean we must go, *in terms of standard-deviation units,* in order to include a certain proportion of *cases.* Knowing the mean and the standard error of the mean for the sampling distribution of the mean, we can also specify how far above or below the sample mean we must go, in terms of standard errors, in order to include a certain proportion of *sample means.* (The sampling distribution of the mean is a distribution of all possible means from samples of a certain size.) Just how far above or below the sample mean we must go to include a certain proportion of "cases" depends upon how large we want to make the *confidence interval.*

A confidence interval is an interval, established around the sample mean, which theoretically includes a given proportion of sample means and which includes the population mean at a certain level of probability. It makes sense to say that the larger we make the confidence interval, the more likely it is that the population parameter will be included within it, and conversely, the smaller the confidence interval, the less likely it is that the population parameter will be included. How large to make the confidence interval, then, will depend upon how much risk we will be willing to take that the parameter will *not* be included by the interval.

If 10 percent of the time, we are willing to have the parameter of the population excluded from the confidence interval, then we should establish 90-percent *confidence limits.* If we want to permit probable exclusion only 5 percent of the time, then we should establish 95-percent confidence limits for the interval.

Since a confidence interval extends an equal distance on either side of the sample mean, we are interested in a Z value which will cut off a given distance from the mean, leaving a *total* of 10 percent of the area in the tails of the distribution if a 90-percent confidence interval is desired, or leaving a total of 5 percent of the area in the tails of the distribution if a 95-percent confidence interval is desired. Let us say that we want to establish a confidence interval of 95 percent. Splitting the remaining 5 percent into two equal parts will leave 2.5 percent of the curve in each end of the distribution. We are, therefore, looking for a Z value which includes the proportion .4750. Turning to the Table of Areas under the Normal Curve, Table A.3 of Appendix A, we find that such a Z value is 1.96.

And since the value of the standard error of the mean is .57, we must multiply 1.96 by the standard error; thus

$$(1.96)(.57) = 1.12.$$

Adding this value to the mean of the sample will give us the upper limit of the 95-percent confidence interval, while subtracting this value from the mean will give us the lower limit of the interval.

What we have just done is illustrated below:

$$\begin{aligned}\text{95-percent confidence interval} &= \bar{X} \pm (1.96)(s_{\bar{X}})\\ &= 30 \pm (1.96)(.57)\\ &= 28.88 \text{ to } 31.12.\end{aligned}$$

We conclude that the population mean falls somewhere between 28.88 and 31.12. This conclusion will be correct 95 times out of every 100 times. In 5 instances out of every 100, however, the population mean will fall outside the interval we have specified.

If our sample were drawn in a nonrandom fashion, then the confidence limits which are established for any statistic computed for that sample would not have the same meaning as confidence limits established for a randomly drawn sample of elements. Also, the larger the sample we draw, the smaller the standard error becomes, and consequently, the confidence limits decrease as we have a larger part of the population as our sample. In other words, the more people we are able to include randomly in our sample from any given population, the more likely it is for statistics computed for that sample to resemble the true parameters of that population. Again, this relation is part of the reason why large samples are desirable in statistical inference.

By way of further examples, suppose we wish to know the confidence limits of the means in each of the two cases below. The sample sizes, standard deviations, and means have been varied, and we want to know the 99-percent confidence limits, the 90-percent confidence limits, and the 80-percent confidence limits for each.

Case I

The information is: $N_1 = 100$, $\overline{X}_1 = 120$, $s_1 = 10$.

Example 1.1: Determining 99-percent confidence limits.

$$\text{99-percent confidence limits} = \overline{X}_1 \pm (2.58)\left(\frac{10}{\sqrt{100-1}}\right)$$
$$= 120 \pm (2.58)\left(\frac{10}{9.9}\right)$$
$$= 120 \pm (2.58)(1.00)$$
$$= 120 \pm 2.58$$
$$= 117.42 \text{ to } 122.58.$$

Example 1.2: Determining 90-percent confidence limits.

$$\text{90-percent confidence limits} = \overline{X}_1 \pm (1.64)\left(\frac{10}{\sqrt{100-1}}\right)$$
$$= 120 \pm (1.64)(1.00)$$
$$= 120 \pm 1.64$$
$$= 118.36 \text{ to } 121.64.$$

Example 1.3: Determining 80-percent confidence limits.

$$\text{80-percent confidence limits} = \overline{X}_1 \pm (1.28)\left(\frac{10}{\sqrt{100-1}}\right)$$
$$= 120 \pm (1.28)(1.00)$$
$$= 120 \pm 1.28$$
$$= 118.72 \text{ to } 121.28.$$

For the first case, the 99-percent, 90-percent, and 80-percent confidence limits are, respectively, 117.42 to 122.58, 118.36 to 121.64, and 118.72 to 121.28. Notice how the interval size *decreases* as the confidence limits are lowered.

Case II

In this case, we have increased the sample size and changed the sample statistics. The information is: $N_2 = 500$, $\overline{X}_2 = 75$, $s_2 = 6$.

Example 2.1: Determining 99-percent confidence limits.

$$\text{99-percent confidence limits} = \overline{X}_2 \pm (2.58)\left(\frac{6}{\sqrt{500-1}}\right)$$
$$= 75 \pm (2.58)(.27)$$
$$= 75 \pm .70$$
$$= 74.30 \text{ to } 75.70.$$

Example 2.2: Determining 90-percent confidence limits.

$$\text{90-percent confidence limits} = \bar{X}_2 \pm (1.64)\left(\frac{6}{\sqrt{500-1}}\right)$$
$$= 75 \pm (1.64)(.27)$$
$$= 75 \pm .44$$
$$= 74.56 \text{ to } 75.44.$$

Example 2.3: Determining 80-percent confidence limits.

$$\text{80-percent confidence limits} = \bar{X}_2 \pm (1.28)\left(\frac{6}{\sqrt{500-1}}\right)$$
$$= 75 \pm (1.28)(.27)$$
$$= 75 \pm .35$$
$$= 74.65 \text{ to } 75.35.$$

The 99-percent, 90-percent, and 80-percent confidence limits for the information in Case II above are 74.30 to 75.70, 74.56 to 75.44, and 74.65 to 75.35. Again, notice how the interval size decreases as the confidence limits are lowered. This relation means that as we lower our confidence limits, we increase our chances of *not* including the population parameter in the sample we draw.

In each of the two cases above, the confidence intervals narrowed as the confidence levels decreased from 90 percent to 80 percent, while the confidence intervals became larger as the confidence levels increased. Note also that the size of the confidence interval depends upon the size of the standard error, which, in turn, depends upon the sample size and the standard deviation of the sample.

In the examples we have been using above, we have proceeded as though the population mean and standard deviation were unknown. This condition is frequently encountered, particularly where large populations are involved. Sometimes, if we are fortunate enough to know the standard deviation of the population, then we can compute the standard error by using the following formula:

$$\sigma_{\bar{X}} = \frac{\sigma}{\sqrt{N}}$$

where σ = the population standard deviation; and
N = the sample size.

Note that in this case the denominator is $\sqrt{N}$ rather than $\sqrt{N-1}$. In the first example, we were using the sample standard deviation and the $\sqrt{N-1}$ in the denominator was used because $s/\sqrt{N}$ consistently *underestimates* $\sigma_{\bar{X}}$. For large samples, the difference between $\sqrt{N}$ and $\sqrt{N-1}$ is negligible.

SUMMARY

In this chapter we have examined certain operations related to the testing of hypotheses. A hypothesis is a statement which specifies the occurrence of an event and which is capable of being either supported or rejected. Two kinds of hypotheses, the research hypothesis and the null hypothesis, were discussed as tools used by the researcher to systematically judge his observations.

Decision rules requiring the specifying of the level of significance, of the sampling distribution, and of the critical region were also surveyed as prerequisites to adequate hypothesis testing.

Finally, statistical inference was briefly treated. Statistical inference is the process of making generalizations about a population by examining a random sample of elements drawn from it. The accuracy of such generalizations depends, in part, upon the type of sampling and the sample size, not to mention the standard error of the statistics used in inference.

The next three chapters of this text treat various *tests of significance* at different levels of measurement. Chapter 7 deals with interval-level tests of significance, while nominal- and ordinal-level tests are covered in Chapters 8 and 9, respectively. Chapter 10 presents an array of measures of association appropriate for nominal, ordinal, and interval measurement levels. It is recommended that the student review thoroughly the material covered in Chapters 5 and 6, as subsequent tests of significance are presented. This review will help toward understanding the various functions each test of significance performs.

QUESTIONS FOR REVIEW AND PROBLEMS TO SOLVE

1. What is a statistical hypothesis? What are two primary functions of statistical hypotheses?
2. What are some differences between research hypotheses and null hypotheses? Why are null hypotheses used in social research?
3. What are three primary decision rules? What is the importance of identifying decision rules prior to conducting research?
4. Construct a sampling distribution of means for samples of size 2 from this information: $N = 6$; $\overline{X} = 14, 12, 10, 8, 6, 4$. (a) What is the value of a sampling distribution? (b) How is it used in social research?
5. Are all sampling distributions symmetrical? Why is the sampling distribution of the mean used so often in research?
6. How much curve area is included in the critical region for the following levels of significance: (a) .01; (b) .10; (c) .005?
7. What is statistical inference? Why should we draw random and representative samples in preparation for making a statistical inference?
8. With a sample size of 65 and a mean of 88, $s = 10$, what is the standard error of the mean?
9. Determine the 95-percent confidence interval for the data in Prob-

lem 8 above. Determine the 80-percent confidence interval. What happens to the size of the confidence interval as the level of significance is raised from 80 to 90 percent?

10. For what are confidence intervals used? Does any particular sample necessarily have to include the mean of the population from which it was drawn? Why or why not?

7 Interval-Level Tests of Significance

In this chapter we shall examine a number of statistical techniques appropriate for data of the interval level of measurement. While the statistical techniques covered here are very good in the sense that they provide a great deal of information about collections of elements, we must be aware of the stringent assumptions underlying their use in social research. We must first demonstrate that we have data of the interval level. There are other assumptions which must be met in addition, and which will be covered in conjunction with certain of the tests to be discussed here.

Statistical techniques to be examined here will include *single-sample tests of significance, two-sample tests for both unrelated and related samples, and k-sample tests of significance for both unrelated and related samples.*

SINGLE-SAMPLE TESTS OF SIGNIFICANCE

When we draw a single sample of elements and we wish to test hypotheses utilizing information provided by this sample, we may use any number of single-sample tests of significance. Frequently, case studies of business organizations or industrial settings will involve a single sample. We may want to be able to say something about elements of business organizations in general (in which case our primary interest would be *inferential*), or we may wish to confine our generalizations to the organization studied.

At least two statistical tests are available which help us test hypotheses concerning a single sample: the Z test, which we have previously examined, and the "t" test, which is very similar.

In Chapter 6 we were concerned with determining confidence intervals. The Z test was useful in determining the limits of these confidence intervals, and an example was provided illustrating the computation of various confidence limits. Here it will be demonstrated that the Z test may be useful to test hypotheses about single samples.

Because samples vary in size, the Z test is not always the best test to use for testing hypotheses about single samples. If the sample is small, difficulty is encountered when we must assume a normal distribution. When small samples are found, that is, fewer than 30 elements, the test employing t, often called "Student's t," is used as a more appropriate alternative to the Z test.

For any given sample, statistics may be computed based upon measurements of any sample characteristic, such as age, years of education, socioeconomic status, sex, or other. With data of the interval level, however, means are frequently computed. When the investigator has computed a mean for some sample characteristic, he may be interested in learning whether or not this mean differs from some hypothesized μ value.

Tests about Population Mean When σ Is Known

The Z test is normally used when σ is known. To illustrate the use of the Z test in testing hypotheses about single samples, the following hypothetical example is provided.

The administrative officials of a large university were very much concerned over the dropout rate at their institution. They believed that if students saw their counselors and advisers more frequently, dropout rates would decrease. The idea was that the more personal attention students receive the more likely they would remain in school. That students withdraw from large universities because of the atmosphere of their anonymity and impersonality was well-known.

Consequently, students received letters from the administration encouraging them to meet frequently with their advisers. Advisers were also urged to invite students to meet with them more often.

Later that year each student at the university completed a questionnaire asking him to list the number of times he had seen his adviser during the year. The μ for the entire student body was 12, with a σ of 3.2. Some months later, a random sample of 40 dropouts from the university was obtained. These dropouts had been part of the original student population participating in the study. Their original questionnaires were obtained, and a mean was computed for the sample. The data were $N = 40$ (the number of dropouts) and $\overline{X} = 9.1$ (the average number of times advisers were seen during year). Is there any reason to believe that the average number of visits to advisers among the sample of dropouts is significantly lower than the average number of visits for the student population as a whole? To answer this question and to test the hypothesis, we hypothesize that:

$$H_0: \quad \overline{X} \geqslant \mu = 12$$

$$H_1: \quad \overline{X} < \mu$$

$$P \leqslant .01 \text{ (one-tailed test).}$$

In this case, H_0 is that the population mean and the sample mean either are identical, both being 12, or that the sample mean is greater than the population mean. We shall test this hypothesis at the .01 level of significance against the alternative hypothesis that the sample mean is less than the population mean. We will use a one-tailed test because we expect dropouts' scores (visits) to be lower than those of the rest of the students. To test this hypothesis we use the following formula:

$$Z = \frac{\overline{X} - \mu}{\sigma/\sqrt{N}}$$

where μ = the population mean;
$\overline{X}$ = the sample mean; and
$\sigma/\sqrt{N}$ = the standard error of the mean.

Carrying out the necessary computations, we have:

$$Z = \frac{9.1 - 12}{3.2/\sqrt{40}} = \frac{-2.9}{3.2/6.3} = \frac{-2.9}{.51}$$
$$= -5.69.$$

In order for the $\overline{X}$ to be significantly different from $\mu = 12$, using a one-tailed test at the .01 level, a Z of -2.33 or greater is required. (See Table A.3 of Appendix A.) Since the observed Z is greater than the critical value of -2.33, being -5.69, we conclude that students who dropped out of the university had significantly fewer contacts with their advisers while in attendance, and we reject H_0 in favor of H_1.

Tests about Population Mean When σ Is Unknown

It is frequently more realistic to treat both μ and σ as *unknown.* Sample statistics as estimates of these parameters are more often encountered in social research where access to total populations is limited or impossible. In the event that both μ and σ are unknown, we again fall back to the "best guess," the *statistics* computed for our samples. Thus, when we do not know the μ and σ of the population, we rely upon the sample estimates of these parameters. In order to test hypotheses about population means based upon sample estimates when we know neither μ nor σ, we may use the t test.

The t test is very similar to the Z test with one modification. Instead of using $\sigma/\sqrt{N}$ for the denominator, $s/\sqrt{N-1}$ is used. It should be evident that $s/\sqrt{N-1}$ is most significant where small samples are drawn, that is, fewer than 30 elements. Where the sample size exceeds 30, $\sqrt{N-1}$ makes little difference to the final result. $\sqrt{N=1}$ is used as a correction for the bias that may result from using the sample standard deviation as a parameter estimate.

The t test formula is

$$t = \frac{\overline{X} - \mu}{s/\sqrt{N-1}}.$$

Suppose we were conducting a study concerned with identifying the occupational aspirations of teen-age boys in a poverty area. Specifically, we are interested in the level of income these boys expect to achieve in adult life.

Our research team enters a poverty area and draws a sample of 17 boys as participants in the study. Through interviews we determine that the mean income expected by these boys as adults is \$6,500, with $s = \$700$. In developing our theory on the culture of poverty, we had originally hypothesized that the income expectation of these boys would be \$8,000. Is there a significant difference between the *hypothesized income expectation* and that which was observed in our study? The hypothesis is:

$$H_0: \quad \bar{X} = \mu = \$8{,}000$$

$$H_1: \quad \bar{X} \neq \mu$$

$$P \leqslant .05 \text{ (two-tailed test).}$$

The null hypothesis states that the population mean is \$8,000, using a two-tailed test of significance at the .05 level. Using the above sample information, we carry out the t test:

$$t = \frac{\$6{,}500 - \$8{,}000}{\$700/\sqrt{17-1}}$$

$$= \frac{-\$1{,}500}{\$700/4} = -\$1{,}500/\$175$$

$$= -8.57.$$

In order to determine the significance of the statistic t, we must turn to Table A.5 of Appendix A, Distribution of t. The left-hand column contains degrees of freedom *(df)*. *Degrees of freedom is defined as the number of values in a set which are free to vary.* In this case, degrees of freedom is determined by $N - 1$. In the example, $N - 1 = 17 - 1 = 16$ *df*. Locating this value down the left-hand column of the table, we next locate the level of significance across the top of the table. Notice that levels of significance are provided for both one- and two-tailed tests. At the point of intersection between the degrees of freedom and level of significance in the body of the table is the t value necessary to reject the null hypothesis. If our observed t is equal to or larger than the t in the table, we reject the hypothesis and conclude that the income aspirations of teen-age boys in our sample differ from what we hypothesized at the .05 level. If the t which we observe is smaller than that found in the table, we conclude that no difference exists between what has been hypothesized and what is observed relative to income aspirations of the boys in our sample.

We need a t equal to or larger than 2.120 in order for our observation to be considered significantly different from what is hypothesized. The observed t is larger than 2.120; therefore, we conclude that a difference exists at $<.05$. The income aspirations of boys in a poverty area are significantly below what was hypothesized.

Assumptions for the Z Test and the* t *Test Proper application of the Z test hinges upon the following assumptions: First, the population should be normally distributed. Second, the sample size should be larger than 30. Finally, the standard deviation of the population should be known. Interval-level measurement has already been assumed.

The t test also assumes a normal distribution of the population. Where small samples (less than 30) are used, this assumption is especially critical. As a second assumption, σ is generally considered unknown. Since this situation is expected more often than situations where σ is known, it seems logical that the t test should be used more often.

***Advantages and Disadvantages of Z and* t** Both the Z test and the t test have the assumption of a normal distribution of the populations being sampled. As N increases, the sampling distribution of the mean tends to approach the normal distribution, and the Z test may be appropriately applied to single-sample tests of significance. When N is less than 30, the t test is the preferred alternative. The correction factor $\sqrt{N-1}$ in the denominator of the t formula helps to overcome some of the bias that accompanies use of the sample standard deviation as a parameter estimator. Also, when Z is used, the population σ is assumed known. This is often an unrealistic assumption because of the inaccessibility of certain elements in any given population. The t test as an alternative is more realistic, then, in the sense that it treats σ as unknown, and the sample standard deviation is used as a part of the single-sample test.

The following chapters present alternative tests of significance which have less stringent assumptions underlying them and which are perfectly acceptable alternatives to either the Z or the t test. For example, see the discussion of the Mann-Whitney U test in Chapter 9 as an alternative to the t test.

TWO-SAMPLE TESTS OF SIGNIFICANCE

Many research designs are concerned with examining differences between two samples of elements. Is one sample different from another according to some trait or characteristic which has been measured by some method? Is one class of students older than another class, on the average? Are the grades of one student group higher or lower than those of another group? Are there differences between delinquent and nondelinquent boys with respect to the presence or absence of fathers in the home? Is one kind of leadership better than another in relation to high and low productivity in an industrial plant? Do small problem-solving groups solve problems more quickly with five members than with ten members? Does one region of the country differ from another with respect to crime rates or other characteristics?

This list of questions could go on indefinitely. But the above questions have at least one thing in common: all deal with differences in some characteristic between two samples of elements. We will now examine a number of tests which help us to determine the significance of difference between two collections of elements according to some characteristic measured at the interval level.

The type of test chosen will depend, in part, upon whether or not the two samples are related in some fashion or are independent. Related samples are those which have something other than the tested characteristic in common with one another. Related samples are found where elements serve as their own control in before-after experiments or designs, or where two samples have been matched according to some trait. For example, the elements in both samples are matched according to age, sex, socioeconomic status, civilian or military status, race, education, or any other meaningful variable. Independent samples are selected in such a way as to permit the assumption that they are unrelated to one another according to any variable.

Tests to be presented in this section include a further extension of *the t test, the randomization test for related samples, and the randomization test for independent samples.*

Differences between Means: Independent Samples, Unequal Standard Deviations

Several variations of the t test exist. One variety involves a test of the difference between two sample means when σ's are unknown and presumed to be unequal. The t formula is:

$$t = \frac{\overline{X}_1 - \overline{X}_2}{s_{\overline{X}_1 - \overline{X}_2}}$$

where

$s_{\overline{X}_1 - \overline{X}_2}$ = the standard error of the difference between the two means

$$= \sqrt{\frac{s_1^2}{N_1} + \frac{s_2^2}{N_2}}$$

and where s_1^2 and s_2^2 are the variances for the first and second samples, and N_1 and N_2 are the sample sizes for the first and second samples.

In the above formula, the standard error of the difference between two means performs the same function as the standard error of the mean. This makes sense inasmuch as two sample means are being used in this formula instead of just one. What this amounts to is a "pooling" of the standard errors of each of the means in order that we may more properly evaluate the differences between them. This "pooling" of the standard errors takes into account (1) the difference in sample size, and (2) the difference in sample standard deviations or variances.

As an example, suppose we were to examine community-development projects in India in terms of their success or failure in reducing the incidence of certain diseases within various communities. Specifically, we wish to know which method of introducing change is associated with the greatest decrease in disease—whether one method of introducing the change is better than the other method. Two contrasting notions of how change ought to be brought about are involved here. One way of introducing change is through the Indian government, its agents bringing information to the communities and seeing that certain practices are started relative to community health and sanitation. Another way of introducing change is to work through important community representatives at the "grass-roots" level, to make the people less suspicious of new practices which they are expected to acquire.

For the samples, 80 communities are selected at random, 35 receiving stimulus to change from Indian government officials and 45 receiving stimulus to change from the grass-roots program. One year later, the following information is recorded for the communities:

Communities with Government Change Program: $N_1 = 35$; mean disease rate per 1,000 people $= 117.3$; $s_1 = 14.7$.

Communities with "Grass-Roots" Change Program: $N_2 = 45$; mean disease rate per 1,000 people $= 99.4$; $s_2 = 10.8$.

Is there a significant difference between the means of the communities experiencing different change programs? Is there less disease as a result of one change program compared to the other? To test for this difference, we will want to use the t test and the following hypothesis:

$$H_0: \quad \mu_1 = \mu_2 \text{ or } \bar{X}_1 = \bar{X}_2{}^*$$

$$H_1: \quad \mu_1 \neq \mu_2 \text{ or } \bar{X}_1 \neq \bar{X}_2$$

$$P \leqslant .01 \text{ (two-tailed test).}$$

The null hypothesis states that there is no difference between community means with respect to disease, at the .01 level of significance, using a two-tailed test.

Carrying out the necessary operations, we have:

$$t = \frac{117.3 - 99.4}{\sqrt{\frac{(14.7)^2}{35} + \frac{(10.8)^2}{45}}}$$

$$= \frac{17.9}{\sqrt{\frac{216.09}{35} + \frac{116.64}{45}}}$$

$$= \frac{17.9}{\sqrt{6.17 + 2.59}} = \frac{17.9}{\sqrt{8.76}} = \frac{17.9}{2.96}$$

$$= 6.05.$$

---

*The null hypothesis uses μ's instead of $\bar{X}$'s because the $\bar{X}$'s are supposed to be *estimates* of μ's. If the $\bar{X}$'s are found to be unequal, the *inference* is that the parameters also differ at some probability level. The samples, therefore, are presumed to be representative of the "universe" of change programs from which they were randomly drawn.

Again, we turn to the table of Distribution of t, Table A.5 in Appendix A, to determine whether the t observed is significant at .01. This time, however, degrees of freedom is determined as follows:

$$\begin{aligned} df_{\text{two samples}} &= (N_1 - 1) + (N_2 - 1) \\ &= (35 - 1) + (45 - 1) \\ &= 78. \end{aligned}$$

For our particular sample, $df = 78$, we need a t equal to or greater than 2.66 in order for a significant difference to exist between the two means. Since our observed t of 6.05 is greater than that needed at the .01 level, we reject the null hypothesis and conclude that there is a significant difference between the communities with respect to rate of disease. We might also speculate that the way in which the change program was administered was the significant factor in promoting this difference. It is possible that change programs administered at the "grass-roots" level are more successful, in the long run, than government-sponsored programs to decrease disease in Indian communities. Caution is required here, for our observational design did not rule out the possibility that the two samples of communities differed in their disease rates to begin with.

Differences between Means:
Independent Samples, Equal Standard Deviations

In the previous example, it was assumed that the standard deviations of two samples were unequal. This is perhaps the most common situation found by investigators. At times, however, investigators may be able to assume that two sample standard deviations are equal. They may be different in reality, but the difference is so small as to be negligible in affecting the final result of the t test. When researchers have drawn two samples with the assumption that the standard deviations are equal, the following t test is used:

$$t = \frac{\overline{X}_1 - \overline{X}_2}{\sqrt{(s^2)\dfrac{N_1 + N_2}{N_1 N_2}}}$$

where $s^2 = \dfrac{(N_1 - 1)s_1^2 + (N_2 - 1)s_2^2}{N_1 + N_2 - 2}$.

To illustrate, suppose two samples of infantrymen were obtained for the purpose of determining the effect of a training film on their combat efficiency. One group is shown the film; the other group does not see it. Assuming equal standard deviations, the following information is derived relevant to combat efficiency:

Group Not Shown Film: $N_1 = 15$; combat efficiency $\overline{X}_1 = 12.4$; $s_1 = 3.5$.

Group Shown Film: $N_2 = 22$; combat efficiency $\overline{X}_2 = 14.3$; $s_2 = 3.1$.

What was the effect of the training film on the combat efficiency of the two groups of infantrymen? We are assuming that combat efficiency is measured according to some interval-level characteristic, that the higher the combat efficiency, the higher the score, and that the standard deviations of each group are equal. Since we expect the group seeing the training film to have the higher combat-efficiency rating or $\overline{X}$, we use a one-tailed test of the following hypothesis:

$$H_0: \quad \mu_1 \geqslant \mu_2 \text{ or } \overline{X}_1 \geqslant \overline{X}_2$$

$$H_1: \quad \mu_1 < \mu_2 \text{ or } \overline{X}_1 < \overline{X}_2$$

$$P \leqslant .01 \text{ (one-tailed test).}$$

Carrying out the necessary operations, we first of all compute s^2:

$$\begin{aligned} s^2 &= \frac{(15-1)(3.5)^2 + (22-1)(3.1)^2}{15+22-2} \\ &= \frac{(14)(12.25) + (21)(9.61)}{35} \\ &= \frac{171.50 + 201.81}{35} = \frac{373.31}{35} \\ &= 10.67. \end{aligned}$$

Substituting s^2 for the symbol in the t formula, we have:

$$\begin{aligned} t &= \frac{12.4 - 14.3}{\sqrt{(10.67)\dfrac{15+22}{(15)(22)}}} \\ &= \frac{-1.9}{\sqrt{1.195}} = \frac{-1.9}{1.09} \\ &= -1.74 \end{aligned}$$

$$df = N_1 + N_2 - 2, \text{ or } 15 + 22 - 2 = 35.$$

Turning to Table A.5 of Appendix A, we find that we must have an observed t equal to or greater than -2.457 in order to reject the null hypothesis.* Since our observed t is not as large as -2.457, being only -1.74, we conclude that the two groups of infantrymen do not differ with respect to combat efficiency at the .01 level of significance, using a one-tailed test.

It should be noted that often we are not able to find exact degrees of freedom according to the size of samples which we have. If our sample

* Since all values of t shown in the table are positive, we simply assign a negative sign (−) to our critical t value to compare it with the observed t, if the t is negative *and* in the predicted direction according to the hypothesis.

size is 75, we note that the *df* column does not contain 75 degrees of freedom specifically. Rather, $df = 60$ and $df = 120$ are provided. We must either interpolate or else use as our significant *t* the closest *df* value below the size of sample we have. Since the jump in degrees of freedom is from 60 to 120, we use the degrees of freedom appropriate for 60. It is more accurate to interpolate, however. To illustrate, let us assume that we are using the .01 level of significance with a one-tailed test. Since no significant *t* value is provided for 75, we must interpolate. The *t* value for 60 is 2.390 and the *t* value for 120 is 2.358. Since 75 is one-quarter of the distance between 60 and 120, we can take one-quarter of the difference between 2.390 and 2.358; thus $2.390 - 2.358 = .032$ and $.032/4 = .008$. We subtract this amount from 2.390; thus $2.390 - .008 = 2.382$. The critical value of *t* for 75 degrees of freedom is 2.382. In this case, we have made it slightly easier to reject the null hypothesis by reducing the size of the critical value of *t*.

Some Large-Sample Considerations

In the two examples of the *t* test above, the formulas presented were especially appropriate for small samples, that is, fewer than 30. When large samples are encountered, that is, greater than 30, *t* approximates the normal distribution, and the *t* observed value may be treated more like a *Z* value. Table A.3 in Appendix A, Areas under the Normal Curve, may be used, in which case we do not need to determine degrees of freedom. If a *t* of 2.38 were observed in a particular difference-of-means test, with a total *N* of 80, for example, we could enter the normal-distribution table, using the *t* as a *Z*, and we could therefore identify whether or not our observed *t* fell in the critical region of the distribution. Again, with an *N* greater than 30, the *t* distribution approximates the normal distribution, and *t* and *Z* become increasingly equivalent in function. Notice how similar the formulas for the two statistical tests are.

The Randomization Test for Matched Pairs: Related Samples

When the researcher has a study design where each element or subject will act as his own control in a before-and-after experiment, or when the two samples involved have been matched according to some underlying characteristic and we must assume that the samples are related, the randomization test for matched pairs may be used. This test is designed to determine the probability associated with our observations. Specifically, we are interested in knowing whether or not our observations are due to chance or to the effect of some experimental variable.

Suppose we are interested in determining the effectiveness of programmed-learning methods compared with learning through lectures. For our purposes, we bring together two groups of college students who have been matched according to a number of salient characteristics—age, sex, grade-point average, academic major, general interests, year in school, and so on. In our study, 6 pairs of students are involved. The first group of students is exposed to programmed learning of history; the other group is given a series of lectures on the same material. At the end of the term, we compare the final-examination scores of the students in both groups. Because of the nature of programmed-learning situations, we think that the students involved in programmed learning will have higher scores than those students learning history through the lecture method. We test this hypothesis by stating it in null form:

H_0: Students taking a history examination after a lecture method of instruction will do as well as or better than students taught by programmed learning.

H_1: The programmed-learning group will do better on the examination.

$$P \leqslant .05 \text{ (one-tailed test).}$$

We observe the information in Table 7.1.

Table 7.1. History-Examination Scores between Two Groups Exposed to Different Learning Methods.

Lecture Method Group A	*Programmed-Learning Method Group B*	d[a]
45	49	+4
48	49	+1
43	51	+8
48	55	+7
45	42	−3
46	51	+5
		$\Sigma d = 22$

[a] d represents the differences in scores between pairs of individuals.

The magnitude of differences in scores between the two groups above constitutes the observations we wish to evaluate. We are interested in determining whether or not such observations were expected as a result of programmed learning of history. Signs (+ or −) are given each score difference according to the direction in which the difference in scores is observed between the pairs of students. We are interested in determining how unusual or different our observations are compared to what otherwise might be expected according to chance.

In the randomization test, there are 2^N possible outcomes for our observations, where N = the number of paired elements. The outcomes refer to the *possible sums of the magnitudes of score differences* which could occur in our illustration in Table 7.1. In our example, there are 6 pairs of elements, and therefore, $(2)^6 = 64$ possible outcomes. Under chance conditions, some of these outcomes are expected more often than others. For example, if there were no difference affecting examination grades between lectures and programmed-learning methods, we might expect little or no differences between scores of the matched pairs of individuals. If one learning method affects examination grades, we might expect differences between pairs of subjects. And logically, the greater the effect, the greater the score difference.

If scores for some individuals in one group are higher and lower than those for individuals in the other group, it would be difficult to determine any systematic effect of a learning method upon examination performance. Under the null-hypothesis model, such a situation would be expected. In order to reject the null hypothesis, we are therefore interested in the more unexpected or extreme arrangements of score differences. Using our research hypothesis as a guideline, we need to identify the extreme arrangements of score differences in the predicted direction.

Inasmuch as we are using the .05 level of significance to test the H_0, we multiply .05 by the number of possible outcomes, $(2)^N$, in the present case 64:

$$(.05)(64) = 3.2.$$

This procedure gives us the number of outcomes of extreme arrangements of score differences which we shall use as our critical region. Since we now are interested in the three most extreme outcomes in the predicted direction, we set up a table similar to that in Table 7.2, showing the three most extreme arrangements of score differences which can arise from the data in Table 7.1. Also included in the table are two additional outcomes which are not as extreme.

Table 7.2. The Most Extreme Outcomes.

							Σd_i
(1)	+4	+1	+8	+7	+3	+5	28
(2)	+4	−1	+8	+7	+3	+5	26
(3)	+4	+1	+8	+7	−3	+5	22[a]
(4)	+4	−1	+8	+7	−3	+5	20
(5)	−4	+1	+8	+7	+3	+5	20

[a]This arrangement or outcome matches our observed arrangement of score differences.

The extreme arrangements of score differences are determined as follows. First, we assign positive signs to all score differences, because our research hypothesis specifies that the programmed-learning group will have higher scores (+) than the group learning by lectures. This is the most extreme arrangement of score differences. Next, we assign a negative sign to the smallest score difference, and positive signs to all other score differences. This observation is the second most extreme arrangement. Next, we assign a negative sign or signs to the next larger number or *combination* of smaller numbers which, when summed, will give us the next smaller Σd_i. This becomes our third most extreme favorable observation. It should be noted that each time we identify a new arrangement of score differences, the sum of these differences usually changes. In Table 7.2 we have provided sums of score differences for each extreme-score arrangement. As we change one score from positive to negative, the sum of score differences for that particular arrangement changes, exceptions being outcomes (4) and (5) above.

In this case, it happens that one of the extreme favorable outcomes shown in Table 7.2 is exactly what was observed in our sample. We conclude, therefore, that our observations are significantly different from chance at the .05 level. Had our observation *not* been included as one of these extreme observations, we would have concluded that there was no significant difference between the two student groups with respect to programmed-learning and lecture methods and the resultant final-examination scores in history.

In the example presented in Table 7.2, positive signs were assigned to all score differences, regardless of what the sign of the score difference was in reality. It should be noted that we could have assigned negative signs to all score differences for an equally extreme outcome at the other end of the distribution of possible positive and negative signs. Such a procedure is used in testing a nondirectional hypothesis with the randomization test for matched pairs. In this case, the level of significance would be halved, $\alpha/2$, in order to determine the extreme outcomes for a two-tailed test.

Assumptions for the Randomization Test for Matched Pairs Interval-level data must be used and the samples should be related in order for the randomization test for matched pairs to be used appropriately. No assumptions need be met concerning normalcy of the distribution.

Advantages and Disadvantages of the Randomization Test The primary advantage of the randomization test for matched pairs is that it makes no assumptions pertaining to the distribution of elements. It is a useful test for determining probabilities associated with the occurrence of specific observations. It is very useful in before-and-after study designs, where subjects act as their own controls, and where the level of measurement associated with a particular characteristic is at least interval.

Where samples are compared, however, matching can be a rather difficult task. As the number of characteristics used in matching increases, the resultant sample size decreases. Also, the randomization test becomes rather unmanageable if $N = 10$ or more. This is because the number of possible outcomes, 2^N, becomes quite large. Large samples may be used, but carrying out the randomization test becomes extremely tedious. When $N = 10$, $(2)^{10} = 1{,}024$ outcomes, and when $N = 11$, $(2)^{11} = 2{,}048$ outcomes, and so on.

A useful alternative to the randomization test for matched pairs, one which handles larger samples with little difficulty, is the Wilcoxon matched-pairs-signed-ranks test, to be discussed in Chapter 9. This alternative test uses rank differences to differentiate between samples according to some experimental variable.

The Randomization Test for Independent Samples

When it cannot be assumed that two samples are related according to some underlying trait or characteristic, several alternatives are available to the investigator. He may compute a t test, but in doing so he makes certain assumptions concerning the distribution of elements. A second alternative is the randomization test for two independent samples, which makes no assumption concerning the distribution of elements. This statistical test is designed to determine whether or not two samples have come from the same population. Specifically, this test tells us the probability associated with the occurrence of our observations, and whether or not they are expected by chance. Do two groups have the same mean scores, or have the groups been drawn from populations having significantly different means?

Suppose we have the following information pertaining to a small-group problem-solving experiment. A social investigator has conducted an experiment involving two independent samples of college students participating in small-group problem-solving sessions. One group leader is highly authoritarian and permits little discussion as the group deals with the problem. The second group leader is very democratic, and consequently everyone in the group has the opportunity to participate freely in the problem-solving effort. At the end of the experiment, the students of each group are given a series of individual problems to solve. The investigator believes that those students who were a part of the group with authoritarian leadership would not do as well at solving the new problems as would the students from the democratically led group. His results are shown in Table 7.3.

We are interested in testing the following hypothesis:

H_0: The authoritarian-led group will do as well as or better than the democratically led group with respect to solving new problems.
H_1: The authoritarian-led group will do less well than the democratically led group with respect to solving new problems.

$$P \leqslant .05 \text{ (one-tailed test).}$$

In order to test this hypothesis, we must determine *how different* our observations in Table 7.3 are from observations due to chance. With

Table 7.3. Comparisons of Problem Solving between Groups under Authoritarian and Democratic Leadership.

	Authoritarian-Led Group	*Democratically Led Group*
N	$N_1 = 4$	$N_2 = 4$
Number of problems correctly solved	15 13 14 19	18 22 17 16

these particular scores, what are all the possible observations which could occur? If there were no significant effect upon one's success at problem solving as a result of the kind of group experience one has, we might expect that high and low scores would be *randomly* distributed between the two groups of students. The more random the distribution of the scores, the more likely it is that our observations are due to chance. The less random the distribution of the scores, the less likely that they are due to chance. We are interested, therefore, in the *extreme* observations which could possibly occur in our present example; we had a similar problem when discussing the randomization test for matched pairs. After identifying the most extreme possible observations, we can make a comparison between these extreme outcomes and the observations we have in the present instance.

To determine the number of possible outcomes given a particular number of scores in each sample, we may apply the following formula:

$$\binom{N_1 + N_2}{N_1}$$

where N_1 and N_2 are the respective sample sizes.

This formula involves factorials. The symbol for a factorial is (!) and its use is illustrated below:

$$\binom{a}{b} = \frac{a!}{b!(a-b)!}.$$

An example of what to do with numbers followed by the factorial sign is

$$4! = (4)(3)(2)(1) = 24$$

$$7! = (7)(6)(5)(4)(3)(2)(1) = 5{,}040$$

and in the general case,

$$N! = N(N-1)(N-2)(N-3)\ldots 1.$$

In some instances, we are confronted with 0!. By definition, 0! = 1.

As used in the present instance,

$$\binom{N_1 + N_2}{N_1} \text{ becomes } \binom{4+4}{4} \text{ or } \binom{8}{4}$$

or

$$\frac{8!}{4!(8-4)!} = \frac{(8)(7)(6)(5)(4)(3)(2)(1)}{(4)(3)(2)(1)(4)(3)(2)(1)},$$

which becomes a simple division problem where we can cancel out most of the terms, and where our final result is

$$\frac{8!}{4!(8-4)!} = 70.$$

For our present problem, where $N_1 = 4$ and $N_2 = 4$, the number of possible outcomes is 70.

Next, we must determine how many extreme outcomes will constitute the region of rejection for the null hypothesis. Since we are using a one-tailed test at the .05 level, we simply multiply the significance level, .05, by the number of possible outcomes, or .05(70) = 3.5. We may round this result to *the closest even number,* or 4 outcomes. Our rejection region becomes the four most extreme outcomes in the predicted direction (according to our research hypothesis).

The most extreme outcome we can think of would be for one group of students to have the four *highest* scores and for the other group of students to have the four *lowest* scores. In our example, for the authoritarian-led group to have the four lowest scores while the democratically led group had the four highest scores would be the most extreme outcome in the predicted direction. And because this observation would lie in the region of rejection, we would reject the null hypothesis.

In Table 7.4 we have identified the four most extreme outcomes from our observations in Table 7.3.

Table 7.4. Extreme Outcomes for Problem Solving by Two Groups, One-Tailed Test.

	Extreme Score Arrangements		
	Authoritarian-Led Group (Group A)	*Democratically Led Group (Group B)*	$\Sigma A - \Sigma B$
(1)	13 14 15 16	17 18 19 22[a]	18
(2)	13 14 15 17	16 18 19 22	16
(3)	13 14 15 18	16 17 19 22	14
(4)	13 14 15 19	16 17 18 22	12

[a] Most extreme arrangement or outcome.

The question we must ask is whether or not the observed outcome in Table 7.3 is found among the four most extreme outcomes. In the present example, it happens that the fourth extreme outcome corresponds to our observations in Table 7.3, and in that event, we conclude that our observations lie in the region of rejection. Therefore, we reject the null hypothesis that the authoritarian-led group did as well as or better than the democratically led group with respect to the solving of new problems. In this case, the democratically led group did better at solving new problems than the group with authoritarian leadership at the .05 level of significance.

Had we used a two-tailed test, we would have had to determine the four most extreme outcomes in terms of *both* types of extremes: that is, where the authoritarian-led group would receive the highest scores and the democratically led group would receive the lowest scores, rather than the reverse as is shown in Table 7.4. Table 7.5 shows the most extreme scores for the observations above in the two-tailed case.

Table 7.5. Extreme Outcomes for Problem Solving by Two Groups, Two-Tailed Test.

	Extreme Score Arrangements	
	Authoritarian-Led Group	*Democratically Led Group*
(1)	13 14 15 16	17 18 19 22[a]
(2)	17 18 19 22	13 14 15 16[a]
(3)	13 14 15 17	16 18 19 22[a]
(4)	16 18 19 22	13 14 15 17[a]

[a]Most extreme outcomes.

In both the one-tailed and the two-tailed cases, the number of possible outcomes was obtained identically. In the one-tailed case, the four extreme outcomes in one direction were taken into account, while in the two-tailed case, the two most extreme outcomes in each direction were identified. Each procedure identifies the four most extreme outcomes, but which particular outcomes are used depends upon whether the test of the hypothesis is one- or two-tailed.

Assumptions for the Randomization Test for Two Independent Samples The primary assumption underlying the randomization test for two independent samples is that the data be at least interval. No assumptions exist concerning the homogeneity of the sample variances or the normalcy of the sample distributions.

Advantages and Disadvantages of the Randomization Test Because so few assumptions exist for application of the randomization test, it is quite useful under a variety of conditions where very small samples exist.

The test reveals exact probabilities associated with particular observations as well.

Like its counterpart, the randomization test for matched pairs, the randomization test for independent samples becomes cumbersome to apply when $N_1 + N_2 > 10$. For example, suppose N_1 and N_2 were 6 and 6 respectively. The number of possible outcomes would be

$$\binom{6+6}{6} \text{ or 924 possible outcomes.}$$

If we were to continue to use the .05 level of significance, the number of extreme outcomes needed to test the hypothesis would be (.05)(924) or about 46. This means that the work involved would be quite time-consuming.

Siegel (1956) suggests an approximation of the *t* test for the randomization test for two independent samples when sample size becomes large. A more useful alternative, however, would be the Mann-Whitney *U* test, to be discussed in Chapter 9.

TESTS FOR *k* SAMPLES: INDEPENDENT SAMPLES

Sometimes investigators draw more than two samples of elements. When more than two samples of elements of size *N* are drawn, we refer to the number of samples drawn as *k* samples of size *N*. The researcher may wish to evaluate differences between *k* classes of introductory sociology students, between *k* groups of policemen from different cities, between *k* groups of workers in an industrial plant, between *k* groups exposed to different teaching methods, or others of the kind. In other words, the investigator is faced with the problem of evaluating differences between *k* samples of size *N* or *k* samples with *N*'s of different sizes.

To deal with this problem, he may use the *t* test or the *Z* test, comparing *pairs* of samples, and identifying differences between each pair. This procedure can become rather time-consuming, particularly if a large number of samples is involved. The possible number of samples which can be compared, two at a time, is

$$\frac{N(N-1)}{2}$$

where $N =$ the number of samples.

This means that for six groups of elements, for example, the number of possible comparisons between two means without repetition is

$$\frac{6(6-1)}{2} \text{ or 15 comparisons.}$$

This also means that there are 15 possible *t* or *Z* tests.

There is a much better way to evaluate differences between each of the

k sample means, however. The method which is often used in situations such as this is called the *analysis of variance,* which is a method for determining the significance of difference between k sample means simultaneously.

Simple Analysis of Variance

The analysis-of-variance test specifically tests the hypothesis that there are no differences between k sample means. The statistic F is used to determine whether or not differences exist between k sample means. Sometimes, the investigators call such a test the F test. An example of simple analysis of variance will now be presented.

Suppose we have three work groups in a given industrial plant. The company manager suspects that one or more of these groups are restricting output, or are not producing as much per day as accords with predetermined production standards. He wishes to have statistical confirmation that certain groups are not producing according to company expectations. He collects information on each individual's as well as each work group's productivity level, and he presents their productivity scores during a given month in a table similar to the one in Table 7.6. With this information, we are interested in testing the following hypothesis:

H_0: There is no difference between the mean productivity scores of the three groups of workers.
H_1: There will be a difference between the mean productivity scores of the three groups of workers.

$$P \leqslant .01.$$

Is there any reason for the manager to suspect that some work groups are restricting output or production according to apparent differences in their mean productivity scores as shown in Table 7.6? To answer this question, we could take each pair of means and test for differences between them with either t or Z. But we decide to use the analysis-of-variance test instead. The results will be comparable, and the test itself will take much less time to compute.

The phrase *analysis of variance* means that we will be analyzing the variation between sample mean productivity as well as the variation of productivity within each of the work groups. The analysis-of-variance test will tell us whether the variation between means of k samples is significant, in this case, at the .01 level.

Procedure for the Analysis-of-Variance Test There are several ways of obtaining the information we need for carrying out an analysis-of-variance test. A long method and a short method will be presented here.

For the long method, we need to construct a table similar to that shown in Table 7.6. Thus we need to have each individual's score, the group

Table 7.6. Productivity Scores for Three Work Groups.

Work Group A		*Work Group B*		*Work Group C*	
X_1	X_1^2	X_2	X_2^2	X_3	X_3^2
4	16	6	36	5	25
5	25	6	36	3	9
5	25	8	64	2	4
7	49	8	64	3	9
4	16	7	49	2	4
$\Sigma X_1 = 25$	$\Sigma X_1^2 = 131$	$\Sigma X_2 = 35$	$\Sigma X_2^2 = 249$	$\Sigma X_3 = 15$	$\Sigma X_3^2 = 51$
$\overline{X}_1 = 5.00$		$\overline{X}_2 = 7.00$		$\overline{X}_3 = 3.00$	
		$\overline{X}_T = 5.00$			

$N = 5 =$ the number of workers in each sample
$k = 3 =$ the number of samples

$\Sigma X_k^2 = 431$[a]
$\Sigma X_T = 75$[b]
$\Sigma(\Sigma X_k)^2 = 2{,}075$[c]

[a] $\Sigma X_k^2 = \Sigma X_1^2 + \Sigma X_2^2 + \Sigma X_3^2 \cdots + \Sigma X_k^2$
[b] $\Sigma X_T = \Sigma X_1 + \Sigma X_2 + \Sigma X_3 \cdots + \Sigma X_N$
[c] $\Sigma(\Sigma X_k)^2 = (\Sigma X_1)^2 + (\Sigma X_2)^2 + (\Sigma X_3)^2 \cdots + (\Sigma X_k)^2$

mean, and the grand mean for all work groups. Since there is an equal number of workers in each sample, the grand mean is found by either (a) summing the group means and dividing by the number of groups, or (b) adding each individual score and dividing by the total number of scores for all samples. Either method will yield the correct result.

We also need to square each individual score and place this value in a column X^2 in juxtaposition to the column containing the scores, X. These X^2's are summed and placed in the table as shown. We can now determine the sum of the scores (ΣX_T), the sum of the squared scores (ΣX_T^2), and the grand mean ($\overline{X}_T$). The last value we will need will be the sum of all $(\Sigma X_k)^2$ or $\Sigma(\Sigma X_k)^2$, as is shown in the lower right-hand corner of the table (above the footnotes).

It is obvious that a certain amount of variation exists between individual scores across all groups as well as within each group. If there were no variation, all scores and group means would be identical. The analysis-of-variance test constitutes, in part, a test of the significance of the ratio of the variation found to exist between the groups and within them. This statement will have greater meaning as we move toward the completion of the test. Therefore, in order to complete the test we need to determine the amount of variation *between* groups and *within* them.

Between-group variation refers to the sum of the variations of each sample mean from the grand mean, the mean of all samples. This sum is determined by squaring the difference of each mean from the grand mean, multiplying this difference by N (the sample size), and summing these products.

In our example, the between-group variation, often termed "the between-group sum of squares" or "SS_{bet}" is determined as follows:

$$SS_{bet} = (5)(5-5)^2 + (5)(7-5)^2 + (5)(3-5)^2$$
$$= 0 + 20 + 20$$
$$= 40.$$

It is important to understand the procedure as explained verbally before the numerical example; but for those who desire an algebraic statement:

$$SS_{bet} = \Sigma N_k(\overline{X}_k - \overline{X}_T)^2$$

where k = the sample size for the kth sample;
$\overline{X}_k$ = the mean for the kth sample; and
$\overline{X}_T$ = the grand mean of all elements.

Within-group variation or the sum of squares within groups, SS_{within}, refers to the sum of the squared variations of each individual score from its sample mean. Again, referring to our present example, SS_{within} is computed as follows:

$$SS_{within} = (4-5)^2 + (5-5)^2 + (5-5)^2 + (7-5)^2 + (4-5)^2 + (6-7)^2 + (6-7)^2 + (8-7)^2 + (8-7)^2 + (7-7)^2 + (5-3)^2 + (3-3)^2 + (2-3)^2 + (3-3)^2 + (2-3)^2$$
$$= 1 + 0 + 0 + 4 + 1 + 1 + 1 + 1 + 1 + 0 + 4 + 0 + 1 + 0 + 1$$
$$= 16.$$

If an algebraic statement is wanted:

$$SS_{within} = \Sigma(X_{ik} - \overline{X}_T)^2$$

where X_{ik} = each individual score across k samples (that is, ith score, kth sample); and
$\overline{X}_T$ = the grand mean.

Combining SS_{bet} and SS_{within}, we have SS_{total}, which is defined as *the total variation for these k samples.*

$$40 + 16 = 56 = SS_{total}.$$

The *total sum of squares* is determined by squaring the difference of each score from the grand mean and summing these products, or more simply,

$$SS_{total} = (4-5)^2 + (5-5)^2 + (5-5)^2 + (7-5)^2 + (4-5)^2 + (6-5)^2 + (6-5)^2 + (8-5)^2 + (8-5)^2 + (7-5)^2 + (5-5)^2 + (3-5)^2 + (2-5)^2 + (3-5)^2 + (2-5)^2$$
$$= 1 + 0 + 0 + 4 + 1 + 1 + 1 + 9 + 9 + 4 + 0 + 4 + 9 + 4 + 9$$
$$= 56.$$

Therefore,

$$SS_{total} = SS_{within} + SS_{bet}.$$

After we have determined SS_{bet} and SS_{within}, we are now ready to construct an analysis-of-variance summary table, often called an *ANOV summary*. Table 7.7 is an ANOV Summary. Across the top of the table is indicated the *source of variation, sums of squares (SS), degrees of freedom (df), mean squares (MS), and F.*

Table 7.7. An ANOV Summary.

Source of Variation	*SS*	*df*	*MS*	*F*
Between samples (SS_{bet})	40.00	2 $(k-1)$	20.00	15.037
Within samples (SS_{within})	16.00	12 $k(N-1)$	1.33	
Total variation (SS_{total})	56.00	14 $(Nk-1)$		

We have previously identified the sources of variation. Variation originates *between* samples and *within* them. We therefore list these two sources of variation in the first column, *Source of Variation.* In the second column, *SS,* we place the sums of squares which we have just computed. $SS_{bet} = 40$, $SS_{within} = 16$, and $SS_{total} = 56$.

The degrees-of-freedom column *df* contains the respective degrees of freedom for between- and within-sample variation. Between-sample degrees of freedom are determined by k samples minus 1. This is shown by the $(k-1)$ in the table. In this case, the number of samples is 3 and *df* for SS_{bet} becomes $3 - 1 = 2$. For within-sample variation, degrees of freedom is equal to $k(N-1)$, or the number of samples multiplied by the sample size minus 1. For our data, $k(N-1) = (3)(5-1) = 12$. We place these degrees of freedom in their respective places in the table as is shown.

The fourth column, *Mean Square (MS),* contains the sums of squares (of SS_{bet} and SS_{within}) divided by their respective degrees of freedom. $SS_{bet}/df_{bet} = 40/2 = 20$. Therefore, $MS_{bet} = 20$. Also, $SS_{within}/df_{within} = 16/12 = 1.33$. Therefore, $MS_{within} = 1.33$.

We are now ready to make the F test to determine whether or not there is a significant difference between the sample means. The hypothesis we are testing is:

H_0: There is no difference between k sample means.

H_1: There is a difference between k sample means.

$$P \leqslant .01.$$

We are testing the null hypothesis that there is no difference between three sample means at the .01 level of significance. The test of this hypothesis is the F test, consisting of the ratio of MS_{bet} to MS_{within}, or

$$F = \frac{MS_{bet}}{MS_{within}}.$$

For our particular sample,

$$F = \frac{20}{1.33} = 15.037.$$

F is a statistic which tells us whether or not differences exist between k sample means at some level of significance. The larger the F, the more likely that significant differences exist between k sample means.

The significance of F is determined by turning to Table A.16 in Appendix A, 5 Percent and 1 Percent Points for the Distribution of F. First of all, we locate the appropriate degrees of freedom corresponding to MS_{bet} by moving across the top of the table. Next, we move down the left-hand column of the table until we find the degrees of freedom corresponding to MS_{within}. With respective df 2 and 12, the F value which we must have in order for the differences between the means to be significant at the .01 level (indicated in boldface type) is 6.93, the point where the two df points intersect within the table.

Since our observed F value is *larger* than 6.93, being 15.037, we may reject the null hypothesis and conclude that there is a significant difference between the means of the three groups at the .01 level.

Before continuing any further, let us examine the *short method* for determining F. The first method of carrying out an analysis of variance was rather tedious. Imagine the complexity of larger samples, larger scores, and so on! A much shorter method is available which circumvents much of this lengthy procedure.

To use the shorter method, we construct the table containing the worker's scores as shown in Table 7.6. We list the scores; we also square each of the scores in each sample, placing the squares of the scores in a column labeled X^2. The squares of the scores for each sample are summed as is shown, ΣX^2. Each of these sums of squares is summed, and the total sum of squares is placed to the bottom of the table at the right, ΣX^2_k. Finally, each of the sample-score totals is squared and the sum of these squares for all samples is placed to the bottom and right of the table as shown, $\Sigma(\Sigma X_k)^2$.

With these three values and with the other information provided in the table, we determine the following values:

$$(\Sigma X_T)^2/kN = (75)^2/(3)(5) = 5{,}625/15 = 375. \quad (1)$$

$$\Sigma X^2_k = 131 + 249 + 51 = 431. \quad (2)$$

$$\Sigma(\Sigma X_k)^2/N = \frac{[(25)^2 + (35)^2 + (15)^2]}{5} = 2{,}075/5 = 415. \quad (3)$$

We can now directly determine SS_{bet}, SS_{within}, and SS_{total} by using these values:

$$SS_{bet} = (3) - (1) = 415 - 375 = 40.$$

$$SS_{within} = (2) - (3) = 431 - 415 = 16.$$

$$SS_{total} = (2) - (1) = 431 - 375 = 56.$$

Placing these values in the ANOV summary will give the same result as the other method for carrying out analysis of variance. This method is much faster than the first presented, because in this instance, we do not have to determine deviation of each score from sample or grand means. We work directly with the squares of scores and the score totals.

Analysis of Variance for Unequal Sample Sizes In the example of analysis of variance illustrated above, the sample sizes were equal to one another. However, it is often the case that samples to be compared with one another will be of unequal size; real-life settings in business and industry present work groups of various sizes to be examined and compared with one another.

Suppose we have the information presented in Table 7.8 relating to the efficiency of three groups of bank employees. A bank president is interested in learning whether or not there are differences between groups of

Table 7.8. Efficiency Scores of Three Groups of Bank Employees.

Branch A		*Branch B*		*Branch C*	
X_1	X_1^2	X_2	X_2^2	X_3	X_3^2
2	4	9	81	4	16
4	16	8	64	4	16
8	64	7	49	4	16
6	36	8	64	3	9
3	9	6	36	5	25
		5	25	3	9
				7	49
				4	16
$\Sigma X_1 = 23$	$\Sigma X_1^2 = 129$	$\Sigma X_2 = 43$	$\Sigma X_2^2 = 319$	$\Sigma X_3 = 34$	$\Sigma X_3^2 = 156$
	$X_1 = 4.60$		$X_2 = 7.17$		$X_3 = 4.25$
	$N_1 = 5$		$N_2 = 6$		$N_3 = 8$
$X_T = 5.26$					

employees at three of the bank's branches with respect to general efficiency. Let us assume that we have measured efficiency according to some interval scale, and we have the efficiency scores of three groups of bank employees as they appear in Table 7.8.

Again, the *between-group variation* is defined as the sum of the squared differences of each sample mean from the grand mean, multiplied by the sample size. Since the sample size varies in each sample in Table 7.8, we must multiply the squared difference of each sample mean from the grand mean by each respective sample size. The grand mean is determined by summing all of the scores across samples and dividing this sum by the total number of scores, or

$$\overline{X}_T = (2 + 4 + 8 + 6 \cdots + 3 + 7 + 4)/(5 + 6 + 8) = 100/19$$
$$= 5.26.$$

Another way of expressing this symbolically would be:

$$\overline{X}_T = \frac{\Sigma X_i}{\Sigma N_k}$$

where ΣX_i = the sum of all sample scores;
ΣN_k = the sum of all elements across samples; and
k = the total number of samples.

What this procedure amounts to is *weighting* each sample mean according to sample size. A problem similar to this was discussed in Chapter 3, Measures of Central Tendency. SS_{bet} is therefore determined as follows:

$$SS_{bet} = (N_1)(\overline{X}_1 - \overline{X}_T)^2 + (N_2)(\overline{X}_2 - \overline{X}_T)^2 + (N_3)(\overline{X}_3 - \overline{X}_T)^2$$
$$= (5)(4.60 - 5.26)^2 + (6)(7.17 - 5.26)^2 + (8)(4.25 - 5.26)^2$$
$$= 2.18 + 21.90 + 8.16$$
$$= 32.24.$$

The *within-group variation* is determined in the same manner as before. Each score is subtracted from its respective mean, this difference is squared, and each of these squares is summed, giving us SS_{within}.

SS_{within} is equal to 45.52 when we carry out this procedure. The verification of this value is left as an exercise.

The short method of determining SS_{bet} and SS_{within} is basically the same as before. Only minor adjustments need be made in the formulas. These adjustments are shown below:

$$(\Sigma X_T)^2/N = (100)^2/19 = 10{,}000/19 = 526.32. \quad (1)$$
$$\Sigma X_k^2 = 129 + 319 + 156 = 604. \quad (2)$$
$$\Sigma(\Sigma X_k)^2/N_k = (23)^2/5 + (43)^2/6 + (34)^2/8$$
$$= 105.8 + 308.2 + 144.5 = 558.5. \quad (3)$$

Then,

$$SS_{bet} = (3) - (1) = 558.5 - 526.32 = 32.18.$$
$$SS_{within} = (2) - (3) = 604 - 558.5 = 45.5.$$
$$SS_{total} = (2) - (1) = 604 - 526.32 = 77.68.$$

The slight differences in SS_{bet} and SS_{within} as a result of using the short method are due to rounding error and will not significantly affect the result. An ANOV summary is shown in Table 7.9. Degrees of freedom

Table 7.9. An ANOV Summary.

Source of Variation	*SS*	*df*	*MS*	*F*
Between groups	32.24	2 $k-1$	16.12	5.676
Within groups	45.52	16 $\Sigma(N_k-1)$	2.84	
Total	77.76	18 $\Sigma N_k - 1$		

for *between-group variation* are determined in the same manner as before, that is, by $k-1$. For *within-group variation*, degrees of freedom are determined by $\Sigma(N_k-1)$. In this case, degrees of freedom for SS_{within} become $(5-1)+(6-1)+(8-1)=16$.

The F test is carried out in the same manner as before, where

$$F=\frac{MS_{bet}}{MS_{within}}=\frac{16.12}{2.84}=5.676.$$

The null hypothesis which we are interested in testing is:

H_0: There is no difference between mean efficiency scores among the three groups of bank employees.

H_1: There is a difference between mean efficiency scores among the three groups of bank employees.

$$P \leqslant .01.$$

With an observed F of 5.676, we turn to Table A.16 of Appendix A to determine the significance of it. For the .01 level of significance, we need an observed F of 6.23. This we have determined by entering the table with 2 and 16 degrees of freedom respectively. Since our observed F value does not equal or exceed 6.23, we are not able to reject the null hypothesis, and we conclude that there are no significant differences between the means of the three groups at the .01 level.

Assumptions for the Analysis-of-Variance Test The assumptions underlying the analysis-of-variance test are essentially the same as those required for the t test. The researcher must be able to assume interval-level data, and the elements should be normally distributed. The samples should be random and independently drawn. A further requirement is that the variances between samples be equal. This equality is often difficult to demonstrate. A number of tests exist to test for equal variances, or *homogeneity of variance* as it is usually called. Bartlett's test, Hartley's test, and Cochran's test are three methods used for determining homogeneity of variance among samples. Perhaps the simplest of the three tests for homogeneity of variance is Hartley's F_{max} test. This is defined as:

$$F_{max} = \frac{s^2_{max}}{s^2_{min}}$$

where s^2_{max} = the largest observed variance among k samples; and
s^2_{min} = the smallest observed variance among k samples.

The ratio of the largest and smallest variances, F_{max}, tells us whether or not the variances are similar enough to assume homogeneity of variance. We determine whether the two variances differ by using Table A.22 of Appendix A. Critical values are given for the .05 and .01 levels of significance.* For any given *df* and k, if the critical value is exceeded by our observed F_{max}, then the two variances are considered *not equal to one another.*†

For example, suppose the largest observed variance were 4.00 and the smallest observed variance were 2.00. Assuming that $k = 4$ and $df = 15$, a critical value of 4.01 or larger is needed in order for us to conclude that the variances differ at the .05 level of significance. Since our observed F_{max} is equal to 4.00/2.00 or 2.00, we conclude that homogeneity of variance can be assumed among the k samples.

When sample size varies, the largest sample size is generally used when determining *df* in Table A.22 of Appendix A, because as the sample size increases the critical value decreases. This is a conservative interpretation. If the researcher demonstrates homogeneity of variance by using the largest sample size, then homogeneity of variance would always exist if any smaller sample size were used. Other homogeneity-of-variance tests are discussed in Winer (1962).

Advantages and Disadvantages of the Analysis-of-Variance Test The analysis of variance has a certain advantage over the t test, particularly when more than two samples are studied. An F may be computed and the difference between means of all samples determined in one test. This procedure is certainly more efficient than carrying out separate t tests for all possible pairs of means among several samples.

---

*The levels of significance correspond to alpha or α. In Table A.22 and others, the probability level may be reported as $1 - \alpha$ or .95 and .99 for the respective significance levels of .05 and .01.

† $df = N - 1$ where sample sizes are equal. Hartley's F_{max} test becomes less appropriate where unequal sample sizes are found. If it is used for cases involving unequal sample sizes, then $df = N - 1$ is used where N = the largest sample size. This means the largest sample size, *regardless* of whether or not the largest and/or the smallest variances come from the largest sample.

On the other hand, carrying out separate t tests will tell the investigator which means are significantly different from one another. The analysis-of-variance test simply says that there is a difference between several means. It does not say *where* the differences are. It is obvious that if a significant difference between eight means is observed as a result of an F test, *at least* the difference between the largest and the smallest means among the samples will be significant. But what about the next smallest mean and the largest mean? Does a significant difference exist here as well? The F test cannot answer this question, but a t test can. A simple procedure will soon be discussed, however, which may be used in conjunction with the analysis-of-variance test. This procedure will show an easy method for determining which pairs of means are significantly different from one another without having to compute individual t tests.

The analysis of variance is a test of significance, and it is valuable in the sense that it helps to describe the differences between several means simultaneously. It is computed rather quickly, and F is interpreted easily. It may probe for differences among any number of means. All in all, the analysis of variance is very useful in social research and this usefulness has been demonstrated in the literature.

The Newman-Keuls Procedure

When the analysis-of-variance test is made to determine if significant differences exist between k sample means, it is apparent that if an F is significant at a particular level, say .01, *at least* the two extreme means (the smallest and the largest) will be different from one another significantly. But it is possible that other significant differences exist between k sample means. Rather than go to the trouble of computing separate t tests for all other mean differences, the Newman-Keuls procedure may be used. This procedure enables the investigator to determine specifically where the significant differences between means lie.

To illustrate the Newman-Keuls procedure, we shall use a situation where seven sample means are found. Suppose we have the following means as shown below:

$$\bar{X}_1 = 3.00$$
$$\bar{X}_2 = 3.50$$
$$\bar{X}_3 = 4.00$$
$$\bar{X}_4 = 4.50$$
$$\bar{X}_5 = 7.00$$
$$\bar{X}_6 = 8.50$$
$$\bar{X}_7 = 9.00$$

Further suppose that $N = 3$ for all samples, and that $MS_{within} = 1.47$.

To determine which means differ from one another significantly, we must construct a *table of ordered means*. Such a table is shown in Table 7.10. A table of ordered means is a simple arrangement of means from

Table 7.10. A Table of Ordered Means.

	3.00	*3.50*	*4.00*	*4.50*	*7.00*	*8.50*	*9.00*	$q_{.99}(r, 14)$	$(s_{\bar{T}})q_{.99}(r, 14)$
3.00		.50	1.00	1.50	4.00	5.50*	6.00*	6.08	4.256 ($r = 7$)
3.50			.50	1.00	3.50	5.00*	5.50*	5.88	4.116 ($r = 6$)
4.00				.50	3.00	4.50*	5.00*	5.63	3.941 ($r = 5$)
4.50					2.50	4.00*	4.50*	5.32	3.724 ($r = 4$)
7.00						1.50	2.00	4.89	3.423 ($r = 3$)
8.50							.50	4.21	2.947 ($r = 2$)
9.00									

* See explanation in text.

largest to smallest across the top of the table, and the same arrangement down the left-hand side of the table, as is illustrated in Table 7.10. The body of the table contains the differences between each pair of means. It is essential *that the proper order of means be maintained in order that the Newman-Keuls test may be made correctly.*

With these mean differences determined and placed appropriately in the body of the table, we now want to know which mean differences are significant and which ones are not significant. The Newman-Keuls test can help us to answer this question.

In the column immediately to the right of the mean differences, we need to determine the statistic q, which varies for the number of steps (r) between ordered pairs of sample means at a particular level of significance.

The number of steps (r) between ordered pairs of means is determined by the number of sample means. If there are ten sample means, then there are ten steps between the first and the tenth sample mean. In this case, $r = 10$. If there are seven sample means as in our example, then there are seven steps between the smallest and the largest sample mean.* In this case, $r = 7$. In order to find the fixed value of q, we need to know the degrees of freedom for MS_{within}. Also, we need to know the

* The number of steps in this situation is established by definition. B. J. Winer, the author of the book from which this Neuman-Keuls procedure was obtained, specifies that r = the number of steps between ordered pairs of sample means. He states that "In this notation $T_{(1)}$ designates the smallest treatment total and $T_{(7)}$ the largest treatment total. $T_{(7)}$ is defined as being seven steps from $T_{(1)}$, $T_{(6)}$ is six steps from $T_{(1)}$, etc.; $T_{(7)}$ is six steps from $T_{(2)}$, $T_{(6)}$ is five steps from $T_{(2)}$, etc. In general, the number of steps between the ordered totals $T_{(j)}$ and $T_{(i)}$ is $j - i + 1$." (Winer, 1962, p. 80.) In the foregoing he was referring to score totals, but the same thing applies to means. $\bar{X}_1$ is six steps from $\bar{X}_6$ even though it *looks* as if it should only be five steps.

value of r, the number of steps between ordered pairs of means. Degrees of freedom for MS_{within} is equal to $k(N-1)$ or

$$df = 7(3 - 1) = 14.$$

In our example, $r = 7$.

With these values we turn to Table A.17 of Appendix A, Distribution of the Studentized Range Statistic. This table contains various values of q. These values correspond to particular numbers of degrees of freedom, a particular r, and a certain level of significance. It will be noted that *degrees of freedom* is found down the left-hand column of the table. In the second column $(1-\alpha)$ are various probabilities, in this case .95 and .99. These probabilities correspond to the .05 and .01 levels of significance. Across the top of the table are included various values of r from 2 to 15. Therefore, this table may handle comparisons of up to 15 different means.

Let us continue to use the .01 level of significance as one of our decision rules to judge the significance of differences between ordered pairs of means in this instance.

With this information we may now determine q. We enter Table A.17 with $df = 14$ and $r = 7$. Where these two values intersect in the body of the table are found two values, one for .95 and one for .99. We select the value for .99, which is 6.08. We enter this value in Table 7.10 in the column headed $q_{.99}(r, 14)$. This is the first value of q when $r = 7$. But we are not through, yet. We need to find q when $r = 6$, $r = 5$, $r = 4$, $r = 3$, and $r = 2$. This is an easy procedure. We simply move to the left in Table A.17 where we originally found q when $r = 7$. Each appropriate column will give us the q we are looking for. When $r = 6$, q becomes 5.88 when $df = 14$ at the .01 level of significance. When $r = 5$, q becomes 5.63. When $r = 4$, q becomes 5.32, and so on.

The final column, $(s_{\bar{t}})q_{.99}(r, 14)$, contains the values by which the mean differences in the body of the table will be compared and evaluated as to their significance. We needed to determine q for various values of r in order to derive these values. $s_{\bar{t}}$ is the standard error of the sample means. It is determined by the following formula:

$$s_{\bar{t}} = \sqrt{\frac{MS_{within}}{N}}$$

where N = the size of the samples, if the sample sizes are identical; or
N = the smallest sample size, if several samples of unequal size are compared.

In our example, $N = 3$ and $MS_{within} = 1.47$. Substituting these values in the formula, we have:

$$s_{\bar{t}} = \sqrt{\frac{1.47}{3}} = \sqrt{.49} = .70.$$

We shall multiply $s_{\bar{T}}$ or .70 by each q in Table 7.10. For example, (6.08)(.70) = 4.256, (5.88)(.70) = 4.116, and so on. These have been computed and have been placed in their proper places in the table.

We are now ready to see how many means differ from one another at the .01 level of significance. We compare the value in the right-hand column $(s_{\bar{T}})q_{.99}(r, 14)$ with all mean differences to the left of it horizontally. Thus we first move horizontally, from the right to the left, comparing 4.256 with the mean differences 6.00, 5.50, 4.00, 1.50, 1.00, and .50. Each time we come to a mean difference which equals or exceeds 4.256, we mark it with an asterisk (*) to note that that particular mean difference is significant at the .01 level. If a mean difference is smaller than 4.256, then that particular mean difference is not significant. Continuing, we take the $(s_{\bar{T}})q_{.99}(r, 14)$ value, 4.116, and compare this with all mean differences and horizontally to the left of it: we compare 4.116 with 5.50, 5.00, 3.50, 1.00, and .50. Again, as before, we place an asterisk next to those mean differences which are equal to or larger than 4.116. We work down the right-hand column likewise for each of the mean differences. *At no time do we compare the mean differences at one horizontal level with the $(s_{\bar{T}})q_{.99}(r, df)$ value of another horizontal level.*

It should be noted that when the investigator is comparing mean differences with the relevant $(s_{\bar{T}})q_{.99}(r, df)$ value, once he has come to a mean difference which is not significant—that is, not equal to or larger than $(s_{\bar{T}})q_{.99}(r, df)$—then all successive mean differences to the left of and below the first nonsignificant mean difference will also be *not significant*. For example, in Table 7.10, the first nonsignificant mean difference encountered is 4.00 (between the means 3.00 and 7.00). All values to the left of and below this nonsignificant mean value are also nonsignificant.

All significant mean differences have been asterisked (*) in Table 7.10. The investigator can now specify which mean differences are significant at the .01 level. From the standpoint of time alone, the Newman-Keuls procedure is a valuable statistical technique to employ. Its results are comparable to the completion of t tests for each of the pairs of sample means. In other words, the conclusions of the t tests and the Newman-Keuls procedure will be similar.

SUMMARY

In this chapter we have examined a number of tests of significance for data of the interval level. Such tests include the t test and the Z test, particularly useful when means of samples are being compared. Other two-sample tests of significance include the randomization test for matched pairs and the randomization test for two independent samples. These techniques enable the researcher to specify probabilities associated with his observations of differences between groups.

The analysis-of-variance procedure for identifying differences between k samples was also presented, both for equal sample sizes and for unequal sample sizes. Such a procedure specifies whether or not differences exist between k sample means, but it does not say where the differences occur. For this special problem, the Newman-Keuls procedure for determining where significant differences between means lie was presented. This procedure is relatively easy to apply, and it saves much time compared to the computation of several t tests for the same purpose. A test for homogeneity of variance was also illustrated.

QUESTIONS FOR REVIEW AND PROBLEMS TO SOLVE

1. Using the t test, test the following hypothesis for this information: $N = 25$; $s = 40$; $\overline{X} = 560$.

$$H_0: \qquad \mu = 500$$
$$P \leqslant .05.$$

2. Changing the sample size to 101 in Problem 1 above, compute a Z for the same information. Discuss the difference between t and Z as results.

3. Carry out an analysis of variance for the following information and determine where the significant differences between means lie by using the Newman-Keuls procedure.

		Groups		
#1	*#2*	*#3*	*#4*	*#5*
9	7	2	10	1
6	7	5	6	2
5	4	4	8	8
7	3	3	9	6
9	6	2	5	3
8	5	7	7	3

$$P \leqslant .05.$$

(a) Does homogeneity of variance exist for the samples above?

4. Two groups of elements received the following scores:

Group 1	*Group 2*
5	10
6	7
3	0
7	9
4	8

$$P \leqslant .05.$$

Assuming that the two groups are related, determine the significance of difference between the two groups using the randomization test for matched pairs. (a) Are there differences between the two groups using the randomization test for independent samples? Use the same level of significance.

5. What are some advantages of using the Newman-Keuls procedure instead of the t test when several means of samples are being compared simultaneously?

6. Carry out an analysis-of-variance test for the following information:

Group 1	*Group 2*	*Group 3*
12	9	6
13	10	5
11	8	7
15	8	7
14	11	4
11	10	
15		

$$P \leqslant .01.$$

7. Test the following hypothesis for this information: $N_1 = 55$; $\overline{X}_1 = 92.3$; $s_1 = 4.5$. $N_2 = 87$; $\overline{X}_2 = 96.8$; $s_2 = 5.6$.

$$H_0: \qquad \overline{X}_1 = \overline{X}_2$$

$$P \leqslant .01 \text{ (two-tailed test).}$$

8. What are some assumptions underlying the t test? What are some disadvantages of the Z test when small samples are found?

9. Using a two-tailed test, test the following hypothesis for this information: $N = 60$; $X = 41$; $s = 3$.

$$H_0: \qquad \mu = 45$$

$$P \leqslant .05.$$

10. The largest and smallest variances among several groups are 8.32 and 4.61; $N = 12$; $k = 5$. Does homogeneity of variance exist at $\leqslant .05$? What other alternatives exist for computing homogeneity of variance? (Use F_{max} in the present problem.)

8 Nominal-Level Tests of Significance

This chapter presents a number of nominal-level tests of significance. It will be remembered that nominal-level information may be categorized only, and that numerical values used to represent nominal-level information simply serve to distinguish between categories of elements according to some trait such as sex, race, religious affiliation, or the like. The meaning of numbers in this sense is one of differentiating one category of elements from another. We cannot mathematically manipulate the numbers by adding, subtracting, dividing, or multiplying them by one another, as was previously illustrated in Chapter 1.

When nominal-level data are converted to proportions or percentages, certain manipulations are possible. In addition, we may count the number of people found in a given category, and we may hypothesize a number of things concerning how these elements are categorized.

In previous chapters we have used chance as a standard with which to compare our observations. When our observations depart markedly from what we expect according to chance, we say that our observations differ from chance at a certain level of probability. Through the establishment of certain decision rules, among them levels of significance, we may determine whether or not our observations are different from what is expected by chance at a particular level of significance.

The tests in this chapter also are geared to tell us whether or not departures from our hypothesized chance expectations are different at a particular level of significance. In other words, the tests presented here will help us to evaluate differences between what we expect under null hypotheses and what we actually find as observations.

The nominal-level tests of significance to be examined in this chapter include the chi-square test, the Z test for differences between proportions, the McNemar test for significance of changes, Fisher's exact test, the Cochran Q test, and an extension of the chi-square test.

SINGLE-SAMPLE TEST

The Chi-Square Test

One of the most widely used tests of significance is the chi-square test. The chi-square statistic, χ^2, tells us whether our observations differ from what is expected by chance, when chance is defined according to a particular set of rules. It is sometimes called a *goodness-of-fit* statistic. Goodness of fit refers to a statistical evaluation of the difference between our sample observations and some distribution of observations provided by a hypothesized model.

The popularity of the chi-square test is chiefly due to the fact that there are no assumptions which need to be made concerning the underlying distributions of the variables. Also, the variables may be either discrete or continuous, and data of the nominal level are appropriate for analysis.

On many occasions, we are interested in determining whether our observations are significantly different from what we would otherwise expect according to the laws of chance or according to some null hypothesis. For example, a simple problem we may have is determining whether or not we have a *biased* coin—a coin which, when tossed, tends to land heads up more often than tails up, or vice versa.

We flip a coin 100 times to find out whether or not the coin is biased. If the coin is *not* biased, we *expect* 50 heads and 50 tails out of 100 flips of the coin. Our reason is that the hypothesized probability model specifies that the probability of getting a head is 1/2, or .50. Exactly one-half of 100 is 50. But we may actually find that out of 100 flips of the coin we obtain 55 heads and 45 tails. Is the coin biased? We can obviously see that our observations are *different* from what we theoretically expect according to our probability model, in this case a 50-50 split between heads and tails. Indeed discrepancies usually exist between what we observe and what we expect under an ideal theoretical model. Evaluating the significance of such discrepancies when they occur is an important function of goodness-of-fit tests. Minor or moderate departures from the expectations of a model often occur by chance. The important question is, therefore, "Do our observations constitute a *significant* departure from what would be expected by chance?" Or in terms of goodness of fit, "To what extent do our observations fit the probability model which we have hypothesized?"

One popular goodness-of-fit test of significance for data of the nominal level is the chi-square test. The chi-square test has many uses, among which is the basic test for determining whether what is observed differs from what is expected by chance at a particular level of significance.

When we obtain a sample of elements and we have identified this sample according to certain nominal characteristics, we test a number of hypotheses concerning this sample pertaining to the *distribution* of these characteristics. The distribution of nominal characteristics is essentially a *proportional distribution.* Consequently, for any given sample, we may be interested in testing whether some observed proportional distribution of characteristics differs from some hypothesized proportional distribution of them, at some level of significance.

In addition to evaluating such proportional differences as those involved in the flipping of coins, the chi-square test helps to evaluate differences in the sex distributions of various groups, racial distributions in neighborhoods or schools or larger geographical areas, general ethnic differences existing in urban or rural settings, educational differences of people under a variety of group and situational conditions, and so on.

The chi-square test takes the general form

$$\chi^2 = \Sigma \frac{(O-E)^2}{E}$$

where O = the frequency of observations in any particular category; and
E = the frequency of observations *expected* under the probability model in any particular category.

χ^2 is the numerical value which tells us whether or not our observations could have occurred by chance. Null hypotheses are used extensively in goodness-of-fit tests such as the chi-square test.

Consider the following example. We are interested in testing the hypothesis that in Group A, males and females are equally represented in a particular sample. The null hypothesis is:

H_0: The number of males is equal to the number of females in Group A.
H_1: The number of males is not equal to the number of females in Group A.

$$P \leqslant .05 \text{ (two-tailed test).}$$

We examine Group A and we find that the sex distribution is as follows:

Group A (Observed)

Males	15
Females	25
Total (N)	40

Under the null hypothesis, we would expect the following sex distribution among the 40 people in Group A:

Group A (Expected)

Males	20
Females	20
Total (N)	40

Given our null hypothesis, the total N, namely 40, is divided by 2, the number of categories into which the group is divided, that is, male and female. The result, 20, represents *how many observations we should expect in each category under the null hypothesis of no difference in sex distribution.*

Carrying out our test of this hypothesis using the chi-square formula shown above, we have:

$$\begin{aligned}\chi^2 &= \frac{(15-20)^2}{20} + \frac{(25-20)^2}{20} \\ &= 25/20 + 25/20 \\ &= 1.25 + 1.25 \\ &= 2.50.\end{aligned}$$

To evaluate this χ^2 value, we must turn to Table A.4 of Appendix A, Distribution of χ^2.* We are looking for a critical value of χ^2 with which we can evaluate our observed χ^2 value. Across the top of the table are various levels of significance or probabilities. Since we are using the .05 level of significance in this case, we select the appropriate column, headed .05. Next, we need to determine the row we must enter. The column down the left-hand side of the table contains the degrees of freedom. For applications like the one being discussed, degrees of freedom are determined by $k-1$, where $k=$ the number of categories. Since the number of categories in this case is 2, male and female, the degrees of freedom for our example are $k-1$ or $2-1=1$. We find the appropriate row with 1 degree of freedom. Where the level of significance or probability (across the top of the table) and the degrees of freedom (down the left-hand column) intersect in the body of the table is the critical value we must have in order to test the hypothesis.

Looking at the value in the table, we must have a χ^2 value equal to or larger than 3.841 in order for our observations to be significantly different from chance at the .05 level with 1 *df*. Since our observed χ^2 is only 2.50, we conclude that the observed difference in sex distribution in Group A is not significant at the .05 level, and therefore we fail to reject H_0.

Let us use another illustration. Suppose we are interested in testing the hypothesis that in Community X there is religious balance, that is, that no one religious denomination predominates over the others to a significant degree. We collect the necessary information from the community and we tabulate the information as follows:

Observed Information

Protestants	26
Catholics	59
Jews	15
Total community residents (N)	100

*Table A.4 provides two-tailed probabilities. For one-tailed applications, simply *halve* the probability shown.

We will test the following hypothesis:

H_0: There is an equal representation of religious denominations in Community X.
H_1: There is an unequal distribution of religious denominations throughout Community X.

$$P \leqslant .01.$$

Under the null hypothesis, we would expect the following distribution of religious denominations in Community X:

Expected Information

Protestants	33.3
Catholics	33.3
Jews	33.3
Total community residents (N)	99.9

Carrying out the test of the hypothesis using the formula

$$\chi^2 = \Sigma \frac{(O - E)^2}{E},$$

we have

$$\chi^2 = \frac{(26 - 33.3)^2}{33.3} + \frac{(59 - 33.3)^2}{33.3} + \frac{(15 - 33.3)^2}{33.3}$$
$$= (7.3)^2/33.3 + (25.7)^2/33.3 + (18.3)^2/33.3$$
$$= 53.29/33.3 + 660.49/33.3 + 334.89/33.3$$
$$= 1.6 + 19.834 + 10.056$$
$$= 31.490.$$

Turning to Table A.4 of Appendix A, we find that the .01 level of significance or probability with $k - 1$ or $3 - 1 = 2$ degrees of freedom requires a χ^2 value equal to or larger than 9.21 in order for our observations to be different from chance. Since our observed χ^2 value exceeds this critical value, we conclude that there is religious imbalance in Community X and therefore, we reject the null hypothesis at the .01 level of significance.

Assumptions for the Chi-Square Test In order to meaningfully apply the chi-square statistic in research, the investigator must obtain a sample of independent observations. Data can be of any level of measurement. Also, *no cell should have an expected frequency of less than 5*. When χ^2's are computed for data where cell frequencies drop below 5, the resulting χ^2 value becomes grossly inflated and does not reveal a true picture of the way things are distributed. Sometimes, the investigator may be able to "collapse" categories in order to raise expected cell frequencies above 5. This operation is illustrated below.

Suppose the researcher had divided his data into six categories:

A. Six Categories

Very low	3
Low	2
Moderately low	4
Moderately high	6
High	3
Very high	6
Total (N)	24

In order to compute the expected frequencies for these data, we must divide the total N, 24, by the number of categories, 6, and we obtain 24/6 or 4 expected frequencies for each category. Computing a χ^2 for these data, we have

$$\begin{aligned}\chi_A^2 &= \frac{(3-4)^2}{4} + \frac{(2-4)^2}{4} + \frac{(4-4)^2}{4} + \frac{(6-4)^2}{4} + \frac{(3-4)^2}{4} + \frac{(6-4)^2}{4} \\ &= 1/4 + 1 + 0 + 1 + 1/4 + 1 \\ &= 3.5.\end{aligned}$$

For purposes of comparison, we shall now collapse the six categories into three categories. These are:

B. Three Categories

Very low-Low	5
Moderately low-Moderately high	10
High-Very high	9
Total (N)	24

To obtain the expected frequencies, we again divide the total N, 24, by the new number of categories, 3, and we obtain 24/3 = 8 expected frequencies for each category. Computing a χ^2 for these data in this new form, we have

$$\begin{aligned}\chi_B^2 &= \frac{(5-8)^2}{8} + \frac{(10-8)^2}{8} + \frac{(9-8)^2}{8} \\ &= 9/8 + 4/8 + 1/8 \\ &= 1.75.\end{aligned}$$

Comparing these chi-squares, we find that χ_A^2 is, in this instance, twice as large as χ_B^2. It should be noted that any chi-square value is, in part, a function of the number of categories, the number of elements, and the extent to which the observed frequencies differ from the expected ones. The researcher should exercise caution when collapsing categories. This operation should be done as *logically* as possible to minimize bias which could result from a more favorable breakdown of categories. With the data above, it would have been possible to group the frequencies in such a way as to make it appear that a significant difference exists. Perhaps we could have lumped together the categories Moderately low, Moderately high, High, and Very high, and compared these frequencies with the categories Low and Very low. This would have involved a 19–5 breakdown. Suffice it to say that any type of breakdown is possible, but ways of collapsing categories are not all equally accurate at portraying the true nature of things.

Advantages and Disadvantages of the Chi-Square Test Since there is so little restriction on the use of the chi-square test, it has become a very popular measure of the significance of difference for nominal-level information. A table is provided which makes it easy to interpret various observed values of χ^2.

Chi-square has one important disadvantage: The smaller one's sample, the more distorted the χ^2 value is likely to be. Distortion is introduced when any expected frequency is less than 5. The resulting χ^2 actually becomes an overestimate of the way things "really are." The researcher should be acutely aware of this problem when he is dealing with small samples.

TWO-SAMPLE TESTS

The Z Test for Differences between Proportions

The Z test has been used previously in order to evaluate differences between means of samples. In a modified form, the Z test may also be used to evaluate differences between two proportions. The resulting Z value is interpreted according to the values in Table A.3 of Appendix A, Areas under the Normal Curve.

Suppose we were conducting a study of voting behavior between two communities, one predominantly Democratic and the other predominantly Republican. These communities are presumed to have been matched according to several salient characteristics, perhaps age distribution, social class, educational level, and population size. In a recent gubernatorial election, residents of both communities voted in the following way, as illustrated by a random sample of them:

	Democratic ($N_1 = 70$)	*Republican* ($N_2 = 80$)
For Governor Doe	.77 ($= p_1$)	.65 ($= p_2$)
Against Governor Doe	.23 ($= q_1$)	.35 ($= q_2$)
	1.00	1.00

Note that p and q are proportions and that $p_i + q_i = 1$.

We are interested in learning whether or not there is a significant difference between the Democratic and Republican communities in their relative support of Governor Doe. The hypothesis which we want to test is:

H_0: There is no difference in the proportion of people supporting Governor Doe in the Democratic and Republican communities.
H_1: There is a difference in the proportion of people supporting Governor Doe in the Democratic and Republican communities.

$$P \leqslant .05 \text{ (two-tailed test).}$$

We may use the Z test to test this hypothesis. The formula for the Z test is

$$Z = \frac{p_1 - p_2}{s_{p_1-p_2}}$$

where p_1 = the proportion of the community for Governor Doe in Sample 1, the Democratic community;
p_2 = the proportion of the community for Governor Doe in Sample 2, the Republican community; and
$s_{p_1-p_2}$ = the standard error of the difference between the two proportions.

The standard error is computed from the formula

$$s_{p_1-p_2} = \sqrt{\frac{p_1q_1}{N_1} + \frac{p_2q_2}{N_2}}$$

where $q_1 = 1 - p_1$; and
$q_2 = 1 - p_2$.

Substituting values for symbols of these formulas, we first of all compute $s_{p_1-p_2}$:

$$\begin{aligned} s_{p_1-p_2} &= \sqrt{\frac{(.77)(.23)}{70} + \frac{(.65)(.35)}{80}} \\ &= \sqrt{.1771/70 + .2275/80} \\ &= \sqrt{.0025 + .0028} = \sqrt{.0053} \\ &= .073. \end{aligned}$$

Then,

$$\begin{aligned} Z &= \frac{p_1 - p_2}{s_{p_1-p_2}} = \frac{.77 - .65}{.073} = .12/.073 \\ &= 1.64. \end{aligned}$$

In order to determine the significance of Z, we must turn to Table A.3 of Appendix A. We find that in order for our Z to be significant at $\leqslant .05$, we must have an observed Z equal to or larger than 1.96. Since our observed Z is less than this value, being 1.64, we cannot reject the null hypothesis, and we conclude that the two communities do not differ significantly with respect to their proportional support of Governor Doe. To enlarge on this explanation: Since we are using the .05 level of significance and a two-tailed test (because direction is not relevant, only *difference*), we need to locate a Z which leaves one-half of .05, or .025, of the curve area in each tail of the curve. An area of .4750 on either side of the mean will leave a total area of .05 in the tails of the curve, with .0250 of the area in each tail. This proportion is equivalent to the Z of 1.96. Any Z observed which is equal to or larger than this Z will fall in the critical region or region of rejection, and will result in rejecting the null hypothesis. If the Z is smaller than 1.96, we will fail to reject the null hypothesis. Such is the case in the present example with an observed Z of 1.64.

Suppose we have some information which leads us to suspect that Governor Doe will receive more support in one community than in the other. If Mr. Doe is a Democrat, we might suspect that the largely Democratic community will reflect greater proportional support for him than would be the case in the Republican community. The null hypothesis which we would test could be that Governor Doe will receive the same proportion of votes or a greater proportion of votes in the Republican community compared to the Democratic community. This hypothesis would involve a one-tailed test of the hypothesis, whereas in the first example we were making a two-tailed test of the hypothesis. The one-tailed test is made in this instance since we *expect* a greater proportion of votes in the Democratic community compared to the other. It will be seen that in order to reject the null hypothesis, we will need a Z equal to or larger than 1.64, at the .05 level of significance. Since our observed Z value is 1.64, we reject the null hypothesis and conclude that Governor Doe received a significantly greater proportion of votes in the Democratic community. This example illustrates again that the more information we have at our disposal, the "easier" it becomes to reject the null hypothesis.

Small Sample Sizes Where sample size is particularly small, that is, when $N < 30$, a modification of the Z test is used. In this case, the t test is adapted as a test for significance of difference between two proportions, using the equation

$$t = \frac{p_1 - p_2}{s_{p_1 - p_2}}$$

where $s_{p_1-p_2} = \sqrt{pq\left(\frac{1}{N_1} + \frac{1}{N_2}\right)}$.

p is determined as follows:

$$p = \frac{p_1 N_1 + p_2 N_2}{N_1 + N_2}.$$

If $N_1 = 10$ and $N_2 = 20$, and if $p_1 = .50$ and $p_2 = .65$, then

$$p = \frac{(.50)(10) + (.65)(20)}{10 + 20} = \frac{5 + 13}{30} = 18/30$$
$$= .60.$$

Then,

$$q = 1.00 - .60 = .40.$$

Determining $s_{p_1-p_2}$, we have

$$s_{p_1-p_2} = \sqrt{(.60)(.40)(1/10 + 1/20)}$$
$$= \sqrt{(.24)(.15)} = \sqrt{.0360}$$
$$= .19.$$

Substituting these values in the t formula, we have:

$$t = \frac{.50 - .65}{.19} = \frac{-.15}{.19} = -.79.$$

To determine the significance of $t = -.79$, we enter Table A.5 of Appendix A, The Distribution of t, with 28 degrees of freedom ($N_1 + N_2 - 2 = 10 + 20 - 2 = 28$). Let us make a two-tailed test of the hypothesis that the two proportions p_1 and p_2 are equal. Let us also set the level of significance at $\leqslant .10$. Entering the table with 28 degrees of freedom, we find that we must have an observed t of ± 1.701 in order to reject our hypothesis that the two proportions are equal. Since our observed t is less than this value, being $-.79$, we fail to reject the hypothesis, and we conclude that the two proportions are equal at the .10 level.

Assumptions for the Z Test for Differences between Proportions In order to apply the Z test accurately in this instance, the investigator must have fairly large N's ($N > 30$). When sample size is small, the t test may be used as a satisfactory alternative. The researcher may simply have nominal-level information expressed as percentages or proportions.

Advantages and Disadvantages of the Z Test A primary advantage is that tables exist which allow the researcher to test null hypotheses concerning differences between two proportions using either one- or two-tailed tests of significance. For large samples, Z values may be determined and used in conjunction with the unit normal distribution.

The McNemar Test for Significance of Changes

In before-and-after research designs, the investigator may wish to determine the effect of some variable upon his sample. First of all, he measures some characteristic behavior of his sample before the experimental variable is introduced, and then, after the sample has been exposed to the experimental variable, he measures the behavioral characteristic again to see to what extent a change in behavior has taken place from one time period to the next. If a significant change *has* taken place, the introduction of the particular experimental variable may be considered as a possible cause of the change.

The McNemar test will enable him to evaluate the impact of experimental variables on samples. Suppose an investigator wishes to determine the effect of a class in human-relations skills upon a group of nursing supervisors in several hospitals. Specifically, the researcher wishes to determine whether the skills class would have any effect on changing the nursing supervisors' supervisory style in relation to their subordinates at their respective hospitals.

By collecting information from various subordinates at these hospitals, the investigator is able to identify the nursing supervisors' supervisory style both before and after the class in human-relations skills is taken. He pays particular attention to whether the supervision given subordinates by nursing supervisors is *close* or *general. Close* supervision means that the subordinates are given little authority and that the superior supervises the details of the subordinates' work to a high degree. *General* supervision, on the other hand, is characterized by greater freedom on the part of subordinates, the supervisor seeing them relatively less often during each day. The investigator feels that the class in human-relations skills should have the effect of encouraging more nursing supervisors to practice general supervision rather than close supervision.

The following hypothesis is tested:

H_0: There is no change in supervisory behavior among nursing supervisors as a result of a class in human-relations skills.

H_1: Nursing supervisors will practice general supervision over their subordinates after a class in human-relations skills.

$$P \leq .05 \text{ (one-tailed test).}$$

To test this hypothesis, the investigator may use the McNemar test for significance of changes. Such a test is applied as follows:

First, we must construct a 2 × 2 table. Such a table appears in Table 8.1. A 2 × 2 table has two rows and two columns. There are four cells in such a table. Beginning in the upper left-hand corner of Table 8.1, the

Table 8.1. A 2 × 2 Table.

		Variable X		
		Column 1	*Column 2*	*Marginal Totals of Rows*
Variable Y	*Row 1*	a	b	$a + b$
	Row 2	c	d	$c + d$
Marginal Totals of Columns		$a + c$	$b + d$	*Grand Total* = $a + b + c + d$

cells are labeled by the letters *a, b, c,* and *d* as is shown. The 2 × 2 table is one of the most frequently used tables in social research. In certain formulas to follow, the 2 × 2 table is required, and the cell letters are used in the formulas as in Table 8.1.

The sums of the cells *a* and *b, c* and *d, a* and *c,* and *b* and *d* are called the *marginal totals.* The sums of either of the marginal totals equal the total number of observations, or the grand total in the 2 × 2 table. (For a check on subsequent work, $a + b$ and $c + d$, the marginal *row* totals, should equal $a + c$ and $b + d$, the marginal *column* totals.) X and Y stand for any particular variables which we use. The values within any given table are called *cell frequencies.*

Setting up a 2 × 2 table for the test of our hypothesis, we have the following information provided in Table 8.2. In carrying out the McNemar test, we are interested only in those nurses whose supervisory style *changed* from one time period to the next. These changes are reflected in

Table 8.2. Changes in Supervisory Style of Nursing Supervisors.

		Supervisory Style after Skills Course		
		General	*Close*	
Supervisory Style before Skills Course	*Close*	21	8	29
	General	9	5	14
		30	13	43

cells *a* and *d* of Table 8.2. In cell *a* are those nursing supervisors whose supervisory style changed from close to general, while cell *d* contains those nursing supervisors whose supervisory style changed from general to close.

With this information, we apply the formula

$$\chi^2 = \frac{(|a - d| - 1)^2}{a + d}$$

where $|a - d|$ = the absolute difference in frequencies in cells *a* and *d* without regard to sign.

Supplying the information in Table 8.2 above for symbols in the formula, we have

$$\chi^2 = \frac{(|21 - 5| - 1)^2}{21 + 5}$$

$$= (15)^2/26 = 225/26$$

$$= 8.65.$$

To interpret this χ^2 value, we enter Table A.4 of Appendix A with $(r-1)(c-1)$ degrees of freedom, where r = the number of rows in the table and c = the number of columns in the table. Since there is $(2-1)(2-1)=1$ degree of freedom for a 2×2 table, we compare our observed χ^2 value with those critical values of χ^2 for 1 degree of freedom. We note that our observed χ^2 exceeds all critical values up to and including the critical value for the .01 level of significance or probability.

Because the table only provides two-tailed critical values of χ^2 for various levels of significance, we must *halve* the probability associated with the last critical value we exceed in the row, 1 degree of freedom, to determine the one-tailed probability which our observed χ^2 exceeds. Therefore, $\frac{1}{2}(.01) = .005$, which is the probability associated with our observation. Since this probability is less than .05, the original level of significance used to test the hypothesis, we reject the null hypothesis and conclude that there was a change in supervisory style among nursing supervisors, possibly as a result of having taken the course in human-relations skills.

Two-Tailed Test Application Had we carried out the McNemar test without suspecting that a change in behavior would occur in either one direction or the other, then our null hypothesis and our alternative hypothesis would be:

H_0: There is no change in supervisory behavior among nursing supervisors as a result of a class in human-relations skills.

H_1: There will be a change in supervisory behavior among nursing supervisors as a result of a class in human-relations skills.

In this instance we are not predicting a behavioral change in any specific direction. We simply expect that a behavioral change will occur. This expectation calls for a two-tailed test of the null hypothesis. The computational procedure for a two-tailed test is the same as that for a one-tailed test. The primary difference is with respect to interpreting our observed χ^2. We enter the table as before, locating the appropriate degrees of freedom (*df* will always be 1 for the McNemar test) and the largest critical value which our observed χ^2 exceeds. Whichever probability is associated with this value is the probability at which the observed χ^2 is significant. We do not halve the probability as was the case in the one-tailed test of the hypothesis. That is, if the probability level associated with the critical value exceeded by our observed χ^2 is .10, then our observed χ^2 is significant at the .10 level, and we may reject the null hypothesis at that level. (In the one-tailed test, our null hypothesis could have been rejected at $\frac{1}{2}$ (.10), or .05, as an example.)

Assumptions for the McNemar Test The primary assumption underlying the McNemar test is that the samples selected are related to one another in some meaningful way. The ideal situation for application of this test is one where each person acts as his own control in a before-and-after design.

Advantages and Disadvantages of the McNemar Test One advantage of the McNemar test is that it may be applied to both discrete and continuous data. When data are continuous, they should be dichotomized in some natural way. Also, when subjects act as their own control, this feature of the design eliminates the problem of having to *match* pairs of subjects. Matching can pose a significant obstacle to any research design. There are always factors over which the investigator has little control, even though samples have been matched according to five or even ten salient characteristics. If small frequencies exist, that is, where $(a + d)/2$ is less than 5, then the McNemar test is not appropriate.

The Chi-Square Test for Two Independent Samples

Frequently we are interested in determining whether or not our observations are significantly different from what we would expect according to chance. Suppose we enter a state prison for the purpose of determining whether significant differences in social-class background exist between prisoners confined for a variety of offenses. Through questionnaires and prison records, we determine the information presented in the 2 × 2 table in Table 8.3, in which we have identified and divided 200 prisoners according to whether they have middle-upper- or working-lower-class backgrounds. We have also classified them according to

Table 8.3. Prisoners' Social-Class Background and Type of Crime.

		Prisoner Social Class		
		Upper or Middle Class	*Working or Lower Class*	
Prisoners with Records of	*Crimes against Property*	75	40	115
	Crimes against Person	25	60	85
		100	100	200

whether their offenses are crimes against persons (assault, robbery) or against property (auto theft, burglary, larceny). These data constitute our observations. We now want to find whether or not these data significantly differ from what we would expect to find according to chance. Assume that we are testing the following hypothesis:

H_0: There is no difference in the type of crime committed by prisoners of different social-class backgrounds.

H_1: There is a difference in the type of crime committed by prisoners of different social-class backgrounds.

$$P \leqslant .05 \text{ (two-tailed test).}$$

Since we already know the values of our observations, we must determine what values would be expected by chance according to the model provided. According to this model provided by chance, each cell in Table 8.3 has an *expected value*. The expected values or expected frequencies are determined from the marginal totals and the grand total of observations for the table. In Table 8.3 the observed value in cell *a* is 75. We obtain the expected value for cell *a* by multiplying the total row observations by the total column observations in which cell *a* is found, and then dividing this product by the total number of observations in the table. The computations for each expected value in Table 8.3 are given.

Cell	*General Model*			*Expected Value*
a	$(a + c)(a + b)/N$	or	(100)(115)/200	57.5
b	$(b + d)(a + b)/N$	or	(100)(115)/200	57.5
c	$(a + c)(c + d)/N$	or	(100)(85)/200	42.5
d	$(b + d)(c + d)/N$	or	(100)(85)/200	42.5

(The values are usually rounded to the nearest tenth.)

We are now ready to compute χ^2 for the data in Table 8.3. We now have the observed and the expected values for the table. Let us label each observed value in Table 8.3 with an O and each expected value with an E. As before, the formula for χ^2 is

$$\chi^2 = \Sigma\frac{(O - E)^2}{E}$$

where O = the observed value for each cell; and
E = the expected value for each cell.

Substituting values in the table for symbols in the formula, we have

$$\begin{aligned}\chi^2 &= \frac{(75 - 57.5)^2}{57.5} + \frac{(40 - 57.5)^2}{57.5} + \frac{(25 - 42.5)^2}{42.5} + \frac{(60 - 42.5)^2}{42.5} \\ &= (17.5)^2/57.5 + (17.5)^2/57.5 + (17.5)^2/42.5 + (17.5)^2/42.5 \\ &= 306.25/57.5 + 306.25/57.5 + 306.25/42.5 + 306.25/42.5 \\ &= 5.326 + 5.326 + 7.205 + 7.205 \\ &= 25.062.\end{aligned}$$

Turning to Table A.4 of Appendix A, we enter the table with the .05 level of probability and degrees of freedom equal to $(r - 1)(c - 1) = (2 - 1)(2 - 1) = 1$ degree of freedom. We need to have a χ^2 value equal to or larger than 3.841 in order for there to be a significant difference between prisoners of different social-class backgrounds pertaining to type of crime. Clearly, 25.062 exceeds this value; consequently, we conclude that there is a significant difference at the .05 level and we reject the null hypothesis.

The assumptions, advantages, and disadvantages of the chi-square test for two independent samples are the same as those for the chi-square test in the one-sample case. It should be noted that the smaller one's sample becomes, the more distorted χ^2 becomes. Distortion is introduced when any cell in a table has an expected frequency of less than 5. The resulting χ^2 value actually becomes an *overestimate* of the way things "really are."

The Yates Correction for Continuity Yates (1934) has devised a *correction for continuity* to help modify the overestimate of χ^2 when the expected cell frequencies are small. This correction is applicable only in the 2 × 2 table situation. For larger tables, the Yates correction for continuity cannot be applied.

To make the correction, the researcher simply reduces the distance between the observed and the expected frequencies by .5. The expected value is moved .5 closer to its respective observed value. Therefore, χ^2 is reduced accordingly.

Suppose we have the following information:

Observed Frequencies

5	9	14
8	6	14
13	15	28

Expected Frequencies

6.5	7.5	14
6.5	7.5	14
13.0	15.0	28

When the expected frequency is *larger* than its corresponding observed value, we subtract .5 from it. Where the expected frequency is *smaller* than its respective observed value, we add .5 to it. In the illustration, since 6.5 is larger than its corresponding value of 5, we subtracted .5 from it. The "corrected" value is now 6. Making all of the necessary corrections, we have:

Observed Frequencies

5	9	14
8	6	14
13	15	28

Corrected Expected Frequencies

6	8	14
7	7	14
13	15	28

As an exercise, compute χ^2 for both illustrations, uncorrected and corrected for continuity. Observe the resulting χ^2 value difference. The χ^2 resulting from the *corrected* procedure will be the more conservative one.

It should be noted in this procedure that when the expected cell frequencies are large, whether a researcher adds or subtracts .5 from the expected values will make little difference to the χ^2 value. This correction for continuity is only applied where frequencies are small, and where the data are in 2 × 2 tables.

It should also be noted that χ^2 is not restricted to 2 × 2 tables. χ^2's may be computed for tables of any size. In a later portion of this chapter, chi-square will be demonstrated for tables larger than 2 × 2. Where tables larger than 2 × 2 are found, the Yates correction for continuity cannot be applied.

Fisher's Exact Test

When we have 2 × 2 tables which have cells for which the expected frequencies are less than 5, we are obliged to use an alternative test for the significance of difference instead of the chi-square test. One such procedure is called Fisher's exact test, and it results in an exact probability for any given set of observations.

For the chi-square test we were interested in determining whether or not our data depart from chance beyond a particular level of significance. With Fisher's exact test, we can now determine the exact probability associated with a given set of observations occurring if chance conditions are assumed.

Suppose we have the following observations:

2	4	6
7	3	10
9	7	16

We shall test the following hypothesis:

H_0: Our observations do not differ from what is expected by chance.
H_1: Our observations differ from what is expected by chance.

$$P \leqslant .05 \text{ (two-tailed test).}$$

In order to determine the probability for this table, we must use the formula

$$P = (2)\frac{(a+b)!\,(c+d)!\,(a+c)!\,(b+d)!}{N!\,a!\,b!\,c!\,d!}$$

where a, b, c, and d = the respective cell frequencies; and
N = the total number of frequencies in the table.

Ordinarily, we will be concerned with the probability of getting our particular set of observations *and* all other more extreme sets of observations which might possibly occur, assuming that the marginal totals in the table remain fixed. In the illustration of three 2 × 2 tables, there are only two additional ways in which the data in the original table can be distributed "more extremely."

Original Table

2	4	6
7	3	10
9	7	16

Next Most Extreme Form

1	5	6
8	2	10
9	7	16

Most Extreme Form

0	6	6
9	1	10
9	7	16

In the set of three tables, we have simply changed cell *a* by reducing it by 1, then modified all other cell values in the table to fit the original marginal totals. We carry out this procedure until we arrive at the table which presents the observations in their most extreme form; doing this means reducing one of the cells of the table to 0. Any table originally containing a 0 in a cell is in its most extreme form.

To obtain the probability of getting our original observations and all other more unusual observations, we compute P (= probability) for each table and sum the respective probabilities obtained. For a two-tailed test which we are making, we double the probability value. It is on the basis of this doubled cumulative probability value that we reject or fail to reject our hypothesis that there is no difference between our observations and what would be expected by chance, at a particular level of significance.

Carrying out the procedure for determining P for each form of the table above, we have

$$P_1 = \frac{6!\,10!\,9!\,7!}{16!\,2!\,4!\,7!\,3!}(2) = \frac{45}{286}(2) \quad = .1573(2) = .3146$$

$$P_2 = \frac{6!\,10!\,9!\,7!}{16!\,1!\,5!\,8!\,2!}(2) = \frac{27}{1{,}144}(2) = .0236(2) = .0472$$

$$P_3 = \frac{6!\,10!\,9!\,7!}{16!\,0!\,6!\,9!\,1!}(2) = \frac{1}{1{,}144}(2) = .0009(2) = .0018$$

$$P_c = .3636.$$

The sum P_c = the cumulative probability.

When the factorial sign (!) follows any number, the following procedure is carried out. For example, 6! (read: Six factorial) is:

$$6! = (6)(5)(4)(3)(2)(1) = 720.$$

In the general case,

$$N! = N(N-1)(N-2)(N-3)\cdots(4)(3)(2)(1).$$

With our observed probability $P_c = .3636$, we cannot reject the null hypothesis, and we must conclude that our observations do not differ from what would be expected by chance at the .05 level of significance.

Had we made a one-tailed test of the hypothesis, the observed probability would be equal to one-half the probability for a two-tailed test, or simply,

$$P = \frac{(a+b)!\,(c+d)!\,(a+c)!\,(b+d)!}{N!\,a!\,b!\,c!\,d!}.$$

In this event, our observed probability would be (.3636)/2, or .1818, and again, we would not be able to reject the null hypothesis at the .05 level. We need a cumulative probability value equal to or less than .05 in order to reject the hypothesis, and .1818 is much too large.

If we assume that cell a will always contain the fewest frequencies, as a general statement, the number of probabilities to be computed for any given set of observations using Fisher's exact test will always be equal to $a + 1$. In our example above, the smallest observation is 2. Therefore, three separate probabilities $(2 + 1 = 3)$ must be computed to obtain an over-all P.

The use of factorials makes the Fisher's exact test an extremely laborious procedure particularly where some of the frequencies are quite large. Because of its greater accuracy compared with the chi-square test for small samples, however, it is recommended. For small samples, it is more conservative than the chi-square test.

Assumptions for Fisher's Exact Test The data may be nominal-level and discrete for appropriate application of Fisher's exact test. The data must be organized in a 2×2 table.* Where large samples are involved, the process of computing probabilities using this test becomes extremely tedious.

Advantages and Disadvantages of Fisher's Exact Test The primary advantage of Fisher's exact test is that it may be applied to 2×2 tables with fewer than 5 frequencies in the cells. It is especially appropriate for small samples. In this sense, it is more accurate than the chi-square test. It gives an exact probability associated with one's observations.

One disadvantage of this test is that it is very cumbersome to carry out when N's become fairly large.

A SIGNIFICANCE TEST FOR *k* RELATED SAMPLES

The Cochran *Q* Test

An extension of the McNemar test for significance of changes is the Cochran Q test. This test is designed to determine whether there are proportionate differences between k related samples with respect to some measured characteristic. The characteristic is usually a classification of

* An extension of Fisher's exact test for 2×3 tables is discussed in Albert Pierce, *Fundamentals of Non-Parametric Statistics: A Sample Space Approach* (Encino, Calif.: Dickenson Publishing Co., 1969).

some sort expressed as a dichotomy. Such classifications may include male-female, yes-no, agree-disagree, church member-nonmember, and the like.

This test is designed to determine whether one group has a greater proportion of some trait which has been categorized or classified compared with k other groups. For this test it is assumed that the samples are related. In the case of k related samples, each subject may act as his own control through several phases of an experiment, or several samples may have been matched according to certain criteria.

Suppose we are conducting a study of racial minorities. We are interested in determining the effect of integrated housing tracts compared to segregated tracts and corresponding favorable-unfavorable attitudes of majority-group tract residents toward minority groups in general. (This could be a study of the effect of increased integration on attitudes of such tract residents toward minority-group members, in which case we would be interested in *attitude change* over time. We would divide the time period into specific segments, where different proportions of minority-group members would become residents of the same housing tract over a two-year period. We would then attempt to match the change in proportion of minority-group members with concurrent changes in attitudes of majority-group tract residents toward them during that period. Each subject would act as his own control in this case, and each sample would be made up of the same individuals, but would be taken in different phases of housing-tract integration.)

The general problem is, Does the proportion of favorable-unfavorable attitudes of majority-group tract residents toward minority-group members change in a corresponding manner as the proportion of minority-group members changes in the housing tract? We might hypothesize the following:

H_0: There is no difference between k samples with respect to favorable-unfavorable attitudes toward minority-group members in differentially integrated housing tracts.

H_1: There will be a difference between k samples with respect to favorable-unfavorable attitudes toward minority-group members in differentially integrated housing tracts.

$$P \leq .10 \text{ (two-tailed test).}$$

What we are hypothesizing, in essence, is that k samples are the same with respect to majority-group attitudes toward minority-group members, *regardless of how integrated the housing tracts are*. We expect that there *will* be differences, however. We have information from three related samples of residents in three housing tracts which differ according to the proportion of minority-group members in them. In Table 8.4 we have differentiated between housing tracts according to the degree of integration. Under each of the three types of housing tracts are the numbers 0 and 1. A 0 is indicative of an unfavorable response toward minority-group members, while a 1 stands for a favorable response toward them. In column F the number of favorable responses for each individual are summed horizontally. Column F^2 is the sum of each individual's favorable responses squared. The sums of each of these columns are shown at the bottom of the table.

Table 8.4. Attitudes of Majority-Group Residents toward Minority-Group Members in Varying Integrated Housing Tracts.

Sets of Matched Individuals ($N = 15$)	*Housing Tracts* *Low Integration*	*Moderate Integration*	*High Integration*	F	F^2
1	0	0	1	1	1
2	0	0	1	1	1
3	0	1	1	2	4
4	0	0	1	1	1
5	1	1	0	2	4
6	0	1	1	2	4
7	0	0	1	1	1
8	1	1	1	3	9
9	0	0	1	1	1
10	1	1	0	2	4
11	0	1	1	2	4
12	0	1	1	2	4
13	1	0	0	1	1
14	1	1	1	3	9
15	0	0	1	1	1
	$S_1 = 5$	$S_2 = 8$	$S_3 = 12$	$\Sigma F = 25$	$\Sigma F^2 = 49$

To test whether or not there are differences between the three samples with respect to their attitudes toward minority-group members, depending upon the degree of integration of their housing tract, we may apply the formula

$$Q = \frac{(k-1)[k\Sigma S_i^2 - (\Sigma S_i)^2]}{k(\Sigma F) - \Sigma F^2}$$

where k = the number of samples;
S_i = the total number of favorable responses for each sample; and
F = the total number of favorable responses for each matched set of individuals across samples.

Substituting the values in the table above for symbols in the Q formula, we have

$$Q = \frac{(3-1)[(3)(5^2 + 8^2 + 12^2) - (25)^2]}{(3)(25) - 49}$$

$$= \frac{(2)[(3)(233) - (625)]}{75 - 49} = \frac{(2)(699 - 625)}{26}$$

$$= (2)(74)/26 = 148/26$$

$$= 5.69.$$

Q is interpreted in the same way that χ^2 values are interpreted. If we turn to Table A.4 of Appendix A with $k - 1$ or $3 - 1$ or 2 degrees of freedom, we then find that at the .10 level of probability we must have a Q value equal to or larger than 4.60 in order for the difference in the proportion of favorable-unfavorable responses among the three groups to be significant. Since our observed Q is larger than 4.60, being 5.69, we reject the null hypothesis and we conclude that at the .10 level there are significant differences between the samples pertaining to their attitudes toward minority-group members.* In this case, attitudes are more favorable where a greater degree of integration is found.

Assumptions for the Cochran* Q *Test Cochran's Q test is appropriate for data which are of the nominal level of measurement and which fall into a natural dichotomy. Again, such data as pass-fail, yes-no, more-less, increase-decrease, favorable-unfavorable, present-absent, and agree-disagree are appropriate. Data which are not naturally dichotomous may also be used, however, provided that the investigator can give a reasonable rationale for establishing a dichotomy for the data. Social class is a continuous variable, but often it is treated as though it were discrete, and thus it is rendered amenable to dichotomizing. No assumptions concerning distribution need be met. Sample sizes should not be too small, although the effect of small samples upon various values of Q has not been systematically investigated.

Advantages and Disadvantages of the Cochran* Q *Test The Cochran Q test is a conservative test for determining the significance of differences in the distribution of some measured nominal-level characteristic between k samples. It does not require stringent assumptions, and thus it may be used extensively for data of the nominal level with little limitation on sample size. It is easy to apply and readily interpreted by using the chi-square table, because Q approximates the chi-square distribution. Q is also conservative in the sense that it requires rather large differences between k samples before these differences reach a given level of significance.

There is no convenient way by which to compare the Q statistic with other tests of significance at higher levels of measurement. This should

* For one-tailed applications, where direction of difference is predicted, the probability level in Table A.4 is halved; that is, .10 (two-tailed) becomes .05 (one-tailed), and so on.

not be too disadvantageous, however, for when the investigator has data of a higher level, he should apply a more appropriate statistical technique in order to maximize his information. For data of the nominal level, the Q statistic is a conservative helper in evaluating differences in proportions between k related samples.

A SIGNIFICANCE TEST FOR *k* INDEPENDENT SAMPLES

An Extension of the Chi-Square Test

We have already presented a rather flexible statistical technique known as the chi-square test. It has been demonstrated that such a technique allows us to evaluate the difference between what we observe and what is expected according to some theoretical model under the laws of chance. This technique is appropriate for one-sample cases and has been illustrated as appropriate for the two-sample case as well. A third instance where the chi-square test may be used is the k-sample case where samples are presumed to be independent.

The k-sample case is where tables larger than 2×2 exist. For situations where tables are larger than 2×2, as 3×3, 2×3, 6×7, 10×10, and so on, we may follow a procedure identical to the two-sample case for determining our χ^2 value. Consider the following example.

In Table 8.5, we have a sample of 154 people whom we have divided into three subsamples according to age. We have also divided these people according to their support or opposition to Issue X. We are interested in testing the following hypothesis:

H_0: There is no difference in opinion toward Issue X among various age groups.

H_1: There is a difference in opinion toward Issue X among various age groups.

$$P \leq .01 \text{ (two-tailed test).}$$

Table 8.5. Age and Opinion toward Issue X.

		Age			
		Old	*Middle-Aged*	*Young*	
Opinion toward Issue X	*Strongly Oppose*	15	10	7	32
	Oppose	20	10	9	39
	Support	8	11	20	39
	Strongly Support	5	13	26	44
		48	44	62	154

Since we already know what our observed frequencies are by examining Table 8.5, our next task is to determine the expected frequencies for each of the above cells. We will want to see whether there is any departure from what we expect under the theoretical model of our null hypothesis, and if so, whether the departure is significantly different at the .01 level. We again employ the familiar χ^2 formula:

$$\chi^2 = \Sigma \frac{(O - E)^2}{E}$$

where O = the observed frequency for each cell; and
E = the expected frequency for each cell.

To find the expected frequencies for the observed values in Table 8.5, we must multiply the row and column totals for each cell in the table, and divide this product by the total N of the table. To find the expected frequency for the first cell (cell *a*, those who are old and who strongly oppose Issue X), we multiply the column total, 48, by the row total, 32, and divide this product by N, or 154. The expected frequency becomes

cell *a* expected frequency = (48)(32)/154 = 10.0.

For cell *b*, we repeat this process as follows:

cell *b* expected frequency = (32)(44)/154 = 9.1.

The following computational format for cells *a* to *l* is provided for determining the χ^2 value for the entire table (see Table 8.6):

Cell	O	E	$O - E$	$(O - E)^2$	$\frac{(O - E)^2}{E}$
a	15	10.0	5.0	25.0	25/10.0 = 2.500
b	10	9.1	.9	.81	.81/9.1 = .089
c	7	12.9	5.9	34.81	34.81/12.9 = 2.698
d	20	12.2	7.8	60.84	60.84/12.2 = 4.986
e	10	11.1	1.1	1.21	1.21/11.1 = .109
f	9	15.7	6.7	44.89	44.89/15.7 = 2.859
g	8	12.2	4.2	17.64	17.64/12.2 = 1.445
h	11	11.1	.1	.01	.01/11.1 = .000
i	20	15.7	4.3	18.49	18.49/15.7 = 1.177
j	5	13.6	8.6	73.96	73.96/13.6 = 5.438
k	13	12.7	.3	.09	.09/12.7 = .007
l	26	17.7	8.3	68.89	68.89/17.7 = 3.892
					χ^2 = 25.200

With a χ^2 of 25.200, we enter the χ^2 table, Table A.4 of Appendix A, with $(r - 1)(c - 1)$ degrees of freedom or $(4 - 1)(3 - 1) = 6$ degrees of freedom at the .01 level of significance, and we find that we must have a χ^2 equal

Table 8.6. Expected Frequencies for Table 8.5.

		Age			
		Old	*Middle-Aged*	*Young*	
Opinion toward Issue X	*Strongly Oppose*	10.0	9.1	12.9	32.0
	Oppose	12.2	11.1	15.7	39.0
	Support	12.2	11.1	15.7	39.0
	Strongly Support	13.6	12.7	17.7	44.0
		48.0	44.0	62.0	154.0

to or larger than 16.812 in order for our observed frequencies to be considered different from what would be expected by chance. Since our observed $\chi^2 = 25.200$, we conclude that the observations are different from chance at the .01 level of significance, and we reject the null hypothesis that there is no difference in opinion toward Issue X among different age groups. There is some reason to believe that attitude toward Issue X is contingent upon age.

It should be noted at this point that a large χ^2 value does not necessarily mean that a strong *relation* exists between age and Issue X. A large χ^2 value means merely that we are confident that the difference between what we observe and what we expect by chance is significant at a particular probability level. In order to determine the size of the relationship between the variables in the table, we must use some appropriate *measure of association.* Measures of association will be discussed in Chapter 10. An appropriate measure for determining the magnitude of the relation between variables where χ^2 has been used to determine significance is the coefficient of contingency, C, or Guttman's coefficient of predictability, lambda (λ). Each of these measures will be discussed in detail in Chapter 10.

Assumptions, Advantages, and Disadvantages of the Chi-Square Test Assumptions underlying the χ^2 statistic for k independent samples are identical to those for the one-sample and two-sample cases where the chi-square test was used.

The chi-square test is a most flexible statistical technique for determining whether one's observations differ from what would be expected according to chance. Wherever expected observations can be determined or predicted, a χ^2 value may be computed. Also, tables are provided which allow the researcher to determine directly the significance of any given χ^2 value with the appropriate number of degrees of freedom. It is apparent that because few assumptions exist for chi-square, it may be applied to virtually every instance where data may be categorized.

A primary limitation of chi-square pertains to small *N*'s. When the *expected* frequency in any cell in a table is less than 5, the resulting χ^2 value becomes an overestimate of the probability that the observed frequencies are significantly different from chance. When *any* expected cell frequency is less than 5, the χ^2 test should not be used, but rather Fisher's exact test if the table is 2×2, or 2×3.

The distortion introduced by small cell frequencies may be corrected by the Yates correction for continuity discussed in a previous section of this chapter, provided the expected frequencies are not less than 5. Such a procedure is appropriate only for data in 2×2 tabular form. But when tables are larger than 2×2, "collapsing" may be done to enlarge expected cell frequencies.

In Table 8.5, it would be quite possible to combine the frequencies for those who strongly oppose and oppose Issue X into one cell, and we could do the same for those who support and strongly support Issue X. We might also combine the old and middle-aged individuals in the table, and thus we would be comparing them with the younger individuals. Such collapsing of information may be done to eliminate the distortion introduced as a result of small expected cell frequencies. But when collapsing is done, a certain amount of information is lost. This loss *always* occurs when collapsing of cells takes place. The measurement becomes more crude. Any combination of cells may be made if a logical justification exists for doing so, although the researcher must decide which alternative to follow in the final analysis.

SUMMARY

In this chapter we have examined a number of nominal-level tests of significance. Nominal-level tests of significance are appropriate for data which can be categorized. Particularly amenable to nominal treatment are percentages and proportions.

When the investigator has a single sample, he may use a variation of the chi-square test. This test tells the researcher whether his observations differ from what is expected by chance, when chance is defined according to a particular set of rules in a theoretical model.

When the researcher has two samples, he may use the Z or t tests for differences between proportions. These tests tell the researcher whether an observed proportion of frequencies differs significantly from a theorized one. The Z test is used when samples are large, that is, when $N > 30$, and the t test is employed when $N < 30$. The McNemar test for significance of changes also can be used. This test is particularly useful in before-and-after experimental designs, and it enables the researcher to evaluate the impact of experimental variables on samples.

When samples are independent of one another, another variation of the chi-square test may be used. When small expected cell frequencies are involved, the Yates correction for continuity may be used. This is a useful correction factor when 2×2 tables are encountered, but for larger tables, this technique cannot be employed. When samples are extremely small and any expected cell frequency is less than 5, Fisher's exact test may be used. This test renders an exact probability associated with one's observations.

When the researcher has k related samples, the Cochran Q test may be used. This test is designed to determine whether or not there are proportionate differences between k related samples with respect to some measured characteristic. When k independent samples exist, a third variation of the chi-square test may be used, one which is basically the same format used in the chi-square test for two independent samples. The assumptions underlying the application of χ^2 are the same for all conditions.

In the following chapter, statistical methods appropriate for the ordinal level of measurement will be discussed. Any test in the present chapter is also appropriate for data of the ordinal level of measurement as well.

QUESTIONS FOR REVIEW AND PROBLEMS TO SOLVE

1. Using the data below, test the following hypothesis:

H_0: There is no difference between Sample A and Sample B with respect to proportion of foreign-born.

$$P \leqslant .05.$$

Sample A: $N_1 = 52$; $p_1 = .49$. *Sample B*: $N_2 = 68$; $p_2 = .59$. p_i = the proportion of foreign-born. (a) Which test of significance did you use? Why?

2. What is meant by "goodness of fit"? What are "expected frequencies"? Identify three primary uses of the chi-square statistical test.

3. Two matched sets of boys are used in an experiment. One group is exposed to a training film and the other group is not. Later, the boys take a test based, in part, upon some of the information presented in the film. Both groups of boys received identical information, but one group received part of the information by film. Their scores on the test are compared below. Using the Z test, determine if one group of boys has proportionately more scoring high on the test than the other group.

Group Exposed to Film: $N_1 = 30$; high score, .67; low score, .33. *Group Not Exposed to Film:* $N_2 = 30$; high score, .60; low score, .40. $P \leqslant .05$.

4. Thirty individuals take a course in marriage and the family. Using the .01 level of significance, determine the significance of change in their equalitarian-traditional family views.

		After Course		
		Equalitarian Views	*Traditional Views*	
Before Course	*Equalitarian Views*	10	5	15
	Traditional Views	14	1	15
		24	6	30

5. Using the chi-square test, determine whether the following observations differ from what would be expected by chance at the .01 level.

	Variable X				
Variable Y	20	15	10	5	50
	10	10	10	10	40
	5	10	15	20	50
	35	35	35	35	140

6. Using Fisher's exact test, compute the probability of obtaining the following observations and all observations which are more extreme. Use a one-tailed probability.

	Tall	*Short*
Heavy	3	9
Light	7	6

7. Assuming that χ^2 will be computed, how many degrees of freedom are associated with the following tables: (a) 2×3; (b) 4×8; (c) 5×5; (d) 10×12?

8. For the following observations, compute χ^2 and determine whether or not the data depart from what would be expected by chance at the .01 level of significance:

	Education		
	High School	*No High School*	
Delinquent	8	12	20
Nondelinquent	5	5	10
	13	17	30

(a) Correct the above data by applying the Yates correction for continuity, and compare the χ^2 values obtained under both conditions. Why was the correction for continuity made?

9. Test the hypothesis that there is no difference between the following three samples with respect to yes-no responses to the question as to whether the city should fluoridate the water supply. Use the Cochran Q test.

Sample A	*Sample B*	*Sample C*
0	1	1
0	0	1
0	1	0
0	0	1
1	0	1
0	0	1
0	1	1
0	0	1
0	1	0
1	0	1

Yes = 1; no = 0; $p \leqslant .05$.

10. What are some of the primary assumptions underlying the Cochran Q test? The chi-square test? The McNemar test? Identify some of the advantages and disadvantages of the above statistical methods.

9 Ordinal-Level Tests of Significance

In this chapter we shall examine several ordinal-level tests of significance. Such tests are appropriate where data are available that can be ranked in some fashion. Such things as social class, attitudinal variables, and the like are variables which may be amenable to the tests in this chapter.

We shall consider a one-sample test of significance, the Kolmogorov-Smirnov one-sample test. Two two-sample tests for related samples will be examined: the sign test and the Wilcoxon matched-pairs-signed-ranks test. For two-sample tests where samples are considered independent, the Wald-Wolfowitz runs test, the Kolmogorov-Smirnov two-sample test, and the Mann-Whitney U test will be presented. Finally, for k related samples and k independent samples, the Friedman two-way analysis-of-variance test and the Kruskal-Wallis one-way analysis-of-variance test will be illustrated.

ONE-SAMPLE TEST OF SIGNIFICANCE

The Kolmogorov-Smirnov One-Sample Test

When the investigator possesses ordinal-level information for a single sample, he may wish to use the Kolmogorov-Smirnov one-sample test to determine whether or not his distribution of observations is significantly different from a theoretical distribution. The test is concerned with the degree of correspondence between a theorized distribution and the actual distribution of observations.

Suppose a researcher wished to study the degree of social distance which prison guards maintain between themselves and inmates. In this case, social distance refers to the degree of familiarity and friendliness which guards permit between themselves and the prisoners. The researcher suspects that guards hold themselves aloof from inmates, and that social distance would be great between them. A sample of prison guards is obtained, and their social-distance scores are ranked in the following way in Table 9.1. We are interested in testing the following hypothesis:

H_0: There is an equal distribution of social-distance scores among the prison guards.

H_1: The prison guards are not distributed equally among the various social-distance categories.

$$P \leq .05 \text{ (two-tailed test).}$$

Table 9.1. Social-Distance Rankings for 16 Prison Guards.

	Social-Distance Ranks			
	Low	*Moderately Low*	*Moderately High*	*High*
Number of guards with various scores ($N = 16$)	0	4	9	3

To test the null hypothesis, we must first determine the theoretical distribution of social-distance scores for these guards. Since there are 4 ($= k$) categories into which social-distance scores may be ranked, and if $N = 16$, then, given our null hypothesis, we should expect N/k or 16/4 or four frequencies in each of the four categories. *Dividing the number of observations by the number of categories into which the observations are ranked will give us the expected number of frequencies per category.*

Next, we must set up a cumulative frequency distribution for both the observed and the expected frequencies. Table 9.2 shows this more clearly. In this table it will be observed that a discrepancy exists between what is observed and what is expected by chance. Our primary concern

Table 9.2. Cumulative Frequency Distribution of Observed and Expected Frequencies.

	Social-Distance Ranks			
	Low	*Moderately Low*	*Moderately High*	*High*
Observed frequencies	0/16	4/16	9/16	3/16
Expected frequencies	4/16	4/16	4/16	4/16
Cumulative observed f	0/16	4/16	13/16	16/16
Cumulative expected f	4/16	8/16	12/16	16/16
Difference between cumulative and expected frequencies	4/16	4/16	1/16	0/16

here will be with the *largest absolute difference between the observed and expected cumulative frequencies.* The largest absolute difference is 4/16, and we shall label this difference D. D is defined as the largest absolute difference between expected and observed cumulative frequencies. Turning to Table A.9 of Appendix A, Critical Values of D, we first identify the level of significance at which we are testing the null hypothesis, in this case .05. Next, we identify N in the left-hand column of the table. Where these points intersect in the body of the table is the critical value of D, the difference between what is observed and what is expected.

If our observed D is equal to or greater than the D in the table, we can reject the null hypothesis. In this case, with $N = 16$, we need a D equal to or greater than the value .328. Since our observed $D = 4/16 = .250$, we cannot reject the null hypothesis. We conclude, therefore, that the sample of prison guards does not have an "uneven" distribution of social-distance scores.

Assumptions for the Kolmogorov-Smirnov One-Sample Test Random sampling is a prerequisite to proper application of the Kolmogorov-Smirnov test. The variable under investigation, in this case social distance, should be such that an underlying continuum can be assumed. If the test is used for discrete variables, Goodman (1954) has shown the test to be a conservative one. If we are able to reject the null hypothesis for discrete data at a given level of significance, we are even more confident that the distribution of the discrete variable is an unexpected one.

Advantages and Disadvantages of the Kolmogorov-Smirnov Test Perhaps the chief advantage of the Kolmogorov-Smirnov test is that it is appropriate for extremely small samples of elements. There are no restrictions on sample size, either large or small. Compared to the chi-square test which performs a similar function, the Kolmogorov-Smirnov Test is better in the sense that it uses more information. For extremely small samples, the chi-square test simply is not appropriate. Further, the chi-square test does not use all the information provided by ordinal data. Finally, the Kolmogorov-Smirnov test is relatively easy to apply and tables are conveniently available for interpreting observed D values.

TWO-SAMPLE TESTS: RELATED SAMPLES

In this section two two-sample tests for related samples will be presented. Both tests assume that either (a) subjects act as their own controls in some type of before-and-after experimental design or succession of treatment conditions, or (b) the investigator has matched individuals according to a number of salient traits. *In both situations the investigator will be able to determine whether score differences can be attributed to treatment conditions rather than to differences between the individuals exposed to the treatment conditions.*

The Sign Test

A very gross measure of the significance of difference between two treatment conditions where two related samples are involved is the sign test. This test uses the direction of score differences (indicated by a plus or minus difference) under different conditions to establish whether the samples are different from one another. It is assumed that the samples under investigation are related, either because each subject acts as his own control or because samples have been carefully matched before being exposed to different treatment conditions.

Suppose we are interested in determining whether or not increased automation in a business setting would result in significant changes of attitudes of employees toward remaining on the job. We use a *readiness-to-change* questionnaire which presumably reflects the degree to which an employee is ready to change his present job assignment. Such a questionnaire is a potential indicator of an employee's satisfaction or dissatisfaction with present job conditions. A low readiness-to-change score would reflect an employee's desire to remain with the present job, while a high readiness-to-change score would be indicative of an employee wanting to change the job he is presently performing.

We obtain information from 15 employees pertaining to their degree of readiness to change before and after increased automation takes place on their jobs, and this information is presented in Table 9.3. We shall test the following null hypothesis:

H_0: There is no effect of increased automation upon employees' readiness-to-change scores.

H_1: There will be an effect of increased automation upon employees' readiness-to-change scores.

$$P \leqslant .05 \text{ (two-tailed test).}$$

Table 9.3. Readiness-to-Change Scores for 15 Employees.

Readiness-to-Change Scores		
Before Automation	*After Automation*	*Sign Associated with Change in Score*
50	62	+
48	46	−
51	58	+
53	59	+
45	44	−
50	55	+
47	70	+
35	40	+
51	46	−
55	65	+
56	56	0
56	64	+
67	52	−
60	66	+
54	56	+
$N = 14$		Sum of fewest signs $= 4 = m$

To test this hypothesis, we construct a table similar to Table 9.3. We identify readiness-to-change scores for each individual under both treatment conditions, in this case before and after increased automation. In the right-hand column, we identify the score change in terms of an increase (+) or decrease (−) or no change at all (0).

Next, we sum the number of the signs (+ or −) which occur *least frequently*. In this case, there are only 4 minuses. We label the number of least frequent signs m. Our N is determined by the number of people who experience a *score change* from one condition to the next. Where no change in a person's score occurs, that is, where a person's score remains the same from one condition to the next, we omit this person from our N. N, therefore, consists exclusively of those persons experiencing a change in score, either + or −. Omitting the person whose readiness-to-change score did not change from one time period to the next, we have an $N = 14$ and an $m = 4$. With these values, we enter Table A.21 of Appendix A. This table contains probabilities for observed values of N and m under the null hypothesis.

To determine the probability for our present observations, we enter the table with $m = 4$ which we identify across the top of the table. The N value, in this case 14, is located down the left-hand column of the table. Where these two values, $N = 14$ and $m = 4$, intersect defines the probability associated with these observations under the null hypothesis. The probability associated with our observations is .090. If this probability is equal to or less than the level of significance which we have established in the test of our hypothesis, then we can reject the null hypothesis. Since we decided to work at the .05 level of significance, we must conclude that we have been unable to find a significant effect of increased automation upon employees' readiness-to-change scores. We are unable to reject the null hypothesis.

For larger samples, that is, where $N > 25$, a Z test of significance may be used in order to determine the significance of difference in sign changes. The formula is

$$Z = \frac{2m - N}{\sqrt{N}}$$

where m = the sum of the least frequent signs; and
N = the total number of elements whose scores change.

The following example is provided to illustrate this kind of problem. Suppose we are interested in determining the effect of a tour through a poverty area of a community on influencing a group of citizens to support increased appropriations to ameliorate the poverty conditions. A sample of 50 citizens is randomly selected and shown the poverty area. Their views toward supporting legislation favoring additional appropriations for the community are obtained before and after the tour, and compared. The results are shown in Table 9.4. We shall test the following hypothesis:

H_0: A tour through a poverty area will have no effect on attitudes among a group of citizens toward financial support of poverty legislation.
H_1: A tour through a poverty area will change attitudes among a group of citizens toward financial support of poverty legislation.

$$P \leq .01 \text{ (one-tailed test).}$$

Table 9.4. Citizens' Support for Poverty Legislation.

		After Tour	
		Favor Legislation	*Oppose Legislation*
Before Tour	*Favor Legislation*	8	3
	Oppose Legislation	30	9

In testing this hypothesis, we are again interested *only* in those individuals whose attitudes toward legislation *changed.* We shall ignore those individuals whose scores did not change. Since 3 individuals changed from favoring to opposing legislation, and since 30 individuals changed from opposing to favoring such legislation, our N becomes $3 + 30 = 33$. Our m for these data will be 3, the fewest changes in sign. Substituting these values in our formula above, we have:

$$Z = \frac{(2)(3) - 33}{\sqrt{33}} = \frac{-27}{5.74}$$
$$= -4.70.$$

We interpret this Z value by using Table A.3 of Appendix A. Entering this table with a Z of -4.70, we find that this value clearly enables us to reject the null hypothesis at the .01 level of significance: we need a Z of 2.33 or larger (disregarding sign) in order for the difference to be considered significant at .01 using a one-tailed test. We conclude that the tour through the poverty area was instrumental in changing the views of the citizens.

Assumptions for the Sign Test Only three assumptions underlie the sign test. Our subjects must constitute a random sample from a larger universe. Our measures are assumed to fall along some underlying continuum. The two sets of observations are related to each other in some meaningful way. In our example, subjects acted as their own controls in a before-and-after design.

Advantages and Disadvantages of the Sign Test The sign test is a simple and rather rapid method for determining differences between related samples exposed to some treatment condition. Ease of application and ready tables for interpretation of sign changes make this test an attractive one.

The sign test is a gross measure of the significance of difference, however. It does not take into account the magnitude of change in scores under different conditions. For this problem, the Wilcoxon matched-pairs-signed-ranks test may be used. This will be discussed next.

The Wilcoxon Matched-Pairs-Signed-Ranks Test

A useful ordinal test for determining the significance of difference between two related samples according to some measured trait is the Wilcoxon matched-pairs-signed-ranks test. This test is designed to take into account ranked differences between two samples, where ranks have been assigned according to the *magnitude of difference* between matched pairs of subjects.

It should be evident that this experimental situation is similar to those where the subjects act as their own controls in before-and-after designs. Careful matching of pairs of individuals can lead to appropriate application of the test as well.

Suppose we are interested in examining the extent to which perception of self changes as the result of professionalization. Specifically, we want to know whether or not a two-year internship period will modify the self perceptions of physicians. Some research indicates that the physician upon leaving medical school perceives his future role as an ideal one, but that a confrontation with the world of actual medical practice alters the ideal self perception the physician may have.

Through projective techniques, we examine the self perceptions of 15 physicians before and after a two-year internship period. We measure the ideality of the self perceptions of these physicians and cast the information into Table 9.5. The larger the score, the more the physicians perceive their roles to be ideal ones. We shall test the following hypothesis:

H_0: There is no difference in physicians' ideal self perceptions before and after a two-year internship period.

H_1: Physicians' ideal self perceptions will decrease after a two-year internship period.

$$P \leqslant .025 \text{ (one-tailed test).}$$

In order to test this hypothesis, we must determine the change in each physician's self-perception score after the two-year internship period. We identify each change in score by listing it in a column labeled *D*, as in Table 9.5. In a column labeled *Rank of* $|D|$ we rank the *absolute*

Table 9.5. Changes in Scores of Ideal Self Perception for 15 Physicians.

Ideality Scores		*Difference in Scores*	*Rank of*	*Rank with Less Frequent Sign*
Before Internship	*After Internship*	(*D*)	$\|D\|$	(*T*)
41	35	−6	−7	
38	44	6	7	7
56	49	−7	−10	
51	50	−1	−1.5	
50	45	−5	−5	
60	52	−8	−12	
49	39	−10	−14	
35	44	9	13	13
47	40	−7	−10	
43	41	−2	−3.5	
55	48	−7	−10	
46	44	−2	−3.5	
49	43	−6	−7	
52	53	1	1.5	1.5
57	46	−11	−15	
$N = 15$				$\Sigma T = 21.5$

differences in scores, assigning a 1 to the smallest score change (either an increase or a decrease), a 2 to the next smallest score change, and so on. When ties occur, the *average rank* is assigned each of the tied scores. Also, in this column we give a sign (+ or −) to each score change. If the score is larger after the internship period, we identify the rank of the score change as *positive*. If the score becomes smaller after the internship period, we assign a negative sign to the score change, as is indicated above. In the last column, we list all of the ranks with the *less frequent sign*. In other words, if more negative ranks than positive ranks occur, we list in this column all the ranks with the positive signs or score changes. On the other hand, if there are more positive signs, we list all negative ranks in the column.

Next, we sum the ranks with the less frequent sign. Now we are able to interpret the significance of changes in physician's self-perception scores. Simply using the sum of the ranks with the less frequent sign, we enter Table A.23 of Appendix A at the selected level of significance, in this case .025, and we identify the critical value associated with the particular size of N in our example. Since our $N = 15$, we must have a ΣT (sum of the ranks with the less frequent sign) *equal to or less than 25* in order for the changes in physicians' scores to be significant at the .025 level. Since our observed $\Sigma T = 21.5$, we conclude that there was a significant change in scores after the two-year internship period. In this case, it appears that the physicians' self perception became less ideal, and so we reject the null hypothesis and support H_1.

Table A.23 of Appendix A is designed for sample sizes of 25 or less. When larger samples are encountered, this table cannot be used. An alternative formula exists, however, which makes it possible to complete the Wilcoxon matched-pairs-signed-ranks test for larger samples. This formula is a modification of the Z test in which

$$Z = \frac{\Sigma T - \dfrac{N(N+1)}{4}}{\sqrt{\dfrac{N(N+1)(2N+1)}{24}}}$$

where ΣT = the sum of the ranks with the less frequent sign; and
N = the number of pairs of scores.

The Z is interpreted according to Table A.3 of Appendix A as either a one- or a two-tailed test of the null hypothesis.

For example, suppose we have the sample in Table 9.6 with an $N = 26$.

Table 9.6. Job-Satisfaction Scores of 26 Employees before and after Isolation on the Job.

Worker Job Satisfaction				
Before Isolation	*After Isolation*	*D*	*Rank of* $\lvert D \rvert$	*Rank with Less Frequent Sign*
80	78	−2	−6	
68	71	3	9.5	9.5
72	70	−2	−6	
75	74	−1	−2	
81	75	−6	−17.5	
79	72	−7	−19.5	
84	80	−4	−11.5	
80	85	5	14.5	14.5
80	72	−8	−21	
79	78	−1	−2	
67	62	−5	−14.5	
62	60	−2	−6	
45	52	7	19.5	19.5
82	84	2	6	6.0
57	55	−2	−6	
65	60	−5	−14.5	
63	53	−10	−25	
75	69	−6	−17.5	
78	69	−9	−23	
72	73	1	2	2.0
62	65	3	9.5	9.5
67	62	−5	−14.5	
84	80	−4	−11.5	
69	52	−17	−26	
69	60	−9	−23	
79	70	−9	−23	
$N = 26$				$\Sigma T = 61.0$

The scores represent the degree of job satisfaction of employees exposed to increased isolation on the job. Measures of job satisfaction before isolation are compared with job-satisfaction scores after isolation. The magnitude of the change in scores from one time period to the next is recorded in column D as before. These D's are ranked in terms of their absolute value, the smallest D receiving the rank of 1 and so on. The ranks with the less frequent sign are listed in the final column as shown, and these ranks are summed.

With this information, we may carry out the Z test of the following null hypothesis:

H_0: There is no change in job-satisfaction scores as a result of increased isolation among workers.

H_1: Job-satisfaction scores will change as a result of increased isolation among workers.

$$P \leqslant .01 \text{ (two-tailed test).}$$

$$Z = \frac{61 - \left(\frac{(26)(27)}{4}\right)}{\sqrt{\frac{(26)(27)(53)}{24}}} = \frac{61 - 175.5}{\sqrt{1550.25}}$$

$$= -114.5/39.37$$

$$= -2.91.$$

Turning to Table A.3 of Appendix A, we find that we must have an observed Z of ± 2.58 or larger in order for the difference in job-satisfaction scores to be considered significant at the .01 level using a two-tailed test. Since our observed $Z = -2.91$, we conclude that job-satisfaction scores significantly changed after increased isolation. We can reject the null hypothesis at the .01 level of significance.

Assumptions for the Wilcoxon Matched-Pairs-Signed-Ranks Test One assumption of this test is that the investigator must have interval-level information. This level is required because the test takes into account the *magnitude* of changes in scores. Some researchers use this test when their data *approach* the interval level, however. "Equal-appearing interval" data or information which can be measured according to some ordered metric scale are analyzed with this test. Data of these types lie somewhere between ordinal and interval measurement levels. Some attitudinal measures purportedly approach the interval level.

Another assumption of this test is that the samples are related in some meaningful way. Either the subjects should act as their own controls in a before-and-after design, or the investigator must demonstrate that he has sufficiently well-matched pairs of individuals according to some pertinent variables.

Advantages and Disadvantages of the Wilcoxon Test The Wilcoxon matched-pairs-signed-ranks test has a definite advantage over the sign test previously discussed. Not only is the *direction of the difference* in scores taken into account, but the *magnitude of the change* is also observed. This test is very popular, in part because of this characteristic. A table exists which makes the interpretation of test results easy. The test is also easy to apply and to understand. When sample size exceeds 25, a modification of the Z test may be used to identify significant changes in scores. This characteristic also enhances the popularity of the test.

TWO-SAMPLE TESTS: INDEPENDENT SAMPLES

The Wald-Wolfowitz Runs Test

The Wald-Wolfowitz runs test is a test for determining whether or not two samples could have come from the same population of elements. Specifically, the test answers the question: Are the two samples so similar with respect to some measured characteristic that they can be assumed to have been drawn from the same population of elements?

The procedure of the Wald-Wolfowitz runs test is relatively easy. Consider the following example: Suppose the National Aeronautics and Space Administration (NASA) is interested in determining the effect of a new space-fitness program on several groups of astronaut trainees. Two groups of astronaut trainees are selected randomly, one which will participate in the new program, the other group participating in the old fitness program. The question is: Do the groups differ with respect to scores which they receive on a general space-fitness test administered at the completion of their respective programs?

Assuming ordinal-level measurement for the space-fitness test, the scores shown in Table 9.7 are observed among the two groups of astro-

Table 9.7. Scores on a Space-Fitness Test for Two Groups of Astronaut Trainees.

Group 1 $N_1 = 12$ *New Program*	*Group 2* $N_2 = 10$ *Old Program*
20	2
12	14
8	6
11	17
18	4
7	10
22	9
21	1
19	3
16	13
15	
5	

naut trainees. We are interested in testing the following null hypothesis:

H_0: There is no difference between the two groups of astronaut trainees with respect to their scores on a space-fitness test.

H_1: There will be a difference between the two groups of astronaut trainees with respect to their scores on a space-fitness test.

$$P \leqslant .05 \text{ (two-tailed test).}$$

To test this hypothesis using the Wald-Wolfowitz runs test, we must arrange all of the scores in Table 9.7 into some order of size, irrespective of group, from the largest to the smallest. After doing this, we draw a line *under* all scores from Group 1 and a line *over* all scores from Group 2. This operation is illustrated as follows:

1	*1*	*1*	*1*		*3*			*5*	*5*
1	2	3	4	5	6	7	8	9	10
				2		*4*	*4*		

		7	*7*			*9*					
11	12	13	14	15	16	17	18	19	20	21	22
6	*6*			*8*	*8*		*10*	*10*	*10*	*10*	*10*

It will be observed that several scores from the same group "run" together. These are called *runs*. The more runs there are, the more homogeneous the two samples are, and the greater the likelihood that they have come from the same population of elements. A relatively small number of runs means that there is relatively great differentiation between groups, which is to say that one group has more large scores than the other, with consequent less mixing of scores.

In the example above, some runs contain one score while other runs contain as many as five scores. A run may consist of *any* number of scores. Each of the runs is numbered as is shown. In order to determine whether the two groups are different with respect to some measured characteristic, in this case space-fitness scores, we must determine whether there is a significantly small number of runs involved in the distribution of all the scores.

When the N in the larger of the two samples is equal to or smaller than 20, Table A.13 of Appendix A may be used: Critical Values of R in the Runs Test. This table contains critical values of R, or the number of runs, for various sizes of N at the .05 level of significance. In the present example, $N_1 = 12$ and $N_2 = 10$. There is a total of 10 runs; thus $R = 10$. Turning to the table, we first of all locate the value of N_1 in the left-hand column. Next, we locate the value of N_2 across the top of the table. The body of the table contains various values of R, the number of runs. Where the two N's intersect in the body of the table, the critical value of R is found. If our observed R *is equal to, or smaller than* the critical value of

R given in the table, we conclude that the two groups are *not* from the same population.

With $N_1 = 12$ and $N_2 = 10$, we need 7 or fewer runs in order for the two groups to be considered different at the .05 level of significance. Since our observed $R = 10$, we conclude that there is no significant difference between the two groups of astronaut trainees with respect to their space-fitness scores at the .05 level. In other words, high scores and low scores appear to be randomly distributed throughout the two groups. Consequently, we fail to reject the null hypothesis.

As long as the N in either sample does not exceed 20, Table A.13 may be used to determine critical values of R. When sample sizes exceed 20, however, we must turn to an alternative procedure for determining the significance of R. Such a procedure utilizes the Z test of significance with the following formula:

$$Z = \frac{\left|R - \left(\frac{2N_1N_2}{N_1 + N_2} + 1\right)\right| - .5}{\sqrt{\frac{2N_1N_2(2N_1N_2 - N_1 - N_2)}{(N_1 + N_2)^2(N_1 + N_2 - 1)}}}$$

where R = the number of runs; and
N_1 and N_2 = the number of elements in each sample.

Z may be interpreted by turning to Table A.3 of Appendix A, using a two-tailed test of significance.

Suppose two classes of AFROTC students take the Air Force Officer Qualification Test and their test scores are subsequently arranged from high to low. Further, suppose that we consider this test as one which provides ordinal-level data. Drawing a line over all runs of scores from Group 1 and a line under all scores from Group 2, we want to find out whether the two groups of students came from the same population, that is, whether the scores are equally distributed throughout the two groups. With $N_1 = 25$ and $N_2 = 16$, the following runs are observed:

86 87 88 89 90 91 92 93 94 115 (underlined)
1

2
116 118 (overlined)

119 120 121 122 (underlined)
3

4
123 124 125 126 127 128 129 130 (overlined)

131 132 133 134 135 136 137 138 139 140 141 (underlined)
5

6
142 143 144 145 146 147 (overlined)

Computing Z, we have:

$$Z = \frac{\left|6 - \left(\frac{(2)(25)(16)}{25 + 16} + 1\right)\right| - .5}{\sqrt{\frac{[(2)(25)(16)][(2)(25)(16) - 25 - 16]}{(25 + 16)^2(25 + 16 - 1)}}}$$

$$= \frac{14}{\sqrt{9.03}}$$

$$= 4.67.$$

With a Z this large, we conclude that there is a difference between the two groups at the .05 level of significance.

Special Situation: Ties When ties occur among the scores of elements from two groups, a question arises as to which scores should be included in which runs? Suppose we were to observe a tie among four individuals on some characteristic. Such ties may be due to the crudeness of our measuring instrument. A conservative way of dealing with these ties as we determine the significance of a number of runs (R) is to *maximize* the number of runs which could conceivably occur among them. For example, the following series of scores is observed:

$$\underbrace{10\quad 12}_{A}\quad \overbrace{15\quad 16}^{B}\quad 19\quad 19\quad 19\quad 19\quad \underbrace{20\quad 23}_{A}\quad \overbrace{25\quad 27\quad 40}^{B}$$

Suppose two individuals from each of two different groups possess identical scores of 19. How should we divide them? We could put the individuals' scores from Group B next to the other scores of 15 and 16 for Group B, and this would leave Group A scores of 19 to be placed next to Group A scores of 20 and 23. This arrangement would mean a total of four runs. Such is the case below.

$$\underbrace{10\quad 12}_{A}\quad \overbrace{15\quad 16\quad 19\quad 19}^{B}\quad \underbrace{19\quad 19\quad 20\quad 23}_{A}\quad \overbrace{25\quad 27\quad 40}^{B}$$

On the other hand, we could divide the scores in such a way as to maximize the number of runs in this sequence of scores. For example, we might arrange the number of runs in the following manner:

$$\underbrace{10\quad 12}_{A}\quad \overbrace{15\quad 16}^{B}\quad \underbrace{19}_{A}\quad \overbrace{19}^{B}\quad \underbrace{19}_{A}\quad \overbrace{19}^{B}\quad \underbrace{20\quad 23}_{A}\quad \overbrace{25\quad 27\quad 40}^{B}$$

Now we have a total of eight runs. Some researchers recommend that the *average* number of runs be used to enter Table A.13 of Appendix A. When N's are averaged, all possible ways of making the runs are explored, and these will yield a different number of runs each time. These runs are averaged and this value is used as R for the data. This averaging reduces the possibility of failing to reject the null hypothesis if, in fact, it is false. Maximizing the number of runs is a more conservative procedure, and for this reason is recommended.

Assumptions for the Wald-Wolfowitz Runs Test The Wald-Wolfowitz runs test is appropriate for data of the ordinal level. In addition, the samples should be independent and randomly drawn. Also, it is assumed that the characteristic measured is continuous.

Advantages and Disadvantages of the Wald-Wolfowitz Runs Test One primary advantage of the Wald-Wolfowitz runs test is that it is appropriate for detecting any differences whatsoever between two samples of elements. The difference may pertain to central tendency or skewness, but may nevertheless be detected by using this test. This fact can also be considered a disadvantage. When we conclude that two samples are "different," we are not able to say in what respect they are "different."

Another advantage is that the samples to be compared may be of different sizes. Some tests of significance are restrictive in the sense that the N's to be compared must be identical in size. Such is not the case with the Wald-Wolfowitz runs test. Tables exist when sample size is 20 or less. When $N > 20$, a Z test may be computed to determine the significance of R, the number of runs.

A fourth advantage of the test is that it is very easy to use and requires little mathematical computation, if any. Also, no assumptions need be made concerning the distribution of the characteristic under investigation.

One disadvantage is that ties often occur among scores from two groups. When the number of ties is excessive, the Wald-Wolfowitz runs test is inappropriate, unless the ties all occur conveniently within the same group. Also, since one assumption underlying the test is that the characteristic under investigation be continuous, the Wald-Wolfowitz runs test is less appropriate when discrete information of the ordinal level is encountered.

The Kolmogorov-Smirnov Test for Small Independent Samples

An extension of the Kolmogorov-Smirnov test has been developed for two samples. The test to be presented here is a test of whether two independent samples could have come from the same distribution. Again, like the one-sample test, this procedure utilizes cumulative frequency distributions of two independent samples according to some measured ordinal characteristic.

It should be noted that several varieties of this test exist, one variety for small samples and another for large samples. When small samples exist, the investigator will find that this variety of the Kolmogorov-Smirnov test (like the one-sample test) will be more appropriate than chi-square tests, simply because fewer restrictions are associated with it than with the other ordinal-level two-sample tests of significance. And since other ordinal procedures such as the Mann-Whitney U test are better for large samples, as when $N > 40$, only the small-sample case of the Kolmogorov-Smirnov test will be presented here.

Suppose the investigator wishes to determine whether there are differences between males and females with respect to resolving role-conflict situations. Through a series of hypothetical role-conflict examples, he records responses of 20 males and 20 females according to certain behavioral responses as alternatives. He classifies the behavioral responses according to a continuum of mild and extreme alternatives. He divides the continuum of responses into five segments, each representing a particular degree of response as determined by a mild-to-extreme score. The scores and frequencies for males and females are presented in Table 9.8. We want to know whether the males and females come from populations with different frequency distributions of mild and extreme scores. The

Table 9.8. Male and Female Scores on Resolution of Role Conflict.

	Role-Conflict Scores				
Sex	*Mild (0–4)*	*(5–9)*	*(10–14)*	*(15–19)*	*Extreme (20–24)*
Male	2	5	3	9	1
Female	6	2	11	0	1

following null hypothesis is tested:

H_0: Males and females come from the same population with respect to resolution of role conflicts.

H_1: Males and females resolve role conflicts differently.

$$P \leq .05 \text{ (two-tailed test).}$$

To test this hypothesis we must recast the data in Table 9.8 into two cumulative frequency distributions and record the differences between them. This we have done in Table 9.9. We may test the null hypothesis by paying attention to the numerator of the largest absolute difference

Table 9.9. Comparison of Cumulative Frequency Distributions of Males and Females Regarding Role-Conflict Resolution.

	Role-Conflict Scores—Cumulative Frequency				
	Mild (0–4)	*(5–9)*	*(10–14)*	*(15–19)*	*Extreme (20–24)*
$N_1 = 20$ males	2/20	7/20	10/20	19/20	20/20
$N_2 = 20$ females	6/20	8/20	19/20	19/20	20/20
Absolute differences	4/20	1/20	9/20	–	–

between the two cumulative frequency distributions for males and females. In this case, the numerator of the largest difference is 9. Turning to Table A.10 of Appendix A, we need to locate the level of significance across the top of the table. Since we simply wish to determine whether the differences between males and females are significant regardless of the direction, we are using a two-tailed test of significance at the .05 level.

It is a requirement for using Table A.10 that samples should be equal. For this reason, either N may be used to enter the table. With an $N = 20$ in the present instance, the critical value of D (= the largest absolute difference) for the .05 level of significance is 9. In other words, the numerator of the largest cumulative frequency difference between distributions should be 9 or larger, in order for us to reject the null hypothesis. Since our observed $D = 9$, we may reject the null hypothesis and conclude that there is a difference in role-conflict resolution between males and females. Had we predicted as an alternative hypothesis that males will give more extreme responses than females, a one-tailed test of significance would have been in order. And in that case, we would need only a numerator difference (D) of 8 in order to reject the null hypothesis that males and females respond similarly.

Assumptions for the Kolmogorov-Smirnov Test The Kolmogorov-Smirnov test assumes ordinal-level data which are continuously distributed, although continuity is not essential to apply the technique appropriately. The two samples should be independent and randomly drawn.

Advantages and Disadvantages of the Kolmogorov-Smirnov Test The primary advantage of this test is its usefulness for determining differences between small samples. In this sense it is much better than many other ordinal-level tests of significance performing a similar function. It is a conservative test as well.

For large samples, however, the Kolmogorov-Smirnov test is weaker than other ordinal-level tests in the sense that it is less sensitive to sample differences where $N > 40$. If the investigator wishes to apply the technique to large samples, however, he will find that the chi-square distribution is approximated and the chi-square table may be used with the following formula, with $df = 2$ in *all* two-sample comparisons:

$$\chi^2 = (4D^2)\left(\frac{N_1 N_2}{N_1 + N_2}\right)$$

where D = the largest proportional difference between the two cumulative frequency distributions (one-tailed test).

Table A.11 is provided for two-tailed, large-sample tests where $N_1 \neq N_2$. Since this technique is rather straightforward, no example will be provided here. For more extensive treatment of this test, see Siegel (1956), pp. 127–136.

The Mann-Whitney *U* Test

When the researcher is interested in evaluating the difference between two means of independent samples of elements, he may select the *t* test. Such a test involves meeting assumptions pertaining to the interval level of measurement and to the normal distribution of the samples. When these assumptions cannot be met, the researcher is obligated to select an alternative test with fewer restrictions, but one which will give him similar information about the differences between two independent samples.

The Mann-Whitney *U* test is designed to perform a function similar to that of the *t* test, and it makes no assumptions concerning the distributions involved. This test assumes that the investigator has at least ordinal-level information at his disposal. This means that he will be able to rank elements according to some measurable dimension.

The Mann-Whitney *U* test is a test for the significance of difference between two samples where the elements have been ranked according to some ordinal-level variable. Specifically, it is designed to determine whether the various ranked values for any given variable are equally distributed throughout both samples. In this sense, it is similar to the runs test, where the object was to find out if some trait is equally distributed throughout two samples of elements.

For the Mann-Whitney *U* test, the null hypothesis is that two independent samples do not differ according to the distribution of high and low ranks according to some measured characteristic. In other words, it is hypothesized that there are approximately the same number of high and low ranks in each sample.

The following formula is used to test the null hypothesis:

$$U = N_1 N_2 + \frac{N_1(N_1 + 1)}{2} - \Sigma R_1$$

and

$$U' = N_1 N_2 + \frac{N_2(N_2 + 1)}{2} - \Sigma R_2$$

where ΣR_1 = the sum of ranks for N_1, or the first group; and
ΣR_2 = the sum of ranks for N_2, or the second group.

It should be noted that *both* formulas are used in the computation of the *U* statistic. The reason is that we need to find the *smaller U* of the two. Since we are dealing with two *N*'s possibly of different sizes, it is generally the case that the two formulas will render different *U* values. In any case, we carry out both tests for *U*; then whichever *U* is the smaller will be used as our observed value to enter one of the tables A.8.1 through A.8.10 of Appendix A, Probabilities Associated with Values as Small as Observed Values of *U* in the Mann-Whitney Test or Critical Values of U in the Mann-Whitney Test. Which table we use is determined by our sample sizes. An alternative exists for computing U' once U has been computed. This method is as follows:

$$N_1N_2 - U = U'.$$

To illustrate the Mann-Whitney U test, consider the following example. Suppose we are hypothesizing that people who join voluntary organizations (Red Cross, P.T.A., Human Relations Council, and the like) are different according to some personality trait from those who do not join such organizations. We may feel that people vary according to their degree of altruism, as manifested perhaps by their donating their time for the benefit of other people. We therefore set out to measure altruism among two samples of individuals, one sample consisting of people who voluntarily join several organizations, and the other sample consisting of people who join no organizations. We collect the information for our two samples as is indicated in Table 9.10.

We are interested in testing the following null hypothesis:

H_0: Two samples are the same with respect to the degree of altruism.
H_1: Joiners have a greater degree of altruism than nonjoiners.

$$P \leqslant .05 \text{ (one-tailed test)}.$$

Table 9.10. Altruism Scores of Joiners and Nonjoiners.

Altruism Scores and Ranks			
Joiners		*Nonjoiners*	
Raw Score	*Rank*	*Raw Score*	*Rank*
45	4	42	7
52	1	39	10
41	8	44	5
48	3	36	12
49	2	32	13
43	6	31	14
		21	15
		40	9
		38	11
$N_1 = 6$	$\Sigma R_1 = 24$	$N_2 = 9$	$\Sigma R_2 = 96$

Applying the formula above, we compute U and U' for our two samples:

$$\begin{aligned} U &= (6)(9) + \frac{(6)(6+1)}{2} - 24 \\ &= 54 + 42/2 - 24 = 54 + 21 - 24 \\ &= 51. \end{aligned}$$

$$U' = (6)(9) + \frac{(9)(9+1)}{2} - 96$$
$$= 54 + 90/2 - 96$$
$$= 54 + 45 - 96$$
$$= 3.$$

Had we used the formula $N_1N_2 - U = U'$, after the first computation, we would have:

$$U' = (6)(9) - 51 = 54 - 51 = 3.$$

The answers are identical.

Since the smaller of the two U's above is 3, we use 3 to enter one of the Tables A.8 of Appendix A. It will be observed that several tables exist. Tables A.8.1 through A.8.6 contain exact probabilities associated with particular values of U where $N_1 = 3, 4, 5, 6, 7$, and 8. Tables A.8.7 through A.8.10 contain critical values of U for one- and two-tailed tests at .05, .025, .01, and .001 significance levels respectively, for samples ranging in size from 9 to 20. In all cases throughout this last series of tables, N_1 is considered to be the *larger* sample size in any comparison of two samples, regardless of which sample the researcher designates as N_1 and N_2.

In the present example, N_1 is 6 in Table 9.10, but for entering Tables A.8.1-A.8.10, N_2 is used because it is the larger sample, being 9.

In the case of U, the procedure of rejecting the null hypothesis is somewhat different from what we have been doing. In the past, we have rejected the null hypothesis if our observed statistic has been equal to or larger than the critical value in the appropriate table of Appendix A. For U, however, if our observed U is *equal to or smaller than* the critical value shown in Table A.8.7 through A.8.10, *then* we reject the null hypothesis. This decision applies only when the larger sample size is between 9 and 20. Exact probabilities exist for observed values of U where sample size is less than 9 for the larger N. The smaller the U, the greater chance there is that the two samples are different with respect to some variable. Where U and U' are equal, complete heterogeneity exists among the two samples with respect to some commonly shared characteristic.

For our problem, we have at least one N between 9 and 20, since $N_1 = 6$ and $N_2 = 9$, and we therefore select Table A.8.10, which is appropriate for a one-tailed test at .05. Since our research hypothesis as an alternative is that joiners will have a greater degree of altruism than nonjoiners, we make a one-tailed test of the null hypothesis. We must have a U of 12 or less in order for a significant difference between groups to exist regarding their degree of altruism. This critical value is determined where N_1 and N_2 intersect in the body of Table A.8.10. Actually, whichever N is used, either across the top of the table or down the left-hand column, the result will be the same. For example, the same U is required if $N_1 = 10$

and $N_2 = 14$ or if $N_1 = 14$ and $N_2 = 10$. Where these two N's intersect in the body of the table defines an identical U value whichever way we enter the table.

In the present case, since our observed $U = 3$, we reject the null hypothesis that altruism is equally distributed among the two samples, and we may conclude that joiners are more altruistic at the .05 level of significance.

To use the tables where the larger $N = 8$ or less, the researcher simply selects the table containing the larger N, then he selects the appropriate N_2 across the top of the table. Then he finds the appropriate U value in the left-hand column. Finally, where these two points intersect in the body of the table defines the exact probability at which he may reject the null hypothesis. It should be noted that the larger the U becomes, the lower becomes the probability of rejecting the null hypothesis.

Suppose we enter Table A.8.5 with the larger $N = 7$. Further suppose that we are testing the null hypothesis that two groups are the same with respect to some measured characteristic, at the .05 level of significance. Our hypothetical U value which is observed is 6. With $N_1 = 7$ and $N_2 = 4$, we find that the probability associated with this U value is .082. We cannot reject the null hypothesis at the .05 level of significance since .082 is greater than .05.

Large Sample Sizes When one sample exceeds 20, a modification of the Z test may be used. This formula is as follows:

$$Z = \frac{U - \dfrac{N_1 N_2}{2}}{\sqrt{\dfrac{(N_1 N_2)(N_1 + N_2 + 1)}{12}}}.$$

The resulting Z may be interpreted using Table A.3 of Appendix A for either a one- or a two-tailed test.

To illustrate this procedure where large N's are involved, consider the following example: Suppose we have two samples, $N_1 = 23$ and $N_2 = 21$, consisting of union stewards representing two major unions, the International Typographical Union (ITU) and the Printing Pressmen's Union (PPU). We are interested in whether or not there are any differences between the two samples with respect to the job seniority of the union stewards. We rank two samples of union stewards according to their job seniority (number of months on the job) and we rank these for each of the union stewards in Table 9.11. We test the following null hypothesis:

H_0: There are no differences in seniority between two groups of union stewards.

H_1: Union stewards from two unions differ according to job seniority.

$$P \leqslant .05 \text{ (two-tailed test).}$$

Table 9.11. Ranks of Seniority Scores for Union Stewards in Two Unions.

ITU Steward Seniority ($N_1 = 23$)	*Rank* (R_1)	*PPU Steward Seniority* ($N_2 = 21$)	*Rank* (R_2)
92	8.5	81	16.5
88	10.5	36	38.5
76	21.0	41	36.0
64	26.0	58	28.0
79	18.0	78	19.0
104	4.0	21	44.0
34	40.0	36	38.5
82	14.5	49	30.5
86	12.0	100	6.0
71	24.0	82	14.5
45	34.0	77	20.0
103	5.0	67	25.0
48	32.0	46	33.0
55	29.0	31	41.0
74	22.0	39	37.0
73	23.0	42	35.0
88	10.5	83	13.0
94	7.0	92	8.5
109	3.0	23	42.0
117	2.0	49	30.5
221	1.0	60	27.0
22	43.0		
81	16.5		
	$\Sigma R_1 = 406.5$		$\Sigma R_2 = 583.5$

Computing U for these data, we have:

$$U = (23)(21) + \frac{(23)(23+1)}{2} - 406.5$$
$$= 483 + 552/2 - 406.5 = 483 + 276 - 406.5$$
$$= 352.5.$$

Computing U', we have:

$$U' = (23)(21) + \frac{(21)(21+1)}{2} - 583.5$$
$$= 483 + 462/2 - 583.5 = 483 + 231 - 583.5$$
$$= 130.5.$$

As a check on our work, we have:

$$N_1N_2 - U = U' \qquad \text{or} \qquad 483 - 352.5 = 130.5.$$

Now we are ready to compute Z:

$$Z = \frac{352.5 - \frac{(23)(21)}{2}}{\sqrt{\frac{[(23)(21)][23 + 21 + 1]}{12}}}$$

$$= \frac{111}{\sqrt{\frac{21,735}{12}}} = \frac{111}{\sqrt{1811.25}} = 111/42.559$$

$$= 2.61.$$

We need a Z equal to or larger than 1.96 in order to reject the null hypothesis at the .05 level of significance. With an observed Z of 2.61, we conclude that there is a significant difference between the two groups of union stewards pertaining to job seniority.

Assumptions for the Mann-Whitney* U *Test The Mann-Whitney U test assumes at least ordinal-level data. Also, the samples should be independent and randomly drawn. The data should be continuous.

Advantages and Disadvantages of the Mann-Whitney* U *Test The primary advantage of the Mann-Whitney U test is that it is a very good nonparametric counterpart to the t test. The researcher makes no unrealistic assumptions concerning the distribution of the data, and the test is quite appropriate for both large and small samples.

Another advantage pertains to the possibility of tied ranks. When ties in ranks occur, that is, when two or more individuals receive the same score and they are from different groups, a correction factor may be introduced to compensate for ties. Also, the effect of ties on the U value is quite small, even when a large number of ties is present. Because the correction for ties is a somewhat laborious procedure and the result is only to make it slightly easier to reject the null hypothesis, it is recommended that the correction for ties *not* be made. This practice makes the Mann-Whitney U test slightly more conservative when ties are not corrected for. Consequently, if null hypotheses are rejected without correcting for ties, then there would be no question that the same hypotheses would be rejected if the ties were taken into account. The correction for ties is discussed in Siegel (1956), pp. 123–126.

The Friedman Two-Way Analysis-of-Variance Test

In order to determine whether or not k samples are different from one another with respect to some measured characteristic, the Friedman two-way analysis-of-variance test may be used. Such a test is appropriate when k samples are related, as when subjects act as their own controls through a series of experimental conditions, or when different individuals have been matched according to several pertinent characteristics and are exposed to a number of different experimental conditions.

For Small Samples Suppose we were to conduct a study to determine the effect of leadership upon role clarity of group members. We subject six individuals to three different kinds of leadership experiences during a six-week period. The leadership experiences include exposure to an autocratic leader, a laissez-faire leader, and a democratic leader. During each exposure we test the role clarity of each of the six individuals and assign them a role-clarity score. At the end of the experimental period we have role-clarity scores for six individuals under three kinds of leadership conditions. These scores are shown in Table 9.12.

Table 9.12. Role-Clarity Scores under Three Leadership Conditions.

			Leadership Type			
Individual	*Autocratic*	*Rank*	*Laissez-faire*	*Rank*	*Democratic*	*Rank*
A	15	1	8	3	10	2
B	11	2	12	1	10	3
C	14	1	12	2	6	3
D	14	1	9	3	11	2
E	12	2	11	3	13	1
F	16	1	10	2	8	3
$N = 6$						
		$\Sigma R_1 = 8$		$\Sigma R_2 = 14$		$\Sigma R_3 = 14$
$k = 3$						

We make the following null hypothesis:

H_0: There is no difference in role clarity under three different leadership conditions.

H_1: Role clarity will differ under three leadership conditions.

$$P \leqslant .10.$$

To test this hypothesis, we must first of all rank each of the individuals' three scores under each leadership condition. For individual A, we note that he has scores of 15, 8, and 10 under the three conditions. We shall assign a 1 to the largest score, a 2 to the next largest score, and a 3 to the smallest of the three scores, respectively 15, 10, and 8. (It makes no difference whether we assign a 1 to the largest or smallest score, so long as we consistently rank each individual's scores in this fashion throughout the table.) Doing this for all of the individuals, we then sum the ranks of the scores under each of the leadership conditions, as is shown in Table 9.12.

The question is, Are the role-clarity scores significantly different under one kind of leadership compared with another? Does the type of leadership influence role clarity to a significant degree?

To answer this question, we apply the formula

$$\chi_r^2 = \left(\frac{12}{Nk(k+1)}\Sigma(\Sigma R_i)^2\right) - [3N(k+1)]$$

where k = the number of treatment conditions (types of leadership, in this case);
$\Sigma(\Sigma R_i)^2$ = the square of the sum of ranks under each experimental condition (i); and
N = the number of individuals under each treatment condition.

Applying this formula to our data in Table 9.12, we have:

$$\begin{aligned}\chi_r^2 &= \frac{12}{(6)(3)(3+1)}[(8)^2 + (14)^2 + (14)^2] - (3)(6)(3+1)\\ &= \frac{12}{72}(64 + 196 + 196) - 72\\ &= .167(456) - 72 = 76.152 - 72\\ &= 4.152.\end{aligned}$$

With a $\chi_r^2 = 4.152$, we enter Table A.19 of Appendix A, Probabilities Associated with Values as Large as Observed Values of χ_r^2. Table A.19 contains exact probabilities for situations when $k = 3$, $N = 2 \ldots 9$, and when $k = 4$, $N = 2 \ldots 4$. Since our example meets these conditions, we enter the appropriate column where $k = 3$, $N = 6$. In the left-hand column of the table are various values of χ_r^2 which we must have in order for our observations to be significantly different from chance at the probability level shown in the right-hand column.

Since we are testing the null hypothesis at the .10 level of significance, we take the value of p that is nearest .10 and does not exceed it, namely .072. Using this value, we perceive that we must have an χ_r^2 equal to or greater than 5.33 in order to reject the hypothesis. Our observed χ_r^2 value is 4.152; consequently, we cannot reject the null hypothesis, and we conclude that no significant difference exists in role-clarity scores between three types of leadership.

For Larger Samples When either the size of N exceeds 9 or the size of k exceeds 4, Table A.19 cannot be used. Under this condition, the chi-square table, Table A.4 of Appendix A, may be used and entered with $k - 1$ degrees of freedom. In this case, χ_r^2 approximates χ^2 and Table A.4 may be used to determine whether or not the null hypothesis should be rejected.

To illustrate this situation, suppose we are studying the effect of various degrees of participation in the decision-making process upon the extent to which the worker identifies with his company. The extent to which the worker identifies with his company is measured according to his responses to questions dealing with recommending the company to his job-seeking friends, discussing his work at the company off the job, and so on. Participating in decision making is measured by giving the workers three different degrees of responsibility over their work over a twelve-week period.

We obtain a random sample of 14 workers from an industrial plant and we vary their decision-making participation over the twelve-week period. During the first four weeks, we give five of the workers their greatest opportunity to participate in decision making. The next four weeks is characterized by low participation in decision making for these five, and the final four weeks involves a moderate amount of participation in decision making for these same five workers.

The second group of workers, consisting of five different employees, is assigned a different sequence of participation conditions, and the final four workers is assigned still a different sequence. The individual workers are assigned randomly to one of the three sequence groups. We want to know whether these differences in decision-making participation will affect their identification with the company in any way. Their identification scores are presented in Table 9.13 below. High scores indicate greater identification.

Table 9.13. Identification Scores and Three Situations of Decision-Making Participation.

	Participation Conditions					
Individual	*High*	*Rank*	*Low*	*Rank*	*Moderate*	*Rank*
1	35	1	20	3	28	2
2	28	2	26	3	32	1
3	40	1	15	3	19	2
4	36	1	24	3	32	2
5	36	1	29	2	15	3
6	41	1	33	3	34	2
7	39	1	22	3	28	2
8	30	3	33	1	31	2
9	29	1	28	2	24	3
10	44	1	30	3	32	2
11	35	1	30	3	32	2
12	43	1	22	2	21	3
13	40	1	29	2	22	3
14	29	1	24	3	27	2
$N = 14$ $k = 3$	$\Sigma R_1 = 17$		$\Sigma R_2 = 36$		$\Sigma R_3 = 31$	

We want to test the following null hypothesis:

H_0: There is no difference in worker identification with the company under three conditions of participation in decision making.

H_1: Different degrees of decision-making participation will affect worker identification with the company.

$$P \leqslant .01.$$

To test this hypothesis, we apply the formula which we applied earlier:

$$\chi_r^2 = \left(\frac{12}{Nk(k+1)}\Sigma(\Sigma R_i)^2\right) - [3N(k+1)].$$

Applying this formula to our data in Table 9.13, we have

$$\chi_r^2 = \frac{12}{(14)(3)(3+1)}[(17)^2 + (36)^2 + (31)^2] - (3)(14)(3+1)$$

$$= \frac{12}{168}(289 + 1296 + 961) - 168$$

$$= .071(2546) - 168 = 180.766 - 168$$

$$= 12.766.$$

Since our N is greater than 9, in this case 14, we enter Table A.4 of Appendix A with $k - 1$ degrees of freedom, or $3 - 1 = 2df$, and we find that at the .01 level of significance we must have a χ_r^2 equal to or greater than 9.210 in order to reject the null hypothesis. Since our observed χ_r^2 exceeds this value, we reject the null hypothesis and conclude that there is a difference in identification with the company between the three conditions of participation in decision making. In this case, examination of the data reveals that the more participation in decision making, the greater the identification with the company.

Assumptions for the Friedman Two-Way Analysis-of-Variance Test The primary assumptions underlying the Friedman two-way analysis-of-variance test are that the data are of ordinal level and that the samples are related to one another in some meaningful way. Either each subject should act as his own control under several experimental conditions, or the researcher must match individuals carefully under different treatment conditions. If samples were *not* related to one another in some way, the investigator would find it difficult to determine whether the differences in scores under k treatment conditions were due to differences of the treatment conditions, or to differences between individuals. Where subjects act as their own controls, the effects of the experimental conditions can more legitimately be determined.

Advantages and Disadvantages of the Friedman Two-Way Analysis-of-Variance Test The Friedman test is easy to apply to rank-order data. Tables are provided which make it easy to interpret any given χ_r^2 value. The test does not require the stringent assumptions associated with the parametric analysis-of-variance test. It does not require that homogeneity of variance exist, nor does it require normality.

Compared with the parametric analysis-of-variance test, the Friedman test tends to render similar decisions pertaining to the rejection of null hypotheses for any given significance level.

The investigator must show either that subjects act as their own controls or that the individuals comprising the samples have been carefully matched according to a number of pertinent traits. Matching is very difficult, particularly where a large number of traits is used as a basis for matching. Matching, therefore, may be a disadvantage where subjects do not act as their own controls. Other than that difficulty, the Friedman test poses no significant problems for application to ordinal information to test for significant differences between k related samples.

TESTS FOR *k* SAMPLES: INDEPENDENT SAMPLES

Kruskal-Wallis One-Way Analysis-of-Variance Test

When the investigator is interested in determining whether or not k independent samples could have come from the same population with respect to some ordinal-level characteristic, he may use the Kruskal-Wallis one-way analysis-of-variance test. This is essentially a test for the significance of difference between k samples ranked according to some ordinal characteristic.

Suppose we conduct a hypothetical study of occupation and mass-media preference. We identify three general occupational categories: lawyers, professors, and engineers, and we are interested in determining whether there are differences among them according to a scale of cultural discrimination. For our study, cultural discrimination is associated with relative appeal of mass media. Through interviews, we obtain information from members of each general occupational classification pertaining to television programs viewed, papers and magazines read, and cultural events preferred. Through data analysis we are able to give each person a cultural-discrimination score. From these scores we are able to say that one person is more culturally discriminating than another.

We obtain three samples. One sample consists of lawyers, another of professors, and a third of engineers. In Table 9.14 are the cultural-discrimination scores of these individuals. Is there reason to believe that the cultural-discrimination scores of one sample are significantly different from those of the other two samples?

We shall make the test of the following null hypothesis:

H_0: There is no difference between the three occupational groups with respect to cultural discrimination.

H_1: The three occupational groups differ with respect to cultural discrimination.

$$P \leqslant .01.$$

Table 9.14. Cultural-Discrimination Scores for Three Groups.

Group A		*Group B*		*Group C*	
Lawyers	*Ranks*	*Professors*	*Ranks*	*Engineers*	*Ranks*
92	4	81	10	82	9
95	3	90	5	80	11
84	7	85	6	65	13
98	1	83	8	70	12
97	2				
$N_1 = 5$	$\Sigma R_1 = 17$	$N_2 = 4$	$\Sigma R_2 = 29$	$N_3 = 4$	$\Sigma R_3 = 45$

To test this hypothesis, we must first rank each of the individuals *across samples* in the above table. We assign the largest score the rank of 1, the next largest score the rank of 2, and so on. We rank the scores without paying any attention to which group the score lies in. Finally, we apply the following formula:

$$H = \frac{12}{N(N+1)}\left(\frac{\Sigma R_i^2}{N_i}\right) - [3(N+1)]$$

where N = the total number of people in k samples;
N_i = the number of people in ith sample; and
ΣR_i = the sum of ranks for the ith sample.

Carrying out this procedure for the data above, we have:

$$H = \frac{12}{13(13+1)}\left[\frac{(17)^2}{5} + \frac{(29)^2}{4} + \frac{(45)^2}{4}\right] - (3)(13+1)$$

$$= \frac{12}{182}\left(\frac{289}{5} + \frac{841}{4} + \frac{2025}{4}\right) - 42$$

$$= .066(57.8 + 210.25 + 506.25) - 42 = 51.10 - 42$$

$$= 9.1.$$

In order to interpret the significance of H, we turn to Table A.18 of Appendix A. It will be noted that this table is exclusively designed for three samples where no sample size is greater than 5. Since our sample meets these criteria, we may enter the table, in this case, with sample sizes 5, 4, and 4. Locating this particular combination of sample sizes in the left-hand column of the table, we compare our observed H with various values of H in the column adjacent to the sample sizes. If our observed H is equal to or larger than the H in the table, then the samples differ at the level of significance shown in the far right-hand column of the table. Exact probabilities are provided here.

For our example, we see that our observed H of 9.1 exceeds the largest H given for this particular combination of sample sizes, or 7.7604. Since the exact probability of .009 is beyond the .01 level of significance, we reject the null hypothesis and conclude that there is a significant difference between the three samples with respect to cultural discrimination.

Large Samples When large samples exist, in this case when there are more than 5 elements in any given sample, the chi-square distribution is approximated by H, and the chi-square table may be entered with $k-1$ degrees of freedom, where k = the number of samples. The H value is treated as a χ^2 value for interpretive purposes in the table. Table A.4 is used in this case instead of Table A.18.

To illustrate the use of the Kruskal-Wallis H test for large samples, consider the following example. Suppose we have three occupational categories: self-employed, salaried employees, and wage workers. We are interested in determining whether there are any differences pertaining to dependency needs among members of each of these occupational groups. We draw three random samples of individuals from the three occupational categories and we measure their dependency needs according to some ordinal scale. Their scores are portrayed in Table 9.15.

Table 9.15. Dependency Needs for Self-Employed, Salaried Employees, and Wage Workers.

Self-Employed	*Rank 1*	*Salaried Employees*	*Rank 2*	*Wage Workers*	*Rank 3*
32	6	21	17	15	19
26	13.5	27	11.5	20	18
35	3	30	8	28	10
31	7	33	5	26	13.5
37	2	29	9	22	16
39	1	34	4	27	11.5
		25	15		
$N_1 = 6$	$\Sigma R_1 = 32.5$	$N_2 = 7$	$\Sigma R_2 = 69.5$	$N_3 = 6$	$\Sigma R_3 = 88.0$

We are interested in testing the following null hypothesis:

H_0: There is no difference between three occupational groups with respect to dependency needs.

H_1: Three occupational groups will exhibit different dependency needs.

$$P \leqslant .05.$$

To test this hypothesis, we apply the H formula:

$$H = \frac{12}{19(19+1)}\left[\frac{(32.5)^2}{6} + \frac{(69.5)^2}{7} + \frac{(88.0)^2}{6}\right] - (3)(19+1)$$

$$= \frac{12}{380}(176.04 + 690.03 + 1290.67) - 60$$

$$= .032(2156.74) - 60 = 69.016 - 60$$

$$= 9.016.$$

Since our sample sizes exceed 5, we enter Table A.4 of Appendix A with $k - 1$ degrees of freedom, or $3 - 1 = 2df$, and we find that we must have an H value equal to or greater than 5.991 in order for the samples to be different from one another at the .05 level of significance. Since our observed H is 9.016, we conclude that there is a significant difference between the samples with respect to dependency needs, and we reject the null hypothesis at the .05 level.

Assumptions for the Kruskal-Wallis* H *Test The primary assumptions underlying the Kruskal-Wallis H test are that the investigator must have ordinal-level data at his disposal, that the variable to be ranked can be assumed to be continuous rather than discrete, and that the k samples are independent.

Advantages and Disadvantages of the Kruskal-Wallis* H *Test The Kruskal-Wallis H test is quite useful when the researcher has ordinal-level data and wishes to avoid the assumptions of homogeneity of variance and normality associated with the parametric analysis-of-variance test. Scores on some ordinal-level characteristic are ranked within k samples, and the Kruskal-Wallis test determines whether or not there are differences between k samples with respect to the ranks between these samples.

No significant modification of the formula for H needs to be made for the analysis of differences between large and small samples. Tables are available for interpreting the significance of H where samples are small as well as where they are large. The test is easy to apply and requires a minimum of mathematical skill. It is appropriate for unequal as well as for equal sample sizes.

One "disadvantage" of H when compared to equivalent parametric procedures is that it does not utilize as much information. It uses ranks rather than differences between scores. But for ordinal-level data, this can hardly be called a disadvantage.

When an H is significant, this fact merely means that a difference exists *somewhere* between k samples with respect to some measured characteristic. Like the parametric F test for analysis of variance, H does not indicate *where* the difference lies. It is obvious that the difference between the largest and smallest average ranks is significant, but in order to identify further differences between other of the samples, the investigator is obligated to select some two-sample test of significance of difference such as the Mann-Whitney U test. He would then have to compare samples, two by two. Such a procedure is comparable to using the t test to identify differences between means when an over-all F test reveals significant differences between k sample means in an analysis of variance. Again, caution is mandatory when such comparisons are made. There is no Newman-Keuls procedure for ordinal-level data, and so the researcher must use a longer method of determining the significance of difference between two samples at a time.

SUMMARY

In this chapter we have examined several ordinal-level tests of significance. The Kolmogorov-Smirnov one-sample test is appropriate for small samples where the investigator wishes to determine whether his distribution of observations differs significantly from some theorized distribution. Where two samples exist, an extension of the Kolmogorov-Smirnov test may be used to tell whether or not two independent samples have been drawn from the same population distribution.

For the two-sample case where samples are presumed related to each other in some meaningful way, the sign test or the Wilcoxon matched-pairs-signed-ranks test may be used. The sign test is quite simple to apply when the investigator wishes merely to identify gross differences between samples with respect to score changes. For more refined differentiation between two related samples, the Wilcoxon matched-pairs-signed-ranks test takes into account the magnitude of the difference between scores and should be used.

The Wald-Wolfowitz runs test, the Kolmogorov-Smirnov test for two independent samples, and the Mann-Whitney U test may be applied when two independent samples have been differentiated according to some measured ordinal-level characteristic and the investigator wishes to determine whether these samples differ from each other significantly. The Kolmogorov-Smirnov test is more appropriate when the sample size is small; but the Mann-Whitney U test is preferred when sample size is large.

Finally, two tests for k related and k independent samples were presented. The Friedman two-way analysis-of-variance test is useful for identifying differences between k related samples, particularly where individuals act as their own control through a series of experimental conditions, although careful matching by the investigator will have a similar result.

The Kruskal-Wallis one-way analysis-of-variance test should be used when samples are independent of one another and sampling is random. Both tests are good for detecting differences between k treatment conditions, and both are relatively unrestricted as far as N is concerned.

QUESTIONS FOR REVIEW AND PROBLEMS TO SOLVE

1. What are some primary assumptions underlying the Friedman two-way analysis-of-variance test? What are some advantages and disadvantages associated with it?

2. Test the null hypothesis that on the school board described here there are no differences among the members as far as social class is concerned. Use the .05 level of significance and the Kolmogorov-Smirnov one-sample test.

Social Class	*Frequency*
Lower-lower	3
Upper-lower	0
Lower-middle	2
Upper-middle	8
Lower-upper	8
Upper-upper	3

3. Using the sign test, determine whether or not there is a significant difference between scores of individuals on decision-making power before and after a change in plant supervision. $P \leqslant .05$.

Individual	*Decision-Making Score*	
	Before	*After*
1	10	12
2	9	11
3	9	8
4	12	15
5	8	13
6	7	7
7	13	12
8	15	16
9	12	14

(a) Carry out the Wilcoxon matched-pairs-signed-ranks test for the same data. Are there any differences between the two groups at the .05 level of significance?

4. Compare the Wald-Wolfowitz runs test with the Mann-Whitney U test in terms of their respective advantages and disadvantages. Think of five situations where each technique might be applied satisfactorily.

5. What does it mean for samples to be related? Give an example different from those used in this chapter.

6. Two groups of people take the Graduate Record Examination. Each group represents graduate students of two different universities. Using the runs test, determine whether the groups differ at the .10 level of significance. (Data at top of next page.)

7. Carry out the Mann-Whitney U test for the data in Problem 6 above, and determine whether there are any differences in your conclusions. What are some things which may be said concerning the two groups of graduate students? (Data at top of next page.)

8. Some social psychologists were experimenting with small groups. They selected four individuals matched according to certain salient characteristics, and exposed them to five different group climates. They took measures of frustration for these individuals under each treatment condi-

Scores on Graduate Record Examination

Group 1	*Group 2*
88	78
72	75
42	65
69	91
88	79
80	92
74	93
65	81
59	83
80	68
72	94
20	
75	

tion. Is there a significant difference with respect to frustration level between the individuals under the five treatment conditions below? Use the Friedman two-way analysis-of-variance test, $P \leqslant .05$, to determine the significance of these differences, if any.

Individual	*Treatment 1*	*Treatment 2*	*Treatment 3*	*Treatment 4*	*Treatment 5*
1	14	12	9	13	11
2	15	16	6	10	11
3	9	15	4	11	12
4	11	16	7	12	11

9. Compare the Friedman two-way analysis-of-variance test with the Kruskal-Wallis *H* test. What are some primary functions of each of the statistical tests? What are their similarities and differences?

10. Using the Kolmogorov-Smirnov two-sample test, determine whether Samples A and B could have come from the same distribution at the .05 level of significance:

Scores	*Sample A*	*Sample B*
50–54	3	2
45–49	0	5
40–44	0	6
35–39	2	9
30–34	8	1
25–29	0	9
20–24	3	2
15–19	7	4

10 Measures of Association

In research work it is frequently necessary to measure the extent to which two or more variables are "related" to one another—how much association exists between them. For example, we may wish to know the extent to which age is related to the frequency of delinquent acts, or how closely social status is associated with the number of admissions to mental hospitals, or the like. Several techniques have been devised to provide us with numerical representations of such relationships. These techniques are often called *measures of association.*

The numerical values rendered by such statistical techniques are called *association coefficients,* and generally they can range in value from −1.00 to +1.00. The coefficient of association −1.00 means that there is a perfect *inverse* relation between the two variables. For example, suppose that in a given city, as the number of policemen assigned to patrol a particular neighborhood *increases,* the number of crimes committed in that area *decreases.* This relationship is called "negative" or "inverse" because one variable increases while the other decreases. All negative or inverse relationships are identified by a minus sign (−) preceding the coefficient of association. No association is indicated by a 0 or .00.

When an association coefficient is positive, this sign means that there is a direct relation between two variables. For example, as the number of years a person attends school *increases,* the number of job opportunities for that person *increases* as well. Perfect associations between variables are indicated by either +1.00 (positive or direct) or −1.00 (negative or inverse). In social research, however, perfect associations between variables occur very infrequently. Social investigators find coefficients ranging between +1.00 and −1.00 such as .42, −.86, −.12, or .98. Determining the strength of association or interpreting the magnitude of it will depend upon such things as the size of the sample and the type of statistical technique used.

Association coefficients simply indicate the degree to which two variables are associated with each other. By themselves they do not imply that there is a causal relation between the two variables. The terms "relationship," "association," and "correlation" do not always imply that the occurrence of one variable means that the other variable will occur. For example, suppose that each time the price of tea rises in India, the pineapple-crop yield in Hawaii increases as well. It is unlikely that any direct causal relation exists between these two variables. It cannot necessarily be said that one is causing the other to occur.

The investigator will sometimes want to determine the existence of a cause-effect association between variables. He is only able to do this, conservatively, by adequately demonstrating *logically and theoretically* that such a relation can be predicted. He uses the numerical value or coefficient of association to back up his theoretical argument, and to help verify or reject hypotheses generated by his theory.

In a given sample, the observation of an association coefficient of .95 between two variables may be due to chance or to a variety of other conditions. If the investigator were to construct a *matrix of intercorrelations,* a table showing the coefficient values of all possible relationships between the variables in his study, a certain number of the larger values would be due to chance. Associating each variable in any study would give us $N(N-1)/2$ possible coefficients of association. If there were 20 variables, he might possibly wind up with $(20)(20-1)/2 = 190$ coefficients of association. Some of these coefficients would be relatively large simply because of chance.

The important thing to remember is that the coefficient of association means very little by itself. It must be viewed within an appropriate theoretical framework. A good foundation in research methodology and theory construction is essential to anyone conducting scientific investigations.

In this chapter, several coefficients of association will be examined. One of the primary assumptions which we must meet before selecting any coefficient formula involves the *level-of-measurement* characteristic of our observations. Measures of association appropriate for interval-, nominal-, and ordinal-level data will now be presented.

INTERVAL-LEVEL MEASURE OF ASSOCIATION

The Pearson *r*

The Pearson *r* or *product-moment correlation coefficient* is the best-known parametric measure of association. In addition to having interval-level data, the researcher must meet several other assumptions before he can correctly interpret *r*. These assumptions will be discussed after a presentation of the computational procedure for *r*.

Suppose an investigator wants to determine the extent to which a relationship exists between size of income and the number of years of education the individual has completed. Table 10.1 shows the incomes of 10 individuals (expressed in hundreds of dollars) along with their respective years of education. To facilitate the computation of *r*, these columns have been labeled *X* and *Y* respectively, standing for *income* and *education.* A third and a fourth column have been labeled X^2 and Y^2. These columns simply contain the squares of each value in columns *X* and *Y*. The last

Table 10.1. The Association between Income and Education.

Individual	*Income (\$100's)* X	*Education (Years)* Y	X^2	Y^2	XY
1	45	20	2,025	400	900
2	63	19	3,969	361	1,197
3	36	16	1,296	256	576
4	52	20	2,704	400	1,040
5	29	12	841	144	348
6	33	14	1,089	196	462
7	48	16	2,304	256	768
8	55	18	3,025	324	990
9	72	20	5,184	400	1,440
10	66	22	4,356	484	1,452
$N = 10$	$\Sigma X = 499$	$\Sigma Y = 177$	$\Sigma X^2 = 26{,}793$	$\Sigma Y^2 = 3{,}221$	$\Sigma XY = 9{,}173$

column contains the product of each X by its respective Y value.

The following formula is used to compute Pearson r for such data:

$$r = \frac{N\Sigma XY - (\Sigma X)(\Sigma Y)}{\sqrt{[N\Sigma X^2 - (\Sigma X)^2][N\Sigma Y^2 - (\Sigma Y)^2]}}$$

Substituting the values in Table 10.1 for symbols in the formula, we have

$$r = \frac{(10)(9{,}173) - (499)(177)}{\sqrt{[(10)(26{,}793) - (499)^2][(10)(3{,}221) - (177)^2]}}$$

$$= \frac{91{,}730 - 88{,}323}{\sqrt{(267{,}930 - 249{,}001)(32{,}210 - 31{,}329)}}$$

$$= \frac{3{,}407}{\sqrt{(18{,}929)(881)}} = 3{,}407/4{,}083.68$$

$$= .83.$$

The interpretation here would be that there is a high association between one's income and years of education.

The Pearson* r *Computation for Grouped Data When we have data in grouped form, we employ a variation of the r formula to obtain the coefficient of association between two variables. In Table 10.2, a *scatter diagram* is shown. This scatter diagram contains two frequency distributions. Let us assume that each of the frequency distributions represents the scores of 49 individuals on two college-entrance examinations. Actually, the scores may be representative of any pair of interval-level variables.

Examine Table 10.2 in order to see how we have arranged the two frequency distributions. *You will note that the intervals for one frequency*

Table 10.2. A Scatter Diagram Showing Frequency Distributions of College-Entrance-Examination Scores for 49 Students.

Variable Y: Scores on Entrance Examination II	*Variable X: Scores on Entrance Examination I*																		
	20–21	*22–23*	*24–25*	*26–27*	*28–29*	*30–31*	*32–33*	*34–35*	*36–37*	*38–39*	*40–41*	*42–43*	*44–45*	*46–47*	f_y	y'	$f_y y'$	$f_y y'^2$	$x'y'$
105–109														//	2	12	24	288	312
100–104													/		1	11	11	121	132
95–99									/	///	/	/			6	10	60	600	560
90–94			/			/	/		/	/					5	9	45	405	270
85–89						/	//	/							4	8	32	256	192
80–84				/			/	//							4	7	28	196	161
75–79						/	/	/	//						5	6	30	180	204
70–74			/		//		//		/						6	5	30	150	150
65–69			//	/				//							5	4	20	80	84
60–64					//		/								3	3	9	27	42
55–59			//					/		/					4	2	8	16	40
50–54		//		/											3	1	3	3	5
45–49	/														1	0	0	0	0
															$\Sigma f_y = 49$		$\Sigma f_y y' = 300$	$\Sigma f_y y'^2 = 2{,}322$	$\Sigma x'y' = 2{,}152$
f_x	1	2	6	3	4	3	8	7	5	5	1	1	1	2	$\Sigma f_x = 49$				
x'	0	1	2	3	4	5	6	7	8	9	10	11	12	13					
$f_x x'$	0	2	12	9	16	15	48	49	40	45	10	11	12	26	$\Sigma f_x x' = 295$				
$f_x x'^2$	0	2	24	27	64	75	288	343	320	405	100	121	144	338	$\Sigma f_x x'^2 = 2{,}251$				

distribution do not have to be of the same size as the intervals for the other, nor does there necessarily have to be the same number of intervals in the two distributions.

In the body of the table the individual's scores are cross tabulated. For example, in the upper right-hand corner of the table are two tallies representing individuals who received scores on one examination which lie within the interval, 105–109, and who received scores on the other examination which lie within the interval, 46–47. When all tallies have been entered in the body of the table, the tallies are summed for each column and row and placed in respective positions to the right (for row totals) and below (for column totals). These tallies are found in the column marked f_y, for variable Y, and in the row marked f_x for variable X.

Next, we begin with the interval in each distribution containing the smallest scores, and we number these intervals consecutively 0, 1, 2, 3, and so on, until the interval containing the largest scores is reached. This has been done for both variables, and these numbers have been entered in the column marked y' and in the row marked x'.

The next step involves multiplying each y' by its respective f_y for variable Y, and multiplying each x' by its respective f_x for variable X. The products of f_y and y' and f_x and x' are entered in the next column and row as in Table 10.2. These columns and rows are marked $f_y y'$ and $f_x x'$.

Now we must multiply each $f_y y'$ by y' and each $f_x x'$ by x'. These products are placed in respective positions in the columns labeled $f_u y'^2$ and $f_x x'^2$, as shown in the table. Finally, we must multiply each x' by its corresponding y'. *This involves a calculation for each tally in the table.* The procedure is as follows:

For convenience and to be systematic, we shall begin in the upper right-hand corner of the table with the two tallies cross tabulated for intervals 105–109 and 46–47. We notice that these tallies are also in a particular x' row and a particular y' column. We must multiply the x' value by its corresponding y' value *for each tally.* Since each tally lies where $x' = 13$ and $y' = 12$ intersect, we multiply $(13)(12) = 156$. Because there are two tallies in this space, we repeat this process, $(13)(12) = 156$, and we sum these two products, $156 + 156 = 312$. Since there are no other tallies in this first row, we enter 312 in the column $x'y'$, as is shown. For the next row, there is only one tally. It lies where $x' = 12$ and $y' = 11$ intersect.

Multiplying these values, we have $(12)(11) = 132$. We enter 132 in the appropriate place in column $x'y'$ as is shown.

For the next row, there are six tallies. Carrying out these computations, we have $(8)(10) + (9)(10) + (9)(10) + (9)(10) + (10)(10) + (11)(10) = 80 + 90 + 90 + 90 + 100 + 110 = 560$. We enter 560 in its appropriate place in column $x'y'$. We carry out these computations for all rows of tallies and sum all $x'y'$ products; the sum of $x'y' = 2{,}152$, as is shown in Table 10.2.

For these data, Pearson r is computed by using the following formula:

$$r = \frac{\Sigma x'y' - [(\Sigma f_x x')(\Sigma f_y y')/N]}{\sqrt{\Sigma f_x x'^2 - [(\Sigma f_x x')^2/N]\Sigma f_y y'^2 - [(\Sigma f_y y')^2/N]}}.$$

Computing r, we have

$$\begin{aligned} r &= \frac{2{,}152 - (295)(300)/49}{\sqrt{(2{,}251) - [(295)^2/49](2{,}322) - [(300)^2/49]}} \\ &= \frac{2{,}152 - 1{,}806.1}{\sqrt{(2{,}251 - 1{,}776)(2{,}322 - 1{,}836.7)}} \\ &= \frac{345.9}{\sqrt{(475)(485.3)}} = \frac{345.9}{\sqrt{230{,}517.5}} = 345.9/480.1 \\ &= .72. \end{aligned}$$

With an $r = .72$, there is a high association between student performance on the two college-entrance examinations.

***The Significance of a Pearson* r** How do we know that, for any given sample, the Pearson r which we compute is *significant,* or not due to chance? When $N < 50$ as is the case in our example above, we may compute t, defined as

$$t = \frac{r}{\sqrt{1 - r^2}}\sqrt{N - 2}.$$

We can then enter the table for the t distribution, Table A.5 of Appendix A, and determine the significance of r for several different levels of significance. For the first example above (income-education) we may test the following hypothesis:

$$H_0: \qquad r \leqslant 0$$

$$H_1: \qquad r > 0$$

$$P \leqslant .05 \text{ (one-tailed test).}$$

To test this hypothesis, we use the t formula above with $r = .83$ and $N = 10$:

$$\begin{aligned} t &= \frac{.83}{\sqrt{1 - (.83)^2}}\sqrt{10 - 2} \\ &= \frac{.83}{\sqrt{1 - .6889}}(2.83) \\ &= \frac{.83}{\sqrt{.3111}}(2.83) = \frac{.83}{.56}(2.83) = (1.48)(2.83) \\ &= 4.19. \end{aligned}$$

With our observed t of 4.19, we enter Table A.5 of Appendix A with $N - 2$ or $10 - 2$ or 8 degrees of freedom in this case. We find that we must have an observed t equal to or larger than 1.860 in order for our r to be significantly different from zero at the .05 level, using a one-tailed test. Since our observed t exceeds 1.860, being 4.19, we can reject the null hypothesis and conclude that $r = .83$ is significantly greater than zero at the .05 level.

Let us use another example to illustrate this process further. Suppose we have the following hypothetical information: $r = .36$; $N = 38$. Is this r significantly different from zero at the .01 level? Our hypothesis which we shall test becomes:

$$H_0: \quad r \leqslant 0$$
$$H_1: \quad r > 0$$
$$P \leqslant .01 \text{ (one-tailed test).}$$

Using the t formula, we have:

$$\begin{aligned} t &= \frac{.36}{\sqrt{1-(.36)^2}}(\sqrt{38-2}) \\ &= \frac{.36}{\sqrt{1-.1296}}(6) = \frac{.36}{\sqrt{.8704}}(6) = \frac{.36}{.93}(6) \\ &= 2.16/.93 \\ &= 2.32. \end{aligned}$$

To interpret this t, we must enter Table A.5 with $N - 2$ or $38 - 2$ or 36 degrees of freedom at the .01 level of significance, using a one-tailed test. Since there are no degrees of freedom provided exactly for 36, we must interpolate. The t values we must have for the .01 level of significance (one-tailed test) for 30 and 40 are 2.457 and 2.423, respectively. For 36 degrees of freedom, we need an observed t equal to or larger than 2.437 in order to reject H_0 at the .01 level of significance. Since our observed t is less than this value, we fail to reject the null hypothesis and conclude that our observed r is not significantly different from zero at the .01 level.

When $N > 50$, a Z may be computed and interpreted directly from the normal-curve table, Table A.3 of Appendix A. In this case, the observed r is divided by the standard error of r, s_r, using the formula

$$s_r = \frac{1}{\sqrt{N-1}}.$$

To illustrate, suppose we have an $N = 101$, $r = .70$. Our null hypothesis which we shall test is

$$H_0: \quad r \leqslant 0$$
$$H_1: \quad r > 0$$
$$P \leqslant .001 \text{ (one-tailed test).}$$

We test this hypothesis with a Z test as follows:

$$Z = \frac{.70}{1/\sqrt{101-1}} = \frac{.70}{1/10} = .70/.10$$
$$= 7.00.$$

Turning to Table A.3 of Appendix A, we find that we are able to reject the null hypothesis at the .001 level and conclude that $r = .70$ is significantly greater than zero.

***Assumptions for the Pearson* r** For r to be meaningfully interpreted, the investigator must demonstrate that his data meet certain assumptions. First, he must demonstrate that his data are at least of the interval level of measurement. Another important assumption is that the association between the two variables is *linear.* Linearity exists when the intersectional points between the two variables lie roughly in a straight line. To understand this assumption more clearly, consider the graph of the data in Table 10.1 as illustrated in Figure 10.1. This graph, which is sometimes called a scatter plot, is nothing more than a diagram showing the intersection points of scores on each variable. The horizontal axis usually stands for the independent variable, while the vertical axis con-

Figure 10.1. A Graph of Income and Education.

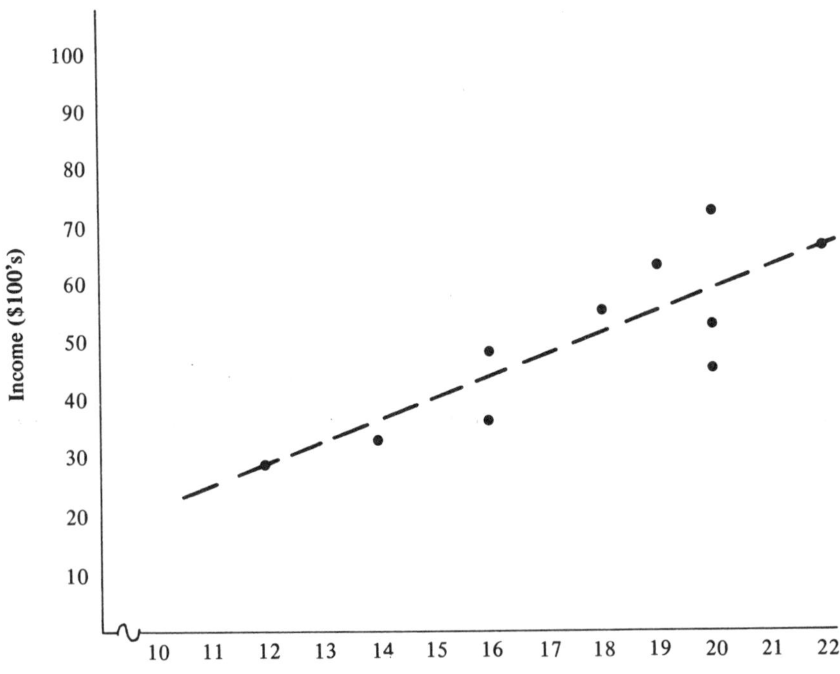

ventionally stands for the dependent variable. In this case, the horizontal axis represents years of education and the vertical axis represents income. In Figure 10.1, the intersection points roughly lie in a straight line. Linearity may be assumed.

Linearity may frequently be observed visually, but when the association between the two variables is weak, it becomes increasingly difficult to see linearity. Under these conditions, linearity may be tested for. The test for linearity involves computations beyond the scope of this text. A good discussion of the test for linearity may be found in Dixon and Massey (1957), pp. 197–198, and in Walker and Lev (1953), pp. 245–246.

When associations between variables are not directly linear, *curvilinearity* may exist. To illustrate a curvilinear relation between two variables, consider the scatter plot in Figure 10.2. When the relation between two variables is curvilinear or has no linear quality, the computed r cannot be interpreted accurately. Other measures of association are recommended such as *eta* (η), the correlation ratio. A good discussion of eta is found in Blalock (1960), pp. 311–317.

Advantages and Disadvantages of **r** When the assumptions underlying its use are met, the Pearson r is perhaps the best coefficient of association to use. Most statisticians and researchers are familiar with r, and for this reason, more has been done to develop its interpretation than has been done for other measures of association.

It can be seen from the discussion above that r is generally interpreted

Figure 10.2. A Curvilinear Relation between Variables.

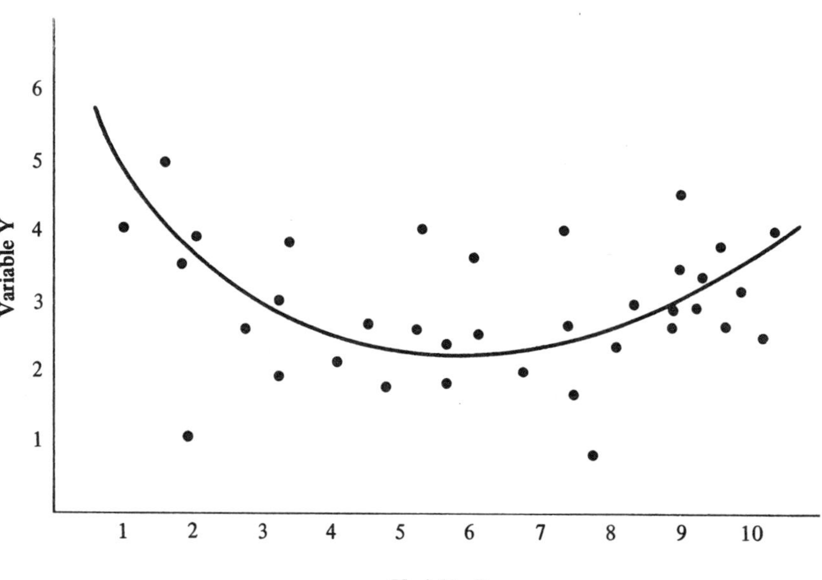

as the degree of relation between two variables. Other interpretations have been suggested, however, which seem to fit better with respect to predicting one variable from another. One interpretation has to do with the *amount of error* involved in predicting one variable from another. If we examine Figure 10.1, we will note that a straight line has been drawn to roughly approximate the successive intersection points of income and education. It appears that linearity exists between the two variables. But we also note that several of the intersection points *do not* lie directly on the straight line which we have drawn. There is a certain amount of deviation of the intersection points from the line. In trying to predict income from years of education, a high association between the variables exists, but we have not found a perfect relation of 1.00 between them. The degree of association was .83. Under these conditions, we say that there was a certain amount of error involved in our prediction of one variable from the other. "Error" or variation from what was predicted between the two variables is measured by $1 - r^2$. In the first example above, with an $r = .83$, the proportion of the variance in income not predictable from the relation between income and education is $1 - (.83)^2 = 1 - .69 = .31$. Another way of saying this is that 31 percent of the variation in income is unexplained by the relation between income and education. *Unexplained variation is measured by* $1 - r^2$.

Another way of interpreting the relation between the two variables is in terms of the *proportional reduction in error* made possible by using one of the variables as a predictor variable. The variable acting as the predictor variable in the example cited above was education. The variable to be predicted was income. If we square r, then r^2 becomes a measure of the proportional reduction in error which we may attribute to the relation between the two variables, income and education. Thus r^2 becomes $(.83)^2$ or .69. We can now say that 69 percent of the variation in income has been accounted for by using education as the independent or predictor variable.

This possible interpretation is an important advantage of r. It will be seen that for a number of measures of association to follow, the same interpretation of proportional reduction in error may be made. Some of the measures of association to be discussed are not amenable to such an interpretation. Costner (1965) suggests that by adopting a proportional-reduction-in-error interpretation of measures of association, we can focus upon a more explicit guide for choosing among alternative measures and we will be able to interpret measures within a more general framework.

The primary disadvantages of r inhere in the stringent assumptions which underlie it. We have discussed briefly two important assumptions: interval-level measurement and linearity of the relation between the two variables. There are other assumptions which must be met for special applications of r. The tests for these assumptions are quite complex when the investigator uses them. Often, however, the Pearson r is computed without examining or meeting the assumptions. The practice of indiscriminately applying r can result in misleading information, and should be avoided. If the investigator is in doubt as to whether his data meet the assumptions underlying Pearson r, he may elect to use a measure of association which has less stringent assumptions. This caution is certainly justified, and in the long run probably more accurate.

***The Significance of Difference between Two* r's** Suppose we have computed two r's and we wish to know whether they differ from one another at some level of significance. In order to determine whether there is a significant difference between the two r's, Fisher devised a statistical method whereby r's are transformed into Z_F's and a Z test is performed. This is called Fisher's Z_F transformation.

Suppose we have the following information relating to age and education in two different populations: $N_1 = 67$, $N_2 = 52$, $r_1 = .66$, $r_2 = .73$. We hypothesize:

$$H_0\colon r_1 = r_2$$
$$H_1\colon r_1 \neq r_2$$
$$P \leqslant .05 \text{ (one-tailed test).}$$

To carry out the test of this hypothesis, we must convert each r to a Z_F. Turning to the Table of Values of Z_F for Given Values of r, Table A.6 of Appendix A, we find:

	r	Z_F
$r_1 =$	$.66 =$	$.793$
$r_2 =$	$.73 =$	$.929$

The left-hand column of the table contains values of r ranging from .000 to .990. We simply find our respective r_1 and r_2 in the left-hand column and then find the corresponding Z_F value in the body of the table to the right. We must then divide the difference between the two Z_F's by the standard error of the difference between the Z_F's, or s_{DZ}, where

$$s_{DZ} = \sqrt{\left(\frac{1}{\sqrt{N_1 - 3}}\right)^2 + \left(\frac{1}{\sqrt{N_2 - 3}}\right)^2}.$$

With our information above, we compute s_{DZ}:

$$\begin{aligned} s_{DZ} &= \sqrt{\left(\frac{1}{\sqrt{67 - 3}}\right)^2 + \left(\frac{1}{\sqrt{52 - 3}}\right)^2} \\ &= \sqrt{(1/8)^2 + (1/7)^2} = \sqrt{.015625 + .020408} = \sqrt{.036033} \\ &= .19. \end{aligned}$$

Making the Z test of significance between the two Z_F's, we have:

$$Z = \frac{Z_{F_1} - Z_{F_2}}{s_{DZ}} = \frac{.929 - .793}{.19} = .136/.19$$

$$= .71.$$

Since a Z of 1.96 (see Table A.3 of Appendix A) would ordinarily be required in order for the difference between r's to be significant at the .05 level using a two-tailed test, we conclude that there is no significant difference between r_1 and r_2.

NOMINAL-LEVEL MEASURES OF ASSOCIATION

Coefficient of Contingency

The coefficient of contingency, C, is a measure of the degree of association which exists between variables for which we only have categorical information. C is used in close conjunction with the chi-square statistic, χ^2. As previously defined, the chi-square statistic tells us whether or not our observations differ from what would ordinarily be expected by chance. If the resulting χ^2 is significant, we may want to compute C to determine the magnitude of association which exists between the two variables. In other words, C is an index of the degree of association between two nominal-level variables.

One of the most simple forms in which data appear is the 2×2 table. Such tables have been discussed previously with reference to the chi-square statistic. Table 10.3 portrays the relationship between education and social status. The χ^2 for these data is 57.26, which is significant at $\leq .01$. Confident that these data are significantly different from chance,

Table 10.3. A 2×2 Table Showing Relationship between Education and Social Status.

		Social Status		
		High	*Low*	
Education	*High*	50	10	60
	Low	15	65	80
		65	75	140

we will now want to determine the magnitude of the relation that exists between a person's education and his social status. Up to now, we know only that the data are different from what would be expected by chance. We still do not know *how strongly the variables are related.*

The following formula is used to find C:

$$C = \sqrt{\frac{\chi^2}{N + \chi^2}}.$$

With an $N = 140$ and a $\chi^2 = 57.26$, we may compute C directly.

$$C = \sqrt{\frac{57.26}{140 + 57.26}} = \sqrt{.2902}$$
$$= .54.$$

There is a weakness of this coefficient of association, however, for it can be shown that no matter *how far* one's observations depart from what would be expected by chance, the highest value that C may achieve is always less than 1.00. The more rows and columns a table has, the closer C approaches 1.00. The fewer rows and columns associated with any given table, the less closely C approaches 1.00.

For tables which have the same number of rows and columns (that is, 2×2, 3×3, 4×4, and so on), it can be demonstrated that the highest value C may achieve is:

$$\sqrt{\frac{r - 1}{r}}$$

where r = the number of rows. For example, a 5×5 table would achieve a maximum C of .894 ($\sqrt{(5 - 1)/5} = .894$ *regardless of how radically the data were distributed.*

A *correction factor* has been suggested to enable the investigator using C to make a more systematic appraisal of the strength of the association between variables. The correction factor will make C more systematic in the sense that we will be able to evaluate it in relation to 1.00. The formula for correcting the original size of C is:

$$\overline{C} = \frac{C}{\text{divisor}}$$

where $\overline{C}$ is to be read "C bar" or "C corrected," and the divisor is chosen according to the number of rows (r) and columns (c) in the table. For tables of any $r \times c$ size, where $r = c$, the formula $\sqrt{(r - 1)/r}$ may be used. When tables are found where $r \neq c$ (that is, 2×3, 3×5, 4×7, and so on), this formula cannot be used. Correction factors for tables where $r = c$ and where $r \neq c$ are provided in Table 10.4 for tabular situations up to and including size 10×10. For tables larger than 10×10, the correction factor makes little difference to the final result and is generally not necessary.

Table 10.4. Correction for Coefficient of Contingency.*

Table Size	*(Divisor) Correction*	*Table Size*	*(Divisor) Correction*	*Table Size*	*(Divisor) Correction*
2 × 2	.707	3 × 9	.843	6 × 6	.913
2 × 3	.685	3 × 10	.846	6 × 7	.930
2 × 4	.730	4 × 4	.866	6 × 8	.936
2 × 5	.752	4 × 5	.863	6 × 9	.941
2 × 6	.765	4 × 6	.877	6 × 10	.945
2 × 7	.774	4 × 7	.888	7 × 7	.926
2 × 8	.779	4 × 8	.893	7 × 8	.947
2 × 9	.783	4 × 9	.898	7 × 9	.952
2 × 10	.786	4 × 10	.901	7 × 10	.955
3 × 3	.816	5 × 5	.894	8 × 8	.935
3 × 4	.786	5 × 6	.904	8 × 9	.957
3 × 5	.810	5 × 7	.915	8 × 10	.961
3 × 6	.824	5 × 8	.920	9 × 9	.943
3 × 7	.833	5 × 9	.925	9 × 10	.966
3 × 8	.838	5 × 10	.929	10 × 10	.949

* All correction factors for tables where $r \neq c$ have been determined by a procedure described in Peters and Van Voorhis (1940, pp. 393–399) and McCormick (1941, pp. 207–208).

Correcting for C in the example shown in Table 10.3, we have

$$\overline{C} = \frac{.54}{.707} = .76.$$

We obtained .707 as our divisor (correction factor) in the present instance because the table in our example was 2 × 2. It is apparent that by correcting the original C we have increased the numerical measure of the strength of the relationship between education and social status. Within the limits of the theoretical framework, the investigator concludes that there is a strong relation between social status and education in this instance.

***Assumptions for* C** The popularity of C rests upon the fact that there are very few assumptions underlying it. This coefficient may be computed for nominal data, and nothing need be assumed concerning the shape of the distribution or the nature of the variables.

***Advantages and Disadvantages of* C** The primary advantage of this measure of association is that it may be computed for any data which can be categorized. Also, there is no limit as to the number of rows or columns of tables. For example, the columns may be divided into four gradations such as *strongly agree, agree, disagree, strongly disagree,* or any other number of gradations. As long as a χ^2 can be computed for data, a C can be computed.

The major disadvantage of C is that it really has no precise interpretation. C is simply an *index number.* Even when the correction factor is introduced as illustrated above, comparisons cannot be made directly.

C's may be compared with one another, however, providing that each has been computed from tables of identical size in terms of (a) degrees of freedom, (b) sample size, and (c) identical marginal totals. When an investigator has several tables of varying sizes, C's cannot be meaningfully compared.

Because C can be computed directly from a χ^2 value, it has been a rather popular index of association. More recently, however, other measures of association have been developed for nominal data which have certain advantages over C.

Yule's *Q*

Another frequently used measure of association between variables is Yule's Q. Q is used exclusively with tables of size 2×2; each variable must be expressed as a dichotomy. Such dichotomies may be black-white, yes-no, agree-disagree, male-female, joiner-nonjoiner, graduate-nongraduate, and so on.

Q is defined as the ratio of the differences of the products of the diagonal cell frequencies to the sum of the products of the diagonal cell frequencies. The following formula may be used for computing Q:

$$Q = \frac{(ad - bc)}{(ad + bc)}$$

where a, b, c, and d are the frequencies found in cells a, b, c, and d of a 2×2 table.

Suppose an investigator were interested in determining whether or not driving cars on campus would affect students' grade-point averages. The data in Table 10.5 show the relation between grades and driving cars for a sample of college students. Substituting values in Table 10.5 for the symbols in the formula for Q, we have

$$\begin{aligned} Q &= \frac{[(20)(20) - (40)(40)]}{[(20)(20) + (40)(40)]} \\ &= \frac{(400 - 1{,}600)}{(400 + 1{,}600)} = \frac{-1{,}200}{2{,}000} \\ &= -.60. \end{aligned}$$

The degree of association between driving cars and grade average is $-.60$, a moderately high inverse association. This statistic means that for this sample of students, those who drive cars receive lower grades. As one variable increases, the other decreases, or so it would appear. The inverse association is indicated by the negative sign (−).

***Assumptions for* Q** The Q coefficient is like C in that it is a distribution-free statistic. It makes no assumption other than that the data can be

Table 10.5. The Relation between Driving Cars and Grades.

		Drive Cars		
		Yes	*No*	
Grade-Point Average	*High*	*a* 20	*b* 40	60
	Low	*c* 40	*d* 20	60
		60	60	120

dichotomized. Such variables as sex, years of education, status, and the like can be meaningfully dichotomized.

Yule originally devised this measure of association for variables which have two and only two values. Male-female, yes-no, for-against, and the like are of this type. Status, however, can be infinitely divided. Often, even though certain things can assume more than two values (as can status, years of education, age), the investigator may want to force these variables into dichotomies. The procedure employed in constructing the dichotomies will affect the value of Q depending upon *how* the originally available categories are collapsed.

***Advantages and Disadvantages of* Q** One advantage of Q is that no correction need be made for it, as is the case with C. Also, Q may be computed directly from a 2×2 table without first having to compute chi-square. It is probably most meaningfully applied where data naturally fall into dichotomies. It does not require stringent assumptions for its application, and it is computed quickly and easily.

Another advantage of Q is that it constitutes a measure of the proportional reduction in error associated with predicting one variable from the other. The *absolute value* of Q is directly interpretable as a proportional-reduction-in-error measure. In the problem dealt with above, we were interested in learning the degree of association between driving cars and grade-point averages. In one sense, we were interested in predicting grade-point average by paying attention to the effect of an independent variable such as driving cars on campus. By taking this variable into account, we can say that 60 percent of the error in predicting grade-point average has been reduced. The coefficient of contingency, C, does not lend itself to this sort of interpretation.

In a general sense, then, Q is similar to r^2 in that both measures allow us to specify the proportionate amount of error reduced as a result of using certain predictive variables. In this sense, greater uniformity in interpretation of Q is introduced as a result of this proportional-reduction-in-error criterion.

One disadvantage of Q is that it is limited to 2×2 tables. Often, the investigator's data fit into larger tables, say of size 4 × 6. Yule's Q cannot be computed unless the data are "collapsed" into 2 × 2 tabular form. But to collapse data into fewer categories may sacrifice important information. For this reason, it is recommended that collapsing be avoided. For the researcher wishing to get a general impression of how his data are associated, Q may be used if he is willing to give up a certain amount of information. Other measures of association are available when the investigator has larger tables. One of these measures is *gamma*, γ, a coefficient of ordinal association. It can be demonstrated that Yule's Q is gamma for the 2 × 2 tabular case. Gamma, however, may be computed for tables larger than 2 × 2. This will be discussed in a later portion of this chapter.

The Phi Coefficient, ϕ

Another popular measure of association for nominal variables is called the phi coefficient, ϕ. The phi coefficient measures the degree of association between two nominal variables when each is expressed as a dichotomy. The formula for ϕ is

$$\phi = \frac{(ad - bc)}{\sqrt{(a + b)(c + d)(a + c)(b + d)}}$$

where a, b, c, and d are the cells of a 2 × 2 table.

Suppose we were interested in determining the association between interfaith marriages and family stability. We obtain a random sample of families from government records and divide them into intrafaith and interfaith marriages. Intrafaith marriages are marriages where both partners are of the same religious faith, while interfaith marriages are marriages in which the partners are of different religious faiths. Family stability is defined as whether or not the partners are separated or divorced. In Table 10.6 we have a hypothetical sample of marriages with data on interfaith and intrafaith marriages and family stability.

Table 10.6. A 2 × 2 Table Showing Association between Type of Marriage and Family Stability.

		Type of Marriage		
		Intrafaith	*Interfaith*	
Type of Family Stability	*Stable*	a 35	b 30	$65 = (a + b)$
	Unstable	c 10	d 20	$30 = (c + d)$
		$45 = (a + c)$	$50 = (b + d)$	95

Substituting formula symbols with values in the table, we may compute ϕ.

$$\phi = \frac{(35)(20) - (30)(10)}{\sqrt{(65)(30)(45)(50)}}$$

$$= \frac{700 - 300}{\sqrt{4,387,500}} = 400/2,095$$

$$= .19.$$

With a value of $\phi = .19$, we may conclude that there is a low association between family stability and interfaith marriages.

Significance of Phi The significance of the phi value may be tested for by using chi-square with 1 degree of freedom. The formula is

$$\chi^2 = N\phi^2.$$

Testing for the significance of phi, we have

$$\chi^2 = (95)(.19)^2 = 3.430.$$

If we use the .05 level of significance to test the χ^2 value, we find that we must have a χ^2 value equal to or greater than 3.841 in order to conclude that our observed ϕ is significant. Since our observed χ^2 value is smaller than 3.841, we say that no significant association between family stability and interfaith marriages exists at the .05 level. That is, our obtained ϕ of .19 can be considered as a chance departure from zero association.

Assumption for Phi The primary assumption underlying the phi statistic is that the variables under analysis should be naturally dichotomous.

Advantages and Disadvantages of Phi The phi coefficient is easy to compute. One of its advantages is that it has a proportional-reduction-in-error interpretation. In order for us to make this interpretation of phi, we must *square* it. In the example above, $\phi^2 = (.19)^2 = .04$. This .04 means that we have accounted for only 4 percent of the error in predicting family stability by using interfaith marriage as an independent or predictor variable. In this instance, interfaith marriage does not constitute a very useful variable for explaining family stability.

A disadvantage of phi is that it is limited to 2×2 tables. For applications where larger tables are involved, other measures of association are more appropriate. One of these measures is Guttman's coefficient of predictability, *lambda*, λ.

Guttman's Coefficient of Predictability, Lambda, λ

A more recent nominal measure of association is lambda, λ, the coefficient of predictability. λ measures the degree to which one variable may be accurately predicted with a knowledge of the other. Being able to predict one variable from a knowledge of the other is one way of looking at association between variables.

Suppose an investigator had information pertaining to 100 boys, 50 of whom are delinquent and 50 of whom are not delinquent. For example, he may be interested in learning the association between delinquency and a boy's motivation to read. In Table 10.7, the 100 boys are divided according to whether or not they are delinquent. The table is further divided to show whether the boys have a high motivation to read. To

Table 10.7. The Relation between Delinquency and Reading Motivation.

		Delinquent		
		Yes	*No*	
Motivation to Read	*High*	10	35	45
	Low	40	15	55
		50	50	100

obtain the association between these two variables as shown in Table 10.7, we may use the following lambda formula:

$$\lambda = \frac{\Sigma f_r + \Sigma f_c - (F_r + F_c)}{2N - (F_r + F_c)}$$

where f_r = the largest frequency occurring in a row;
f_c = the largest frequency occurring in a column;
F_r = the largest marginal frequency occurring among the rows;
F_c = the largest marginal frequency occurring among the columns; and
N = the number of observations.

Substituting the values in Table 10.7 in our formula, we have:

$$\lambda = \frac{(35 + 40) + (35 + 40) - (55 + 50)}{2(100) - (55 + 50)} = \frac{45}{95}$$

$$= .47.$$

With a $\lambda = .47$ we can say that there is a moderate association between delinquency and motivation to read in this instance.

We shall now look at two additional problems. To what extent can we predict a person's motivation to read by knowing whether or not he is delinquent? Also, to what extent can we predict delinquency by knowing a person's motivation to read? In the first instance, we shall treat *delinquency* as the independent variable. In the second instance, we shall treat *motivation to read* as the independent variable. This treatment will mean altering the construction of Table 10.7 slightly and a different formula will be used to compute λ. The new formula is

$$\lambda = \frac{\Sigma f_i - F_d}{N - F_d}$$

where f_i = the largest frequency occurring within each subclass of the independent variable;
F_d = the largest frequency found within the dependent variable totals; and
N = the total number of observations.

This formula is "asymmetric." This means that different values of λ are rendered depending upon how we view the variables involved. If we use *motivation to read* as an independent variable and *delinquency* as the dependent variable, a different λ value may be obtained compared to the situation where *motivation to read* constitutes the dependent variable and *delinquency* is the independent one. The first formula used to compute λ was "symmetrical," which means that it provided an index of association or *mutual predictability* between the two variables.

First, we shall compute λ for Table 10.7, where delinquency is considered the independent variable. Using the values in the table in our formula above, we have

$$\lambda = \frac{(40 + 35) - 55}{100 - 55} = 20/45$$
$$= .44.$$

In this case we can say that by using delinquency as the independent variable to "predict" motivation to read, 44 percent of the error in our prediction has been reduced. Knowledge of delinquency improved the accuracy of our prediction by 44 percent.

The effect of *motivation to read* on *delinquency* is portrayed in Table 10.8. Again, the formula

$$\lambda = \frac{\Sigma f_i - F_d}{N - F_d}$$

is used. Using the values in the table, we have:

$$\lambda = \frac{(35 + 40) - 50}{100 - 50} = 25/50$$
$$= .50.$$

In this case, by using *motivation to read* as the independent variable, we find that we are able to reduce the error of predicting *delinquency* by 50 percent. It would appear that *motivation to read* is a slightly better predictor of *delinquency* than *delinquency* is at predicting *motivation to read.*

Table 10.8. The Effect of Motivation to Read on Delinquency.

		Motivation to Read		
		High	*Low*	
Delinquent	*Yes*	10	40	50
	No	35	15	50
		45	55	100

In Tables 10.7 and 10.8 above we have consistently utilized the variable across the *top* of the table as the *independent variable.* In social research it is *conventional* to do so. This convention makes it easier for the reader to determine how the variables are being discussed and also makes it easier to apply our formulas consistently and correctly.

Assumptions for λ A nominal-level measure of association, λ makes no assumption concerning the distribution of variables. It may be computed whenever data can be categorized.

Advantages and Disadvantages of λ Like C, one advantage λ has over some other nominal-level measures of association is that it is not restricted to 2×2 tables. It may be computed for tables of any $r \times c$ size.

Another advantage of λ is that it has a direct proportional-reduction-in-error interpretation. In this sense it is comparable to Yule's Q and to phi. In a more general sense, it is comparable to r^2. It is an index of the reduction in error of predicting one variable from another.

λ may also be interpreted directly without being modified by some correction factor like C. It is relatively easy to compute and to understand, and it is becoming an increasingly popular measure of nominal-level association.

ORDINAL-LEVEL MEASURES OF ASSOCIATION

Often in sociological research the investigator will have data which can be ranked in some fashion. For example, he may have job-satisfaction scores, social-class or socioeconomic-status scores, productivity scores, and so on. He may wish to dichotomize or divide his data into tabular form such as we have previously discussed, but he will find that by doing so he loses a certain amount of information. If he can keep his data close to their original form during the analysis stage of his research, he will not lose as much information and his findings will have correspondingly more meaning.

If he has the scores of several individuals on two dimensions, *job satis-*

faction and *level of information,* he may wish to know the degree of association which exists between these two ordinal-level variables. One measure of association enabling him to accomplish this task is called Spearman's rho, r_s.

Spearmen's Rho, r_s

Spearman's rho is frequently called the rank-order-correlation coefficient. It measures the degree of association between two sets of ranked data. Suppose an investigator has the information in Table 10.9 pertaining to job satisfaction and level of information for 10 workers in Factory X.

Table 10.9. Job Satisfaction and Level of Information for 10 Workers in Factory X.

Individual	*Job-Satisfaction Score*	*Level-of-Information Score*	*Rank 1*	*Rank 2*	*D*	D^2
1	45	46	1	1	0	0
2	41	37	2	3.5	1.5	2.25
3	40	45	3	2	1	1
4	36	21	4	8	4	16
5	34	37	5	3.5	1.5	2.25
6	33	32	6	5	1	1
7	25	30	7	6	1	1
8	21	19	8	9	1	1
9	18	26	9	7	2	4
10	17	17	10	10	0	0
$N = 10$						$\Sigma D^2 = 28.50$

In this case we shall be interested in learning whether or not job satisfaction is associated with level of information. Table 10.9 is constructed in the following three-step way:

1. Each person's job-satisfaction score is placed in order from the largest to the smallest. In this case, the larger the scores, the greater the job satisfaction *and* the higher one's level of information. Each person's level-of-information score is correspondingly placed alongside his job-satisfaction score, as is shown. It is apparent that the information-level scores do not necessarily occur from the highest to lowest in their column. *We wish to know how closely the ranking of one set of scores resembles the ranking of the other.*

2. In the next column entitled *Rank 1* we rank the scores in the job-satisfaction column from 1 to N. In the column labeled *Rank 2* we place the corresponding ranks of information-level scores from 1 to N (=10). This placement makes it apparent that the information rankings do not necessarily occur in numerical order. If both sets of ranks were

identical, a perfect association would exist between them, and we would not need to make any computation. But in the present example, such is not the case.

3. Next, we determine the *difference* (D) between each pair of ranks. This computation involves subtracting the smaller of the two ranks in columns *Rank 1* and *Rank 2* from the larger rank; it does not matter which is larger. Each difference between pairs of ranks for each individual is placed in column D. Each of these differences between ranks is squared and the square is placed in column D^2 as is shown. The squares of the differences between the ranks are then summed, and the following formula is applied:

$$r_s = 1 - \frac{6\Sigma D^2}{N(N^2 - 1)}.$$

Using the values in the table, we have:

$$r_s = 1 - \frac{(6)(28.50)}{(10)(100 - 1)} = 1 - \frac{171.0}{990} = 1 - .173$$
$$= .83.$$

In this case we make the interpretation that a high degree of association exists between job satisfaction and information in Factory X.

When ties occur in either set of ranked scores (where two or more scores in the same column are identical), a correction is suggested to compensate for these ties. Such a correction is described in Siegel (1956). The general effect of correcting for ties is to slightly reduce the size of r_s. When r_s is corrected for ties, the effect on r_s is almost negligible; only a very large number of ties would change r_s significantly. If the number of ties is quite large, say, more than 5, Kendall's tau is suggested as an alternative measure of association. This procedure will be discussed shortly.

The Significance of Spearman's Rho When $N < 30$, Table A.14, Critical Values of r_s, may be used for interpreting the level of significance for any r_s. If $N > 30$, the sampling distribution of r_s tends to be normal, and the standard deviation may be computed by using the formula

$$s = \frac{1}{\sqrt{N - 1}}$$

with a $Z = r_s/s$. To determine the significance of a given r_s, simply compute the standard deviation, determine Z, then use Table A.3 of Appendix A, Areas under the Normal Curve, to locate the significance level under the normal distribution.

For the example referring to Table 10.9, $N < 30$; therefore we need to turn to Table A.14 of Appendix A to determine the significance of r_s. Our observed $r_s = .83$. Both the .05 and .01 levels of significance are provided in the table. With an $N = 10$, we must have an $r_s = .564$ or larger for our observed r_s to be significant at .05. For the .01 level, the observed r_s should be equal to or larger than .746. Since our observed $r_s = .83$, we conclude that the r_s is significant at $< .01$, and that there is a significant association between job satisfaction and level of information.

Assumptions for Spearman's Rho The value of Spearman's rho is very similar to that of certain parametric measures of association. The Pearson r has already been discussed as one of these. In this sense, it is a strong measure of association and is used extensively. Also, it is appropriate when ties in ranks occur. If the number of ties is quite large, say, more than 5, then other more appropriate measures of association such as Kendall's tau should be used.

While Spearman's rho has commonly been included as an ordinal-level measure of association, the computation of subtracting ranks from one another actually assumes *interval-level data.* This contradiction has led some researchers to question the appropriateness of this statistic for ordinal-level data. However, r_s is easy to compute and is a well-known measure of association. More recent measures have been suggested which have fewer limitations than r_s.

Kendall's Tau, τ

A somewhat more difficult computation for measuring association between ordinal variables is involved with Kendall's tau. Like r_s, τ is based upon ranked observations, but it is computed differently.

To offer some comparison between the two coefficients of association, we shall use the data from Table 10.9, Job Satisfaction and Level of Information for Ten Workers in Factory X. Let us further assume that we have already ranked both variables and they appear as such below in Table 10.9a. For τ it is also important that one of the variables (in this case, job satisfaction) be ordered from high to low as shown in Table 10.9. The following formula is applied:

$$\tau = \frac{S}{\frac{1}{2}(N)(N-1)}.$$

The value S is computed in the following way:

Beginning with the highest rank, 1, in the unordered column, *Level of Information* in this case, all *larger* ranks in that column are counted, and from these are subtracted all *smaller* ranks. This operation is done for each rank in the column, and each of these sums is summed. For these data, the following illustration is provided.

In the column *Level of Information,* the first rank is 1. There are nine ranks below it which are larger, while no ranks below it are smaller. Therefore, we have $(9 - 0) = 9$. For the next rank, 3.5, six ranks below it are larger, while only one rank is smaller. (There is one tie, but this will

Table 10.9a. Job Satisfaction and Level of Information for 10 Workers in Factory X.

Individual	*Job Satisfaction: Rank 1*	*Level of Information: Rank 2*
1	1	1
2	2	3.5
3	3	2
4	4	8
5	5	3.5
6	6	5
7	7	6
8	8	9
9	9	7
10	10	10

be discussed later.) Therefore, we have $(6-1)=5$. Working through the entire process, we have $(9-0)+(6-1)+(7-0)+(2-4)+(5-0)+(4-0)+(3-0)+(1-1)+(1-0)+(0-0)=9+5+7-2+5+4+3+0+1+0=32$. $S=32$.

Applying the formula for τ to this information, we have:

$$\tau=\frac{32}{\frac{1}{2}(10)(10-1)}$$

$$=\frac{32}{\frac{1}{2}(10)(9)}=\frac{32}{45}$$

$$=.71.$$

There is a moderately high association between job satisfaction and information for the ten workers in Factory X. It is apparent that some differences exist between r_s and τ. In this instance, r_s was .83 while τ was .71. It must be assumed, therefore, that these two measures of association are not directly comparable.

The Correction for Tied Ranks Like r_s, τ may be corrected when tied ranks are present. In many cases the correction will not change the original τ significantly. But where a large number of ties exist, the correction should be made. The formula for this correction is

$$\tau=\frac{S}{\sqrt{\frac{1}{2}N(N-1)-T_x}\sqrt{\frac{1}{2}N(N-1)-T_y}}$$

where $T_x=\frac{1}{2}t_x(t_x-1)$
(t_x being the number of tied ranks on the X variable); and
$T_y=\frac{1}{2}t_y(t_y-1)$
(t_y being the number of tied ranks on the Y variable).

In our previous example of the relation between job-satisfaction and information-level scores, there were no tied ranks on the X or job-satisfaction variable. There was one pair of tied ranks on the Y or information-level variable, however. Two scores were tied for the third and fourth ranks and received the average rank of 3.5. In this case $T_y = \frac{1}{2}(2)(2-1)$ or $(1)(1) = 1$. Because there were no tied ranks on the X variable, job satisfaction, $T_x = 0$. Substituting these values for our formula above, we have:

$$\tau = \frac{32}{\sqrt{1/2(10)(10-1)-0}\sqrt{1/2(10)(10-1)-1}}$$

$$= \frac{32}{\sqrt{45}\sqrt{44}}$$

$$= 32/44.49$$

$$= .72.$$

In this particular case, the original τ, .71, was relatively unaffected by the correction for ties. However, as the number of ties increases, this correction factor becomes increasingly important.

Assumption for τ In order to compute τ, we must be able to meet the assumption of ordinal-level measurement for our data.

Advantages and Disadvantages of τ A primary advantage of τ is that it is appropriately used when a large number of ties is present within ranks. When a large number of ties is present, τ should be computed rather than r_s.

One disadvantage of τ is that it is slightly more difficult to compute compared with other measures of association. Compared with Spearman's rho, where ranks are subtracted from one another, τ is more laborious in computation.

The Significance of τ ***When*** $N > 10$ Kendall (1955) provides a procedure for testing the significance of τ when the sample size is larger than 10. The formula is as follows:

$$Z = \frac{S - 0}{\sqrt{\sigma_s^2}}$$

where $\sigma_s^2 = 1/18(N)(N-1)(2N+5) =$ the variance of τ.

The probability value rendered by Z is based upon a one-tailed test of significance when using the normal distribution tables. For our example above, we may make the test for the significance of τ:

$$\sigma_s^2 = (1/18)(10)(9)(25) = 1/18(2{,}250)$$

$$= 125.$$

Then we apply the Z formula:

$$Z = \frac{S - 0}{\sqrt{\sigma_s^2}}$$

or

$$Z = \frac{32 - 0}{\sqrt{125}} = \frac{32}{11.18}$$
$$= 2.86.$$

Table A.3 of Appendix A is entered with this $Z = 2.86$. A Z of 2.33 or larger is needed in order for our τ of .72 to be significant at $\leqslant .01$, using a one-tailed test. With a Z this large, we may conclude that our $\tau = .72$ is significant.

Goodman's and Kruskal's Gamma, γ

One of the most useful measures of association between two ordinal-level variables is gamma, γ. γ measures the degree of agreement or association between two ordinal-level variables.

Suppose we are interested in learning the association between the degree of automation and the extent to which employees are depersonalized. Automation may be measured by the degree to which computers and other electronic equipment are used in the work setting. Depersonalization is determined by a numerical total of the subject's responses to ten Likert-type questions and is defined as the perceived control one has over the outcome of his work. As a result of our investigations, we find five organizations which are automated to varying degrees. We may rank these organizations which are automated in order of how much automation is used from greatest (1) to least (5). After giving the employees of each of these organizations the depersonalization questionnaire, we are able to determine a median depersonalization score for each organization. Table 10.10 shows the information which we have collected.

Table 10.10. Degree of Automation and Depersonalization.

Organization	*Degree of Automation Rank 1*	*Degree of Depersonalization Rank 2*	*Agreements*	*Inversions*
Smith Co.	1	1	0	0
Brown & Son	2	5	1	0
Jones, Inc.	3	2	1	1
Roe & Hoe	4	4	2	1
Doe & Buck	5	3	2	2
			$\Sigma f_a = 6$	$\Sigma f_i = 4$

In Table 10.10 we have ranked the organizations according to the degree to which automation is used. In a corresponding column we have listed their respective employee-depersonalization ranks. If there were a perfect positive association between these variables, the depersonalization rankings would be identical to the automation rankings. A perfect negative or inverse relation would obtain if one set of ranks was exactly opposite from the other. In this case, there is neither a perfect positive nor a perfect negative association between these variables. We determine the degree of association by using the formula

$$\gamma = \frac{\Sigma f_a - \Sigma f_i}{\Sigma f_a + \Sigma f_i}$$

where f_a = the frequency of agreements, and
f_i = the frequency of inversions.

To determine Σf_a and Σf_i, the following procedure is used: After ranking one variable in perfect order (the degree of automation has been ranked in this fashion), the rankings of the other variable are placed in juxtaposition with their respective organizations. We have already noted that the median depersonalization scores are not in the same order as the automation ranks.

To determine the frequency of agreements, Σf_a, we pay exclusive attention to the column of ranks which is not in perfect order. In this case, we would examine the depersonalization-ranks column. Beginning with the first rank in that column, 1, we ask, "How many ranks above it are smaller?" Since no ranks occur above it, we enter a zero in the column which we have labeled *Agreements*, as is shown in Table 10.10. The next rank in the depersonalization column is 5. Only one rank above it is smaller, therefore, we enter a 1 in the *Agreements* column. The next rank is 2, and only one rank above it is smaller; therefore, we enter another 1 in the *Agreements* column. The next rank is 4, and this time two ranks above it are smaller, namely 2 and 1. Therefore, we enter a 2 in the *Agreements* column. The last rank, 3, also has two ranks above it which are smaller. Another 2 is entered in the *Agreements* column. Totaling the number of agreements will give us Σf_a.

To determine the frequency of inversions, Σf_i, we again pay attention to the depersonalization-ranks column. This time we see how many *larger* ranks occur above another rank. Beginning with the first rank, 1, we have no ranks above it which are larger. We enter a zero in a column labeled *Inversions*. The next rank, 5, has no larger ranks above it. Another zero is entered in the *Inversions* column. The next rank in the table, 2, has one rank above it which is larger, namely 5. A 1 is entered in the *Inversions* column. The next rank, 4, has one rank above it which is larger, and another 1 is entered in the *Inversions* column. The final rank in the depersonalization column, 3, has two ranks above it which are larger, namely 4 and 5. A 2 is entered in the *Inversions* column. The total number of inversions will give us Σf_i.

The total number of agreements for Table 10.10 is 6, while the total number of inversions is 4. Substituting these values for symbols in the γ formula, we have:

$$\gamma = \frac{6-4}{6+4} = 2/10$$
$$= .20.$$

There is a low degree of association between the two sets of ranks. Only 20 percent of the error was reduced in the mutual predictability of automation and depersonalization. In terms of agreement, there was only 20 percent agreement between the two sets of ranks.

The above method for computing γ applies only when no ties are present in either variable. When ties exist, the same formula is employed, but a slightly different way of arriving at Σf_a and Σf_i is involved. To illustrate the computation of γ when numerous ties exist, consider the following example.

Suppose we are interested in determining the association between the social standing of fathers and the achievement motivation of their sons. We might hypothesize that the higher the social standing of fathers, the higher the achievement motivation of their sons. Presumably, greater motivation to achieve is associated with middle- and upper-class values. We want to see to what extent such agreement exists in a sample of boys we have drawn. Table 10.11 shows the relation between achievement motivation and social standing of father.

It will be observed that we have divided achievement motivation and

Table 10.11. Relation between Achievement Motivation and Social Standing of Father.

		Social Standing of Father				
		High	*Moderately High*	*Moderately Low*	*Low*	
Achievement Motivation	*High*	6	3	4	2	15
	Moderately High	4	5	1	2	12
	Moderately Low	2	4	6	1	13
	Low	1	3	7	5	16
		13	15	18	10	56

social standing into four categories each. Because of our sample size, several boys are tied at certain points in the table. For example, 6 boys are tied at high achievement motivation and high social standing of father. Seven boys are tied at low achievement motivation and moderately low social standing of father, and so on. To determine γ, the following formula is used:

$$\gamma = \frac{\Sigma f_a - \Sigma f_i}{\Sigma f_a + \Sigma f_i}$$

where f_a = the frequency of agreements, and
f_i = the frequency of inversions.

Computation of Σf_a: In order to compute Σf_a, we must take each number in the table beginning with the 6 in the upper left-hand corner, and *multiply it by the sum of all numbers below and to the right of it.* All numbers within the table below and to the right of 6 are 5, 1, 2, 4, 6, 1, 3, 7, and 5. Thus 6 times the sum of these values is $(6)(5+1+2+4+6+1+3+7+5) = (6)(34) = 204$. Systematically doing this for each number in the table, we have (working across from left to right):

$(6)(5 + 1 + 2 + 4 + 6 + 1 + 3 + 7 + 5) = (6)(34) = 204$

$(3)(1 + 2 + 6 + 1 + 7 + 5) = (3)(22) = 66$

$(4)(2 + 1 + 5) = (4)(8) = 32$

$(2)(0) = 0$ (No numbers are below and to the right of this 2.)

$(4)(4 + 6 + 1 + 3 + 7 + 5) = (4)(26) = 104$

$(5)(6 + 1 + 7 + 5) = (5)(19) = 95$

$(1)(1 + 5) = 6$

$(2)(0) = 0$ (No numbers are below and to the right of this 2.)

$(2)(3 + 7 + 5) = (2)(15) = 30$

$(4)(7 + 5) = (4)(12) = 48$

$(6)(5) = 30$

The rest of the numbers—that is, 1, 1, 3, 7, and 5—have no numbers below and to the right of them.

Summing these products will give us Σf_a:

$$\Sigma f_a = 204 + 66 + 32 + 104 + 95 + 6 + 30 + 48 + 30 = 615.$$

Computation of Σf_i: To compute Σf_i we must reverse the process above; this time, we begin in the upper right-hand corner of the table, *and we must multiply each number by the sum of all numbers below and to the left of it.* Systematically doing this for all values in the table, we have:

$$(2)(4+5+1+2+4+6+1+3+7) = (2)(33) = 66$$
$$(4)(4+5+2+4+1+3) = (4)(19) = 76$$
$$(3)(4+2+1) = (3)(7) = 21$$
$$(2)(2+4+6+1+3+7) = (2)(23) = 46$$
$$(1)(2+4+1+3) = (1)(10) = 10$$
$$(5)(2+1) = (5)(3) = 15$$
$$(1)(1+3+7) = (1)(11) = 11$$
$$(6)(1+3) = (6)(4) = 24$$
$$(4)(1) = 4$$

The numbers 1, 3, 7, and 5 (the *Low* row) do not have other numbers below and to the left of them; therefore, we do not need to list them above. The sum of the above products will give us Σf_i:

$$\Sigma f_i = 66 + 76 + 21 + 46 + 10 + 15 + 11 + 24 + 4 = 273.$$

We are now ready to substitute these values in our formula to determine γ:

$$\gamma = \frac{615 - 273}{615 + 273} = 342/888$$
$$= .385.$$

There is a moderately low association between social standing of fathers and achievement motivation of sons. We have reduced the error by about 38 percent in the mutual predictability of achievement motivation and father's social standing. There is 38 percent "agreement" between these variables. Whenever Σf_i is larger than Σf_a, an *inverse* association will be found between the variables. This will be indicated by a minus sign (−).

Assumption for γ In order for γ to be computed, the investigator must be able to assume that both variables are at least of the ordinal level of measurement.

Advantages and Disadvantages of γ γ is very useful in that it is designed to fit tables of any size. No corrections need be made for ties with the exception of the change as to how Σf_a and Σf_i are determined. This modification does not involve elaborate computations. The simplicity in the computation of γ for both tied and untied sets of ranks is a strong advantage over other measures of association suited for data of the ordinal level. Compared to other measures of association previously discussed, γ is a most flexible and useful statistical technique. γ readily reflects both positive and negative associations between variables and is directly interpretable. γ may also handle small cell frequencies, whereas these provide a restriction for other measures.

γ is also interpretable as a proportional-reduction-in-error measure. In this sense it has an interpretation analogous to that of r^2. In fact, among the ordinal measures of association discussed in this chapter, γ is *most* amenable to the proportional-reduction-in-error interpretation.

ASSOCIATION BETWEEN TWO OR MORE SETS OF VARIABLES

Up to now we have examined measures of association which exclusively apply to situations where only two sets of variables are involved. Sometimes the investigator will wish to determine the degree of association between more than two sets of variables simultaneously. For this purpose, under certain conditions, he may use W, Kendall's coefficient of concordance.

Kendall's Coefficient of Concordance, W

Kendall's coefficient of concordance, W, measures the extent to which there is agreement between the rankings on any number of variables. For example, suppose we have information for five individuals in Company A. This information pertains to their degree of job satisfaction, their decision-making power, and their staff popularity. The data in Table 10.12 represent each person's rank on each of these three dimensions.

W represents the degree of agreement between ranked sets of scores for each individual. In Table 10.12 we have assigned each individual a rank based upon a presumed raw score which reflects the degree of a particular variable (job satisfaction, decision-making power, or staff popularity). The final column contains the sum of the three ranks for each individual.

If there were perfect agreement between the variables for each individual (if individual #1 was highest on all three variables, #2 was second high, and so on), then the *Rank Sum* scores for each individual, from the highest (1) to the lowest (5), would be 3, 6, 9, 12, and 15. Table 10.13 shows a hypothetical perfect agreement for each individual on all three dimensions.

Table 10.12. Job-Satisfaction, Decision-Making, and Staff-Popularity Scores for Five Staff Members of Company A.

Individual	*Job Satisfaction*	*Decision-Making Power*	*Staff Popularity*	*Rank Sum*
1	1	2	1	4
2	3	4	5	12
3	5	5	4	14
4	4	3	3	10
5	2	1	2	5
				Σ Rank Sum = 45

Table 10.13. Perfect Agreement between Variables for Five Individuals.

Individual	*Job Satisfaction*	*Decision-Making Power*	*Staff Popularity*	*Rank Sum*
1	1	1	1	3
2	2	2	2	6
3	3	3	3	9
4	4	4	4	12
5	5	5	5	15
$N = 5$			Σ Rank Sum = 45	

It may likewise be assumed that if absolutely no agreement was found to exist between the three variables for each individual, each person would have the same total score for each of the three variables, namely 9. There is a variance which exists, therefore, between what would be expected when absolutely no agreement existed between variables and what is observed. W is based upon this variance.

We shall test the following null hypothesis:

H_0: No agreement exists between the individuals with respect to job-satisfaction, decision-making, and staff-popularity scores.

H_1: Agreement does exist between the individuals according to the three variables.

$$P \leqslant .05.$$

To test this hypothesis we may compute W, the coefficient of concordance. In computing W, we must find the *expected* sum of ranks for each individual. Since this will be equal for all individuals, we simply take the grand sum of all possible ranks for all variables and divide this sum by the number of individuals in our sample. For our example in Tables 10.12 and 10.13, this means that we should divide the grand rank sum, 45, by 5, the total N, and this becomes $45/5 = 9$. Each person would therefore receive a rank sum of 9, representing the sum of the person's ranks on each of the variables, job satisfaction, decision making, and staff popularity.

The following formula is then applied to compute W:

$$W = \frac{S}{(1/12)k^2(N^3 - N)}$$

where S = the sum of the squares of the observed deviations from the expected sum of ranks;

k = the number of variables ranked; and

N = the number of individuals in the sample being ranked.

We first compute S, taking the squares of the differences between the individual rank sums in Table 10.12 and Table 10.13:

$$
\begin{aligned}
S &= (4-9)^2 + (12-9)^2 + (14-9)^2 + (10-9)^2 + (5-9)^2 \\
&= (-5)^2 + (3)^2 + (5)^2 + (1)^2 + (-4)^2 \\
&= 25 + 9 + 25 + 1 + 16 \\
&= 76.
\end{aligned}
$$

Substituting values for symbols in the W formula, we have:

$$
\begin{aligned}
W &= \frac{76}{(1/12)(3)^2(5^3 - 5)} \\
&= \frac{76}{(.75)(125 - 5)} = 76/90 \\
&= .84.
\end{aligned}
$$

This W is interpreted like other measures of association between two variables. There is a relatively high degree of association (or agreement) between the rankings of the three variables, job satisfaction, decision-making power, and staff popularity for each individual in Company A.

For purposes of testing our hypothesis, the significance of W may be easily tested by using the following chi-square test with $N - 1$ degrees of freedom:

$$
\chi^2 = \frac{S}{(1/12)kN(N+1)}
$$

where N = the number of individuals being ranked; and
k = the number of variables.

We may use our S as computed from the W formula above. In this case,

$$
\begin{aligned}
\chi^2 &= \frac{76}{1/12(3)(5)(5+1)} \\
&= \frac{76}{(.25)(30)} = 76/7.50 \\
&= 10.133.
\end{aligned}
$$

With this χ^2 value we enter Table A.4 of Appendix A with $N - 1 = 5 - 1 = 4$ degrees of freedom, and we find that in order to reject the null hypothesis at the .05 level, we must have a χ^2 equal to or larger than 9.488. Since our observed χ^2 value exceeds 9.488, being 10.133, we conclude that $W = .84$ is significant at the .05 level and we reject the null hypothesis. Where small sample sizes are found, Table A.15 of Appendix A may be used. It is appropriate when $k = 3$ to 20, and when $N = 3$ to 7. Critical values are provided for .05 and .01 respectively. In this case, we may use our observed S value to enter the table. In our present example, $S = 76$. With $k = 3$, $N = 5$, we enter Table A.15 and observe that if we have an S equal to or larger than 64.4, our W is significant at .05. Hence, both procedures give comparable results.

***Assumption for* W** The primary assumption underlying W is that the variables be of ordinal level. W is perhaps the best nonparametric measure of the extent to which association exists for any number of individuals ranked according to k variables.

***Advantages of* W** The main advantage of W is that it offers a coefficient of association for k variables, thus demonstrating the amount of agreement between persons according to any number of dimensions. It eliminates the necessity of having to average individual r_s's, as some researchers have done. W is also relatively easy to compute and is directly interpretable.

MULTIPLE AND PARTIAL CORRELATION

Thus far we have covered various measures of association geared to tell us something about the relation between two variables and a special case of the relation between k variables for ranked data. Other statistical measures exist, however, which allow us to specify more precisely the relation between k variables. Researchers have labeled these statistical procedures as measures of *multiple correlation* and *partial correlation.*

Multiple-correlation measures are geared to reveal the degree of association between three or more variables simultaneously. For example, we may be interested in learning the degree of association between delinquency, social class, and the condition of parental supervision of adolescents. Or we may be interested in learning the degree of association between aggressiveness and certain other personality dimensions such as anxiety level or sociability. In terms of prediction, we may feel that we can better predict variable Y not only by paying attention to the effect of variable X, but also the effects of variables A, B, C, and D upon variable Y simultaneously. Multiple correlation, or "regression" as it is often called, is designed to tell us the degree of association between k variables.

Partial-correlation measures are geared to tell us the degree of association between two variables after the influence of other variables has been controlled. To illustrate the general problem, suppose we found that a relation exists between type of supervision and job satisfaction. We observe the following relation between these variables:

	Supervision	
Job Satisfaction	*Close*	*General*
High	25	50
Low	50	25

It would appear that high job satisfaction is associated with general supervision, while low job satisfaction is associated with close supervision. But suppose that the relation between these two variables was actually attributable to the presence of a *third* variable. We might be able to show that, in reality, no systematic relation exists between job satisfaction and type of supervision, but rather that salary is the overriding factor in determining job satisfaction. We might find the above data in a different form with the addition of salary:

	High Salary		*Low Salary*	
Job Satisfaction	*Close Supervision*	*General Supervision*	*Close Supervision*	*General Supervision*
High	25	50	0	0
Low	0	0	50	25

This display of data presents a story quite different from the first relation between variables which was observed.

Determining the relation between two variables with a third variable "partialed-out" is the function of partial-correlation measures.

The example we have employed illustrates the nature of the problem to which such measures are addressed. The particular measure that an investigator employs depends on the assumptions that can be made about the data: level of measurement, distribution, and the like. Both the multiple-correlation and the partial-correlation measures are valuable statistical techniques. We will not attempt to cover these statistical methods in this text. Such statistical procedures are treated in advanced statistics courses. By mastering the fundamentals of statistics presented here, however, the student is in the position to begin a study of these more elaborate statistical procedures geared to handle intricate research problems.

SUMMARY

In this chapter we have examined several measures of association appropriate for interval, nominal, and ordinal levels of measurement. Association does not necessarily mean that a cause-effect relation is established between any two variables. One characteristic or variable is associated with another to a particular degree. The numerical representation of the degree to which two variables are associated is called a coefficient of association, and can range in value from +1.00 to −1.00.

An interval-level measure of association is the Pearson r. This statistic is appropriate when there is a linear association between two variables. When r is squared, it is interpretable as a proportional-reduction-in-error measure. A test also exists to determine the significance of difference between two r's. The Pearson r is perhaps the most popular measure of association discussed in this chapter.

Nominal-level measures of association include: the coefficient of contingency, C; Yule's Q; the phi coefficient; and Guttman's coefficient of predictability, lambda. C, the coefficient of contingency, is most often used in conjunction with chi-square as an index of association between two nominal variables. C is flexible in that it can be computed for tables of any size, but certain disadvantages are associated with it. Under extreme conditions where cell frequencies are radically distributed, C may only reach a value of .85. It must be corrected in order to be "raised" to 1.00. Even so, it is not directly comparable with other measures of association.

Yule's Q and the phi coefficient, ϕ, are appropriate when tables are of size 2×2. They are both indices of association between two nominal variables, when these variables are expressed as dichotomies. Like the Pearson r, both Yule's Q and the phi coefficient are subject to a proportional-reduction-in-error interpretation. Yule's Q is directly interpretable as such, while the phi coefficient must be squared to render such an interpretation.

Guttman's lambda is perhaps the most versatile of the measures discussed in this section. It is directly interpretable as a proportional-reduction-in-error measure, and it may be computed directly for tables of any size. It has no restrictions concerning the distribution of variables and is not limited by specific sizes of N nor by small cell frequencies. It measures the degree to which one variable may be predicted with a knowledge of the other.

Ordinal-level measures of association discussed in this chapter include Spearman's rho, Kendall's tau, and Goodman's and Kruskal's gamma. Spearman's rho, r_s, is comparable to the Pearson r, but it is primarily applicable to data which can be ranked. Although classified as an ordinal-level measure, it involves computations which parallel the interval level, and consequently, some researchers have questioned its appropriateness for ordinal data. It is well known, however, and is easy to compute. It is not appropriate when a large number of ties in ranks exist.

Kendall's tau is equipped to handle the association between two sets of ranked data even when large numbers of ties are present. In this sense it is better than Spearman's rho. Kendall's tau is slightly more difficult to compute than Spearman's rho, however.

Goodman's and Kruskal's gamma is one of the most useful measures of association between ordinal-level variables. It can handle large numbers of ties in ranks and can be computed for tables of any size. No corrections need be made for the original gamma coefficient. It is also directly interpretable as a proportional-reduction-in-error measure.

Kendall's coefficient of concordance, W, was discussed as an ordinal-level measure of the degree of agreement between ranked sets of scores for individuals. It is geared to handle k variables and is easy to compute and interpret. W is perhaps the best nonparametric measure of association between k ordinal-level variables.

QUESTIONS FOR REVIEW AND PROBLEMS TO SOLVE

1. Compute a coefficient of contingency, C, for the following information:

		Social Participation		
		High	Low	
Age	Young	44	15	59
	Old	12	64	76
		56	79	135

2. Compute $\overline{C}$ for the information you obtain from Problem 1 above. Compute lambda and phi for these data and compare the three coefficients.

3. What is a measure of association? How is an inverse association identified? In a study with 15 variables, how many possible coefficients of association could be obtained by pairing each of the variables with one another?

4. Compute Yule's Q for the information in the following table:

		Attitude		
		Favorable	Unfavorable	
Sex	Male	75	25	100
	Female	40	60	100
		115	85	200

5. What are some advantages and disadvantages associated with Spearman's rho? With Kendall's tau?

6. Twelve individuals have been assigned the following scores on two attitudinal measures. Is there a significant association between the two sets of scores at the .05 level? (Use the Spearman's rho for these data.)

Individual	Attitude 1	Attitude 2
1	15	19
2	34	28
3	24	27
4	25	29
5	22	23
6	19	26
7	28	31
8	33	40
9	33	40
10	25	36
11	21	22
12	20	21

7. Compute gamma for the following information. What is the extent of agreement between the two sets of ranks?

Rank 1	*Rank 2*
1	4
2	3
3	2
4	1
5	5
6	8
7	7
8	6

8. What are some assumptions underlying gamma? What are some important advantages and disadvantages of it?

9. Compute a Pearson r for the following two sets of scores:

X	Y	X	Y	X	Y
15	45	23	35	23	41
20	47	25	40	14	34
18	41	27	45	15	36
12	37	19	51	30	57
28	50	29	49	29	54
12	28	26	43	24	48
21	32	25	46	24	47

10. Compute W for the following three sets of ranks. Interpret W. What are some advantages of W?

Individual	*Rank 1*	*Rank 2*	*Rank 3*
1	1	7	4
2	2	5	5
3	6	6	1
4	3	1	7
5	7	4	2
6	5	3	3
7	4	2	6

11 A Short Summary and a Look Ahead

Throughout this text a variety of statistical techniques has been surveyed. Each statistical technique is designed to play a particular role in data analysis. However, the process of data analysis involves considerably more than merely matching a statistical procedure with a given problem. The text has emphasized the importance of meeting the assumptions underlying statistical procedures as a prerequisite to their meaningful application in social research. Accordingly, the social investigator has the responsibility of determining at the beginning whether statistical analysis is necessary, and if so, which techniques ought to be used for particular problems. This decision involves weighing and sifting the relative advantages and disadvantages of the various statistical methods.

The researcher often finds himself in a dilemma concerning which statistical technique to use. He may need to decide whether to choose statistical technique A (which is easy to apply but requires large samples and is costly) or to choose statistical technique B (which is more difficult to apply but is appropriate for smaller samples and is less costly). Decisions such as this are often difficult to make and the justifications are not always clear-cut. Because there are so many statistical techniques available with overlapping functions, advantages, and disadvantages, the decision generally becomes a matter of judgment about which technique renders the most information about the data at the least cost. Thus the process of selecting a statistical technique is in some part a matter of practicality rather than sheer arbitrariness.

The process of selecting a statistical technique usually involves the following steps:

1. Decide what you want to do with your data. What is the purpose of your research? What are the goals of your study design?
2. Determine the level of measurement of the data to be analyzed. This will narrow the range of the statistical tests and techniques which can be used for your particular problem.
3. Focus your choice upon a general block of statistical techniques which appear to fit the kind of analysis you wish to make.

4. Select the most appropriate technique in terms of: (a) the assumptions you must meet in order to apply the technique appropriately; (b) the kind of sample or population you are dealing with; (c) the kind of sampling procedure used; and (d) the decision rules you require.

This text contains a number of statistical techniques which are suited for many of the problems which you will encounter in social research. Where a specific problem is encountered, it may be necessary to turn to a more advanced or detailed source. Some of these sources are listed in Appendix B. Sometimes you may have a problem for which no standard statistical procedure is appropriate. It is then wise to consult a statistician in order to determine whether it is possible and/or feasible to devise a new technique or modify an old one to handle the kind of analysis you wish to make. Remember that not all research situations have been covered by statistical procedures, and that statistical procedures are continuing to be developed for novel research circumstances.

Statistical techniques are not panaceas for all of your research problems. The application of a statistical procedure does not make up for sloppy research methodology and poor scientific thinking. It is necessary that the investigator make every effort to insure that the research he conducts is soundly conceived and that the research design clearly defines the type of data analysis which should be made. Statistical procedures are primarily aids to good thinking and not substitutes for it. They are aids in the sense that they enable the researcher to have numerical evidence and confirmation for decisions he makes pertaining to his data analysis.

A final note is in the nature of a caution. The interpretation of any numerical value as a statistic should be tempered with a degree of conservatism. Where numbers are assigned to information and then manipulated mathematically, there is always the possibility that the numbers do not mean what they seem to mean. A good rule of thumb is never to base your conclusions on the statistical analysis alone. Consider statistical information as supplementary and treat it as such. Be aware of the limitations of statistical methods throughout the research process, and particularly when the time comes to interpret what you think you have found.

Some Answers to Selected Problems

Chapter One

No problems.

Chapter Two

5. (a) 25.5; (b) .87; (c) 66.5; (d) 574.5; (e) 12; (f) .002.
6. (a) 567.5; (b) 46.775; (c) .45; (d) .815; (e) 8,999.45; (f) .0015; (g) 2.75.
8. (a) .34; (b) .70; (c) 1.00; (d) 1.00; (e) .50; (f) .97; (g) .80.
9. (a) 33.1%; (b) 1%; (c) .02%; (d) 47.6%; (e) 50%; (f) 10%; (g) 10,000%.
10. (a) .3367; (b) .00998; (c) .00099; (d) .03841; (e) .10; (f) .000001.

Chapter Three

1. $\overline{X} = 68.1$; mode = 64.5; median = 65.2.
3. $\overline{X} = 90$; mode = 91; median = 90.
5. $\overline{X}_T = 127.4$.
7. $\overline{X} = 5.7$; mode = 5; median = 5.4.
9. Midpoints: 114.5, 104.5, 94.5, 84.5, 74.5, 64.5, 54.5, 44.5, 34.5, 24.5, and 14.5; 10, 9, 8, 7, 6, 5, 4, 3, 2.
10. Median = 119.

Chapter Four

1. Interquartile range = 70.9 − 52.2 = 18.7; standard deviation = 12.3; modes = 67 and 57.
5. $IQV = 94.3\%$.
8. $AD = 10.47$ (with a $\overline{X} = 61.9$).
9. Standard deviation = 33.34.

Chapter Five

1. (a) .7525; (b) .0870; (c) .3472; (d) .0175; (e) .9166.
3. (a) −1.25; (b) 1.00; (c) 1.92; (d) −1.92; (e) .46; (f) 1.51.
5. (a) 43.24; (b) 55.74; (c) 50.20; (d) 47.62; (e) 53.74; (f) 54.86; (g) 58.5.

9. (a) 42; (b) 55; (c) 54.8; (d) 50.8; (e) 60.
10. First class: $Z = 1.71$. Second class: $Z = 1.67$. The student in the first class did *relatively* better than the student in the other class in relation to their respective student groups.

Chapter Six

8. $s_{\bar{X}} = 1.25$.
9. 95% C.I. = 85.55 to 90.45; 80% C.I. = 86.40 to 89.60.

Chapter Seven

1. $t = 7.352$.
2. $Z = 15.00$.
3. $F = 4.95$; $MS_{bet} = 19.383$, $MS_{within} = 3.913$. Significant differences between means: Between both 3.8's and 7.3, 7.5; or between means of groups 1 and 3, 1 and 5, 3 and 4, and 4 and 5. (a) Homogeneity of variance exists.
4. Not significant.
6. $F = 35.71$.
7. $t = 5.275$.
9. $t = 10.256$.
10. Yes, homogeneity of variance exists. Other alternatives include Bartlett's test and Cochran's test.

Chapter Eight

1. $Z = 1.10$; not significant.
3. Not significant; $Z = .56$. The boys do not significantly differ from one another with respect to their test scores.
4. Chi square = 3.368 (not significant at .01). The individuals do not significantly change their views as a result of the course in marriage and the family.
5. Chi square = 20. Significant at less than .01, 6 *df*.
7. (a) 2; (b) 21; (c) 16; (d) 99.
8. Not significant. The boys with and without high-school education do not differ with respect to delinquent behavior. (a) Using Yates's correction factor will further reduce the difference between what is observed and what is expected. Any difference now remaining will be even *less* significant than that before Yates's correction was applied.
9. $Q = 5.6$. There are no significant differences between groups at .05.

Chapter Nine

2. Reject the null hypothesis.
3. Not significant. (a) Significant; reject the null hypothesis at .05, one-tailed test.

6. Not significant.
7. $U = 35$.
8. $\chi_r^2 = 10.35$; significant at .05.
10. Significant; samples A and B do not come from the same population. We must reject the null hypothesis at .05.

Chapter Ten

1. $C = .51$.
2. $\bar{C} = .72$; lambda = .53; phi = .59.
4. $Q = .64$.
6. $r_s = .84$.
7. Gamma = .36.
9. $r = .69$.
10. $W = .02$. No agreement.

Chapter Eleven

No problems.

Appendix A
Tables

Table A.1. Squares, Square Roots, and Reciprocals of Integers from 1 to 1,000

n	n^2	$\sqrt{n}$	$\frac{1}{n}$	$\frac{1}{\sqrt{n}}$
1	1	1.0000	1.000000	1.0000
2	4	1.4142	.500000	.7071
3	9	1.7321	.333333	.5774
4	16	2.0000	.250000	.5000
5	25	2.2361	.200000	.4472
6	36	2.4495	.166667	.4082
7	49	2.6458	.142857	.3780
8	64	2.8284	.125000	.3536
9	81	3.0000	.111111	.3333
10	100	3.1623	.100000	.3162
11	121	3.3166	.090909	.3015
12	144	3.4641	.083333	.2887
13	169	3.6056	.076923	.2774
14	196	3.7417	.071429	.2673
15	225	3.8730	.066667	.2582
16	256	4.0000	.062500	.2500
17	289	4.1231	.058824	.2425
18	324	4.2426	.055556	.2357
19	361	4.3589	.052632	.2294
20	400	4.4721	.050000	.2236
21	441	4.5826	.047619	.2182
22	484	4.6904	.045455	.2132
23	529	4.7958	.043478	.2085
24	576	4.8990	.041667	.2041
25	625	5.0000	.040000	.2000
26	676	5.0990	.038462	.1961
27	729	5.1962	.037037	.1925
28	784	5.2915	.035714	.1890
29	841	5.3852	.034483	.1857
30	900	5.4772	.033333	.1826
31	961	5.5678	.032258	.1796
32	1024	5.6569	.031250	.1768
33	1089	5.7446	.030303	.1741
34	1156	5.8310	.029412	.1715
35	1225	5.9161	.028571	.1690
36	1296	6.0000	.027778	.1667
37	1369	6.0828	.027027	.1644
38	1444	6.1644	.026316	.1622
39	1521	6.2450	.025641	.1601
40	1600	6.3246	.025000	.1581
41	1681	6.4031	.024390	.1562
42	1764	6,4807	.023810	.1543
43	1849	6.5574	.023256	.1525
44	1936	6.6332	.022727	.1508
45	2025	6.7082	.022222	.1491
46	2116	6.7823	.021739	.1474
47	2209	6.8557	.021277	.1459
48	2304	6.9282	.020833	.1443
49	2401	7.0000	.020408	.1429
50	2500	7.0711	.020000	.1414

Source: "Table M" (Squares, Square Roots and Reciprocals of Integers from 1 to 1000) from *Introduction to Applied Statistics* by John G. Peatman (Harper & Row, 1963).

Table A.1. *(continued)*

n	n^2	$\sqrt{n}$	$\frac{1}{n}$	$\frac{1}{\sqrt{n}}$
51	2601	7.1414	.019608	.1400
52	2704	7.2111	.019231	.1387
53	2809	7.2801	.018868	.1374
54	2916	7.3485	.018519	.1361
55	3025	7.4162	.018182	.1348
56	3136	7.4833	.017857	.1336
57	3249	7.5498	.017544	.1325
58	3364	7.6158	.017241	.1313
59	3481	7.6811	.016949	.1302
60	3600	7.7460	.016667	.1291
61	3721	7.8102	.016393	.1280
62	3844	7.8740	.016129	.1270
63	3969	7.9373	.015873	.1260
64	4096	8.0000	.015625	.1250
65	4225	8.0623	.015385	.1240
66	4356	8.1240	.015152	.1231
67	4489	8.1854	.014925	.1222
68	4624	8.2462	.014706	.1213
69	4761	8.3066	.014493	.1204
70	4900	8.3666	.014286	.1195
71	5041	8.4261	.014085	.1187
72	5184	8.4853	.013889	.1179
73	5329	8.5440	.013699	.1170
74	5476	8.6023	.013514	.1162
75	5625	8.6603	.013333	.1155
76	5776	8.7178	.013158	.1147
77	5929	8.7750	.018987	.1140
78	6084	8.8318	.012821	.1132
79	6241	8.8882	.012658	.1125
80	6400	8.9443	.012500	.1118
81	6561	9.0000	.012346	.1111
82	6724	9.0554	.012195	.1104
83	6889	9.1104	.012048	.1098
84	7056	9.1652	.011905	.1091
85	7225	9.2195	.011765	.1085
86	7396	9.2736	.011628	.1078
87	7569	9.3274	.011494	.1072
88	7744	9.3808	.011364	.1066
89	7921	9.4340	.011236	.1060
90	8100	9.4868	.011111	.1054
91	8281	9.5394	.010989	.1048
92	8464	9.5917	.010870	.1043
93	8649	9.6437	.010753	.1037
94	8836	9.6954	.010638	.1031
95	9025	9.7468	.010526	.1026
96	9216	9.7980	.010417	.1021
97	9409	9.8489	.010309	.1015
98	9604	9.8995	.010204	.1010
99	9801	9.9499	.010101	.1005
100	10000	10.0000	.010000	.1000

Table A.1. *(continued)*

n	n^2	$\sqrt{n}$	$\frac{1}{n}$	$\frac{1}{\sqrt{n}}$
101	10201	10.0499	.009901	.0995
102	10404	10.0995	.009804	.0990
103	10609	10.1489	.009709	.0985
104	10816	10.1980	.009615	.0981
105	11025	10.2470	.009524	.0976
106	11236	10.2956	.009434	.0971
107	11449	10.3441	.009346	.0967
108	11664	10.3923	.009259	.0962
109	11881	10.4403	.009174	.0958
110	12100	10.4881	.009091	.0953
111	12321	10.5357	.009009	.0949
112	12544	10,5830	.008929	.0945
113	12769	10.6301	.008850	.0941
114	12996	10.6771	.008772	.0937
115	13225	10.7238	.008696	.0933
116	13456	10.7703	.008621	.0928
117	13689	10.8167	.008547	.0925
118	13924	10.8628	.008475	.0921
119	14161	10.9087	.008403	.0917
120	14400	10.9545	.008333	.0913
121	14641	11.0000	.008264	.0909
122	14884	11.0454	.008197	.0905
123	15129	11.0905	.008130	.0902
124	15376	11.1355	.008065	.0898
125	15625	11.1803	.008000	.0894
126	15876	11.2250	.007937	.0891
127	16129	11.2694	.007874	.0887
128	16384	11.3137	.007813	.0884
129	16641	11.3578	.007752	.0880
130	16900	11.4018	.007692	.0877
131	17161	11.4455	.007634	.0874
132	17424	11.4891	.007576	.0870
133	17689	11.5326	.007519	.0867
134	17956	11.5758	.007463	.0864
135	18225	11.6190	.007407	.0861
136	18496	11.6619	.007353	.0857
137	18769	11.7047	.007299	.0854
138	19044	11.7473	.007246	.0851
139	19321	11.7898	.007194	.0848
140	19600	11.8322	.007143	.0845
141	19881	11.8743	.007092	.0842
142	20164	11.9164	.007042	.0839
143	20449	11.9583	.006993	.0836
144	20736	12.0000	.006944	.0833
145	21025	12.0416	.006897	.0830
146	21316	12.0830	.006849	.0828
147	21609	12.1244	.006803	.0825
148	21904	12.1655	.006757	.0822
149	22201	12.2066	.006711	.0819
150	22500	12.2474	.006667	.0816

Table A.1. *(continued)*

n	n^2	$\sqrt{n}$	$\frac{1}{n}$	$\frac{1}{\sqrt{n}}$
151	22801	12.2882	.006623	.0814
152	23104	12.3288	.006579	.0811
153	23409	12.3693	.006536	.0808
154	23716	12.4097	.006494	.0806
155	24025	12.4499	.006452	.0803
156	24336	12.4900	.006410	.0301
157	24649	12.5300	.006369	.0798
158	24964	12.5698	.006329	.0796
159	25281	12.6095	.006289	.0793
160	25600	12.6491	.006250	.0791
161	25921	12.6886	.006211	.0788
162	26244	12.7279	.006173	.0786
163	26569	12.7671	.006135	.0783
164	26896	12.8062	.006098	.0781
165	27225	12.8452	.006061	.0778
166	27556	12.8841	.006024	.0776
167	27889	12.9228	.005988	.0774
168	28224	12.9615	.005952	.0772
169	28561	13.0000	.005917	.0769
170	28900	13.0384	.005882	.0767
171	29241	13.0767	.005848	.0765
172	29584	13.1149	.005814	.0762
173	29929	13.1529	.005780	.0760
174	30276	13.1909	.005747	.0758
175	30625	13.2288	.005714	.0756
176	30976	13.2665	.005682	.0754
177	31329	13.3041	.005650	.0752
178	31684	13.3417	.005618	.0750
179	32041	13.3791	.005587	.0747
180	32400	13.4164	.005556	.0745
181	32761	13.4536	.005525	.0743
182	33124	13.4907	.005495	.0741
183	33489	13.5277	.005464	.0739
184	33856	13.5647	.005435	.0737
185	34225	13.6015	.005405	.0735
186	34596	13.6382	.005376	.0733
187	34969	13.6748	.005348	.0731
188	35344	13.7113	.005319	.0729
189	35721	13.7477	.005291	.0727
190	36100	13.7840	.005263	.0725
191	36481	13.8203	.005236	.0724
192	36864	13.8564	.005208	.0722
193	37249	13.8924	.005181	.0720
194	37636	13.9284	.005155	.0718
195	38025	13.9642	.005128	.0716
196	38416	14.0000	.005102	.0714
197	38809	14.0357	.005076	.0712
198	39204	14.0712	.005051	.0711
199	39601	14.1067	.005025	.0709
200	40000	14.1421	.005000	.0707

Table A.1. *(continued)*

n	n^2	$\sqrt{n}$	$\frac{1}{n}$	$\frac{1}{\sqrt{n}}$
201	40401	14.1774	.004975	.0705
202	40804	14.2127	.004950	.0704
203	41209	14.2478	.004926	.0702
204	41616	14.2829	.004902	.0700
205	42025	14.3178	.004878	.0698
206	42436	14.3527	.004854	.0697
207	42849	14.3875	.004831	.0695
208	43264	14.4222	.004808	.0693
209	43681	14.4568	.004785	.0692
210	44100	14.4914	.004762	.0690
211	44521	14.5258	.004739	.0688
212	44944	14.5602	.004717	.0687
213	45369	14.5945	.004695	.0685
214	45796	14.6287	.004673	.0684
215	46225	14.6629	.004651	.0682
216	46656	14.6969	.004630	.0680
217	47089	14.7309	.004608	.0679
218	47524	14.7648	.004587	.0677
219	47961	14.7986	.004566	.0676
220	48400	14.8324	.004545	.0674
221	48841	14.8661	.004525	.0673
222	49284	14.8997	.004505	.0671
223	49729	14.9332	.004484	.0670
224	50176	14.9666	.004464	.0668
225	50625	15.0000	.004444	.0667
226	51076	15.0333	.004425	.0665
227	51529	15.0665	.004405	.0664
228	51984	15.0997	.004386	.0662
229	52441	15.1327	.004367	.0661
230	52900	15.1658	.004348	.0659
231	53361	15.1987	.004329	.0658
232	53824	15.2315	.004310	.0657
233	54289	15.2643	.004292	.0655
234	54756	15.2971	.004274	.0654
235	55225	15.3297	.004255	.0652
236	55696	15.3623	.004237	.0651
237	56169	15.3948	.004219	.0650
238	56644	15.4272	.004202	.0648
239	57121	15.4596	.004184	.0647
240	57600	15.4919	.004167	.0645
241	58081	15.5242	.004149	.0644
242	58564	15.5563	.004132	.0643
243	59049	15.5885	.004115	.0642
244	59536	15.6205	.004098	.0640
245	60025	15.6525	.004082	.0639
246	60516	15.6844	.004065	.0638
247	61009	15.7162	.004049	.0636
248	61504	15.7480	.004032	.0635
249	62001	15.7797	.004016	.0634
250	62500	15.8114	.004000	.0632

Table A.1. *(continued)*

n	n^2	$\sqrt{n}$	$\frac{1}{n}$	$\frac{1}{\sqrt{n}}$
251	63001	15.8430	.003984	.0631
252	63504	15.8745	.003968	.0630
253	64009	15.9060	.003953	.0629
254	64516	15.9374	.003937	.0627
255	65025	15.9687	.003922	.0626
256	65536	16.0000	.003906	.0625
257	66049	16.0312	.003891	.0624
258	66564	16.0624	.003876	.0623
259	67081	16.0935	.003861	.0621
260	67600	16.1245	.003846	.0620
261	68121	16.1555	.003831	.0619
262	68644	16.1864	.003817	.0618
263	69169	16.2173	.003802	.0617
264	69696	16.2481	.003788	.0615
265	70225	16.2788	.003774	.0614
266	70756	16.3095	.003759	.0613
267	71289	16.3401	.003745	.0612
268	71824	16.3707	.003731	.0611
269	72361	16.4012	.003717	.0610
270	72900	16.4317	.003704	.0609
271	73441	16.4621	.003690	.0607
272	73984	16.4924	.003676	.0606
273	74529	16.5227	.003663	.0605
274	75076	16.5529	.003650	.0604
275	75625	16.5831	.003636	.0603
276	76176	16.6132	.003623	.0602
277	76729	16.6433	.003610	.0601
278	77284	16.6733	.003597	.0600
279	77841	16.7033	.003584	.0599
280	78400	16.7332	.003571	.0598
281	78961	16.7631	.003559	.0597
282	79524	16.7929	.003546	.0595
283	80089	16.8226	.003534	.0594
284	80656	16.8523	.003521	.0593
285	81225	16.8819	.003509	.0592
286	81796	16.9115	.003497	.0591
287	82369	16.9411	.003484	.0590
288	82944	16.9706	.003472	.0589
289	83521	17.0000	.003460	.0588
290	84100	17.0294	.003448	.0587
291	84681	17.0587	.003436	.0586
292	85264	17.0880	.003425	.0585
293	85849	17.1172	.003413	.0584
294	86436	17.1464	.003401	.0583
295	87025	17.1756	.003390	.0582
296	87616	17.2047	.003378	.0581
297	88209	17.2337	.003367	.0580
298	88804	17.2627	.003356	.0579
299	89401	17.2916	.003344	.0578
300	90000	17.3205	.003333	.0577

Table A.1. *(continued)*

n	n^2	$\sqrt{n}$	$\frac{1}{n}$	$\frac{1}{\sqrt{n}}$
301	90601	17.3494	.003322	.0576
302	91204	17.3781	.003311	.0575
303	91809	17.4069	.003300	.0574
304	92416	17.4356	.003289	.0574
305	93025	17.4642	.003279	.0573
306	93636	17.4929	.003268	.0572
307	94249	17.5214	.003257	.0571
308	94864	17.5499	.003247	.0570
309	95481	17.5784	.003236	.0569
310	96100	17.6068	.003226	.0568
311	96721	17.6352	.003215	.0567
312	97344	17.6635	.003205	.0566
313	97969	17.6918	.003195	.0565
314	98596	17.7200	.003185	.0564
315	99225	17.7482	.003175	.0563
316	99856	17.7764	.003165	.0563
317	100489	17.8045	.003155	.0562
318	101124	17.8326	.003145	.0561
319	101761	17.8606	.003135	.0560
320	102400	17.8885	.003125	.0559
321	103041	17.9165	.003115	.0558
322	103684	17.9444	.003106	.0557
323	104329	17.9722	.003096	.0556
324	104976	18.0000	.003086	.0556
325	105625	18.0278	.003077	.0555
326	106276	18.0555	.003067	.0554
327	106929	18.0831	.003058	.0553
328	107584	18.1108	.003049	.0552
329	108241	18.1384	.003040	.0551
330	108900	18.1659	.003030	.0550
331	109561	18.1934	.003021	.0550
332	110224	18.2209	.003012	.0549
333	110889	18.2483	.003003	.0548
334	111556	18.2757	.002994	.0547
335	112225	18.3030	.002985	.0546
336	112896	18.3303	.002976	.0546
337	113569	18.3576	.002967	.0545
338	114244	18.3848	.002959	.0544
339	114921	18.4120	.002950	.0543
340	115600	18.4391	.002941	.0542
341	116281	18.4662	.002933	.0542
342	116964	18.4932	.002924	.0541
343	117649	18.5203	.002915	.0540
344	118336	18.5472	.002907	.0539
345	119025	18.5742	.002899	.0538
346	119716	18.6011	.002890	.0538
347	120409	18.6279	.002882	.0537
348	121104	18.6548	.002874	.0536
349	121801	18.6815	.002865	.0535
350	122500	18.7083	.002857	.0535

Table A.1. *(continued)*

n	n^2	$\sqrt{n}$	$\frac{1}{n}$	$\frac{1}{\sqrt{n}}$
351	123201	18.7350	.002849	.0534
352	123904	18.7617	.002841	.0533
353	124609	18.7883	.002833	.0532
354	125316	18.8149	.002825	.0531
355	126025	18.8414	.002817	.0531
356	126736	18.8680	.002809	.0530
357	127449	18.8944	.002801	.0529
358	128164	18.9209	.002793	.0529
359	128881	18.9473	.002786	.0528
360	129600	18.9737	.002778	.0527
361	130321	19.0000	.002770	.0526
362	131044	19.0263	.002762	.0526
363	131769	19.0526	.002755	.0525
364	132496	19.0788	.002747	.0524
365	133225	19.1050	.002740	.0523
366	133956	19.1311	.002732	.0523
367	134689	19.1572	.002725	.0522
368	135424	19.1833	.002717	.0521
369	136161	19.2094	.002710	.0521
370	136900	19.2354	.002703	.0520
371	137641	19.2614	.002695	.0519
372	138384	19.2873	.002688	.0518
373	139129	19.3132	.002681	.0518
374	139876	19.3391	.002674	.0517
375	140625	19.3649	.002667	.0516
376	141376	19.3907	.002660	.0516
377	142129	19.4165	.002653	.0515
378	142884	19.4422	.002646	.0514
379	143641	19.4679	.002639	.0514
380	144400	19.4936	.002632	.0513
381	145161	19.5192	.002625	.0512
382	145924	19.5448	.002618	.0512
383	146689	19.5704	.002611	.0511
384	147456	19.5959	.002604	.0510
385	148225	19.6214	.002597	.0510
386	148996	19.6469	.002591	.0509
387	149769	19.6723	.002584	.0508
388	150544	19.6977	.002577	.0508
389	151321	19.7231	.002571	.0507
390	152100	19.7484	.002564	.0506
391	152881	19.7737	.002558	.0506
392	153664	19.7990	.002551	.0505
393	154449	19.8242	.002545	.0504
394	155236	19.8494	.002538	.0504
395	156025	19.8746	.002532	.0503
396	156816	19.8997	.002525	.0503
397	157609	19.9249	.002519	.0502
398	158404	19.9499	.002513	.0501
399	159210	19.9750	.002506	.0501
400	160000	20.0000	.002500	.0500

Table A.1. *(continued)*

n	n^2	$\sqrt{n}$	$\frac{1}{n}$	$\frac{1}{\sqrt{n}}$
401	160801	20.0250	.002494	.0499
402	161604	20.0499	.002488	.0499
403	162409	20.0749	.002481	.0498
404	163216	20.0998	.002475	.0498
405	164025	20.1246	.002469	.0497
406	164836	20.1494	.002463	.0496
407	165649	20.1742	.002457	.0496
408	166464	20.1990	.002451	.0495
409	167281	20.2237	.002445	.0494
410	168100	20.2485	.002439	.0494
411	168921	20.2731	.002433	.0493
412	169744	20.2978	.002427	.0493
413	170569	20.3224	.002421	.0492
414	171396	20.3470	.002415	.0491
415	172225	20.3715	.002410	.0491
416	173056	20.3961	.002404	.0490
417	173889	20.4206	.002398	.0490
418	174724	20.4450	.002392	.0489
419	175561	20.4695	.002387	.0489
420	176400	20.4939	.002381	.0488
421	177241	20.5183	.002375	.0487
422	178084	20.5426	.002370	.0487
423	178929	20.5670	.002364	.0486
424	179776	20.5913	.002358	.0486
425	180625	20.6155	.002353	.0485
426	181476	20.6398	.002347	.0485
427	182329	20.6640	.002342	.0484
428	183184	20.6882	.002336	.0483
429	184041	20.7123	.002331	.0483
430	184900	20.7364	.002326	.0482
431	185761	20.7605	.002320	.0482
432	186624	20.7846	.002315	.0481
433	187489	20.8087	.002309	.0481
434	188356	20.8327	.002304	.0480
435	189225	20.8567	.002299	.0479
436	190096	20.8806	.002294	.0479
437	190969	20.9045	.002288	.0478
438	191844	20.9284	.002283	.0478
439	192721	20.9523	.002278	.0477
440	193600	20.9762	.002273	.0477
441	194481	21.0000	.002268	.0476
442	195364	21.0238	.002262	.0476
443	196249	21.0476	.002257	.0475
444	197136	21.0713	.002252	.0475
445	198025	21.0950	.002247	.0474
446	198916	21.1187	.002242	.0474
447	199809	21.1424	.002237	.0473
448	200704	21.1660	.002232	.0472
449	201601	21.1896	.002227	.0472
450	202500	21.2132	.002222	.0471

Table A.1. *(continued)*

n	n^2	$\sqrt{n}$	$\frac{1}{n}$	$\frac{1}{\sqrt{n}}$
451	203401	21.2368	.002217	.0471
452	204304	21.2603	.002212	.0470
453	205209	21.2838	.002208	.0470
454	206116	21.3073	.002203	.0469
455	207025	21.3307	.002198	.0469
456	207936	21.3542	.002193	.0468
457	208849	21.3776	.002188	.0468
458	209764	21.4009	.002183	.0467
459	210681	21.4243	.002179	.0467
460	211600	21.4476	.002174	.0466
461	212521	21.4709	.002169	.0466
462	213444	21.4942	.002165	.0465
463	214369	21.5174	.002160	.0465
464	215296	21.5407	.002155	.0464
465	216225	21.5639	.002151	.0464
466	217156	21.5870	.002146	.0463
467	218089	21.6102	.002141	.0463
468	219024	21.6333	.002137	.0462
469	219961	21.6564	.002132	.0462
470	220900	21.6795	.002128	.0461
471	221841	21.7025	.002123	.0461
472	222784	21.7256	.002119	.0460
473	223729	21.7486	.002114	.0460
474	224676	21.7715	.002110	.0459
475	225625	21.7945	.002105	.0459
476	226576	21.8174	.002101	.0458
477	227529	21.8403	.002096	.0458
478	228484	21.8632	.002092	.0457
479	229441	21.8861	.002088	.0457
480	230400	21.9089	.002083	.0456
481	231361	21.9317	.002079	.0456
482	232324	21.9545	.002075	.0455
483	233289	21.9773	.002070	.0455
484	234256	22.0000	.002066	.0455
485	235225	22.0227	.002062	.0454
486	236196	22.0454	.002058	.0454
487	237169	22.0681	.002053	.0453
488	238144	22.0907	.002049	.0453
489	239121	22.1133	.002045	.0452
490	240100	22.1359	.002041	.0452
491	241081	22.1585	.002037	.0451
492	242064	22.1811	.002033	.0451
493	243049	22.2036	.002028	.0450
494	244036	22.2261	.002024	.0450
495	245025	22.2486	.002020	.0449
496	246016	22.2711	.002016	.0448
497	247009	22.2935	.002012	.0449
498	248004	22.3159	.002008	.0449
499	249001	22.3383	.002004	.0448
500	250000	22.3607	.002000	.0447

Table A.1. *(continued)*

n	n^2	$\sqrt{n}$	$\frac{1}{n}$	$\frac{1}{\sqrt{n}}$
501	251001	22.3830	.001996	.0447
502	252004	22.4054	.001992	.0446
503	253009	22.4277	.001988	.0446
504	254016	22.4499	.001984	.0445
505	255025	22.4722	.001980	.0445
506	256036	22.4944	.001976	.0445
507	257049	22.5167	.001972	.0444
508	258064	22.5389	.001969	.0444
509	259081	22.5610	.001965	.0443
510	260100	22.5832	.001961	.0443
511	261121	22.6053	.001957	.0442
512	262144	22.6274	.001953	.0442
513	263169	22.6495	.001949	.0442
514	264196	22.6716	.001946	.0441
515	265225	22.6936	.001942	.0441
516	266256	22.7156	.001938	.0440
517	267289	22.7376	.001934	.0440
518	268324	22.7596	.001931	.0439
519	269361	22.7816	.001927	.0439
520	270400	22.8035	.001923	.0439
521	271441	22.8254	.001919	.0438
522	272484	22.8473	.001916	.0438
523	273529	22.8692	.001912	.0437
524	274576	22.8910	.001908	.0437
525	275625	22.9129	.001905	.0436
526	276676	22.9347	.001901	.0436
527	277729	22.9565	.001898	.0436
528	278784	22.9783	.001894	.0435
529	279841	23.0000	.001890	.0435
530	280900	23.0217	.001887	.0434
531	281961	23.0434	.001883	.0434
532	283024	23.0651	.001880	.0434
533	284089	23.0868	.001876	.0433
534	285156	23.1084	.001873	.0433
535	286225	23.1301	.001869	.0432
536	287296	23.1517	.001866	.0432
536	288369	23.1733	.001862	.0432
538	289444	23.1948	.001859	.0431
539	290521	23.2164	.001855	.0431
540	291600	23.2379	.001852	.0430
541	292681	23.2594	.001848	.0430
542	293764	23.2809	.001845	.0430
543	294849	23.3024	.001842	.0429
544	295936	23.3238	.001838	.0429
545	297025	23.3452	.001835	.0428
546	298116	23.3666	.001832	.0428
547	299209	23.3880	.001828	.0428
548	300304	23.4094	.001825	.0427
549	301401	23.4307	.001821	.0427
550	302500	23.4521	.001818	.0426

Table A.1. *(continued)*

n	n^2	$\sqrt{n}$	$\frac{1}{n}$	$\frac{1}{\sqrt{n}}$
551	303601	23.4734	.001815	.0426
552	304704	23.4947	.001812	.0426
553	305809	23.5160	.001808	.0425
554	306916	23.5372	.001805	.0425
555	308025	23.5584	.001802	.0424
556	309136	23.5797	.001799	.0424
557	310249	23.6008	.001795	.0424
558	311364	23.6220	.001792	.0423
559	312481	23.6432	.001789	.0423
560	313600	23.6643	.001786	.0423
561	314721	23.6854	.001783	.0422
562	315844	23.7065	.001779	.0422
563	316969	23.7276	.001776	.0421
564	318096	23.7487	.001773	.0421
565	319225	23.7697	.001770	.0421
566	320356	23.7908	.001767	.0420
567	321489	23.8118	.001764	.0420
568	322624	23.8328	.001761	.0420
569	323761	23.8537	.001757	.0419
570	324900	23.8747	.001754	.0419
571	326041	23.8956	.001751	.0418
572	327184	23.9165	.001748	.0418
573	328329	23.9374	.001745	.0418
574	329476	23.9583	.001742	.0417
575	330625	23.9792	.001739	.0417
576	331776	24.0000	.001736	.0417
577	332929	24.0208	.001733	.0416
578	334084	24.0416	.001730	.0416
579	335241	24.0624	.001727	.0416
580	336400	24.0832	.001724	.0415
581	337561	24.1039	.001721	.0415
582	338724	24.1247	.001718	.0415
583	339889	24.1454	.001715	.0414
584	341056	24.1661	.001712	.0414
585	342225	24.1868	.001709	.0413
586	343396	24.2074	.001706	.0413
587	344569	24.2281	.001704	.0413
588	345744	24.2487	.001701	.0412
589	346921	24.2693	.001698	.0412
590	348100	24.2899	.001695	.0412
591	349281	24.3105	.001692	.0411
592	350464	24.3311	.001689	.0411
593	351649	24.3516	.001686	.0411
594	352836	24.3721	.001684	.0410
595	354025	24.3926	.001681	.0410
596	355216	24.4131	.001678	.0410
597	356409	24.4336	.001675	.0409
598	357604	24.4540	.001672	.0409
599	358801	24.4745	.001669	.0409
600	360000	24.4949	.001667	.0408

Table A.1. *(continued)*

n	n^2	$\sqrt{n}$	$\frac{1}{n}$	$\frac{1}{\sqrt{n}}$
601	361201	24.5153	.001664	.0408
602	362404	24.5357	.001661	.0408
603	363609	24.5561	.001658	.0407
604	364816	24.5764	.001656	.0407
605	366025	24.5967	.001653	.0407
606	367236	24.6171	.001650	.0406
607	368449	24.6374	.001647	.0406
608	369664	24.6577	.001645	.0406
609	370881	24.6779	.001642	.0405
610	372100	24.6982	.001639	.0405
611	373321	24.7184	.001637	.0405
612	374544	24.7386	.001634	.0404
613	375769	24.7588	.001631	.0404
614	376996	24.7790	.001629	.0404
615	378225	24.7992	.001626	.0403
616	379456	24.8193	.001623	.0403
617	380689	24.8395	.001621	.0403
618	381924	24.8596	.001618	.0402
619	383161	24.8797	.001616	.0402
620	384400	24.8998	.001613	.0402
621	385641	24.9199	.001610	.0401
622	386884	24.9399	.001608	.0401
623	388129	24.9600	.001605	.0401
624	389376	24.9800	.001603	.0400
625	390625	25.0000	.001600	.0400
626	391876	25.0200	.001597	.0400
627	393129	25.0400	.001595	.0399
628	394384	25.0599	.001592	.0399
629	395641	25.0799	.001590	.0399
630	396900	25.0998	.001587	.0398
631	398161	25.1197	.001585	.0398
632	399424	25.1396	.001582	.0398
633	400689	25.1595	.001580	.0397
634	401956	25.1794	.001577	.0397
635	403225	25.1992	.001575	.0397
636	404496	25.2190	.001572	.0397
637	405769	25.2389	.001570	.0396
638	407044	25.2587	.001567	.0396
639	408321	25.2784	.001565	.0396
640	409600	25.2982	.001563	.0395
641	410881	25.3180	.001560	.0395
642	412164	25.3377	.001558	.0395
643	413449	25.3574	.001555	.0394
644	414736	25.3772	.001553	.0394
645	416025	25.3969	.001550	.0394
646	417316	25.4165	.001548	.0393
647	418609	25.4362	.001546	.0393
648	419904	25.4558	.001543	.0393
649	421201	25.4755	.001541	.0393
650	422500	25.4951	.001538	.0392

Table A.1. *(continued)*

n	n^2	$\sqrt{n}$	$\frac{1}{n}$	$\frac{1}{\sqrt{n}}$
651	423801	25.5147	.001536	.0392
652	425104	25.5343	.001534	.0392
653	426409	25.5539	.001531	.0391
654	427716	25.5734	.001529	.0391
655	429025	25.5930	.001527	.0391
656	430336	25.6125	.001524	.0390
657	431649	25.6320	.001522	.0390
658	432964	25.6515	.001520	.0390
659	434281	25.6710	.001517	.0390
660	435600	25.6905	.001515	.0389
661	436921	25.7099	.001513	.0389
662	438244	25.7294	.001511	.0389
663	439569	25.7488	.001508	.0388
664	440896	25.7682	.001506	.0388
665	442225	25.7876	.001504	.0388
666	443556	25.8070	.001502	.0387
667	444889	25.8263	.001499	.0387
668	446224	25.8457	.001497	.0387
669	447561	25.8650	.001495	.0387
670	448900	25.8844	.001493	.0386
671	450241	25.9037	.001490	.0386
672	451584	25.9230	.001488	.0386
673	452929	25.9422	.001486	.0385
674	454276	25.9615	.001484	.0385
675	455625	25.9808	.001481	.0385
676	456976	26.0000	.001479	.0385
677	458329	26.0192	.001477	.0384
678	459684	26.0384	.001475	.0384
679	461041	26.0576	.001473	.0384
680	462400	26.0768	.001471	.0383
681	463761	26.0960	.001468	.0383
682	465124	26.1151	.001466	.0383
683	466489	26.1343	.001464	.0383
684	467856	26.1534	.001462	.0382
685	469225	26.1725	.001460	.0382
686	470596	26.1916	.001458	.0382
687	471969	26.2107	.001456	.0382
688	473344	26.2298	.001453	.0381
689	474721	26.2488	.001451	.0381
690	476100	26.2679	.001449	.0381
691	477481	26.2869	.001447	.0380
692	478864	26.3059	.001445	.0380
693	480249	26.3249	.001443	.0380
694	481636	26.3439	.001441	.0380
695	483025	26.3629	.001439	.0379
696	484416	26.3818	.001437	.0379
697	485809	26.4008	.001435	.0379
698	487204	26.4197	.001433	.0379
699	488601	26.4386	.001431	.0378
700	490000	26.4575	.001429	.0378

Table A.1. *(continued)*

n	n^2	$\sqrt{n}$	$\frac{1}{n}$	$\frac{1}{\sqrt{n}}$
701	491401	26.4764	.001427	.0378
702	492804	26.4953	.001425	.0377
703	494209	26.5141	.001422	.0377
704	495616	26.5330	.001420	.0377
705	497025	26.5518	.001418	.0377
706	498436	26.5707	.001416	.0376
707	499849	26.5895	.001414	.0376
708	501264	26.6083	.001412	.0376
709	502681	26.6271	.001410	.0376
710	504100	26.6458	.001408	.0375
711	505521	26.6646	.001406	.0375
712	506944	26.6833	.001404	.0375
713	508369	26.7021	.001403	.0375
714	509796	26.7208	.001401	.0374
715	511225	26.7395	.001399	.0374
716	512656	26.7582	.001397	.0374
717	514089	26.7769	.001395	.0373
718	515524	26.7955	.001393	.0373
719	516961	26.8142	.001391	.0373
720	518400	26.8328	.001389	.0373
721	519841	26.8514	.001387	.0372
722	521284	26.8701	.001385	.0372
723	522729	26.8887	.001383	.0372
724	524176	26.9072	.001381	.0372
725	525625	26.9258	.001379	.0371
726	527076	26.9444	.001377	.0371
727	528529	26.9629	.001376	.0371
728	529984	26.9815	.001374	.0371
729	531441	27.0000	.001372	.0370
730	532900	27.0185	.001370	.0370
731	534361	27.0370	.001368	.0370
732	535824	27.0555	.001366	.0370
733	537289	27.0740	.001364	.0369
734	538756	27.0924	.001362	.0369
735	540225	27.1109	.001361	.0369
736	541696	26.1293	.001359	.0369
737	543169	27.1477	.001357	.0368
738	544644	27.1662	.001355	.0368
739	546121	27.1846	.001353	.0368
740	547600	27.2029	.001351	.0368
741	549081	27.2213	.001350	.0367
742	550564	27.2397	.001348	.0367
743	552049	27.2580	.001346	.0367
744	553536	27.2764	.001344	.0367
745	555025	27.2947	.001342	.0366
746	556516	27.3130	.001340	.0366
747	558009	27.3313	.001339	.0366
748	559504	27.3496	.001337	.0366
749	561001	27.3679	.001335	.0365
750	562500	27.3861	.001333	.0365

Table A.1. *(continued)*

n	n^2	$\sqrt{n}$	$\frac{1}{n}$	$\frac{1}{\sqrt{n}}$
751	564001	27.4044	.001332	.0365
752	565504	27.4226	.001330	.0365
753	567009	27.4408	.001328	.0364
754	568516	27.4591	.001326	.0364
755	570025	27.4773	.001325	.0364
756	571536	27.4955	.001323	.0364
757	573049	27.5136	.001321	.0363
758	574564	27.5318	.001319	.0363
759	576081	27.5500	.001318	.0363
760	577600	27.5681	.001316	.0363
761	579121	27.5862	.001314	.0363
762	580644	27.6043	.001312	.0362
763	582169	27.6225	.001311	.0362
764	583696	27.6405	.001309	.0362
765	585225	27.6586	.001307	.0362
766	586756	27.6767	.001305	.0361
767	588289	27.6948	.001304	.0361
768	589824	27.7128	.001302	.0361
769	591361	27.7308	.001300	.0361
770	592900	27.7489	.001299	.0360
771	594441	27.7669	.001297	.0360
772	595984	27.7849	.001295	.0360
773	597529	27.8029	.001294	.0360
774	599076	27.8209	.001292	.0359
775	600625	27.8388	.001290	.0359
776	602176	27.8568	.001289	.0359
777	603729	27.8747	.001287	.0359
778	605284	27.8927	.001285	.0359
779	606841	27.9106	.001284	.0358
780	608400	27.9285	.001282	.0358
781	609961	27.9464	.001280	.0358
782	611524	27.9643	.001279	.0358
783	613089	27.9821	.001277	.0357
784	614656	28.0000	.001276	.0357
785	616225	28.0179	.001274	.0357
786	617796	28.0357	.001272	.0357
787	619369	28.0535	.001271	.0356
788	620944	28.0713	.001269	.0356
789	622521	28.0891	.001267	.0356
790	624100	28.1069	.001266	.0356
791	625681	28.1247	.001264	.0356
792	627264	28.1425	.001263	.0355
793	628849	28.1603	.001261	.0355
794	630436	28.1780	.001259	.0355
795	632025	28.1957	.001258	.0355
796	633616	28.2135	.001256	.0354
797	635209	28.2312	.001255	.0354
798	636804	28.2489	.001253	.0354
799	638401	28.2666	.001252	.0354
800	640000	28.2843	.001250	.0354

Table A.1. *(continued)*

n	n^2	$\sqrt{n}$	$\frac{1}{n}$	$\frac{1}{\sqrt{n}}$
801	641601	28.3019	.001248	.0353
802	643204	28.3196	.001247	.0353
803	644809	28.3373	.001245	.0353
804	646416	28.3549	.001244	.0353
805	648025	28.3725	.001242	.0352
806	649636	28.3901	.001241	.0352
807	651249	28.4077	.001239	.0352
808	652864	28.4253	.001248	.0352
809	654481	28.4429	.001236	.0352
810	656100	28.4605	.001235	.0351
811	657721	28.4781	.001233	.0351
812	659344	28.4956	.001232	.0351
813	660969	28.5132	.001230	.0351
814	662596	28.5307	.001229	.0351
815	664225	28.5482	.001227	.0350
816	665856	28.5657	.001225	.0350
817	667489	28.5832	.001224	.0350
818	669124	28.6007	.001222	.0350
819	670761	28.6182	.001221	.0349
820	672400	28.6356	.001220	.0349
821	674041	28.6531	.001218	.0349
822	675684	28.6705	.001217	.0349
823	677329	28.6880	.001215	.0349
824	678976	28.7054	.001214	.0348
825	680625	28.7228	.001212	.0348
826	682276	28.7402	.001211	.0348
827	683929	28.7576	.001209	.0348
828	685584	28.7750	.001208	.0348
829	687241	28.7924	.001206	.0347
830	688900	28.8097	.001205	.0347
831	690561	28.8271	.001203	.0347
832	692224	28.8444	.001202	.0347
833	693889	28.8617	.001200	.0346
834	695556	28.8791	.001199	.0346
835	697225	28.8964	.001198	.0346
836	698896	28.9137	.001196	.0346
837	700569	28.9310	.001195	.0346
838	702244	28.9482	.001193	.0345
839	703921	28.9655	.001192	.0345
840	705600	28.9828	.001190	.0345
841	707281	29.0000	.001189	.0345
842	708964	29.0172	.001188	.0345
843	710649	29.0345	.001186	.0344
844	712336	29.0517	.001185	.0344
845	714025	29.0689	.001183	.0344
846	715716	29.0861	.001182	.0344
847	717409	29.1033	.001181	.0344
848	719104	29.1204	.001179	.0343
849	720801	29.1376	.001178	.0343
850	722500	29.1548	.001176	.0343

Table A.1. *(continued)*

n	n^2	$\sqrt{n}$	$\frac{1}{n}$	$\frac{1}{\sqrt{n}}$
851	724201	29.1719	.001175	.0343
852	725904	29.1890	.001174	.0343
853	727609	29.2062	.001172	.0342
854	729316	29.2233	.001171	.0342
855	731025	29.2404	.001170	.0342
856	732736	29.2575	.001168	.0342
857	734449	29.2746	.001167	.0342
858	736164	29.2916	.001166	.0341
859	737881	29.3087	.001164	.0341
860	739600	29.3258	.001163	.0341
861	741321	29.3428	.001161	.0341
862	743044	29.3598	.001160	.0341
863	744769	29.3769	.001159	.0340
864	746496	29.3939	.001157	.0340
865	748225	29.4109	.001156	.0340
866	749956	29.4279	.001155	.0340
867	751689	29.4449	.001153	.0340
868	753424	29.4618	.001152	.0339
869	755161	29.4788	.001151	.0339
870	756900	29.4958	.001149	.0339
871	758641	29.5127	.001148	.0339
872	760384	29.5296	.001147	.0339
873	762129	29.5466	.001145	.0338
874	763876	29.5635	.001144	.0338
875	765625	29.5804	.001143	.0338
876	767376	29.5973	.001142	.0338
877	769129	29.6142	.001140	.0338
878	770884	29.6311	.001139	.0337
879	772641	29.6479	.001138	.0337
880	774400	29.6648	.001136	.0337
881	776161	29.6816	.001135	.0337
882	777924	29.6985	.001134	.0337
883	779689	29.7153	.001133	.0337
884	781456	29.7321	.001131	.0336
885	783225	29.7489	.001130	.0336
886	784996	29.7658	.001129	.0336
887	786769	29.7825	.001127	.0336
888	788544	29.7993	.001126	.0336
889	790321	29.8161	.001125	.0335
890	792100	29.8329	.001124	.0335
891	793881	29.8496	.001122	.0335
892	795664	29.8664	.001121	.0335
893	797449	29.8831	.001120	.0335
894	799236	29.8998	.001119	.0334
895	801025	29.9166	.001117	.0334
896	802816	29.9333	.001116	.0334
897	804609	29.9500	.001115	.0334
898	806404	29.9666	.001114	.0334
899	808201	29.9833	.001112	.0334
900	810000	30.0000	.001111	.0333

Table A.1. *(continued)*

n	n^2	$\sqrt{n}$	$\frac{1}{n}$	$\frac{1}{\sqrt{n}}$
901	811801	30.0167	.001110	.0333
902	813604	30.0333	.001109	.0333
903	815409	30.0500	.001107	.0333
904	817216	30.0666	.001106	.0333
905	819025	30.0832	.001105	.0332
906	820836	30.0998	.001104	.0332
907	822649	30.1164	.001103	.0332
908	824464	30.1330	.001101	.0332
909	826281	30.1496	.001100	.0332
910	828100	30.1662	.001099	.0331
911	829921	30.1828	.001098	.0331
912	831744	30.1993	.001096	.0331
913	833569	30.2159	.001095	.0331
914	835396	30.2324	.001094	.0331
915	837225	30.2490	.001093	.0331
916	839056	30.2655	.001092	.0330
917	840889	30.2820	.001091	.0330
918	842724	30.2985	.001089	.0330
919	844561	30.3150	.001088	.0330
920	846400	30.3315	.001087	.0330
921	848241	30.3480	.001086	.0330
922	850084	30.3645	.001085	.0329
923	851929	30.3809	.001083	.0329
924	853776	30.3974	.001082	.0329
925	855625	30.4138	.001081	.0329
926	857476	30.4302	.001080	.0329
927	859329	30.4467	.001079	.0238
928	861184	30.4631	.001078	.0328
929	863041	30.4795	.001076	.0328
930	864900	30.4959	.001075	.0328
931	866761	30.5123	.001074	.0328
932	868624	30.5287	.001073	.0328
933	870489	30.5450	.001072	.0327
934	872356	30.5614	.001071	.0327
935	874225	30.5778	.001070	.0327
936	876096	30.5941	.001068	.0327
937	877969	30.6105	.001067	.0327
938	879844	30.6268	.001066	.0327
939	881721	30.6431	.001065	.0326
940	883600	30.6594	.001064	.0326
941	885481	30.6757	.001063	.0326
942	887364	30.6920	.001062	.0326
943	889249	30.7083	.001060	.0326
944	891136	30.7246	.001059	.0325
945	893025	30.7409	.001058	.0325
946	894916	30.7571	.001057	.0325
947	896809	30.7734	.001056	.0325
948	898704	30.7896	.001055	.0325
949	900601	30.8058	.001054	.0325
950	902500	30.8221	.001053	.0324

Table A.1. *(continued)*

n	n^2	$\sqrt{n}$	$\frac{1}{n}$	$\frac{1}{\sqrt{n}}$
951	904401	30.8383	.001052	.0324
952	906304	30.8545	.001050	.0324
953	908209	30.8707	.001049	.0324
954	910116	30.8869	.001048	.0324
955	912025	30.9031	.001047	.0324
956	913936	30.9192	.001046	.0323
957	915849	30.9354	.001045	.0323
958	917764	30.9516	.001044	.0323
959	919681	30.9677	.001043	.0323
960	921600	30.9839	.001042	.0323
961	923521	31.0000	.001041	.0323
962	925444	31.0161	.001040	.0322
963	927369	31.0322	.001038	.0322
964	929296	31.0483	.001037	.0322
965	931225	31.0644	.001036	.0322
966	933156	31.0805	.001035	.0322
967	935089	31.0966	.001034	.0322
968	937024	31.1127	.001033	.0321
969	938961	31.1288	.001032	.0321
970	940900	31.1448	.001031	.0321
971	942841	31.1609	.001030	.0321
972	944784	31.1769	.001029	.0321
973	946729	31.1929	.001028	.0321
974	948676	31.2090	.001027	.0320
975	950625	31.2250	.001026	.0320
976	952576	31.2410	.001025	.0320
977	954529	31.2570	.001024	.0320
978	956484	31.2730	.001022	.0320
979	958441	31.2890	.001021	.0320
980	960400	31.3050	.001020	.0319
981	962361	31.3209	.001019	.0319
982	964324	31.3369	.001018	.0319
983	966289	31.3528	.001017	.0319
984	968256	31.3688	.001016	.0319
985	970225	31.3847	.001015	.0319
986	972196	31.4006	.001014	.0318
987	974169	31.4166	.001013	.0318
988	976144	31.4325	.001012	.0318
989	978121	31.4484	.001011	.0318
990	980100	31.4643	.001010	.0318
991	982081	31.4802	.001009	.0318
992	984064	31.4960	.001008	.0318
993	986049	31.5119	.001007	.0317
994	988036	31.5278	.001006	.0317
995	990025	31.5436	.001005	.0317
996	992016	31.5595	.001004	.0317
997	994009	31.5753	.001003	.0317
998	996004	31.5911	.001002	.0317
999	998001	31.6070	.001001	.0316
1000	1000000	31.6228	.001000	.0316

Table A.2. Random Numbers

10097	32533	76520	13586	34673	54876	80959	09117	39292	74945
37542	04805	64894	74296	24805	24037	20636	10402	00822	91665
08422	68953	19645	09303	23209	02560	15953	34764	35080	33606
99019	02529	09376	70715	38311	31165	88676	74397	04436	27659
12807	99970	80157	36147	64032	36653	98951	16877	12171	76833
66065	74717	34072	76850	36697	36170	65813	39885	11199	29170
31060	10805	45571	82406	35303	42614	86799	07439	23403	09732
85269	77602	02051	65692	68665	74818	73053	85247	18623	88579
63573	32135	05325	47048	90553	57548	28468	28709	83491	25624
73796	45753	03529	64778	35808	34282	60935	20344	35273	88435
98520	17767	14905	68607	22109	40558	60970	93433	50500	73998
11805	05431	39808	27732	50725	68248	29405	24201	52775	67851
83452	99634	06288	98083	13746	70078	18475	40610	68711	77817
88685	40200	86507	58401	36766	67951	90364	76493	29609	11062
99594	67348	87517	64969	91826	08928	93785	61368	23478	34113
65481	17674	17468	50950	58047	76974	73039	57186	40218	16544
80124	35635	17727	08015	45318	22374	21115	78253	14385	53763
74350	99817	77402	77214	43236	00210	45521	64237	96286	02655
69916	26803	66252	29148	36936	87203	76621	13990	94400	56418
09893	20505	14225	68514	46427	56788	96297	78822	54382	14598
91499	14523	68479	27686	46162	83554	94750	89923	37089	20048
80336	94598	26940	36858	70297	34135	53140	33340	42050	82341
44104	81949	85157	47954	32979	26575	57600	40881	22222	06413
12550	73742	11100	02040	12860	74697	96644	89439	28707	25815
63606	49329	16505	34484	40219	52563	43651	77082	07207	31790
61196	90446	26457	47774	51924	33729	65394	59593	42582	60527
15474	45266	95270	79953	59367	83848	82396	10118	33211	59466
94557	28573	67897	54387	54622	44431	91190	42592	92927	45973
42481	16213	97344	08721	16868	48767	03071	12059	25701	46670
23523	78317	73208	89837	68935	91416	26252	29663	05522	82562
04493	52494	75246	33824	45862	51025	61962	79335	65337	12472
00549	97654	64051	88159	96119	63896	54692	82391	23287	29529
35963	15307	26898	09354	33351	35462	77974	50024	90103	39333
59808	08391	45427	26842	83609	49700	13021	24892	78565	20106
46058	85236	01390	92286	77281	44077	93910	83647	70617	42941
32179	00597	87379	25241	05567	07007	86743	17157	85394	11838
69234	61406	20117	45204	15956	60000	18743	92423	97118	96338
19565	41430	01758	75379	40419	21585	66674	36806	84962	85207
45155	14938	19476	07246	43667	94543	59047	90033	20826	69541
94864	31994	36168	10851	34888	81553	01540	35456	05014	51176
98086	24826	45240	28404	44999	08896	39094	73407	35441	31880
33185	16232	41941	50949	89435	48581	88695	41994	37548	73043
80951	00406	96382	70774	20151	23387	25016	25298	94624	61171
79752	49140	71961	28296	69861	02591	74852	20539	00387	59579
18633	32537	98145	06571	31010	24674	05455	61427	77938	91936
74029	43902	77557	32270	97790	17119	52527	58021	80814	51748
54178	45611	80993	37143	05335	12969	56127	19255	36040	90324
11664	49883	52079	84827	59381	71539	09973	33440	88461	23356
48324	77928	31249	64710	02295	36870	32307	57546	15020	09994
69074	94138	87637	91976	35584	04401	10518	21615	01848	76938

Source: The RAND corporation. *A Million Random Digits.* The Free Press, Glencoe, Illinois, 1955. By the kind permission of the publishers.

Table A.2. *(continued)*

09188	20097	32825	39527	04220	86304	83389	87374	64278	58044
90045	85497	51981	50654	94938	81997	91870	76150	68476	64659
73189	50207	47677	26269	62290	64464	27124	67018	41361	82760
75768	76490	20971	87749	90429	12272	95375	05871	93823	43178
54016	44056	66281	31003	00682	27398	20714	53295	07706	17813
08358	69910	78542	42785	13661	58873	04618	97553	31223	08420
28306	03264	81333	10591	40510	07893	32604	60475	94119	01840
53840	86233	81594	13628	51215	90290	28466	68795	77762	20791
91757	53741	61613	62269	50263	90212	55781	76514	83483	47055
89415	92694	00397	58391	12607	17646	48949	72306	94541	37408
77513	03820	86864	29901	68414	82774	51908	13980	72893	55507
19502	37174	69979	20288	55210	29773	74287	75251	65344	67415
21818	59313	93278	81757	05686	73156	07082	85046	31853	38452
51474	66499	68107	23621	94049	91345	42836	09191	08007	45449
99559	68331	62535	24170	69777	12830	74819	78142	43860	72834
33713	48007	93584	72869	51926	64721	58303	29822	93174	93972
85274	86893	11303	22970	28834	34137	73515	90400	71148	43643
84133	89640	44035	52166	73852	70091	61222	60561	62327	18423
56732	16234	17395	96131	10123	91622	85496	57560	81604	18880
65138	56806	87648	85261	34313	65861	45875	21069	85644	47277
38001	02176	81719	11711	71602	92937	74219	64049	65584	49698
37402	96397	01304	77586	56271	10086	47324	62605	40030	37438
97125	40348	87083	31417	21815	39250	75237	62047	15501	29578
21826	41134	47143	34072	64638	85902	49139	06441	03856	54552
73135	42742	95719	09035	85794	74296	08789	88156	64691	19202
07638	77929	03061	18072	96207	44156	23821	99538	04713	66994
60528	83441	07954	19814	59175	20695	05533	52139	61212	06455
83596	35655	06958	92983	05128	09719	77433	53783	92301	50498
10850	62746	99599	10507	13499	06319	53075	71839	06410	19362
39820	98952	43622	63147	64421	80814	43800	09351	31024	73167
59580	06478	75569	78800	88835	54486	23768	06156	04111	08408
38508	07341	23793	48763	90822	97022	17719	04207	95954	49953
30692	70668	94688	16127	56196	80091	82067	63400	05462	69200
65443	95659	18288	27437	49632	24041	08337	65676	96299	90836
27267	50264	13192	72294	07477	44606	17985	48911	97341	30358
91307	06991	19072	24210	36699	53728	28825	35793	28976	66252
68434	94688	84473	13622	62126	98408	12843	82590	09815	93146
48908	15877	54745	24591	35700	04754	83824	52692	54130	55160
06913	45197	42672	78601	11883	09528	63011	98901	14974	40344
10455	16019	14210	33712	91342	37821	88325	80851	43667	70883
12883	97343	65027	61184	04285	01392	17974	15077	90712	26769
21778	30976	38807	36961	31649	42096	63281	02023	08816	47449
19523	59515	65122	59659	86283	68258	69572	13798	16435	91529
67245	52670	35583	16563	79246	86686	76463	34222	26655	90802
60584	47377	07500	37992	45134	26529	26760	83637	41326	44344
53853	41377	36066	94850	58838	73859	49364	73331	96240	43642
24637	38736	74384	89342	52623	07992	12369	18601	03742	83873
83080	12451	38992	22815	07759	51777	97377	27585	51972	37867
16444	24334	36151	99073	27493	70939	85130	32552	54846	54759
60790	18157	57178	65762	11161	78576	45819	52979	65130	04860

Table A.2. *(continued)*

03991	10461	93716	16894	66083	24653	84609	58232	88618	19161
38555	95554	32886	59780	08355	60860	29735	47762	71299	23853
17546	73704	92052	46215	55121	29281	59076	07936	27954	58909
32643	52861	95819	06831	00911	98936	76355	93779	80863	00514
69572	68777	39510	35905	14060	40619	29549	69616	33564	60780
24122	66591	27699	06494	14845	46672	61958	77100	90899	75754
61196	30231	92962	61773	41839	55382	17267	70943	78038	70267
30532	21704	10274	12202	39685	23309	10061	68829	55986	66485
03788	97599	75867	20717	74416	53166	35208	33374	87539	08823
48228	63379	85783	47619	53152	67433	35663	52972	16818	60311
60365	94653	35075	33949	42614	29297	01918	28316	98953	73231
83799	42402	56623	34442	34994	41374	70071	14736	09958	18065
32960	07405	36409	83232	99385	41600	11133	07586	15917	06253
19322	53845	57620	52606	66497	68646	78138	66559	19640	99413
11220	94747	07399	37408	48509	23929	27482	45476	85244	35159
31751	57260	68980	05339	15470	48355	88651	22596	03152	19121
88492	99382	14454	04504	20094	98977	74843	93413	22109	78508
30934	47744	07481	83828	73788	06533	28597	20405	94205	20380
22888	48893	27499	98748	60530	45128	74022	84617	82037	10268
78212	16993	35902	91386	44372	15486	65741	14014	87481	37220
41849	84547	46850	52326	34677	58300	74910	64345	19325	81549
46352	33049	69248	93460	45305	07521	61318	31855	14413	70951
11087	96294	14013	31792	59747	67277	76503	34513	39663	77544
52701	08337	56303	87315	16520	69676	11654	99893	02181	68161
57275	36898	81304	48585	68652	27376	92852	55866	88448	03584
20857	73156	70284	24326	79375	95220	01159	63267	10622	48391
15633	84924	90415	93614	33521	26665	55823	47641	86225	31704
92694	48297	39904	02115	59589	49067	66821	41575	49767	04037
77613	19019	88152	00080	20554	91409	96277	48257	50816	97616
38688	32486	45134	63545	59404	72059	43947	51680	43852	59693
25163	01889	70014	15021	41290	67312	71857	15957	68971	11403
65251	07629	37239	33295	05870	01119	92784	26340	18477	65622
36815	43625	18637	37509	82444	99005	04921	73701	14707	93997
64397	11692	05327	82162	20247	81759	45197	25332	83745	22567
04515	25624	95096	67946	48460	85558	15191	18782	16930	33361
83761	60873	43253	84145	60833	25983	01291	41349	20368	07126
14387	06345	80854	09279	43529	06318	38384	74761	41196	37480
51321	92246	80088	77074	88722	56736	66164	49431	66919	31678
72472	00008	80890	18002	94813	31900	54155	83436	35352	54131
05466	55306	93128	18464	74457	90561	72848	11834	79982	68416
39528	72484	82474	25593	48545	35247	18619	13674	18611	19241
81616	18711	53342	44276	75122	11724	74627	73707	58319	15997
07586	16120	82641	22820	92904	13141	32392	19763	61199	67940
90767	04235	13574	17200	69902	63742	78464	22501	18627	90872
40188	28193	29593	88627	94972	11598	62095	36787	00441	58997
34414	82157	86887	55087	19152	00023	12302	80783	32624	68691
63439	75363	44989	16822	36024	00867	76378	41605	65961	73488
67049	09070	93399	45547	94458	74284	05041	49807	20288	34060
79495	04146	52162	90286	54158	34243	46978	35482	59362	95938
91704	30552	04737	21031	75051	93029	47665	64382	99782	93478

Table A.3. Areas under the Normal Curve:
Fractions of Unit Area from 0 to Z

Z	0.00	0.01	0.02	0.03	0.04	0.05	0.06	0.07	0.08	0.09
0.0	0.0000	0.0040	0.0080	0.0120	0.0160	0.0199	0.0239	0.0279	0.0319	0.0359
0.1	.0398	.0438	.0478	.0517	.0557	.0596	.0636	.0675	.0714	.0753
0.2	.0793	.0832	.0871	.0910	.0948	.0987	.1026	.1064	.1103	.1141
0.3	.1179	.1217	.1255	.1293	.1331	.1368	.1406	.1443	.1480	.1517
0.4	.1554	.1591	.1628	.1664	.1700	.1736	.1772	.1808	.1844	.1879
0.5	.1915	.1950	.1985	.2019	.2054	.2088	.2123	.2157	.2190	.2224
0.6	.2257	.2291	.2324	.2357	.2389	.2422	.2454	.2486	.2517	.2549
0.7	.2580	.2611	.2642	.2673	.2704	.2734	.2764	.2794	.2823	.2852
0.8	.2881	.2910	.2939	.2967	.2995	.3023	.3051	.3078	.3106	.3133
0.9	.3159	.3186	.3212	.3238	.3264	.3289	.3315	.3340	.3365	.3389
1.0	.3413	.3438	.3461	.3485	.3508	.3531	.3554	.3577	.3599	.3621
1.1	.3643	.3665	.3686	.3708	.3729	.3749	.3770	.3790	.3810	.3830
1.2	.3849	.3869	.3888	.3907	.3925	.3944	.3962	.3980	.3997	.4015
1.3	.4032	.4049	.4066	.4082	.4099	.4115	.4131	.4147	.4162	.4177
1.4	.4192	.4207	.4222	.4236	.4251	.4265	.4279	.4292	.4306	.4319
1.5	.4332	.4345	.4357	.4370	.4382	.4394	.4406	.4418	.4429	.4441
1.6	.4452	.4463	.4474	.4484	.4495	.4505	.4515	.4525	.4535	.4545
1.7	.4554	.4564	.4573	.4582	.4591	.4599	.4608	.4616	.4625	.4633
1.8	.4641	.4649	.4656	.4664	.4671	.4678	.4686	.4693	.4699	.4706
1.9	.4713	.4719	.4726	.4732	.4738	.4744	.4750	.4756	.4761	.4767
2.0	.4772	.4778	.4783	.4788	.4793	.4798	.4803	.4808	.4812	.4817
2.1	.4821	.4826	.4830	.4834	.4838	.4842	.4846	.4850	.4854	.4857
2.2	.4861	.4864	.4868	.4871	.4875	.4878	.4881	.4884	.4887	.4890
2.3	.4893	.4896	.4898	.4901	.4904	.4906	.4909	.4911	.4913	.4916
2.4	.4918	.4920	.4922	.4925	.4927	.4929	.4931	.4932	.4934	.4936
2.5	.4938	.4940	.4941	.4943	.4945	.4946	.4948	.4949	.4951	.4952
2.6	.4953	.4955	.4956	.4957	.4959	.4960	.4961	.4962	.4963	.4964
2.7	.4965	.4966	.4967	.4968	.4969	.4970	.4971	.4972	.4973	.4974
2.8	.4974	.4975	.4976	.4977	.4977	.4978	.4979	.4979	.4980	.4981
2.9	.4981	.4982	.4982	.4983	.4984	.4984	.4985	.4985	.4986	.4986
3.0	.4987	.4987	.4987	.4988	.4988	.4989	.4989	.4989	.4990	.4990
3.1	.4990	.4991	.4991	.4991	.4992	.4992	.4992	.4992	.4993	.4993
3.2	.4993	.4993	.4994	.4994	.4994	.4994	.4994	.4995	.4995	.4995
3.3	.4995	.4995	.4995	.4996	.4996	.4996	.4996	.4996	.4996	.4997
3.4	.4997	.4997	.4997	.4997	.4997	.4997	.4997	.4997	.4997	.4998
3.6	.4998	.4998	.4999	.4999	.4999	.4999	.4999	.4999	.4999	.4999
3.9	.5000									

Source: Harold O. Rugg. *Statistical Methods Applied to Education.* Boston: Houghton Mifflin Company, 1917. Table III, pp. 389-390. With the kind permission of the publishers. Reproduced by permission from *Statistical Methods,* 6th edition, by George W. Snedecor and William G. Cochran. © 1967 by the Iowa State University Press.

Table A.4. Distribution of χ^2

	Probability (two-tailed)*													
df	.99	.98	.95	.90	.80	.70	.50	.30	.20	.10	.05	.02	.01	.001
1	$.0^3157$	$.0^3628$	.00393	.0158	.0642	.148	.455	1.074	1.642	2.706	3.841	5.412	6.635	10.827
2	.0201	.0404	.103	.211	.446	.713	1.386	2.408	3.219	4.605	5.991	7.824	9.210	13.815
3	.115	.185	.352	.584	1.005	1.424	2.366	3.665	4.642	6.251	7.815	9.837	11.345	16.268
4	.297	.429	.711	1.064	1.649	2.195	3.357	4.878	5.989	7.779	9.488	11.668	13.277	18.465
5	.554	.752	1.145	1.610	2.343	3.000	4.351	6.064	7.289	9.236	11.070	13.388	15.086	20.517
6	.872	1.134	1.635	2.204	3.070	3.828	5.348	7.231	8.558	10.645	12.592	15.033	16.812	22.457
7	1.239	1.564	2.167	2.833	3.822	4.671	6.346	8.383	9.803	12.017	14.067	16.622	18.475	24.322
8	1.646	2.032	2.733	3.490	4.594	5.527	7.344	9.524	11.030	13.362	15.507	18.168	20.090	26.125
9	2.088	2.532	3.325	4.168	5.380	6.393	8.343	10.656	12.242	14.684	16.919	19.679	21.666	27.877
10	2.558	3.059	3.940	4.865	6.179	7.267	9.342	11.781	13.442	15.987	18.307	21.161	23.209	29.588
11	3.053	3.609	4.575	5.578	6.989	8.148	10.341	12.899	14.631	17.275	19.675	22.618	24.725	31.264
12	3.571	4.178	5.226	6.304	7.807	9.034	11.340	14.011	15.812	18.549	21.026	24.054	26.217	32.909
13	4.107	4.765	5.892	7.042	8.634	9.926	12.340	15.119	16.985	19.812	22.362	25.472	27.688	34.528
14	4.660	5.368	6.571	7.790	9.467	10.821	13.339	16.222	18.151	21.064	23.685	26.873	29.141	36.123
15	5.229	5.985	7.261	8.547	10.307	11.721	14.339	17.322	19.311	22.307	24.996	28.259	30.578	37.697
16	5.812	6.614	7.962	9.312	11.152	12.624	15.338	18.418	20.465	23.542	26.296	29.633	32.000	39.252
17	6.408	7.255	8.672	10.085	12.002	13.531	16.338	19.511	21.615	24.769	27.587	30.995	33.409	40.790
18	7.015	7.906	9.390	10.865	12.857	14.440	17.338	20.601	22.760	25.989	28.869	32.346	34.805	42.312
19	7.633	8.567	10.117	11.651	13.716	15.352	18.338	21.689	23.900	27.204	30.144	33.687	36.191	43.820
20	8.260	9.237	10.851	12.443	14.578	16.266	19.337	22.775	25.038	28.412	31.410	35.020	37.566	45.315
21	8.897	9.915	11.591	13.240	15.445	17.182	20.337	23.858	26.171	29.615	32.671	36.343	38.932	46.797
22	9.542	10.600	12.338	14.041	16.314	18.101	21.337	24.939	27.301	30.813	33.924	37.659	40.289	48.268
23	10.196	11.293	13.091	14.848	17.187	19.021	22.337	26.018	28.429	32.007	35.172	38.968	41.638	49.728
24	10.856	11.992	13.848	15.659	18.062	19.943	23.337	27.096	29.553	33.196	36.415	40.270	42.980	51.179
25	11.524	12.697	14.611	16.473	18.940	20.867	24.337	28.172	30.675	34.382	37.652	41.566	44.314	52.620
26	12.198	13.409	15.379	17.292	19.820	21.792	25.336	29.246	31.795	35.563	38.885	42.856	45.642	54.052
27	12.879	14.125	16.151	18.114	20.703	22.719	26.336	30.319	32.912	36.741	40.113	44.140	46.963	55.476
28	13.565	14.847	16.928	18.939	21.588	23.647	27.336	31.391	34.027	37.916	41.337	45.419	48.278	56.893
29	14.256	15.574	17.708	19.768	22.475	24.577	28.336	32.461	35.139	39.087	42.557	46.693	49.588	58.302
30	14.953	16.306	18.493	20.599	23.364	25.508	29.336	33.530	36.250	40.256	43.773	47.962	50.892	59.703

* For one-tailed applications, simply *halve* the probability shown; that is, .10 (two-tailed) becomes .10/2, or .05, for a one-tailed probability.

Source: Ronald A. Fisher and Frank Yates. ***Statistical Tables for Biological, Agricultural and Medical Research.*** **Edinburgh: Oliver & Boyd, Ltd. By permission of the authors and publishers. Table V. Reprinted from *Basic Statistical Methods* (2nd ed.), N. M. Downie and R. W. Heath, Harper & Row, 1965.**

Table A.5. Distribution of *t*

df	Level of significance for one-tailed test					
	.10	.05	.025	.01	.005	.0005
	Level of significance for two-tailed test					
	.20	.10	.05	.02	.01	.001
1	3.078	6.314	12.706	31.821	63.657	636.619
2	1.886	2.920	4.303	6.965	9.925	31.598
3	1.638	2.353	3.182	4.541	5.841	12.941
4	1.533	2.132	2.776	3.747	4.604	8.610
5	1.476	2.015	2.571	3.365	4.032	6.859
6	1.440	1.943	2.447	3.143	3.707	5.959
7	1.415	1.895	2.365	2.998	3.499	5.405
8	1.397	1.860	2.306	2.896	3.355	5.041
9	1.383	1.833	2.262	2.821	3.250	4.781
10	1.372	1.812	2.228	2.764	3.169	4.587
11	1.363	1.796	2.201	2.718	3.106	4.437
12	1.356	1.782	2.179	2.681	3.055	4.318
13	1.350	1.771	2.160	2.650	3.012	4.221
14	1.345	1.761	2.145	2.624	2.977	4.140
15	1.341	1.753	2.131	2.602	2.947	4.073
16	1.337	1.746	2.120	2.583	2.921	4.015
17	1.333	1.740	2.110	2.567	2.898	3.965
18	1.330	1.734	2.101	2.552	2.878	3.922
19	1.328	1.729	2.093	2.539	2.861	3.883
20	1.325	1.725	2.086	2.528	2.845	3.850
21	1.323	1.721	2.080	2.518	2.831	3.819
22	1.321	1.717	2.074	2.508	2.819	3.792
23	1.319	1.714	2.069	2.500	2.807	3.767
24	1.318	1.711	2.064	2.492	2.797	3.745
25	1.316	1.708	2.060	2.485	2.787	3.725
26	1.315	1.706	2.056	2.479	2.779	3.707
27	1.314	1.703	2.052	2.473	2.771	3.690
28	1.313	1.701	2.048	2.467	2.763	3.674
29	1.311	1.699	2.045	2.462	2.756	3.659
30	1.310	1.697	2.042	2.457	2.750	3.646
40	1.303	1.684	2.021	2.423	2.704	3.551
60	1.296	1.671	2.000	2.390	2.660	3.460
120	1.289	1.658	1.980	2.358	2.617	3.373
∞	1.282	1.645	1.960	2.326	2.576	3.291

Source: Abridged from Ronald A. Fisher and Frank Yates. *Statistical Tables for Biological, Agricultural and Medical Research.* Edinburgh: Oliver & Boyd Ltd. By permission of the authors and publishers. Table III. Reprinted from *Nonparametric Statistics for the Behavioral Sciences,* Sidney Siegel, McGraw-Hill Book Company, 1956, by the kind permission of the publishers.

Table A.6. Values of Z for Given Values of r

r	.000	.001	.002	.003	.004	.005	.006	.007	.008	.009
.000	.0000	.0010	.0020	.0030	.0040	.0050	.0060	.0070	.0080	.0090
.010	.0100	.0110	.0120	.0130	.0140	.0150	.0160	.0170	.0180	.0190
.020	.0200	.0210	.0220	.0230	.0240	.0250	.0260	.0270	.0280	.0290
.030	.0300	.0310	.0320	.0330	.0340	.0350	.0360	.0370	.0380	.0390
.040	.0400	.0410	.0420	.0430	.0440	.0450	.0460	.0470	.0480	.0490
.050	.0501	.0511	.0521	.0531	.0541	.0551	.0561	.0571	.0581	.0591
.060	.0601	.0611	.0621	.0631	.0641	.0651	.0661	.0671	.0681	.0691
.070	.0701	.0711	.0721	.0731	.0741	.0751	.0761	.0771	.0782	.0792
.080	.0802	.0812	.0822	.0832	.0842	.0852	.0862	.0872	.0882	.0892
.090	.0902	.0912	.0922	.0933	.0943	.0953	.0963	.0973	.0983	.0993
.100	.1003	.1013	.1024	.1034	.1044	.1054	.1064	.1074	.1084	.1094
.110	.1105	.1115	.1125	.1135	.1145	.1155	.1165	.1175	.1185	.1195
.120	.1206	.1216	.1226	.1236	.1246	.1257	.1267	.1277	.1287	.1297
.130	.1308	.1318	.1328	.1338	.1348	.1358	.1368	.1379	.1389	.1399
.140	.1409	.1419	.1430	.1440	.1450	.1460	.1470	.1481	.1491	.1501
.150	.1511	.1522	.1532	.1542	.1552	.1563	.1573	.1583	.1593	.1604
.160	.1614	.1624	.1634	.1644	.1655	.1665	.1676	.1686	.1696	.1706
.170	.1717	.1727	.1737	.1748	.1758	.1768	.1779	.1789	.1799	.1810
.180	.1820	.1830	.1841	.1851	.1861	.1872	.1882	.1892	.1903	.1913
.190	.1923	.1934	.1944	.1954	.1965	.1975	.1986	.1996	.2007	.2017
.200	.2027	.2038	.2048	.2059	.2069	.2079	.2090	.2100	.2111	.2121
.210	.2132	.2142	.2153	.2163	.2174	.2184	.2194	.2205	.2215	.2226
.220	.2237	.2247	.2258	.2268	.2279	.2289	.2300	.2310	.2321	.2331
.230	.2342	.2353	.2363	.2374	.2384	.2395	.2405	.2416	.2427	.2437
.240	.2448	.2458	.2469	.2480	.2490	.2501	.2511	.2522	.2533	.2543
.250	.2554	.2565	.2575	.2586	.2597	.2608	.2618	.2629	.2640	.2650
.260	.2661	.2672	.2682	.2693	.2704	.2715	.2726	.2736	.2747	.2758
.370	.2769	.2779	.2790	.2801	.2812	.2823	.2833	.2844	.2855	.2866
.280	.2877	.2888	.2898	.2909	.2920	.2931	.2942	.2953	.2964	.2975
.290	.2986	.2997	.3008	.3019	.3029	.3040	.3051	.3062	.3073	.3084
.300	.3095	.3106	.3117	.3128	.3139	.3150	.3161	.3172	.3183	.3195
.310	.3206	.3217	.3228	.3239	.3250	.3261	.3272	.3283	.3294	.3305
.320	.3317	.3328	.3339	.3350	.3361	.3372	.3384	.3395	.3406	.3417
.330	.3428	.3439	.3451	.3462	.3473	.3484	.3496	.3507	.3518	.3530
.340	.3541	.3552	.3564	.3575	.3586	.3597	.3609	.3620	.3632	.3643
.350	.3654	.3666	.3677	.3689	.3700	.3712	.3723	.3734	.3746	.3757
.360	.3769	.3780	.3792	.3803	.3815	.3826	.3838	.3850	.3861	.3873
.370	.3884	.3896	.3907	.3919	.3931	.3942	.3954	.3966	.3977	.3989
.380	.4001	.4012	.4024	.4036	.4047	.4059	.4071	.4083	.4094	.4106
.390	.4118	.4130	.4142	.4153	.4165	.4177	.4189	.4201	.4213	.4225
.400	.4236	.4248	.4260	.4272	.4284	.4296	.4308	.4320	.4332	.4344
.410	.4356	.4368	.4380	.4392	.4404	.4416	.4429	.4441	.4453	.4465
.420	.4477	.4489	.4501	.4513	.4526	.4538	.4550	.4562	.4574	.4587
.430	.4599	.4611	.4623	.4636	.4648	.4660	.4673	.4685	.4697	.4710
.440	.4722	.4735	.4747	.4760	.4772	.4784	.4797	.4809	.4822	.4835
.450	.4847	.4860	.4872	.4885	.4897	.4910	.4923	.4935	.4948	.4961
.460	.4973	.4986	.4999	.5011	.5024	.5037	.5049	.5062	.5075	.5088
.470	.5101	.5114	.5126	.5139	.5152	.5165	.5178	.5191	.5204	.5217
.480	.5230	.5243	.5256	.5279	.5282	.5295	.5308	.5321	.5334	.5347
.490	.5361	.5374	.5387	.5400	.5413	.5427	.5440	.5453	.5466	.5480

Source: Albert E. Waugh. *Statistical Tables and Problems.* New York: McGraw-Hill Book Company, Inc., 1952. Used with the kind permission of the publisher. Table A11, pp. 40-41 in the source.

Table A.6. *(continued)*

r	.000	.001	.002	.003	.004	.005	.006	.007	.008	.009
.500	.5493	.5506	.5520	.5533	.5547	.5560	.5573	.5587	.5600	.5614
.510	.5627	.5641	.5654	.5668	.5681	.5695	.5709	.5722	.5736	.5750
.520	.5763	.5777	.5791	.5805	.5818	.5832	.5846	.5860	.5874	.5888
.530	.5901	.5915	.5929	.5943	.5957	.5971	.5985	.5999	.6013	.6027
.540	.6042	.6056	.6070	.6084	.6098	.6112	.6127	.6141	.6155	.6170
.550	.6184	.6198	.6213	.6227	.6241	.6256	.6270	.6285	.6299	.6314
.560	.6328	.6343	.6358	.6372	.6387	.6401	.6416	.6431	.6446	.6460
.570	.6475	.6490	.6505	.6520	.6535	.6550	.6565	.6579	.6594	.6610
.580	.6625	.6640	.6655	.6670	.6685	.6700	.6715	.6731	.6746	.6761
.590	.6777	.6792	.6807	.6823	.6838	.6854	.6869	.6885	.6900	.6916
.600	.6931	.6947	.6963	.6978	.6994	.7010	.7026	.7042	.7057	.7073
.610	.7089	.7105	.7121	.7137	.7153	.7169	.7185	.7201	.7218	.7234
.620	.7250	.7266	.7283	.7299	.7315	.7332	.7348	.7364	.7381	.7398
.630	.7414	.7431	.7447	.7464	.7481	.7497	.7514	.7531	.7548	.7565
.640	.7582	.7599	.7616	.7633	.7650	.7667	.7684	.7701	.7718	.7736
.650	.7753	.7770	.7788	.7805	.7823	.7840	.7858	.7875	.7893	.7910
.660	.7928	.7946	.7964	.7981	.7999	.8017	.8035	.8053	.8071	.8089
.670	.8107	.8126	.8144	.8162	.8180	.8199	.8217	.8236	.8254	.8273
.680	.8291	.8310	.8328	.8347	.8366	.8385	.8404	.8423	.8442	.8461
.690	.8480	.8499	.8518	.8537	.8556	.8576	.8595	.8614	.8634	.8653
.700	.8673	.8693	.8712	.8732	.8752	.8772	.8792	.8812	.8832	.8852
.710	.8872	.8892	.8912	.8933	.8953	.8973	.8994	.9014	.9035	.9056
.720	.9076	.9097	.9118	.9139	.9160	.9181	.9202	.9223	.9245	.9266
.730	.9287	.9309	.9330	.9352	.9373	.9395	.9417	.9439	.9461	.9483
.740	.9505	.9527	.9549	.9571	.9594	.9616	.9639	.9661	.9684	.9707
.750	.9730	.9752	.9775	.9799	.9822	.9845	.9868	.9892	.9915	.9939
.760	.9962	.9986	1.0010	1.0034	1.0058	1.0082	1.0106	1.0130	1.0154	1.0179
.770	1.0203	1.0228	1.0253	1.0277	1.0302	1.0327	1.0352	1.0378	1.0403	1.0428
.780	1.0454	1.0479	1.0505	1.0531	1.0557	1.0583	1.0609	1.0635	1.0661	1.0688
.790	1.0714	1.0741	1.0768	1.0795	1.0822	1.0849	1.0876	1.0903	1.0931	1.0958
.800	1.0986	1.1014	1.1041	1.1070	1.1098	1.1127	1.1155	1.1184	1.1212	1.1241
.810	1.1270	1.1299	1.1329	1.1358	1.1388	1.1417	1.1447	1.1477	1.1507	1.1538
.820	1.1568	1.1599	1.1630	1.1660	1.1692	1.1723	1.1754	1.1786	1.1817	1.1849
.830	1.1870	1.1913	1.1946	1.1979	1.2011	1.2044	1.2077	1.2111	1.2144	1.2178
.840	1.2212	1.2246	1.2280	1.2315	1.2349	1.2384	1.2419	1.2454	1.2490	1.2526
.850	1.2561	1.2598	1.2634	1.2670	1.2708	1.2744	1.2782	1.2819	1.2857	1.2895
.860	1.2934	1.2972	1.3011	1.3050	1.3089	1.3129	1.3168	1.3209	1.3249	1.3290
.870	1.3331	1.3372	1.3414	1.3456	1.3498	1.3540	1.3583	1.3626	1.3670	1.3714
.880	1.3758	1.3802	1.3847	1.3892	1.3938	1.3984	1.4030	1.4077	1.4124	1.4171
.890	1.4219	1.4268	1.4316	1.4366	1.4415	1.4465	1.4516	1.4566	1.4618	1.4670
.900	1.4722	1.4775	1.4828	1.4883	1.4937	1.4992	1.5047	1.5103	1.5160	1.5217
.910	1.5275	1.5334	1.5393	1.5453	1.5513	1.5574	1.5636	1.5698	1.5762	1.5825
.920	1.5890	1.5956	1.6022	1.6089	1.6157	1.6226	1.6296	1.6366	1.6438	1.6510
.930	1.6584	1.6659	1.6734	1.6811	1.6888	1.6967	1.7047	1.7129	1.7211	1.7295
.940	1.7380	1.7467	1.7555	1.7645	1.7736	1.7828	1.7923	1.8019	1.8117	1.8216
.950	1.8318	1.8421	1.8527	1.8635	1.8745	1.8857	1.8972	1.9090	1.9210	1.9333
.960	1.9459	1.9588	1.9721	1.9857	1.9996	2.0140	2.0287	2.0439	2.0595	2.0756
.970	2.0923	2.1095	2.1273	2.1457	2.1649	2.1847	2.2054	2.2269	2.2494	2.2729
.980	2.2976	2.3223	2.3507	2.3796	2.4101	2.4426	2.4774	2.5147	2.5550	2.5988
.990	2.6467	2.6996	2.7587	2.8257	2.9031	2.9945	3.1063	3.2504	3.4534	3.8002

r	z
.9999	4.95172
.99999	6.10303

Table A.7. Values of r for Different Levels of Significance

df	.1	.05	.02	.01	.001
1	.98769	.99692	.999507	.999877	.9999988
2	.90000	.95000	.98000	.990000	.99900
3	.8054	.8783	.93433	.95873	.99116
4	.7293	.8114	.8822	.91720	.97406
5	.6694	.7545	.8329	.8745	.95074
6	.6215	.7067	.7887	.8343	.92493
7	.5822	.6664	.7498	.7977	.8982
8	.5494	.6319	.7155	.7646	.8721
9	.5214	.6021	.6851	.7348	.8471
10	.4973	.5760	.6581	.7079	.8233
11	.4762	.5529	.6339	.6835	.8010
12	.4575	.5324	.6120	.6614	.7800
13	.4409	.5139	.5923	.6411	.7603
14	.4259	.4973	.5742	.6226	.7420
15	.4124	.4821	.5577	.6055	.7246
16	.4000	.4683	.5425	.5897	.7084
17	.3887	.4555	.5285	.5751	.6932
18	.3783	.4438	.5155	.5614	.6787
19	.3687	.4329	.5034	.5487	.6652
20	.3598	.4227	.4921	.5368	.6524
25	.3233	.3809	.4451	.4869	.5974
30	.2960	.3494	.4093	.4487	.5541
35	.2746	.3246	.3810	.4182	.5189
40	.2573	.3044	.3578	.3932	.4896
45	.2428	.2875	.3384	.3721	.4648
50	.2306	.2732	.3218	.3541	.4433
60	.2108	.2500	.2948	.3248	.4078
70	.1954	.2319	.2737	.3017	.3799
80	.1829	.2172	.2565	.2830	.3568
90	.1726	.2050	.2422	.2673	.3375
100	.1638	.1946	.2301	.2540	.3211

Source: Ronald A. Fisher and Frank Yates. *Statistical Tables for Biological, Agricultural and Medical Research.* Edinburgh: Oliver & Boyd Ltd. By permission of the authors and publishers. Table VI. Reprinted from *Basic Statistical Methods* (2nd ed.), N. M. Downie and R. W. Heath, Harper & Row, 1965.

Table A.8. Probabilities Associated with Values as Small as Observed Values of U in the Mann-Whitney Test

Table A.8.1. $n_1 = 3$ (M & W)

U \ n_2	1	2	3
0	.250	.100	.050
1	.500	.200	.100
2	.750	.400	.200
3		.600	.350
4			.500
5			.650

Table A.8.2. $n_1 = 4$ (M & W)

U \ n_2	1	2	3	4
0	.200	.067	.028	.014
1	.400	.133	.057	.029
2	.600	.267	.114	.057
3		.400	.200	.100
4		.600	.314	.171
5			.429	.243
6			.571	.343
7				.443
8				.557

Source: (M & W; subtables A.8.1 to A.8.6) E. B. Mann and D. R. Whitney. "On a Test of whether One of Two Random Variables is Stochastically Larger than the Other." *Annals of Mathematical Statistics,* 18 (1947), pp. 52-54. Used with the kind permission of the editor; notation modified for this book. (Auble; subtables A.8.7 to A.8.10) D. Auble. "Extended Tables for the Mann-Whitney Statistic." *Bulletin of the Institute of Educational Research at Indiana University,* 1, No. 2. Adapted and abridged; used with the kind permission of the editor. Reprinted from *Nonparametric Statistics for the Behavioral Sciences,* Sidney Siegel, McGraw-Hill Book Company, 1956, by the kind permission of the publishers; notation modified for this book.

Table A.8. *(continued)*

Table A.8.3. $n_1 = 5$ (M & W)

U \ n_2	1	2	3	4	5
0	.167	.047	.018	.008	.004
1	.333	.095	.036	.016	.008
2	.500	.190	.071	.032	.016
3	.667	.286	.125	.056	.028
4		.429	.196	.095	.048
5		.571	.286	.143	.075
6			.393	.206	.111
7			.500	.278	.155
8			.607	.365	.210
9				.452	.274
10				.548	.345
11					.421
12					.500
13					.579

Table A.8.4. $n_1 = 6$ (M & W)

U \ n_2	1	2	3	4	5	6
0	.143	.036	.012	.005	.002	.001
1	.286	.071	.024	.010	.004	.002
2	.428	.143	.048	.019	.009	.004
3	.571	.214	.083	.033	.015	.008
4		.321	.131	.057	.026	.013
5		.429	.190	.086	.041	.021
6		.571	.274	.129	.063	.032
7			.357	.176	.089	.047
8			.452	.238	.123	.066
9			.548	.305	.165	.090
10				.381	.214	.120
11				.457	.268	.155
12				.545	.331	.197
13					.396	.242
14					.465	.294
15					.535	.350
16						.409
17						.469
18						.531

Table A.8. *(continued)*

Table A.8.5. $n_1 = 7$ (M & W)

U \ n_2	1	2	3	4	5	6	7
0	.125	.028	.008	.003	.001	.001	.000
1	.250	.056	.017	.006	.003	.001	.001
2	.375	.111	.033	.012	.005	.002	.001
3	.500	.167	.058	.021	.009	.004	.002
4	.625	.250	.092	.036	.015	.007	.003
5		.333	.133	.055	.024	.011	.006
6		.444	.192	.082	.037	.017	.009
7		.556	.258	.115	.053	.026	.013
8			.333	.158	.074	.037	.019
9			.417	.206	.101	.051	.027
10			.500	.264	.134	.069	.036
11			.583	.324	.172	.090	.049
12				.394	.216	.117	.064
13				.464	.265	.147	.082
14				.538	.319	.183	.104
15					.378	.223	.130
16					.438	.267	.159
17					.500	.314	.191
18					.562	.365	.228
19						.418	.267
20						.473	.310
21						.527	.355
22							.402
23							.451
24							.500
25							.549

Table A.8. *(continued)*

Table A.8.6. $n_1 = 8$ (M & W).

U \ n_2	1	2	3	4	5	6	7	8	t	Normal
0	.111	.022	.006	.002	.001	.000	.000	.000	3.308	.001
1	.222	.044	.012	.004	.002	.001	.000	.000	3.203	.001
2	.333	.089	.024	.008	.003	.001	.001	.000	3.098	.001
3	.444	.133	.042	.014	.005	.002	.001	.001	2.993	.001
4	.556	.200	.067	.024	.009	.004	.002	.001	2.888	.002
5		.267	.097	.036	.015	.006	.003	.001	2.783	.003
6		.356	.139	.055	.023	.010	.005	.002	2.678	.004
7		.444	.188	.077	.033	.015	.007	.003	2.573	.005
8		.556	.248	.107	.047	.021	.010	.005	2.468	.007
9			.315	.141	.064	.030	.014	.007	2.363	.009
10			.387	.184	.085	.041	.020	.010	2.258	.012
11			.461	.230	.111	.054	.027	.014	2.153	.016
12			.539	.285	.142	.071	.036	.019	2.048	.020
13				.341	.177	.091	.047	.025	1.943	.026
14				.404	.217	.114	.060	.032	1.838	.033
15				.467	.262	.141	.076	.041	1.733	.041
16				.533	.311	.172	.095	.052	1.628	.052
17					.362	.207	.116	.065	1.523	.064
18					.416	.245	.140	.080	1.418	.078
19					.472	.286	.168	.097	1.313	.094
20					.528	.331	.198	.117	1.208	.113
21						.377	.232	.139	1.102	.135
22						.426	.268	.164	.998	.159
23						.475	.306	.191	.893	.185
24						.525	.347	.221	.788	.215
25							.389	.253	.683	.247
26							.433	.287	.578	.282
27							.478	.323	.473	.318
28							.522	.360	.368	.356
29								.399	.263	.396
30								.439	.158	.437
31								.480	.052	.481
32								.520		

Table A.8. *(continued)*

Table A.8.7. Critical Values of *U* for a One-Tailed Test at $\alpha = .001$ or for a Two-Tailed Test at $\alpha = .002$ (Auble).

n_2 \ n_1	9	10	11	12	13	14	15	16	17	18	19	20
1												
2												
3									0	0	0	0
4		0	0	0	1	1	1	2	2	3	3	3
5	1	1	2	2	3	3	4	5	5	6	7	7
6	2	3	4	4	5	6	7	8	9	10	11	12
7	3	5	6	7	8	9	10	11	13	14	15	16
8	5	6	8	9	11	12	14	15	17	18	20	21
9	7	8	10	12	14	15	17	19	21	23	25	26
10	8	10	12	14	17	19	21	23	25	27	29	32
11	10	12	15	17	20	22	24	27	29	32	34	37
12	12	14	17	20	23	25	28	31	34	37	40	42
13	14	17	20	23	26	29	32	35	38	42	45	48
14	15	19	22	25	29	32	36	39	43	46	50	54
15	17	21	24	28	32	36	40	43	47	51	55	59
16	19	23	27	31	35	39	43	48	52	56	60	65
17	21	25	29	34	38	43	47	52	57	61	66	70
18	23	27	32	37	42	46	51	56	61	66	71	76
19	25	29	34	40	45	50	55	60	66	71	77	82
20	26	32	37	42	48	54	59	65	70	76	82	88

Table A.8.8. Critical Values of *U* for a One-Tailed Test at $\alpha = .01$ or for a Two-Tailed Test at $\alpha = .02$ (Auble).

n_2 \ n_1	9	10	11	12	13	14	15	16	17	18	19	20
1												
2					0	0	0	0	0	0	1	1
3	1	1	1	2	2	2	3	3	4	4	4	5
4	3	3	4	5	5	6	7	7	8	9	9	10
5	5	6	7	8	9	10	11	12	13	14	15	16
6	7	8	9	11	12	13	15	16	18	19	20	22
7	9	11	12	14	16	17	19	21	23	24	26	28
8	11	13	15	17	20	22	24	26	28	30	32	34
9	14	16	18	21	23	26	28	31	33	36	38	40
10	16	19	22	24	27	30	33	36	38	41	44	47
11	18	22	25	28	31	34	37	41	44	47	50	53
12	21	24	28	31	35	38	42	46	49	53	56	60
13	23	27	31	35	39	43	47	51	55	59	63	67
14	26	30	34	38	43	47	51	56	60	65	69	73
15	28	33	37	42	47	51	56	61	66	70	75	80
16	31	36	41	46	51	56	61	66	71	76	82	87
17	33	38	44	49	55	60	66	71	77	82	88	93
18	36	41	47	53	59	65	70	76	82	88	94	100
19	38	44	50	56	63	69	75	82	88	94	101	107
20	40	47	53	60	67	73	80	87	93	100	107	114

Table A.8. *(continued)*

Table A.8.9. Critical Values of U for a One-Tailed Test at $\alpha = .025$ or for a Two-Tailed Test at $\alpha = .05$ (Auble).

n_2 \ n_1	9	10	11	12	13	14	15	16	17	18	19	20
1												
2	0	0	0	1	1	1	1	1	2	2	2	2
3	2	3	3	4	4	5	5	6	6	7	7	8
4	4	5	6	7	8	9	10	11	11	12	13	13
5	7	8	9	11	12	13	14	15	17	18	19	20
6	10	11	13	14	16	17	19	21	22	24	25	27
7	12	14	16	18	20	22	24	26	28	30	32	34
8	15	17	19	22	24	26	29	31	34	36	38	41
9	17	20	23	26	28	31	34	37	39	42	45	48
10	20	23	26	29	33	36	39	42	45	48	52	55
11	23	26	30	33	37	40	44	47	51	55	58	62
12	26	29	33	37	41	45	49	53	57	61	65	69
13	28	33	37	41	45	50	54	59	63	67	72	76
14	31	36	40	45	50	55	59	64	67	74	78	83
15	34	39	44	49	54	59	64	70	75	80	85	90
16	37	42	47	53	59	64	70	75	81	86	92	98
17	39	45	51	57	63	67	75	81	87	93	99	105
18	42	48	55	61	67	74	80	86	93	99	106	112
19	45	52	58	65	72	78	85	92	99	106	113	119
20	48	55	62	69	76	83	90	98	105	112	119	127

Table A.8.10. Critical Values of U for a One-Tailed Test at $\alpha = .05$ or for a Two-Tailed Test at $\alpha = .10$ (Auble).

n_1 \ n_2	9	10	11	12	13	14	15	16	17	18	19	20
1											0	0
2	1	1	1	2	2	2	3	3	3	4	4	4
3	3	4	5	5	6	7	7	8	9	9	10	11
4	6	7	8	9	10	11	12	14	15	16	17	18
5	9	11	12	13	15	16	18	19	20	22	23	25
6	12	14	16	17	19	21	23	25	26	28	30	32
7	15	17	19	21	24	26	28	30	33	35	37	39
8	18	20	23	26	28	31	33	36	39	41	44	47
9	21	24	27	30	33	36	39	42	45	48	51	54
10	24	27	31	34	37	41	44	48	51	55	58	62
11	27	31	34	38	42	46	50	54	57	61	65	69
12	30	34	38	42	47	51	55	60	64	68	72	77
13	33	37	42	47	51	56	61	65	70	75	80	84
14	36	41	46	51	56	61	66	71	77	82	87	92
15	39	44	50	55	61	66	72	77	83	88	94	100
16	42	48	54	60	65	71	77	83	89	95	101	107
17	45	51	57	64	70	77	83	89	96	102	109	115
18	48	55	61	68	75	82	88	95	102	109	116	123
19	51	58	65	72	80	87	94	101	109	116	123	130
20	54	62	69	77	84	92	100	107	115	123	130	138

Table A.9. Critical Values of D in the Kolmogorov-Smirnov One-Sample Test*

Sample size (N)	Level of significance for D = maximum $\lvert F_0(X) - S_N(X)\rvert$				
	.20	.15	.10	.05	.01
1	.900	.925	.950	.975	.995
2	.684	.726	.776	.842	.929
3	.565	.597	.642	.708	.828
4	.494	.525	.564	.624	.733
5	.446	.474	.510	.565	.669
6	.410	.436	.470	.521	.618
7	.381	.405	.438	.486	.577
8	.358	.381	.411	.457	.543
9	.339	.360	.388	.432	.514
10	.322	.342	.368	.410	.490
11	.307	.326	.352	.391	.468
12	.295	.313	.338	.375	.450
13	.284	.302	.325	.361	.433
14	.274	.292	.314	.349	.418
15	.266	.283	.304	.338	.404
16	.258	.274	.295	.328	.392
17	.250	.266	.286	.318	.381
18	.244	.259	.278	.309	.371
19	.237	.252	.272	.301	.363
20	.231	.246	.264	.294	.356
25	.21	.22	.24	.27	.32
30	.19	.20	.22	.24	.29
35	.18	.19	.21	.23	.27
Over 35	$\frac{1.07}{\sqrt{N}}$	$\frac{1.14}{\sqrt{N}}$	$\frac{1.22}{\sqrt{N}}$	$\frac{1.36}{\sqrt{N}}$	$\frac{1.63}{\sqrt{N}}$

* Two-tailed values.

Source: F. J. Massey, Jr. "The Kolmogorov-Smirnov Test for Goodness of Fit." *Journal of the American Statistical Association,* 46 (1951), p. 70. Used with the kind permission of the publishers. Reprinted from *Nonparametric Statistics for the Behavioral Sciences,* Sidney Siegel, McGraw-Hill Book Company, 1956, by the kind permission of the publishers

Table A.10. Critical Values of K_D in the Kolmogorov-Smirnov Two-Sample Test (Small Samples)*

N	One-tailed test*		Two-tailed test†	
	$\alpha = .05$	$\alpha = .01$	$\alpha = .05$	$\alpha = .01$
3	3	—	—	—
4	4	—	4	—
5	4	5	5	5
6	5	6	5	6
7	5	6	6	6
8	5	6	6	7
9	6	7	6	7
10	6	7	7	8
11	6	8	7	8
12	6	8	7	8
13	7	8	7	9
14	7	8	8	9
15	7	9	8	9
16	7	9	8	10
17	8	9	8	10
18	8	10	9	10
19	8	10	9	10
20	8	10	9	11
21	8	10	9	11
22	9	11	9	11
23	9	11	10	11
24	9	11	10	12
25	9	11	10	12
26	9	11	10	12
27	9	12	10	12
28	10	12	11	13
29	10	12	11	13
30	10	12	11	13
35	11	13	12	
40	11	14	13	

*$N_1 = N_2$.

Sources: (One-Tailed Test) L. A. Goodman. "Kolmogorov-Smirnov Tests for Psychological Research." *Psychological Bulletin* 51 (1954), p. 1677. Reproduced by permission of the American Psychological Association. (Two-Tailed Test) F. J. Massey. "The Distribution of the Maximum Deviation between Two Sample Cumulative Step Functions." *Annals of Mathematical Statistics,* 22 (1951), pp. 126-127. Derived from Table 1. Used with the kind permission of the editor. The table above is reprinted from *Nonparametric Statistics for the Behavioral Sciences,* Sidney Siegel, McGraw-Hill Book Company, 1956 by the kind permission of the publishers.

Table A.11. Critical Values of D in the Kolmogorov-Smirnov Two-Sample Test (Large Samples; Two-Tailed Test)

Level of significance	Value of D so large as to call for rejection of H_0 at the indicated level of significance, where D = maximum $\lvert S_{n_1}(X) - S_{n_2}(X)\rvert$
.10	$1.22\sqrt{\frac{n_1+n_2}{n_1n_2}}$
.05	$1.36\sqrt{\frac{n_1+n_2}{n_1n_2}}$
.025	$1.48\sqrt{\frac{n_1+n_2}{n_1n_2}}$
.01	$1.63\sqrt{\frac{n_1+n_2}{n_1n_2}}$
.005	$1.73\sqrt{\frac{n_1+n_2}{n_1n_2}}$
.001	$1.95\sqrt{\frac{n_1+n_2}{n_1n_2}}$

Source: N. Smirnov. "Tables for Estimating the Goodness of Fit of Empirical Distributions." *Annals of Mathematical Statistics,* 19 (1948), pp. 280-281. Used with the kind permission of the editor. Reprinted from *Nonparametric Statistics for the Behavioral Sciences,* Sidney Siegel, McGraw-Hill Book Company, 1956, by the kind permission of the publishers.

Table A.12. Probabilities Associated with Values as Large as Observed Values of S in the Kendall Rank Correlation Coefficient

S	Values of N				S	Values of N		
	4	5	8	9		6	7	10
0	.625	.592	.548	.540	1	.500	.500	.500
2	.375	.408	.452	.460	3	.360	.386	.431
4	.167	.242	.360	.381	5	.235	.281	.364
6	.042	.117	.274	.306	7	.136	191	.300
8		.042	.199	.238	9	.068	.119	.242
10		.0083	.138	.179	11	.028	.068	.190
12			.089	.130	13	.0083	.035	.146
14			.054	.090	15	.0014	.015	.108
16			.031	.060	17		.0054	.078
18			.016	.038	19		.0014	.054
20			.0071	.022	21		.00020	.036
22			.0028	.012	23			.023
24			.00087	.0063	25			.014
26			.00019	.0029	27			.0083
28			.000025	.0012	29			.0046
30				.00043	31			.0023
32				.00012	33			.0011
34				.000025	35			.00047
36				.0000028	37			.00018
					39			.000058
					41			.000015
					43			.0000028
					45			.00000028

Source: M. G. Kendall. *Rank Correlation Methods.* London: Charles Griffin & Company Ltd. 1948. Appendix Table 1, p. 141. Used with the kind permission of the publishers. Reprinted from *Nonparametric Statistics for the Behavioral Sciences,* Sidney Siegel, McGraw-Hill Book Company, 1956, by the kind permission of the publishers.

Table A.13. Critical Values of R in the Runs Test

In the body of the table are given various critical values of R for various values of N_1 and N_2. For the one-sample runs test, any value of R which is equal to or smaller than that shown in the table is significant at the .05 level. For the Wald-Wolfowitz two-sample runs test, any value of R which is equal to or smaller than that shown in the table is significant at the .05 level.

N_1 \ N_2	2	3	4	5	6	7	8	9	10	11	12	13	14	15	16	17	18	19	20
2											2	2	2	2	2	2	2	2	2
3					2	2	2	2	2	2	2	2	2	3	3	3	3	3	3
4				2	2	2	3	3	3	3	3	3	3	3	4	4	4	4	4
5			2	2	3	3	3	3	3	4	4	4	4	4	4	4	5	5	5
6		2	2	3	3	3	3	4	4	4	4	5	5	5	5	5	5	6	6
7		2	2	3	3	3	4	4	5	5	5	5	5	6	6	6	6	6	6
8		2	3	3	3	4	4	5	5	5	6	6	6	6	6	7	7	7	7
9		2	3	3	4	4	5	5	5	6	6	6	7	7	7	7	8	8	8
10		2	3	3	4	5	5	5	6	6	7	7	7	7	8	8	8	8	9
11		2	3	4	4	5	5	6	6	7	7	7	8	8	8	9	9	9	9
12	2	2	3	4	4	5	6	6	7	7	7	8	8	8	9	9	9	10	10
13	2	2	3	4	5	5	6	6	7	7	8	8	9	9	9	10	10	10	10
14	2	2	3	4	5	5	6	7	7	8	8	9	9	9	10	10	10	11	11
15	2	3	3	4	5	6	6	7	7	8	8	9	9	10	10	11	11	11	12
16	2	3	4	4	5	6	6	7	8	8	9	9	10	10	11	11	11	12	12
17	2	3	4	4	5	6	7	7	8	9	9	10	10	11	11	11	12	12	13
18	2	3	4	5	5	6	7	8	8	9	9	10	10	11	11	12	12	13	13
19	2	3	4	5	6	6	7	8	8	9	10	10	11	11	12	12	13	13	13
20	2	3	4	5	6	6	7	8	9	9	10	10	11	12	12	13	13	13	14

Source: Frieda S. Swed and C. Eisenhart. "Tables for Testing Randomness of Grouping in a Sequence of Alternatives." *Annals of Mathematical Statistics,* 14 (1943), pp. 83-86. Used with the kind permission of the editor. Reprinted from *Nonparametric Statistics for the Behavioral Sciences,* Sidney Siegel, McGraw-Hill Book Company, 1956, by the kind permission of the publisher; slightly modified for this book.

Table A.14. Critical Values of r_s, the Spearman Rank Correlation Coefficient

N	Significance level (one-tailed test)	
	.05	.01
4	1.000	
5	.900	1.000
6	.829	.943
7	.714	.893
8	.643	.833
9	.600	.783
10	.564	.746
12	.506	.712
14	.456	.645
16	.425	.601
18	.399	.564
20	.377	.534
22	.359	.508
24	.343	.485
26	.329	.465
28	.317	.448
30	.306	.432

Sources: E. G. Olds. "Distributions of Sums of Rank Differences for Small Numbers of Individuals." *Annals of Mathematical Statistics,* 9 (1943), pp. 133-148. "The 5% Significance Levels for Sums of Squares of Rank Differences and a Correction." *Annals of Mathematical Statistics,* 20 (1949), pp. 117-118. Used with the kind permission of the editor. Reprinted from *Nonparametric Statistics for the Behavioral Sciences,* Sidney Siegel, McGraw-Hill Book Company, 1956, by the kind permission of the publishers.

Table A.15. Critical Values of s in the Kendall Coefficient of Concordance

Note that additional critical values of s for $N = 3$ are given in the right-hand column of this table.

k	N					Additional values for $N = 3$	
	3	4	5	6	7	k	s
Values at the .05 level of significance							
3			64.4	103.9	157.3	9	54.0
4		49.5	88.4	143.3	217.0	12	71.9
5		62.6	112.3	182.4	276.2	14	83.8
6		75.7	136.1	221.4	335.2	16	95.8
8	48.1	101.7	183.7	299.0	453.1	18	107.7
10	60.0	127.8	231.2	376.7	571.0		
15	89.8	192.9	349.8	570.5	864.9		
20	119.7	258.0	468.5	764.4	1,158.7		
Values at the .01 level of significance							
3			75.6	122.8	185.6	9	75.9
4		61.4	109.3	176.2	265.0	12	103.5
5		80.5	142.8	229.4	343.8	14	121.9
6		99.5	176.1	282.4	422.6	16	140.2
8	66.8	137.4	242.7	388.3	579.9	18	158.6
10	85.1	175.3	309.1	494.0	737.0		
15	131.0	269.8	475.2	758.2	1,129.5		
20	177.0	364.2	641.2	1,022.2	1,521.9		

Source: M. Friedman. "A Comparison of Alternative Tests of Significance for the Problem of M Rankings." *Annals of Mathematical Statistics,* 11 (1940), pp. 86-92. Used with the kind permission of the editor. Reprinted from *Nonparametric Statistics for the Behavioral Sciences,* Sidney Siegel, McGraw-Hill Book Company, 1956, by the kind permission of the publishers.

Table A.16. 5-Percent (Lightface Type) and 1-Percent (Boldface Type) Points for the Distribution of F

f_2	f_1 Degrees of Freedom (for greater mean square)																								f_2
	1	2	3	4	5	6	7	8	9	10	11	12	14	16	20	24	30	40	50	75	100	200	500	∞	
1	161	200	216	225	230	234	237	239	241	242	243	244	245	246	248	249	250	251	252	253	253	254	254	254	1
	4,052	**4,999**	**5,403**	**5,625**	**5,764**	**5,859**	**5,928**	**5,981**	**6,022**	**6,056**	**6,082**	**6,106**	**6,142**	**6,169**	**6,208**	**6,234**	**6,261**	**6,286**	**6,302**	**6,323**	**6,334**	**6,352**	**6,361**	**6,366**	
2	18.51	19.00	19.16	19.25	19.30	19.33	19.36	19.37	19.38	19.39	19.40	19.41	19.42	19.43	19.44	19.45	19.46	19.47	19.47	19.48	19.49	19.49	19.50	19.50	2
	98.49	**99.00**	**99.17**	**99.25**	**99.30**	**99.33**	**99.36**	**99.37**	**99.39**	**99.40**	**99.41**	**99.42**	**99.43**	**99.44**	**99.45**	**99.46**	**99.47**	**99.48**	**99.48**	**99.49**	**99.49**	**99.49**	**99.50**	**99.50**	
3	10.13	9.55	9.28	9.12	9.01	8.94	8.88	8.84	8.81	8.78	8.76	8.74	8.71	8.69	8.66	8.64	8.62	8.60	8.58	8.57	8.56	8.54	8.54	8.53	3
	34.12	**30.82**	**29.46**	**28.71**	**28.24**	**27.91**	**27.67**	**27.49**	**27.34**	**27.23**	**27.13**	**27.05**	**26.92**	**26.83**	**26.69**	**26.60**	**26.50**	**26.41**	**26.35**	**26.27**	**26.23**	**26.18**	**26.14**	**26.12**	
4	7.71	6.94	6.59	6.39	6.26	6.16	6.09	6.04	6.00	5.96	5.93	5.91	5.87	5.84	5.80	5.77	5.74	5.71	5.70	5.68	5.66	5.65	5.64	5.63	4
	21.20	**18.00**	**16.69**	**15.98**	**15.52**	**15.21**	**14.98**	**14.80**	**14.66**	**14.54**	**14.45**	**14.37**	**14.24**	**14.15**	**14.02**	**13.93**	**13.83**	**13.74**	**13.69**	**13.61**	**13.57**	**13.52**	**13.48**	**13.46**	
5	6.61	5.79	5.41	5.19	5.05	4.95	4.88	4.82	4.78	4.74	4.70	4.68	4.64	4.60	4.56	4.53	4.50	4.46	4.44	4.42	4.40	4.38	4.37	4.36	5
	16.26	**13.27**	**12.06**	**11.39**	**10.97**	**10.67**	**10.45**	**10.29**	**10.15**	**10.05**	**9.96**	**9.89**	**9.77**	**9.68**	**9.55**	**9.47**	**9.38**	**9.29**	**9.24**	**9.17**	**9.13**	**9.07**	**9.04**	**9.02**	
6	5.99	5.14	4.76	4.53	4.39	4.28	4.21	4.15	4.10	4.06	4.03	4.00	3.96	3.92	3.87	3.84	3.81	3.77	3.75	3.72	3.71	3.69	3.68	3.67	6
	13.74	**10.92**	**9.78**	**9.15**	**8.75**	**8.47**	**8.26**	**8.10**	**7.98**	**7.87**	**7.79**	**7.72**	**7.60**	**7.52**	**7.39**	**7.31**	**7.23**	**7.14**	**7.09**	**7.02**	**6.99**	**6.94**	**6.90**	**6.88**	
7	5.59	4.74	4.35	4.12	3.97	3.87	3.79	3.73	3.68	3.63	3.60	3.57	3.52	3.49	3.44	3.41	3.38	3.34	3.32	3.29	3.28	3.25	3.24	3.23	7
	12.25	**9.55**	**8.45**	**7.85**	**7.46**	**7.19**	**7.00**	**6.84**	**6.71**	**6.62**	**6.54**	**6.47**	**6.35**	**6.27**	**6.15**	**6.07**	**5.98**	**5.90**	**5.85**	**5.78**	**5.75**	**5.70**	**5.67**	**5.65**	
8	5.32	4.46	4.07	3.84	3.69	3.58	3.50	3.44	3.39	3.34	3.31	3.28	3.23	3.20	3.15	3.12	3.08	3.05	3.03	3.00	2.98	2.96	2.94	2.93	8
	11.26	**8.65**	**7.59**	**7.01**	**6.63**	**6.37**	**6.19**	**6.03**	**5.91**	**5.82**	**5.74**	**5.67**	**5.56**	**5.48**	**5.36**	**5.28**	**5.20**	**5.11**	**5.06**	**5.00**	**4.96**	**4.91**	**4.88**	**4.86**	
9	5.12	4.26	3.86	3.63	3.48	3.37	3.29	3.23	3.18	3.13	3.10	3.07	3.02	2.98	2.93	2.90	2.86	2.82	2.80	2.77	2.76	2.73	2.72	2.71	9
	10.56	**8.02**	**6.99**	**6.42**	**6.06**	**5.80**	**5.62**	**5.47**	**5.35**	**5.26**	**5.18**	**5.11**	**5.00**	**4.92**	**4.80**	**4.73**	**4.64**	**4.56**	**4.51**	**4.45**	**4.41**	**4.36**	**4.33**	**4.31**	
10	4.96	4.10	3.71	3.48	3.33	3.22	3.14	3.07	3.02	2.97	2.94	2.91	2.86	2.82	2.77	2.74	2.70	2.67	2.64	2.61	2.59	2.56	2.55	2.54	10
	10.04	**7.56**	**6.55**	**5.99**	**5.64**	**5.39**	**5.21**	**5.06**	**4.95**	**4.85**	**4.78**	**4.71**	**4.60**	**4.52**	**4.41**	**4.33**	**4.25**	**4.17**	**4.12**	**4.05**	**4.01**	**3.96**	**3.93**	**3.91**	
11	4.84	3.98	3.59	3.36	3.20	3.09	3.01	2.95	2.90	2.86	2.82	2.79	2.74	2.70	2.65	2.61	2.57	2.53	2.50	2.47	2.45	2.42	2.41	2.40	11
	9.65	**7.20**	**6.22**	**5.67**	**5.32**	**5.07**	**4.88**	**4.74**	**4.63**	**4.54**	**4.46**	**4.40**	**4.29**	**4.21**	**4.10**	**4.02**	**3.94**	**3.86**	**3.80**	**3.74**	**3.70**	**3.66**	**3.62**	**3.60**	
12	4.75	3.88	3.49	3.26	3.11	3.00	2.92	2.85	2.80	2.76	2.72	2.69	2.64	2.60	2.54	2.50	2.46	2.42	2.40	2.36	2.35	2.32	2.31	2.30	12
	9.33	**6.93**	**5.95**	**5.41**	**5.06**	**4.82**	**4.65**	**4.50**	**4.39**	**4.30**	**4.22**	**4.16**	**4.05**	**3.98**	**3.86**	**3.78**	**3.70**	**3.61**	**3.56**	**3.49**	**3.46**	**3.41**	**3.38**	**3.36**	
13	4.67	3.80	3.41	3.18	3.02	2.92	2.84	2.77	2.72	2.67	2.63	2.60	2.55	2.51	2.46	2.42	2.38	2.34	2.32	2.28	2.26	2.24	2.22	2.21	13
	9.07	**6.70**	**5.74**	**5.20**	**4.86**	**4.62**	**4.44**	**4.30**	**4.19**	**4.10**	**4.02**	**3.96**	**3.85**	**3.78**	**3.67**	**3.59**	**3.51**	**3.42**	**3.37**	**3.30**	**3.27**	**3.21**	**3.18**	**3.16**	

Source: Reproduced by permission from *Statistical Methods,* 6th Edition, by George W. Snedecor and William G. Cochran. The function, $F = e$ with exponent $2z$, is computed in part from Fisher's Table VI. Additional entries are by interpolation, mostly graphical.

Table A.16. *(continued)*

f_2	1	2	3	4	5	6	7	8	9	10	11	12	14	16	20	24	30	40	50	75	100	200	500	∞	f_2
	f_1 Degrees of Freedom (for greater mean square)																								
14	4.60	3.74	3.34	3.11	2.96	2.85	2.77	2.70	2.65	2.60	2.56	2.53	2.48	2.44	2.39	2.35	2.31	2.27	2.24	2.21	2.19	2.16	2.14	2.13	14
	8.86	**6.51**	**5.56**	**5.03**	**4.69**	**4.46**	**4.28**	**4.14**	**4.03**	**3.94**	**3.86**	**3.80**	**3.70**	**3.62**	**3.51**	**3.43**	**3.34**	**3.26**	**3.21**	**3.14**	**3.11**	**3.06**	**3.02**	**3.00**	
15	4.54	3.68	3.29	3.06	2.90	2.79	2.70	2.64	2.59	2.55	2.51	2.48	2.43	2.39	2.33	2.29	2.25	2.21	2.18	2.15	2.12	2.10	2.08	2.07	15
	8.68	**6.36**	**5.42**	**4.89**	**4.56**	**4.32**	**4.14**	**4.00**	**3.89**	**3.80**	**3.73**	**3.67**	**3.56**	**3.48**	**3.36**	**3.29**	**3.20**	**3.12**	**3.07**	**3.00**	**2.97**	**2.92**	**2.89**	**2.87**	
16	4.49	3.63	3.24	3.01	2.85	2.74	2.66	2.59	2.54	2.49	2.45	2.42	2.37	2.33	2.28	2.24	2.20	2.16	2.13	2.09	2.07	2.04	2.02	2.01	16
	8.53	**6.23**	**5.29**	**4.77**	**4.44**	**4.20**	**4.03**	**3.89**	**3.78**	**3.69**	**3.61**	**3.55**	**3.45**	**3.37**	**3.25**	**3.18**	**3.10**	**3.01**	**2.96**	**2.98**	**2.86**	**2.80**	**2.77**	**2.75**	
17	4.45	3.59	3.20	2.96	2.81	2.70	2.62	2.55	2.50	2.45	2.41	2.38	2.33	2.29	2.23	2.19	2.15	2.11	2.08	2.04	2.02	1.99	1.97	1.96	17
	8.40	**6.11**	**5.18**	**4.67**	**4.34**	**4.10**	**3.93**	**3.79**	**3.68**	**3.59**	**3.52**	**3.45**	**3.35**	**3.27**	**3.16**	**3.08**	**3.00**	**2.92**	**2.86**	**2.79**	**2.76**	**2.70**	**2.67**	**2.65**	
18	4.41	3.55	3.16	2.93	2.77	3.66	2.58	2.51	2.46	2.41	2.37	2.34	2.29	2.25	2.19	2.15	2.11	2.07	2.04	2.00	1.98	1.95	1.93	1.92	18
	8.28	**6.01**	**5.09**	**4.58**	**4.25**	**4.01**	**3.85**	**3.71**	**3.60**	**3.51**	**3.44**	**3.37**	**3.27**	**3.19**	**3.07**	**3.00**	**2.91**	**2.83**	**2.78**	**2.71**	**2.68**	**2.62**	**2.59**	**2.57**	
19	4.38	3.52	3.13	2.90	2.74	2.63	2.55	2.48	2.43	2.38	2.34	2.31	2.26	2.21	2.15	2.11	2.07	2.02	2.00	1.96	1.94	1.91	1.90	1.88	19
	8.18	**5.93**	**5.01**	**4.50**	**4.17**	**3.94**	**3.77**	**3.63**	**3.52**	**3.43**	**3.36**	**3.30**	**3.19**	**3.12**	**3.00**	**2.92**	**2.84**	**2.76**	**2.70**	**2.63**	**2.60**	**2.54**	**2.51**	**2.49**	
20	4.35	3.49	3.10	2.87	2.71	2.60	2.52	2.45	2.40	2.35	2.31	2.28	2.23	2.18	2.12	2.08	2.04	1.99	1.96	1.92	1.90	1.87	1.85	1.84	20
	8.10	**5.85**	**4.94**	**4.43**	**4.10**	**3.87**	**3.71**	**3.56**	**3.45**	**3.37**	**3.30**	**3.23**	**3.13**	**3.05**	**2.94**	**2.86**	**2.77**	**2.69**	**2.63**	**2.56**	**2.53**	**2.47**	**2.44**	**2.42**	
21	4.32	3.47	3.07	2.84	2.68	2.57	2.49	2.42	2.37	2.32	2.28	2.25	2.20	2.15	2.09	2.05	2.00	1.96	1.93	1.89	1.87	1.84	1.82	1.81	21
	8.02	**5.78**	**4.87**	**4.37**	**4.04**	**3.81**	**3.65**	**3.51**	**3.40**	**3.31**	**3.24**	**3.17**	**3.07**	**2.99**	**2.88**	**2.80**	**2.72**	**2.63**	**2.58**	**2.51**	**2.47**	**2.42**	**2.38**	**2.36**	
22	4.30	3.44	3.05	2.82	2.66	2.55	2.47	2.40	2.35	2.30	2.26	2.23	2.18	2.13	2.07	2.03	1.98	1.93	1.91	1.87	1.84	1.81	1.80	1.78	22
	7.94	**5.72**	**4.82**	**4.31**	**3.99**	**3.76**	**3.59**	**3.45**	**3.35**	**3.26**	**3.18**	**3.12**	**3.02**	**2.94**	**2.83**	**2.75**	**2.67**	**2.58**	**2.53**	**2.46**	**2.42**	**2.37**	**2.33**	**2.31**	
23	4.28	3.42	3.03	2.80	2.64	2.53	2.45	2.38	2.32	2.28	2.24	2.20	2.14	2.10	2.04	2.00	1.96	1.91	1.88	1.84	1.82	1.79	1.77	1.76	23
	7.88	**5.66**	**4.76**	**4.26**	**3.94**	**3.71**	**3.54**	**3.41**	**3.30**	**3.21**	**3.14**	**3.07**	**2.97**	**2.89**	**2.78**	**2.70**	**2.62**	**2.53**	**2.48**	**2.41**	**2.37**	**2.32**	**2.28**	**2.26**	
24	4.26	3.40	3.01	2.78	2.62	2.51	2.43	2.36	2.30	2.26	2.22	2.18	2.13	2.09	2.02	1.98	1.94	1.89	1.86	1.82	1.80	1.76	1.74	1.73	24
	7.82	**5.61**	**4.72**	**4.22**	**3.90**	**3.67**	**3.50**	**3.36**	**3.25**	**3.17**	**3.09**	**3.03**	**2.93**	**2.85**	**2.74**	**2.66**	**2.58**	**2.49**	**2.44**	**2.36**	**2.33**	**2.27**	**2.23**	**2.21**	
25	4.24	3.38	2.99	2.76	2.60	2.49	2.41	2.34	2.28	2.24	2.20	2.16	2.11	2.06	2.00	1.96	1.92	1.87	1.84	1.80	1.77	1.74	1.72	1.71	25
	7.77	**5.57**	**4.68**	**4.18**	**3.86**	**3.63**	**3.46**	**3.32**	**3.21**	**3.13**	**3.05**	**2.99**	**2.89**	**2.81**	**2.70**	**2.62**	**2.54**	**2.45**	**2.40**	**2.32**	**2.29**	**2.23**	**2.19**	**2.17**	
26	4.22	3.37	2.98	2.74	2.59	2.47	2.39	2.32	2.27	2.22	2.18	2.15	2.10	2.05	1.99	1.95	1.90	1.85	1.82	1.78	1.76	1.72	1.70	1.69	26
	7.72	**5.53**	**4.64**	**4.14**	**3.82**	**3.59**	**3.42**	**3.29**	**3.17**	**3.09**	**3.02**	**2.96**	**2.86**	**2.77**	**2.66**	**2.58**	**2.50**	**2.41**	**2.36**	**2.28**	**2.25**	**2.19**	**2.15**	**2.13**	

Table A.16. *(continued)*

f_2	f_1 Degrees of Freedom (for greater mean square)																								f_2
	1	2	3	4	5	6	7	8	9	10	11	12	14	16	20	24	30	40	50	75	100	200	500	∞	
27	4.21 **7.68**	3.35 **5.49**	2.96 **4.60**	2.73 **4.11**	2.57 **3.79**	2.46 **3.56**	2.37 **3.39**	2.30 **3.26**	2.25 **3.14**	2.20 **3.06**	2.16 **2.98**	2.13 **2.93**	2.08 **2.83**	2.03 **2.74**	1.97 **2.63**	1.93 **2.55**	1.88 **2.47**	1.84 **2.38**	1.80 **2.33**	1.76 **2.25**	1.74 **2.21**	1.71 **2.16**	1.68 **2.12**	1.67 **2.10**	27
28	4.20 **7.64**	3.34 **5.45**	2.95 **4.57**	2.71 **4.07**	2.56 **3.76**	2.44 **3.53**	2.36 **3.36**	2.29 **3.23**	2.24 **3.11**	2.19 **3.03**	2.15 **2.95**	2.12 **2.90**	2.06 **2.80**	2.02 **2.71**	1.96 **2.60**	1.91 **2.52**	1.87 **2.44**	1.81 **2.35**	1.78 **2.30**	1.75 **2.22**	1.72 **2.18**	1.69 **2.13**	1.67 **2.09**	1.65 **2.06**	28
29	4.18 **7.60**	3.33 **5.42**	2.93 **4.54**	2.70 **4.04**	2.54 **3.73**	2.43 **3.50**	2.35 **3.33**	2.28 **3.20**	2.22 **3.08**	2.18 **3.00**	2.14 **2.92**	2.10 **2.87**	2.05 **2.77**	2.00 **2.68**	1.94 **2.57**	1.90 **2.49**	1.85 **2.41**	1.80 **2.32**	1.77 **2.27**	1.73 **2.19**	1.71 **2.15**	1.68 **2.10**	1.65 **2.06**	1.64 **2.03**	29
30	4.17 **7.56**	3.32 **5.39**	2.92 **4.51**	2.69 **4.02**	2.53 **3.70**	2.42 **3.47**	2.34 **3.30**	2.27 **3.17**	2.21 **3.06**	2.16 **2.98**	2.12 **2.90**	2.09 **2.84**	2.04 **2.74**	1.99 **2.66**	1.93 **2.55**	1.89 **2.47**	1.84 **2.38**	1.79 **2.29**	1.76 **2.24**	1.72 **2.16**	1.69 **2.13**	1.66 **2.07**	1.64 **2.03**	1.62 **2.01**	30
32	4.15 **7.50**	3.30 **5.34**	2.90 **4.46**	2.67 **3.97**	2.51 **3.66**	2.40 **3.42**	2.32 **3.25**	2.25 **3.12**	2.19 **3.01**	2.14 **2.94**	2.10 **2.86**	2.07 **2.80**	2.02 **2.70**	1.97 **2.62**	1.91 **2.51**	1.86 **2.42**	1.82 **2.34**	1.76 **2.25**	1.74 **2.20**	1.69 **2.12**	1.67 **2.08**	1.64 **2.02**	1.61 **1.98**	1.59 **1.96**	32
34	4.13 **7.44**	3.28 **5.29**	2.88 **4.42**	2.65 **3.93**	2.49 **3.61**	2.38 **3.38**	2.30 **3.21**	2.23 **3.08**	2.17 **2.97**	2.12 **2.89**	2.08 **2.82**	2.05 **2.76**	2.00 **2.66**	1.95 **2.58**	1.89 **2.47**	1.84 **2.38**	1.80 **2.30**	1.74 **2.21**	1.71 **2.15**	1.67 **2.08**	1.64 **2.04**	1.61 **1.98**	1.59 **1.94**	1.57 **1.91**	34
36	4.11 **7.39**	3.26 **5.25**	2.86 **4.38**	2.63 **3.89**	2.48 **3.58**	2.36 **3.35**	2.28 **3.18**	2.21 **3.04**	2.15 **2.94**	2.10 **2.86**	2.06 **2.78**	2.03 **2.72**	1.98 **2.62**	1.93 **2.54**	1.87 **2.43**	1.82 **2.35**	1.78 **2.26**	1.72 **2.17**	1.69 **2.12**	1.65 **2.04**	1.62 **2.00**	1.59 **1.94**	1.56 **1.90**	1.55 **1.87**	36
38	4.10 **7.35**	3.25 **5.21**	2.85 **4.34**	2.62 **3.86**	2.46 **3.54**	2.35 **3.32**	2.26 **3.15**	2.19 **3.02**	2.14 **2.91**	2.09 **2.82**	2.05 **2.75**	2.02 **2.69**	1.96 **2.59**	1.92 **2.51**	1.85 **2.40**	1.80 **2.32**	1.76 **2.22**	1.71 **2.14**	1.67 **2.08**	1.63 **2.00**	1.60 **1.97**	1.57 **1.90**	1.54 **1.86**	1.53 **1.84**	38
40	4.08 **7.31**	3.23 **5.18**	2.84 **4.31**	2.61 **3.83**	2.45 **3.51**	2.34 **3.29**	2.25 **3.12**	2.18 **2.99**	2.12 **2.88**	2.07 **2.80**	2.04 **2.73**	2.00 **2.66**	1.95 **2.56**	1.90 **2.49**	1.84 **2.37**	1.79 **2.29**	1.74 **2.20**	1.69 **2.11**	1.66 **2.05**	1.61 **1.97**	1.59 **1.94**	1.55 **1.88**	1.53 **1.84**	1.51 **1.81**	40
42	4.07 **7.27**	3.22 **5.15**	2.83 **4.29**	2.59 **3.80**	2.44 **3.49**	2,32 **3.26**	2.24 **3.10**	2.17 **2.96**	2.11 **2.86**	2.06 **2.77**	2.02 **2.70**	1.99 **2.64**	1.94 **2.54**	1.89 **2.46**	1.82 **2.35**	1.78 **2.26**	1.73 **2.17**	1.68 **2.08**	1.64 **2.02**	1.60 **1.94**	1.57 **1.91**	1.54 **1.85**	1.51 **1.80**	1.49 **1.78**	42
44	4.06 **7.24**	3.21 **5.12**	2.82 **4.26**	2.58 **3.78**	2.43 **3.46**	2.31 **3.24**	2.23 **3.07**	2.16 **2.94**	2.10 **2.84**	2.05 **2.75**	2.01 **2.68**	1.98 **2.62**	1.92 **2.52**	1.88 **2.44**	1.81 **2.32**	1.76 **2.24**	1.72 **2.15**	1.66 **2.06**	1.63 **2.00**	1.58 **1.92**	1.56 **1.88**	1.52 **1.82**	1.50 **1.78**	1.48 **1.75**	44
46	4.05 **7.21**	3.20 **5.10**	2.81 **4.24**	2.57 **3.76**	2.42 **3.44**	2.30 **3.22**	2.22 **3.05**	2.14 **2.92**	2.09 **2.82**	2.04 **2.73**	2.00 **2.66**	1.97 **2.60**	1.91 **2.50**	1.87 **2.42**	1.80 **2.30**	1.75 **2.22**	1.71 **2.13**	1.65 **2.04**	1.62 **1.98**	1.57 **1.90**	1.54 **1.86**	1.51 **1.80**	1.48 **1.76**	1.46 **1.72**	46
48	4.04 **7.19**	3.19 **5.08**	2.80 **4.22**	2.56 **3.74**	2.41 **3.42**	2.30 **3.20**	2.21 **3.04**	2.14 **2.90**	2.08 **2.80**	2.03 **2.71**	1.99 **2.64**	1.96 **2.58**	1.90 **2.48**	1.86 **2.40**	1.79 **2.28**	1.74 **2.20**	1.70 **2.11**	1.64 **2.02**	1.61 **1.96**	1.56 **1.88**	1.53 **1.84**	1.50 **1.78**	1.47 **1.73**	1.45 **1.70**	48

Table A.16. *(continued)*

f_2	f_1 Degrees of Freedom (for greater mean square)																								f_2
	1	2	3	4	5	6	7	8	9	10	11	12	14	16	20	24	30	40	50	75	100	200	500	∞	
50	4.03 **7.17**	3.18 **5.06**	2.79 **4.20**	2.56 **3.72**	2.40 **3.41**	2.29 **3.18**	2.20 **3.02**	2.13 **2.88**	2.07 **2.78**	2.02 **2.70**	1.98 **2.62**	1.95 **2.56**	1.90 **2.46**	1.85 **2.39**	1.78 **2.26**	1.74 **2.18**	1.69 **2.10**	1.63 **2.00**	1.60 **1.94**	1.55 **1.86**	1.52 **1.82**	1.48 **1.76**	1.46 **1.71**	1.44 **1.68**	50
55	4.02 **7.12**	3.17 **5.01**	2.78 **4.16**	2.54 **3.68**	2.38 **3.37**	2.27 **3.15**	2.18 **2.98**	2.11 **2.85**	2.05 **2.75**	2.00 **2.66**	1.97 **2.59**	1.93 **2.53**	1.88 **2.43**	1.83 **2.35**	1.76 **2.23**	1.72 **2.15**	1.67 **2.06**	1.61 **1.96**	1.58 **1.90**	1.52 **1.82**	1.50 **1.78**	1.46 **1.71**	1.43 **1.66**	1.41 **1.64**	55
60	4.00 **7.08**	3.15 **4.98**	2.76 **4.13**	2.52 **3.65**	2.37 **3.34**	2.25 **3.12**	2.17 **2.95**	2.10 **2.82**	2.04 **2.72**	1.99 **2.63**	1.95 **2.56**	1.92 **2.50**	1.86 **2.40**	1.81 **2.32**	1.75 **2.20**	1.70 **2.12**	1.65 **2.03**	1.59 **1.93**	1.56 **1.87**	1.50 **1.79**	1.48 **1.74**	1.44 **1.68**	1.41 **1.63**	1.39 **1.60**	60
65	3.99 **7.04**	3.14 **4.95**	2.75 **4.10**	2.51 **3.62**	2.36 **3.31**	2.24 **3.09**	2.15 **2.93**	2.08 **2.79**	2.02 **2.70**	1.98 **2.61**	1.94 **2.54**	1.90 **2.47**	1.85 **2.37**	1.80 **2.30**	1.73 **2.18**	1.68 **2.09**	1.63 **2.00**	1.57 **1.90**	1.54 **1.84**	1.49 **1.76**	1.46 **1.71**	1.42 **1.64**	1.39 **1.60**	1.37 **1.56**	65
70	3.98 **7.01**	3.13 **4.92**	2.74 **4.08**	2.50 **3.60**	2.35 **3.29**	2.23 **3.07**	2.14 **2.91**	2.07 **2.77**	2.01 **2.67**	1.97 **2.59**	1.93 **2.51**	1.89 **2.45**	1.84 **2.35**	1.79 **2.28**	1.72 **2.15**	1.67 **2.07**	1.62 **1.98**	1.56 **1.88**	1.53 **1.82**	1.47 **1.74**	1.45 **1.69**	1.40 **1.62**	1.37 **1.56**	1.35 **1.53**	70
80	3.96 **6.96**	3.11 **4.88**	2.72 **4.04**	2.48 **3.56**	2.33 **3.25**	2.21 **3.04**	2.12 **2.87**	2.05 **2.74**	1.99 **2.64**	1.95 **2.55**	1.91 **2.48**	1.88 **2.41**	1.82 **2.32**	1.77 **2.24**	1.70 **2.11**	1.65 **2.03**	1.60 **1.94**	1.54 **1.84**	1.51 **1.78**	1.45 **1.70**	1.42 **1.65**	1.38 **1.57**	1.35 **1.52**	1.32 **1.49**	80
100	3.94 **6.90**	3.09 **4.82**	2.70 **3.98**	2.46 **3.51**	2.30 **3.20**	2.19 **2.99**	2.10 **2.82**	2.03 **2.69**	1.97 **2.59**	1.92 **2.51**	1.88 **2.43**	1.85 **2.36**	1.79 **2.26**	1.75 **2.19**	1.68 **2.06**	1.63 **1.98**	1.57 **1.89**	1.51 **1.79**	1.48 **1.73**	1.42 **1.64**	1.39 **1.59**	1.34 **1.51**	1.30 **1.46**	1.28 **1.43**	100
125	3.92 **6.84**	3.07 **4.78**	2.68 **3.94**	2.44 **3.47**	2.29 **3.17**	2.17 **2.95**	2.08 **2.79**	2.01 **2.65**	1.95 **2.56**	1.90 **2.47**	1.86 **2.40**	1.83 **2.33**	1.77 **2.23**	1.72 **2.15**	1.65 **2.03**	1.60 **1.94**	1.55 **1.85**	1.49 **1.75**	1.45 **1.68**	1.39 **1.59**	1.36 **1.54**	1.31 **1.46**	1.27 **1.40**	1.25 **1.37**	125
150	3.91 **6.81**	3.06 **4.75**	2.67 **3.91**	2.43 **3.44**	2.27 **3.14**	2.16 **2.92**	2.07 **2.76**	2.00 **2.62**	1.94 **2.53**	1.89 **2.44**	1.85 **2.37**	1.82 **2.30**	1.76 **2.20**	1.71 **2.12**	1.64 **2.00**	1.59 **1.91**	1.54 **1.83**	1.47 **1.72**	1.44 **1.66**	1.37 **1.56**	1.34 **1.51**	1.29 **1.43**	1.25 **1.37**	1.22 **1.33**	150
200	3.89 **6.76**	3.04 **4.71**	2.65 **3.88**	2.41 **3.41**	2.26 **3.11**	2.14 **2.90**	2.05 **2.73**	1.98 **2.60**	1.92 **2.50**	1.87 **2.41**	1.83 **2.34**	1.80 **2.28**	1.74 **2.17**	1.69 **2.09**	1.62 **1.97**	1.57 **1.88**	1.52 **1.79**	1.45 **1.69**	1.42 **1.62**	1.35 **1.53**	1.32 **1.48**	1.26 **1.39**	1.22 **1.33**	1.19 **1.28**	200
400	3.86 **6.70**	3.02 **4.66**	2.62 **3.83**	2.39 **3.36**	2.23 **3.06**	2.12 **2.85**	2.03 **2.69**	1.96 **2.55**	1.90 **2.46**	1.85 **2.37**	1.81 **2.29**	1.78 **2.23**	1.72 **2.12**	1.67 **2.04**	1.60 **1.92**	1.54 **1.84**	1.49 **1.74**	1.42 **1.64**	1.38 **1.57**	1.32 **1.47**	1.28 **1.42**	1.22 **1.32**	1.16 **1.24**	1.13 **1.19**	400
1000	3.85 **6.66**	3.00 **4.62**	2.61 **3.80**	2.38 **3.34**	2.22 **3.04**	2.10 **2.82**	2.02 **2.66**	1.95 **2.53**	1.89 **2.43**	1.84 **2.34**	1.80 **2.26**	1.76 **2.20**	1.70 **2.09**	1.65 **2.01**	1.58 **1.89**	1.53 **1.81**	1.47 **1.71**	1.41 **1.61**	1.36 **1.54**	1.30 **1.44**	1.26 **1.38**	1.19 **1.28**	1.13 **1.19**	1.08 **1.11**	1000
∞	3.84 **6.64**	2.99 **4.60**	2.60 **3.78**	2.37 **3.32**	2.21 **3.02**	2.09 **2.80**	2.01 **2.64**	1.94 **2.51**	1.88 **2.41**	1.83 **2.32**	1.79 **2.24**	1.75 **2.18**	1.69 **2.07**	1.64 **1.99**	1.57 **1.87**	1.52 **1.79**	1.46 **1.69**	1.40 **1.59**	1.35 **1.52**	1.28 **1.41**	1.24 **1.36**	1.17 **1.25**	1.11 **1.15**	1.00 **1.00**	∞

Table A.17. Distribution of the Studentized Range Statistic

df for $s_{\bar{X}}$	$1-\alpha$	r = number of steps between ordered means													
		2	3	4	5	6	7	8	9	10	11	12	13	14	15
1	.95	18.0	27.0	32.8	37.1	40.4	43.1	45.4	47.4	49.1	50.6	52.0	53.2	54.3	55.4
	.99	90.0	135	164	186	202	216	227	237	246	253	260	266	272	277
2	.95	6.09	8.3	9.8	10.9	11.7	12.4	13.0	13.5	14.0	14.4	14.7	15.1	15.4	15.7
	.99	14.0	19.0	22.3	24.7	26.6	28.2	29.5	30.7	31.7	32.6	33.4	34.1	34.8	35.4
3	.95	4.50	5.91	6.82	7.50	8.04	8.48	8.85	9.18	9.46	9.72	9.95	10.2	10.4	10.5
	.99	8.26	10.6	12.2	13.3	14.2	15.0	15.6	16.2	16.7	17.1	17.5	17.9	18.2	18.5
4	.95	3.93	5.04	5.76	6.29	6.71	7.05	7.35	7.60	7.83	8.03	8.21	8.37	8.52	8.66
	.99	6.51	8.12	9.17	9.96	10.6	11.1	11.5	11.9	12.3	12.6	12.8	13.1	13.3	13.5
5	.95	3.64	4.60	5.22	5.67	6.03	6.33	6.58	6.80	6.99	7.17	7.32	7.47	7.60	7.72
	.99	5.70	6.97	7.80	8.42	8.91	9.32	9.67	9.97	10.2	10.5	10.7	10.9	11.1	11.2
6	.95	3.46	4.34	4.90	5.31	5.63	5.89	6.12	6.32	6.49	6.65	6.79	6.92	7.03	7.14
	.99	5.24	6.33	7.03	7.56	7.97	8.32	8.61	8.87	9.10	9.30	9.49	9.65	9.81	9.95
7	.95	3.34	4.16	4.69	5.06	5.36	5.61	5.82	6.00	6.16	6.30	6.43	6.55	6.66	6.76
	.99	4.95	5.92	6.54	7.01	7.37	7.68	7.94	8.17	8.37	8.55	8.71	8.86	9.00	9.12
8	.95	3.26	4.04	4.53	4.89	5.17	5.40	5.60	5.77	5.92	6.05	6.18	6.29	6.39	6.48
	.99	4.74	5.63	6.20	6.63	6.96	7.24	7.47	7.68	7.87	8.03	8.18	8.31	8.44	8.55
9	.95	3.20	3.95	4.42	4.76	5.02	5.24	5.43	5.60	5.74	5.87	5.98	6.09	6.19	6.28
	.99	4.60	5.43	5.96	6.35	6.66	6.91	7.13	7.32	7.49	7.65	7.78	7.91	8.03	8.13
10	.95	3.15	3.88	4.33	4.65	4.91	5.12	5.30	5.46	5.60	5.72	5.83	5.93	6.03	6.11
	.99	4.48	5.27	5.77	6.14	6.43	6.67	6.87	7.05	7.21	7.36	7.48	7.60	7.71	7.81

Source: This table is abridged from Table II.2 in *The Probability Integrals of the Range and of the Studentized Range*, prepared by H. Leon Harter, Donald S. Klemm, and Robert H. Guthrie. These tables are published in WADC Technical Report 58-484, volume 2, 1959, Wright Air Development Center. Reprinted from *Statistical Principles in Experimental Design*, B. J. Winer, McGraw-Hill Book Company, 1962, by the kind permission of the publishers.

Table A.17. *(continued)*

11	.95	3.11	3.82	4.26	4.57	4.82	5.03	5.20	5.35	5.49	5.61	5.71	5.81	5.90	5.99
	.99	4.39	5.14	5.62	5.97	6.25	6.48	6.67	6.84	6.99	7.13	7.26	7.36	7.46	7.56
12	.95	3.08	3.77	4.20	4.51	4.75	4.95	5.12	5.27	5.40	5.51	5.62	5.71	5.80	5.88
	.99	4.32	5.04	5.50	5.84	6.10	6.32	6.51	6.67	6.81	6.94	7.06	7.17	7.26	7.36
13	.95	3.06	3.73	4.15	4.45	4.69	4.88	5.05	5.19	5.32	5.43	5.53	5.63	5.71	5.79
	.99	4.26	4.96	5.40	5.73	5.98	6.19	6.37	6.53	6.67	6.79	6.90	7.01	7.10	7.19
14	.95	3.03	3.70	4.11	4.41	4.64	4.83	4.99	5.13	5.25	5.36	5.46	5.55	6.64	5.72
	.99	4.21	4.89	5.32	5.63	5.88	6.08	6.26	6.41	6.54	6.66	6.77	6.87	6.96	7.05
16	.95	3.00	3.65	4.05	4.33	4.56	4.74	4.90	5.03	5.15	5.26	5.35	5.44	5.52	5.59
	.99	4.13	4.78	5.19	5.49	5.72	5.92	6.08	6.22	6.35	6.46	6.56	6.66	6.74	6.82
18	.95	2.97	3.61	4.00	4.28	4.49	4.67	4.82	4.96	5.07	5.17	5.27	5.35	5.43	5.50
	.99	4.07	4.70	5.09	5.38	5.60	5.79	5.94	6.08	6.20	6.31	6.41	6.50	6.58	6.65
20	.95	2.95	3.58	3.96	4.23	4.45	4.62	4.77	4.90	5.01	5.11	5.20	5.28	5.36	5.43
	.99	4.02	4.64	5.02	5.29	5.51	5.69	5.84	5.97	6.09	6.19	6.29	6.37	6.45	6.52
24	.95	2.92	3.53	3.90	4.17	4.37	4.54	4.68	4.81	4.92	5.01	5.10	5.18	5.25	5.32
	.99	3.96	4.54	4.91	5.17	5.37	5.54	5.69	5.81	5.92	6.02	6.11	6.19	6.26	6.33
30	.95	2.89	3.49	3.84	4.10	4.30	4.46	4.60	4.72	4.83	4.92	5.00	5.08	5.15	5.21
	.99	3.89	4.45	4.80	5.05	5.24	5.40	5.54	5.56	5.76	5.85	5.93	6.01	6.08	6.14
40	.95	2.86	3.44	3.79	4.04	4.23	4.39	4.52	4.63	4.74	4.82	4.91	4.98	5.05	5.11
	.99	3.82	4.37	4.70	4.93	5.11	5.27	5.39	5.50	5.60	5.69	5.77	5.84	5.90	5.96
60	.95	2.83	3.40	3.74	3.98	4.16	4.31	4.44	4.55	4.65	4.73	4.81	4.88	4.94	5.00
	.99	3.76	4.28	4.60	4.82	4.99	5.13	5.25	5.36	5.45	5.53	5.60	5.67	5.73	5.79
120	.95	2.80	3.36	3.69	3.92	4.10	4.24	4.36	4.48	4.56	4.64	4.72	4.78	4.84	4.90
	.99	3.70	4.20	4.50	4.71	4.87	5.01	5.12	5.21	5.30	5.38	5.44	5.51	5.56	5.61
∞	.95	2.77	3.31	3.63	3.86	4.03	4.17	4.29	4.39	4.47	4.55	4.62	4.68	4.74	4.80
	.99	3.64	4.12	4.40	4.60	4.76	4.88	4.99	5.08	5.16	5.23	5.29	5.35	5.40	5.45

Table A.18. Probabilities Associated with Values as Large as Observed Values of H in the Kruskal-Wallis One-Way Analysis of Variance by Ranks

Sample sizes			H	p
n_1	n_2	n_3		
2	1	1	2.7000	.500
2	2	1	3.6000	.200
2	2	2	4.5714	.067
			3.7143	.200
3	1	1	3.2000	.300
3	2	1	4.2857	.100
			3.8571	.133
3	2	2	5.3572	.029
			4.7143	.048
			4.5000	.067
			4.4643	.105
3	3	1	5.1429	.043
			4.5714	.100
			4.0000	.129
3	3	2	6.2500	.011
			5.3611	.032
			5.1389	.061
			4.5556	.100
			4.2500	.121
3	3	3	7.2000	.004
			6.4889	.011
			5.6889	.029
			5.6000	.050
			5.0667	.086
			4.6222	.100
4	1	1	3.5714	.200
4	2	1	4.8214	.057
			4.5000	.076
			4.0179	.114
4	2	2	6.0000	.014
			5.3333	.033
			5.1250	.052
			4.4583	.100
			4.1667	.105
4	3	1	5.8333	.021
			5.2083	.050
			5.0000	.057
			4.0556	.093
			3.8889	.129
4	3	2	6.4444	.008
			6.3000	.011
			5.4444	.046
			5.4000	.051
			4.5111	.098
			4.4444	.102
4	3	3	6.7455	.010
			6.7091	.013
			5.7909	.046
			5.7273	.050
			4.7091	.092
			4.7000	.101
4	4	1	6.6667	.010
			6.1667	.022
			4.9667	.048
			4.8667	.054
			4.1667	.082
			4.0667	.102
4	4	2	7.0364	.006
			6.8727	.011
			5.4545	.046
			5.2364	.052
			4.5545	.098
			4.4455	.103
4	4	3	7.1439	.010
			7.1364	.011
			5.5985	.049
			5.5758	.051
			4.5455	.099
			4.4773	.102
4	4	4	7.6538	.008
			7.5385	.011
			5.6923	.049
			5.6538	.054
			4.6539	.097
			4.5001	.104
5	1	1	3.8571	.143
5	2	1	5.2500	.036
			5.0000	.048
			4.4500	.071
			4.2000	.095
			4.0500	.119

Table A.18. *(continued)*

Sample sizes			H	p
n_1	n_2	n_3		
5	2	2	6.5333	.008
			6.1333	.013
			5.1600	.034
			5.0400	.056
			4.3733	.090
			4.2933	.122
5	3	1	6.4000	.012
			4.9600	.048
			4.8711	.052
			4.0178	.095
			3.8400	.123
5	3	2	6.9091	.009
			6.8218	.010
			5.2509	.049
			5.1055	.052
			4.6509	.091
			4.4945	.101
5	3	3	7.0788	.009
			6.9818	.011
			5.6485	.049
			5.5152	.051
			4.5333	.097
			4.4121	.109
5	4	1	6.9545	.008
			6.8400	.011
			4.9855	.044
			4.8600	.056
			3.9873	.098
			3.9600	.102
5	4	2	7.2045	.009
			7.1182	.010
			5.2727	.049
			5.2682	.050
			4.5409	.098
			4.5182	.101
5	4	3	7.4449	.010
			7.3949	.011
			5.6564	.049
			5.6308	.050
			4.5487	.099
			4.5231	.103
5	4	4	7.7604	.009
			7.7440	.011
			5.6571	.049
			5.6176	.050
			4.6187	.100
			4.5527	.102
5	5	1	7.3091	.009
			6.8364	.011
			5.1273	.046
			4.9091	.053
			4.1091	.086
			4.0364	.105
5	5	2	7.3385	.010
			7.2692	.010
			5.3385	.047
			5.2462	.051
			4.6231	.097
			4.5077	.100
5	5	3	7.5780	.010
			7.5429	.010
			5.7055	.046
			5.6264	.051
			4.5451	.100
			4.5363	.102
5	5	4	7.8229	.010
			7.7914	.010
			5.6657	.049
			5.6429	.050
			4.5229	.099
			4.5200	.101
5	5	5	8.0000	.009
			7.9800	.010
			5.7800	.049
			5.6600	.051
			4.5600	.100
			4.5000	.102

Source: W. H. Kruskal and W. A. Wallis. "Use of Ranks in One-Criterion Variance Analysis." *Journal of the American Statistical Association,* 47 (1947), pp. 614-617; adapted and abridged. Used with the kind permission of the publisher. Reprinted from *Nonparametric Statistics for the Behavioral Sciences,* Sidney Siegel, McGraw-Hill Book Company, 1956, by the kind permission of the publishers.

Table A.19. Probabilities Associated with Values as Large as Observed Values of χ_r^2 in the Friedman Two-Way Analysis of Variance by Ranks
$k = 3$

$N = 2$		$N = 3$		$N = 4$		$N = 5$	
χ_r^2	p	χ_r^2	p	χ_r^2	p	χ_r^2	p
0	1.000	.000	1.000	.0	1.000	.0	1.000
1	.833	.667	.944	.5	.931	.4	.954
3	.500	2.000	.528	1.5	.653	1.2	.691
4	.167	2.667	.361	2.0	.431	1.6	.522
		4.667	.194	3.5	.273	2.8	.367
		6.000	.028	4.5	.125	3.6	.182
				6.0	.069	4.8	.124
				6.5	.042	5.2	.093
				8.0	.0046	6.4	.039
						7.6	.024
						8.4	.0085
						10.0	.00077

$N = 6$		$N = 7$		$N = 8$		$N = 9$	
χ_r^2	p	χ_r^2	p	χ_r^2	p	χ_r^2	p
.00	1.000	.000	1.000	.00	1.000	.000	1.000
.33	.956	.286	.964	.25	.967	.222	.971
1.00	.740	.857	.768	.75	.794	.667	.814
1.33	.570	1.143	.620	1.00	.654	.889	.865
2.33	.430	2.000	.486	1.75	.531	1.556	.569
3.00	.252	2.571	.305	2.25	.355	2.000	.398
4.00	.184	3.429	.237	3.00	.285	2.667	.328
4.33	.142	3.714	.192	3.25	.236	2.889	.278
5.33	.072	4.571	.112	4.00	.149	3.556	.187
6.33	.052	5.429	.085	4.75	.120	4.222	.154
7.00	.029	6.000	.052	5.25	.079	4.667	.107
8.33	.012	7.143	.027	6.25	.047	5.556	.069
9.00	.0081	7.714	.021	6.75	.038	6.000	.057
9.33	.0055	8.000	.016	7.00	.030	6.222	.048
10.33	.0017	8.857	.0084	7.75	.018	6.889	.031
12.00	.00013	10.286	.0036	9.00	.0099	8.000	.019
		10.571	.0027	9.25	.0080	8.222	.016
		11.143	.0012	9.75	.0048	8.667	.010
		12.286	.00032	10.75	.0024	9.556	.0060
		14.000	.000021	12.00	.0011	10.667	.0035
				12.25	.00086	10.889	.0029
				13.00	.00026	11.556	.0013
				14.25	.000061	12.667	.00066
				16.00	.0000036	13.556	.00035
						14.000	.00020
						14.222	.000097
						14.889	.000054
						16.222	.000011
						18.000	.0000006

Table A.19. *(continued)*
$k = 4$

$N = 2$		$N = 3$		$N = 4$			
χ_r^2	p	χ_r^2	p	χ_r^2	p	χ_r^2	p
.0	1.000	.2	1.000	.0	1.000	5.7	.141
.6	.958	.6	.958	.3	.992	6.0	.105
1.2	.834	1.0	.910	.6	.928	6.3	.094
1.8	.792	1.8	.727	.9	.900	6.6	.077
2.4	.625	2.2	.608	1.2	.800	6.9	.068
3.0	.542	2.6	.524	1.5	.754	7.2	.054
3.6	.458	3.4	.446	1.8	.677	7.5	.052
4.2	.375	3.8	.342	2.1	.649	7.8	.036
4.8	.208	4.2	.300	2.4	.524	8.1	.033
5.4	.167	5.0	.207	2.7	.508	8.4	.019
6.0	.042	5.4	.175	3.0	.432	8.7	.014
		5.8	.148	3.3	.389	9.3	.012
		6.6	.075	3.6	.355	9.6	.0069
		7.0	.054	3.9	.324	9.9	.0062
		7.4	.033	4.5	.242	10.2	.0027
		8.2	.017	4.8	.200	10.8	.0016
		9.0	.0017	5.1	.190	11.1	.00094
				5.4	.158	12.0	.000072

Source: M. Friedman. "The Use of Ranks to Avoid the Assumptions of Normality Implicit in the Analysis of Variance." *Journal of the American Statistical Association,* 32 (1937), pp. 688-689; adapted. Reprinted from *Nonparametric Statistics for the Behavioral Sciences,* Sidney Siegel, McGraw-Hill Book Company, 1956, by the kind permission of the publishers.

Table A.20. Values of the Coefficient of Concordance W Significant at the 20, 10, 5, and 1 Percent Levels

m	α	n = 3	4	5	6	7	8	9	10
3	.20	.78	.60	.53	.49	.47	.46	.45	.44
	.10		.73	.62	.58	.55	.53	.52	.51
	.05	1.00	.82	.71	.65	.62	.60	.58	.56
	.01		.96	.84	.77	.73	.70	.67	.65
4	.20	.56	.40	.38	.37	.36	.35	.34	.33
	.10	.75	.52	.47	.44	.42	.41	.40	.39
	.05	.81	.65	.54	.51	.48	.46	.45	.44
	.01	1.00	.80	.67	.62	.59	.56	.54	.52
5	.20	.36	.34	.30	.29	.28	.28	.27	.27
	.10	.52	.42	.38	.36	.34	.33	.32	.31
	.05	.64	.52	.44	.41	.39	.38	.36	.35
	.01	.84	.66	.56	.52	.49	.46	.44	.43
6	.20	.33	.27	.25	.24	.24	.23	.23	.23
	.10	.44	.36	.32	.30	.29	.28	.27	.26
	.05	.58	.42	.37	.35	.33	.32	.31	.30
	.01	.75	.56	.49	.45	.42	.40	.38	.37
7	.20	.27	.23	.22	.21	.20	.20	.20	.19
	.10	.39	.30	.27	.26	.25	.24	.23	.23
	.05	.51	.36	.32	.30	.29	.27	.26	.26
	.01	.63	.48	.43	.39	.36	.34	.33	.32
8	.20	.25	.20	.19	.18	.18	.17	.17	.17
	.10	.33	.26	.24	.23	.22	.21	.20	.20
	.05	.39	.32	.29	.27	.25	.24	.23	.23
	.01	.56	.43	.38	.35	.32	.31	.29	.28
9	.20	.20	.18	.17	.16	.16	.16	.15	.15
	.10	.31	.23	.21	.20	.19	.19	.18	.18
	.05	.35	.28	.26	.24	.23	.22	.21	.20
	.01	.48	.38	.34	.31	.29	.27	.26	.25
10	.20	.19	.16	.15	.15	.14	.14	.14	.13
	.10	.25	.21	.19	.18	.17	.17	.16	.16
	.05	.31	.25	.23	.21	.20	.20	.19	.18
	.01	.48	.35	.31	.28	.26	.25	.24	.23
12	.20	.14	.13	.13	.12	.12	.12	.11	.11
	.10	.19	.17	.16	.15	.15	.14	.14	.13
	.05	.25	.21	.19	.18	.17	.16	.16	.15
	.01	.36	.30	.26	.24	.22	.21	.20	.19

Table A.20. *(continued)*

m	α	n: 3	4	5	6	7	8	9	10
14	.20	.12	.11	.11	.10	.10	.10	.10	.10
	.10	.17	.15	.14	.13	.13	.12	.12	.12
	.05	.21	.18	.17	.16	.15	.14	.14	.13
	.01	.31	.26	.23	.21	.19	.18	.17	.17
16	.20	.10	.10	.09	.09	.09	.09	.09	.08
	.10	.15	.13	.12	.12	.11	.11	.10	.10
	.05	.19	.16	.15	.14	.13	.12	.12	.12
	.01	.28	.23	.20	.18	.17	.16	.15	.15
18	.20	.09	.09	.08	.08	.08	.08	.08	.07
	.10	.13	.12	.11	.10	.10	.09	.09	.09
	.05	.17	.14	.13	.12	.11	.11	.11	.10
	.01	.25	.20	.18	.16	.15	.14	.14	.13
20	.20	.08	.08	.07	.07	.07	.07	.07	.07
	.10	.11	.10	.10	.09	.09	.08	.08	.08
	.05	.15	.13	.12	.11	.10	.10	.10	.09
	.01	.22	.18	.16	.15	.14	.13	.12	.11
25	.20	.07	.06	.06	.06	.06	.06	.05	.05
	.10	.09	.08	.08	.07	.07	.07	.07	.06
	.05	.12	.10	.09	.09	.08	.08	.08	.07
	.01	.18	.15	.13	.12	.11	.10	.10	.09
30	.20	.05	.05	.05	.05	.05	.05	.05	.04
	.10	.08	.07	.06	.06	.06	.06	.06	.05
	.05	.10	.09	.08	.07	.07	.07	.07	.06
	.01	.15	.12	.11	.10	.09	.09	.08	.08

Source: Values at the left of the stepped line were derived from Appendix Tables 5A, 5B, 5C, and 5D of M. G. Kendall, *Rank Correlation Methods* London: Charles Griffin & Company, Ltd., 1948). Other values were obtained by the method described by Kendall, p. 84 of the same book. Reproduced from M. W. Tate and R. C. Clelland, *Nonparametric and Shortcut Statistics* Danville, Ill.: The Interstate Printers and Publishers, 1957), by the kind permission of the publishers. Used with the further kind permission of Messrs. Charles Griffin & Company.

Table A.21. Cumulative Binomial Probabilities: $P = .5$

N \ m	0	1	2	3	4	5	6	7	8	9	10	11	12	13	14	15
5	031	188	500	812	969	*										
6	016	109	344	656	891	984	*									
7	008	062	227	500	773	938	992	*								
8	004	035	145	363	637	855	965	996	*							
9	002	020	090	254	500	746	910	980	998	*						
10	001	011	055	172	377	623	828	945	989	999	*					
11		006	033	113	274	500	726	887	967	994	*	*				
12		003	019	073	194	387	613	806	927	981	997	*	*			
13		002	011	046	133	291	500	709	867	954	989	998	*	*		
14		001	006	029	090	212	395	605	788	910	971	994	999	*	*	
15			004	018	059	151	304	500	696	849	941	982	996	*	*	*
16			002	011	038	105	227	402	598	773	895	962	989	998	*	*
17			001	006	025	072	166	315	500	685	834	928	975	994	999	*
18			001	004	015	048	119	240	407	593	760	881	952	985	996	999
19				002	010	032	084	180	324	500	676	820	916	968	990	998
20				001	006	021	058	132	252	412	588	748	868	942	979	994
21				001	004	013	039	095	192	332	500	668	808	905	961	987
22					002	008	026	067	143	262	416	584	738	857	933	974
23					001	005	017	047	105	202	339	500	661	798	895	953
24					001	003	011	032	076	154	271	419	581	729	846	924
25						002	007	022	054	115	212	345	500	655	788	885

Source: Helen M. Walker and Joseph Lev. *Statistical Inference.* New York: Henry Holt and Company, 1953. Copyright 1953 by Holt, Rinehart and Winston, Inc. Used with the kind permission of the publishers and Miss Helen M. Walker.

Table A.22. Distribution of the F_{max} Statistic

df for s_X^2	$1-\alpha$	k = number of variances								
		2	3	4	5	6	7	8	9	10
4	.95	9.60	15.5	20.6	25.2	29.5	33.6	37.5	41.4	44.6
	.99	23.2	37.	49.	59.	69.	79.	89.	97.	106.
5	.95	7.15	10.8	13.7	16.3	18.7	20.8	22.9	24.7	26.5
	.99	14.9	22.	28.	33.	38.	42.	46.	50.	54.
6	.95	5.82	8.38	10.4	12.1	13.7	15.0	16.3	17.5	18.6
	.99	11.1	15.5	19.1	22.	25.	27.	30.	32.	34.
7	.95	4.99	6.94	8.44	9.70	10.8	11.8	12.7	13.5	14.3
	.99	8.89	12.1	14.5	16.5	18.4	20.	22.	23.	24.
8	.95	4.43	6.00	7.18	8.12	9.03	9.78	10.5	11.1	11.7
	.99	7.50	9.9	11.7	13.2	14.5	15.8	16.9	17.9	18.9
9	.95	4.03	5.34	6.31	7.11	7.80	8.41	8.95	9.45	9.91
	.99	6.54	8.5	9.9	11.1	12.1	13.1	13.9	14.7	15.3
10	.95	3.72	4.85	5.67	6.34	6.92	7.42	7.87	8.28	8.66
	.99	5.85	7.4	8.6	9.6	10.4	11.1	11.8	12.4	12.9
12	.95	3.28	4.16	4.79	5.30	5.72	6.09	6.42	6.72	7.00
	.99	4.91	6.1	6.9	7.6	8.2	8.7	9.1	9.5	9.9
15	.95	2.86	3.54	4.01	4.37	4.68	4.95	5.19	5.40	5.59
	.99	4.07	4.9	5.5	6.0	6.4	6.7	7.1	7.3	7.5
20	.95	2.46	2.95	3.29	3.54	3.76	3.94	4.10	4.24	4.37
	.99	3.32	3.8	4.3	4.6	4.9	5.1	5.3	5.5	5.6
30	.95	2.07	2.40	2.61	2.78	2.91	3.02	3.12	3.21	3.29
	.99	2.63	3.0	3.3	3.4	3.6	3.7	3.8	3.9	4.0
60	.95	1.67	1.85	1.96	2.04	2.11	2.17	2.22	2.26	2.30
	.99	1.96	2.2	2.3	2.4	2.4	2.5	2.5	2.6	2.6
∞	.95	1.00	1.00	1.00	1.00	1.00	1.00	1.00	1.00	1.00
	.99	1.00	1.00	1.00	1.00	1.00	1.00	1.00	1.00	1.00

Source: This table is abridged from Table 31 in *Biometrika Tables for Statisticians,* volume 1, 2nd edition (New York: Cambridge University Press, 1958), edited by E. S. Pearson and H. O. Hartley. Used with the kind permission of E. S. Pearson and the trustees of Biometrika. Reprinted from *Statistical Principles in Experimental Design,* B. J. Winer, McGraw-Hill Book Company, 1962, by the kind permission of the publishers.

Table A.23. Critical Values of ΣT in the Wilcoxon Matched-Pairs-Signed-Ranks Test

N	Level of significance for one-tailed test		
	.025	.01	.005
	Level of significance for two-tailed test		
	.05	.02	.01
6	0	—	—
7	2	0	—
8	4	2	0
9	6	3	2
10	8	5	3
11	11	7	5
12	14	10	7
13	17	13	10
14	21	16	13
15	25	20	16
16	30	24	20
17	35	28	23
18	40	33	28
19	46	38	32
20	52	43	38
21	59	49	43
22	66	56	49
23	73	62	55
24	81	69	61
25	89	77	68

Source: Adapted from Table I of F. Wilcoxon. *Some Rapid Approximate Statistical Procedures*, p. 13. New York: American Cyanamid Company, 1949. Used with the kind permission of the author and publisher. Reprinted from *Nonparametric Statistics for the Behavioral Sciences*, Sidney Siegel, McGraw-Hill Book Company, 1946, by the kind permission of the publishers.

Appendix B
Bibliography of Texts and Articles

Adams, Joe Kennedy. *Basic Statistical Concepts.* McGraw-Hill, 1955.

Adler, Irving. *Probability and Statistics for Everyman.* New American Library, 1966.

Alder, Henry L., and Edward B. Roessler. *Introduction to Probability and Statistics.* W. H. Freeman, 1964.

Balsley, Howard L. *An Introduction to Statistical Method.* Littlefield, Adams, 1964.

Bartz, Albert E. *Elementary Statistical Methods for Educational Measurement.* Burgess, 1966.

Bernstein, Allen L. *A Handbook of Statistical Solutions for the Behavioral Sciences.* Holt, 1964.

Blalock, Hubert M. *Social Statistics.* McGraw-Hill, 1960.

Bowen, Earl K. *Statistics.* R. D. Irwin, 1960.

Bradley, Jack I., and James McClelland. *Basic Statistical Concepts.* Scott, Foresman, 1963.

Bulmer, M. G. *Principles of Statistics.* M.I.T. Press, 1965.

Cohen, Lillian. *Statistical Methods for Social Scientists.* Prentice-Hall, 1954.

Connolly, T. G., and W. Sluckin. *An Introduction to Statistics for the Social Sciences.* Hafner, 1953.

Cornell, Francis G. *The Essentials of Educational Statistics.* Wiley, 1956.

Costner, Herbert L. "Criteria for Measures of Association." *American Sociological Review,* 30:3 (June, 1965), pp. 341–353.

Cotton, John W. *Elementary Statistical Theory for Behavior Scientists.* Addison-Wesley, 1967.

Croxton, Frederick E., and Dudley J. Cowden. *Applied General Statistics.* Prentice-Hall, 1955.

Dixon, Wilfrid J., and Frank J. Massey. *Introduction to Statistical Analysis.* McGraw-Hill, 1957.

Dornbusch, Sanford M., and Calvin F. Schmid. *A Primer of Social Statistics.* McGraw-Hill, 1955.

Downie, Norville M., and R. W. Heath. *Basic Statistical Methods.* Harper, 1965.

Edwards, Allen L. *Statistical Analysis.* Rinehart, 1958.

Edwards, Allen L. *Statistical Methods.* Holt, 1967.

Ferguson, George A. *Statistical Analysis in Psychology and Education.* McGraw-Hill, 1966.

Fisher, R. A. *Statistical Methods for Research Workers.* Hafner, 1958.

Franzblau, Abraham N. *Primer of Statistics for Non-Statisticians.* Harcourt, 1958.

Freeman, Linton C. *Elementary Applied Statistics.* Wiley, 1965.

Freund, John E. *Modern Elementary Statistics.* Prentice-Hall, 1960.

Freund, John E., and Frank J. Williams. *Dictionary/Outline of Basic Statistics.* McGraw-Hill, 1966.

Fryer, Holly C. *Elements of Statistics.* Wiley, 1954.

Games, Paul A., and George R. Klare. *Elementary Statistics.* McGraw-Hill, 1967.

Garlington, Warren K., and Helen E. Shimota. *Statistically Speaking.* Thomas, 1964.

Garrett, Henry E. *Elementary Statistics.* McKay, 1962.

Garrett, Henry E. *Statistics in Psychology and Education.* McKay, 1958.

Goldfarb, Nathan. *Introduction to Longitudinal Statistical Analysis.* Free Press, 1960.

Goodman, L. A. "Kolmogorov-Smirnov Tests for Psychological Research." *Psychological Bulletin,* 51 (1954), pp. 160–168.

Goulden, Cyril H. *Methods of Statistical Analysis.* Wiley, 1952.

Guest, Lester P. *Beginning Statistics.* Crowell, 1957.

Guilford, Jay P. *Fundamental Statistics in Psychology and Education.* McGraw-Hill, 1956.

Hagood, Margaret J., and Daniel O. Price. *Statistics for Sociologists.* Holt, 1952.

Hirsch, Werner Z. *Introduction to Modern Statistics.* Macmillan, 1957.

Hoel, Paul G. *Elementary Statistics.* Wiley, 1966.

Huff, Darrell. *How to Lie with Statistics.* Norton, 1954.

Johnson, Palmer O., and Robert W. B. Jackson. *Introduction to Statistical Methods.* Prentice-Hall, 1953.

Johnson, Palmer O., and Robert W. B. Jackson. *Modern Statistical Methods.* Rand McNally, 1959.

Johnson, Robert E., and Doris N. Morris. *Guide to Elementary Statistical Formulas.* McGraw-Hill, 1956.

Kendall, Maurice G. *Advanced Theory of Statistics.* Griffin, 1945–48.

Kendall, Maurice G. *Rank Correlational Methods,* 2d ed. Griffin, 1955.

Kendall, Maurice G., and William R. Buckland. *Dictionary of Statistical Terms.* Hafner, 1960.

Koenker, Robert H. *Simplified Statistics for Students in Education and Psychology.* McKnight, 1961.

Lewis, Edward E. *Methods of Statistical Analysis in Economics and Business.* Houghton Mifflin, 1963.

Li, Jerome Ching-ren. *Statistical Inference.* Edwards Bros., 1964.

Loveday, Robert. *First Course in Statistics.* Cambridge University Press, 1966.

McCarthy, Philip J. *Introduction to Statistical Reasoning.* McGraw-Hill, 1957.

McCormick, Thomas C. *Elementary Social Statistics.* McGraw-Hill, 1941.

McCullough, Celeste, and Loche Van Atta. *Introduction to Descriptive Statistics and Correlation.* McGraw-Hill, 1965.

McCullough, Celeste, and Loche Van Atta. *Statistical Concepts.* McGraw-Hill, 1963.

McMilien, Ardee W. *Statistical Methods for Social Workers.* University of Chicago Press, 1952.

McNemar, Quinn. *Psychological Statistics,* 3d ed. Wiley, 1962.

Mandel, John. *Statistical Analysis of Experimental Data.* Interscience, 1964.
Mark, Mary L. *Statistics in the Making.* Ohio State University, 1958.
Mills, Frederick C. *Introduction to Statistics.* Holt, 1956.
Mueller, John H., and Karl F. Schuessler. *Statistical Reasoning in Sociology.* Houghton Mifflin, 1961.
Neyman, Jerzy. *First Course in Probability and Statistics.* Holt, 1950.
Ostle, Bernard. *Statistics in Research.* Iowa State University Press, 1963.
Peatman, John G. *Descriptive and Sampling Statistics.* Harper, 1947.
Peatman, John G. *Introduction to Applied Statistics.* Harper, 1963.
Peters, Charles C., and Walter R. Van Voorhis. *Statistical Procedures and Their Mathematical Bases.* McGraw-Hill, 1940.
Quenouille, M. H. *Fundamentals of Statistical Reasoning.* Hafner, 1958.
Quenouille, M. H. *Rapid Statistical Calculations.* Hafner, 1959.
Ray, William S. *Statistics in Psychological Research.* Macmillan, 1962.
Reichman, William J. *Use and Abuse of Statistics.* Oxford University Press, 1962.
Richmond, Samuel B. *Statistical Analysis.* Ronald, 1964.
Rosander, Arlyn C. *Elementary Principles of Statistics.* Van Nostrand, 1951.
Runyon, Richard P., and Audrey Haber. *Fundamentals of Behavioral Statistics.* Addison-Wesley, 1967.
Savage, Leonard J. *Foundations of Statistics.* Wiley, 1954.
Siegel, Sidney. *Nonparametric Statistics for the Behavioral Sciences.* McGraw-Hill, 1956.
Simpson, George, and Fritz Kafka. *Basic Statistics.* Norton, 1952. (Rev. ed., 1957.)
Smith, George M. *A Simplified Guide to Statistics for Psychology and Education.* Holt, 1962.
Spiegel, Murray R. *Schaum's Outline of Theory and Problems of Statistics.* Schaum, 1961.
Sprowls, R. Clay. *Elementary Statistics for Students of Social Science and Business.* McGraw-Hill, 1955.
Tippett, Leonard. *Methods of Statistics.* Wiley, 1952.
Underwood, Benton J. *Elementary Statistics.* Appleton, 1954.
Walker, Helen Mary, and Joseph Lev. *Elementary Statistical Methods.* Holt, 1958.
Walker, Helen Mary, and Joseph Lev. *Statistical Inference.* Holt, 1953.
Wallis, Wilson A., and Harry Roberts. *The Nature of Statistics.* Free Press, 1965.
Wallis, Wilson A., and Harry Roberts. *Statistics, a New Approach.* Free Press, 1956.
Waugh, Albert E. *Elements of Statistical Method.* McGraw-Hill, 1952.
Wert, James E., *et al. Statistical Methods in Educational and Psychological Research.* Appleton, 1954.
Wilks, Samuel S. *Elementary Statistical Analysis.* Princeton University Press, 1948.
Winer, B. J. *Statistical Principles in Experimental Design.* McGraw-Hill, 1962.
Wyatt, Woodrow W., and Charles M. Bridges. *Statistics for the Behavioral Sciences.* Heath, 1966–67.

Yamane, Taro. *Statistics, an Introductory Analysis.* Harper, 1967.

Yates, F. "Contingency Tables Involving Small Numbers and the χ^2 Test." *Journal of the Royal Statistical Society,* 1 (1934), pp. 217–235.

Yuker, Harold E. *Guide to Statistical Calculations.* Putnam, 1958.

Yule, George U., and M. G. Kendall. *An Introduction to the Theory of Statistics.* Griffin, 1951.

Zeisel, Hans. *Say It with Figures.* Harper, 1957.

Zelditch, Morris. *Basic Course in Sociological Statistics.* Holt, 1959.

Appendix C
Some Selected Symbols

! = factorial sign; $N! = (N)(N-1)(N-2)\cdots(1)$
α = alpha, or the probability of rejecting a true hypothesis
$1-\alpha$ = the probability of failing to reject a true hypothesis
a, b, c, and d = the four cells in a 2×2 table
$\leqslant$ = equal to or less than
$\geqslant$ = equal to or greater than
$=$ = equal to
$\neq$ = not equal to
$|\ |$ = absolute value (ignore sign associated with number)
$<$ = less than
$>$ = greater than
AD = average deviation
β = beta, or the probability of failing to reject a false hypothesis
$1-\beta$ = the power of the test, or the probability of rejecting a false hypothesis
C = centile; or coefficient of contingency
$\bar{C}$ = corrected coefficient of contingency
chi = see below, following $\bar{X}$
D = decile
df = degrees of freedom
η = eta, the correlation ratio
F = statistic used for analysis of variance; ratio of MS_{bet}/MS_{within}
f = frequencies
F_{max} = Hartley's test for homogeneity of variance
γ = gamma, a measure of association between two ordinal variables
H = Kruskal-Wallis test for significance of difference between k sets of ordinal variables
H_1 = research hypothesis
H_0 = null hypothesis
i = interval size; subscript representing the ith score
IQV = index of qualitative variation
k = number of samples or treatments
λ = lambda, Guttman's coefficient of predictability; a measure of association between two nominal variables

M' = arbitrary reference point or guessed mean in a sample distribution
Mdn = median
μ = population mean
N = the number of elements in a distribution
n = (sometimes) the number of elements in a sample
P = probability
ϕ = the phi coefficient; a measure of association between two nominal variables
q = studentized range statistic
Q = Yule's Q; a measure of association between nominal data; or Cochran's Q test for significance of difference between k samples (nominal data); or quartile
$Q_3 - Q_1$ = interquartile range; divided by 2 becomes semi-interquartile range
r = Pearson r, product-moment correlation coefficient; or the number of steps between ordered pairs of means
r_s = Spearman's rank-order correlation coefficient
r^2 = the explained variation between two variables
R = the number of runs in the runs test
s = the sample standard deviation
s^2 = the sample variance
s_{DZ} = the standard error of the difference between two Z's
$s_{\bar{t}}$ = the standard error of sample means
s_X = the standard error of the mean
σ = sigma (lowercase), the population standard deviation
σ^2 = the population variance
Σ = the sum of
t = Student's t; a test for significance of difference between two means
τ = tau, a measure of association between two ordinal variables
U = the statistic for the Mann-Whitney test for significance of difference between ordinal variables
W = Kendall's coefficient of concordance; measures the degree of agreement between k variables which have been ranked
X = any score in a distribution
x = a deviation score where $x = X - \bar{X}$
$\bar{X}$ = the sample mean
χ^2 = chi square; a test for goodness of fit
χ_r^2 = statistic for Friedman two-way analysis of variance for ordinal variables
Z = a standard score; also a test for significance of difference between two means
Z_F = Fisher's Z transformation

Index